AF540452

FOREIGN AID IN INDIA
Effectiveness and Policy

Contents

SECTION II

SECTION II

SECTION I

SECTION II

Foreword

Assisting developing countries in their development process has been the prime role of foreign aid, comprising loans both concessional as well as non-concessional along with outright grants including technical assistance and training. Research into the various aspects of foreign aid such as : whether it has been fruitful for the development process or not; on which terms and conditions it has been received; from where it has been obtained; what is the Govt. policy regarding it; and what are the major constraints in its utilization etc., provides important guidelines to make it more effective and useful.

It is in this context that the challenging work *Foreign Aid in India : Effectiveness and Policy*, accomplished by Dr. Kulwant Singh Phull, providing an exhaustive analysis of these issues faced by the Indian economy, particularly in the recent momentous years, is to be welcomed. The study has been undertaken with the main objectives of analyzing the source-wise and purpose-wise nature, extent and utilization of foreign aid in India, and the changes therein; examining the loan-wise terms and conditions of the same, particularly the loans utilized by India, from both the multilateral and bilateral sources, in order to estimate the grant element inherent therein; assessing the effectiveness of the same through its impact on the various sectors of the economy; reviewing the mechanism and policy of the Govt. of India regarding accepting foreign aid; and identification of various problems in the authorization and utilization of foreign aid which restricted its effectiveness.

The study reported that despite being a smaller proportion of country's GDP, foreign aid has been utilized for financing the basic and strategic development projects involving capital investment of high magnitude, such as : development of industries like steel, chemical fertilizers, petroleum refineries; infrastructural projects like power generation, railways, road network, ports and telecommunications; projects in the social and urban development sectors along with environmental sustenance, etc., which helped in the capacity building of the economy. The author's attempt to estimate grant element implicit in the loans, both multilateral as well as bilateral, committed to/ utilized by India using domestic market sensitive discount rates, with and without incorporating exchange rate variations in rupee in relation to the donor currencies, is laudable and thereby add to the novelty of the book. The results showed that grant element inherent in almost all the loans sanctioned by all the sources proved concessional/highly concessional, when exchange rate variations in rupee were ignored, but grant element was found negative in most of the loans/sources, when depreciation of rupee was accounted for.

Examining empirically, the effectiveness of utilized foreign aid with the help of econometric techniques and using time series data regarding 18 variables, the author argued that it proved fruitful and effective for most of the activities/areas on which it was utilized, especially during the overall study period, and the pre-reforms period. The comprehensive review of the Govt. of India's mechanism, and policy regarding obtaining and utilizing foreign aid has been another main feature of the book. He argued that though the importance of foreign aid has been waning gradually over the years, yet the country is unable to fully end its dependence on the same, not even by the end of the Tenth Plan.

The author has sounded notes of caution regarding various undue, unnecessary and inordinate problems, which constituted serious constraints on the effective utilization of foreign aid in the country. Consequently, a huge quantum of authorized aid amounting to Rs. 81,122.93 crore remained un-disbursed up to the period end-March, 2004. The study also recommended some policy measures for improving the effectiveness of foreign aid in the country, which merit the attention of those engaged in policy formulation and planning.

On the whole, the author has carried out an in-depth, comprehensive and systematic analysis of the various aspects of utilized foreign aid in India. I am confident that the book will prove extremely useful to the students, researchers, teachers, policy-makers and will receive wide acceptance by all those who are interested in the problems of global developmental financing of a developing country like India.

Amritsar

DR. P.S. RAIKHY
Professor,
Former Head, Punjab School of Economics;
Dean, Faculty of Economics and Business,
Guru Nanak Dev University; and
Member, Punjab State Disinvestment Commission

Preface

India has been a recipient of foreign aid from a wide variety of sources, both bilateral and multilateral, to ease out the financial constraints in the process of development, ever since 1951, when the planning process was launched. There is a widespread impression that India received large sums of foreign aid, which of course is true in absolute terms, but is not true if large size of the country and its gargantuan population are taken into consideration. Besides this, the real worth of foreign aid depends upon the terms and conditions under which it has been sanctioned, and utilized. In the present book, an endeavor has been made to estimate the real worth of foreign aid utilized in India, particularly since 1980, when the process of liberalization was espoused in the country. For this purpose 'grant element' inherent in the loans utilized by the country has been worked out by using the domestic market sensitive discount rates. An attempt has also been made to examine the effectiveness of utilized foreign aid in the economy, through its impact on the development of various sectors, especially on which it has been utilized and also on the whole economy, since 1970. A comprehensive review of the Govt. of India's policy regarding obtaining foreign aid along with various problems faced in its utilization, which restricted the effectiveness of foreign aid in the country, has also been carried out.

Though this controversial topic has been widely researched in the past, yet the present study is quite comprehensive and is an explicit case of product differentiation. The use of domestic market sensitive discount rates along with exchange rate variations in rupee vis-a-vis donor currencies for the estimation of grant element implicit in the loans utilized and the examination of aid effectiveness through its impact on the various sectors of the Indian economy constitute a clear cut distinction as contrasted to the previous studies on this topic.

With the grace of the Almighty God ***'Akal Purkh'***, the present study has been accomplished through the help, assistance and cooperation of a galaxy of scholars, experts and persons, who helped me in diverse ways at the different stages of this work.

In the first place, words can hardly express the deep debt of gratitude to my renowned and esteemed teacher Dr. P.S. Raikhy, Professor, Punjab School of Economics, Guru Nanak Dev University, Amritsar, for his invaluable guidance, consistent encouragement, continuous motivation and critical comments during the completion of this project in the present form. I thank him from the core of my heart for examining each and every statement thoroughly, despite being awfully busy in his own work.

I place on record my gratitude to Dr. D.K. Srivastva, Director, Madras School of Economics, Chennai and formerly member, Twelfth Finance Commission, Govt. of India; Dr. Gautam Naresh, Senior Economist, National Institute of Public Finance and Policy, New Delhi; Dr. B.N. Goldar, Professor, Institute of Economic Growth, Delhi; and Dr. A.S. Sethi, Professor of Quantitative Economics, Punjab School of Economics, Guru Nanak Dev University, Amritsar, for constantly solving my conceptual problems and offering valuable suggestions at the various stages of the present study.

I am grateful to Dr. (Mrs.) Paramjeet Kaur Dhindsa, Professor and former Head, Punjab School of Economics, Guru Nanak Dev University, Amritsar, for providing me the requisite facilities for the completion of this book.

I am also thankful to S. Jagat Singh Plahi, Chairman, Managing Committee and S. Inderjit Singh, Principal, Guru Nanak College, Sukhchainana Sahib, Phagwara for granting me the study leave, and the University Grants Commission, New Delhi for awarding me the Teacher Fellowship to complete this work.

During the course of this study, I visited a number of institutions and organizations, mainly at New Delhi, such as: Ministry of Finance, Department of Economic Affairs, Govt. of

India; Aid, Accounts and Audit Division; National Institute of Public Finance and Policy; National Council of Applied Economic Research; Indian Council for Social Sciences Research; Ratan Tata Library, Delhi School of Economics; Institute of Economic Growth; Central Statistical Organization; and Yojna Bhawan, alongwith Punjab School of Economics Library and Bhai Gurdas Library, Guru Nanak Dev University, Amritsar; and Lajpat Rai Library, D.A.V. College, Jalandhar. I gratefully acknowledge the liberal access to the research material, journals, reports and books allowed by the Librarians and staff members of these institutions. My special thanks are due to Ms. Savitari Devi, Librarian, and all other staff members, especially Mr. Ashok Kumar, of the Ministry of Finance Library, New Delhi, and S. Mukhtiar Singh, Librarian, Punjab School of Economics Library, Guru Nanak Dev University, Amritsar, for their bounteous help and cooperation during the completion of this research work. I also express my thanks to Mr. J.P. Singh Arora, Auditor, Office of the Aid, Accounts and Audit Division in the Department of Economic Affairs, Ministry of Finance, New Delhi for useful discussions regarding foreign aid policy of the Govt. of India; and to S. Sukhdev Singh of Computer Centre, Guru Nanak Dev University, Amritsar, for providing me the necessary assistance during the computer work.

My sincere thanks are also due to S. G.S. Bhatia, Managing Director, Deep & Deep Publications Pvt. Ltd., New Delhi for bringing out this edition in an efficient, impressive and lucid format.

Last, but certainly not the least, I shall remain highly indebted to my respected father S. Gurcharan Singh Phull for his consistent inspiration and encouragement, to my wife Mrs. Rajinder Kaur, and both sons for their infinite support and patience during this study.

Any errors of omission or commission in the study are, however, solely the responsibility of the author.

Phagwara (Punjab)

KULWANT SINGH PHULL
Head, Department of Economics,
Guru Nanak College,
Sukhchainana Sahib.

Acronyms and Abbreviations

ACA	:	Additional Central Assistance
ADB	:	Asian Development Bank
AIDS	:	Acquired Immune Deficiency Syndrome
BOP	:	Balance of Payments
CAA & A	:	Controller Aid, Accounts and Audit
DAC	:	Development Assistance Committee
DEA	:	Department of Economic Affairs
EAPs	:	Externally Aided Projects
ECB	:	External Commercial Borrowings
EEC	:	European Economic Community
FDI	:	Foreign Direct Investment
FII	:	Foreign Institutional Investment
FOREX	:	Foreign Exchange Reserves
FYP	:	Five Year Plan
GDP	:	Gross Domestic Product
GNP	:	Gross National Product
GOI	:	Government of India
IBRD	:	International Bank for Reconstruction and Development
ICICI	:	Industrial Credit and Investment Corporation of India
IDA	:	International Development Association
IDBI	:	Industrial Development Bank of India
IFAD	:	International Fund for Agricultural Development
IFCI	:	Industrial Finance Corporation of India

IMF	:	International Monetary Fund
IRBI	:	Industrial Reconstruction Bank of India
LIC	:	Life Insurance Corporation
MDGs	:	Millennium Development Goals
MNCs	:	Multi-National Corporations
MOF	:	Ministry of Finance
NGOs	:	Non-Government Organizations
ODA	:	Official Development Assistance
OECD	:	Organization for Economic Cooperation and Development
OEEC	:	Organization of European Economic Cooperation
OLS	:	Ordinary Least Squares
OPEC	:	Organization of Petroleum Exporting Countries
P	:	Provisional
PPI	:	Private Portfolio Investment
PFI	:	Private Foreign Investment
QE	:	Quick Estimates
RBI	:	Reserve Bank of India
RE	:	Revised Estimates
SARS	:	Severe Acute Respiratory Syndrome
SCICI	:	Shipping Credit and Investment Company of India
SFCs	:	State Financial Corporations
SIDBI	:	Small Industries Development Bank of India
SIDCs	:	State Industrial Development Corporations
TDICI	:	Technology Development and Information Company of India
TFCI	:	Tourism Finance Corporation of India
UNCTAD	:	United Nations Conference on Trade and Development
WB	:	The World Bank
WW-I	:	World War Ist (1914-18)
WW-II	:	World War IInd (1939-45)

1

Foreign Aid : An Overview

Throughout the period of almost six decades since the World War II, development, whatever may be the definition, has been accepted in almost all the countries, whatever may be their political orientations, as the prime national goal. Earlier the development objective was focused mainly on the growth of per capita income. But, in reality, developing countries are now more concerned with the broad improvements in the quality of life, i.e., the reduced poverty, advances in literacy and health, and environmentally sustainable development along with higher incomes. In other words, "the ultimate goal of development is to reduce poverty and improve standards of living" (The World Bank, 1995c: p. 1), which requires sustainable economic growth, investment in capital and human resources.

But, most of the developing countries are faced with the problem of shortage of financial resources as they are "under equipped with capital in relation to their population and natural resources" (Nurkse, 1986: p. 1). Even when economic development has much to do with human endowments, social attitudes, political conditions and historical accidents etc., capital has been termed as a necessary but not a sufficient condition of progress. However, this problem of shortage of capital can mainly be over-ridden through the international flow of financial resources, besides certain other measures. These "external resource flows have a strategic and catalytic role to play only in so far as they supplement and not substitute domestic savings and also, concomitantly, help to bring in essential technology or access to foreign markets, promote export earnings, import substitution, and greater efficiency and competition in the domestic economy." (Chandavarkar, 1980: p. 30).

External resource flow means the transfer of resources, like financial, technical, food products, consultancy services etc., from the advanced industrialized countries, either officially and bilaterally (from government to government) or multilaterally (through international financial institutions) or privately, for the purpose of development investment to the economically backward developing countries. These resource flows can broadly be classified into two categories: (1) *Non-Debt-Creating Flows*, and (2) *Debt-Creating Flows*.

(1) *Non-Debt-Creating Flows* refer to the flow of financial resources in the form of *Private Foreign Investment (PFI)* which do not involve any repayment obligation and hence do not create debt burden in the recipient country. These non-debt-creating flows mainly are of two types: *Foreign Direct Investment (FDI)*, and *Private Portfolio Investment (PPI)*.

Foreign Direct Investment (FDI) forms one of the most significant economic and technological link, since the late 1950s, between the advanced industrialized countries, and the developing countries. The World Bank in its report 'Global Development Finance' has aptly remarked, "like trade, it provides an important channel for global integration and technology transfer. Many developing countries are opening their investment regimes, and enhancing the credibility of earlier trade and investment reforms." (The World Bank[b], 1997, Vol. I : p. 27). FDI consists of direct investment exercise that is made to acquire a lasting management interest (usually 10 percent of the voting stock) in an enterprise located in one country by the investors located in another, the investor's purpose being an effective voice in the management of the enterprise. It is the sum of equity capital, reinvestment of earnings, other long-term as well as short-term capital as shown in the balance of payments (The World Bank[b], 1996, Vol. I : p. 182). Although, such an investment can be made by individuals or partnerships but most of the FDI is undertaken by the Multinational (or Trans-national) Corporations with headquarters in the advanced industrialized countries.

Though FDI has become increasingly an important source in financing the needs of developing countries, yet it has remained mostly concentrated in some selected countries, such as : China, Brazil, Hong Kong, Mexico, Singapore, Malaysia, South Korea, Taiwan and Argentina, etc. The FDI has increased from US $ 51.1 billion in 1992 to US $ 162.1 billion in 2002 for all the developing countries including China. But, the share of India has increased from just 0.5 percent (US $ 233 million) in 1992 to only 2.9 percent (US $ 4.7 billion) in 2002 as against China's 21.8 percent (US $ 11,156 million) to 32.5 percent (US $ 52.7 billion) during the same period (Govt. of India[b], 2003: p. 133). The share of China along with Hong Kong and Taiwan has been 42 percent. The major source of FDI are East Asian newly industrialized countries along with Japan, which ranks as the second largest investor in the region (RBI[c], 2003: p. 154).

But, the FDI is "associated, in the minds of many persons, with imperialism and colonialism, and with foreign dominated enclaves surrounded by an underdeveloped native sector. Moreover, it is charged that gains in output produced by foreign investments are withdrawn from local economy in the form of profits remitted to their foreign owners." (Snider, 1987: p. 438). There is also the possibility of distortions in the production structure, due to investment in the low priority areas, from the point of view of national development plans.

However, the *Private Portfolio Investment (PPI)*, another important part of non-debt-creating flows, consisting of foreign purchase of stocks (equity), certificates of deposits, and commercial papers of developing countries through international markets, such as : institutional investors, Global Depository Receipts (GDRs)* and American Depository Receipts (ADRs).** Institutional investors include institutions like pension funds, investment trusts, asset management companies, nominee

* *GDR* : A GDR is foreign currency denominated instrument traded on a foreign stock exchange. It represents a certain numbers of underlying equity shares.

** *ADR*: An ADR is a US$ denominated instrument traded on foreign stock exchange.

companies and incorporated institutional portfolio managers. An important feature of these instruments is that these are traded in secondary markets and ergo, give investors the possibility of getting out of investment relatively easily. The PPI has been growing rapidly, since 1985, with the opening up of the developing countries. Between 1990 and 1999 total portfolio flows increased by more than 1200 percent, from just US $ 5 billion to US $ 60 billion.... Mexico was a principal beneficiary (and later a conspicuous victim) of these equity flows having received almost 25 percent of its entire external financing in this form (Todaro and Smith, 2004: p. 645). On an average, India received cross border portfolio investment to the tune of US $ 2.2 billion per year between 1992-93 and 2002-03. The cumulative Foreign Institutional Investment (FII) in India is close to US $ 19 billion, which accounted for over 10 percent of the total market capitalization of the Indian stock market (RBIc, 2003: pp. 162-63).

But, the PPI also suffers from certain disadvantages. First, these PPI flows tend to be pro-cyclical, in the sense that these come, when the balance of payments (BOP) position is seen to be strong and go out when the BOP position is expected to weaken. Thus, PPI accentuates the direction of movement of the BOP which can cause serious problems in the macroeconomic management, particularly in a developing country like India, where foreign exchange markets are very thin compared to the international financial market (Govt. of India, 1999, Vol. I : p. 66). Second, inflow of PPI does not necessarily mean that additional investment will take place, it could merely influence the asset prices. Even if investment comes in the form of new issues, no additional investment would occur if receipts are used for debt redemption or incurring current expenditure (Zaidi, 1996: p. 56). Third, a less transparent and less efficient market, in a developing country like India, is an important disadvantage for the PPI because no information is made available on the volume of transactions executed at the highest, and lowest prices. Neither client orders to buy or sell nor trades executed on the floor of exchange are time stamped, which results in the possibility of price manipulation through circular trading and collusion (Brahmbhatt *et al.*, 1996: p. 46). Other areas of concern include the fact that the settlement period is often a few weeks rather than days and that broker's own accounts are often not separated from their clients.

Thus, if any country relies heavily on the PPI to camouflage the structural weaknesses of the body economic, it might face problems like Mexico, where grossly overvalued foreign exchange rate led to high current account deficit and dwindling foreign exchange reserves in December, 1994. India opened its stock market to foreign institutional investors in September, 1992. By the end-March 2002, about four-fifth of FII emanated from the USA, UK and Western Europe. These flows were consistently positive for the first few years, reflective of buoyant stock market conditions, but turned negative in September, 1997 for the first time at the time of Asian crisis. Although there have been a few periods of net outflows during brief episodes of foreign exchange market volatility, they were quickly reversed once stability returned to financial markets (RBI[a], 2003: pp. 94-95). Hence, it would be a mistake to treat PPI as a stable factor in the process of economic growth.

Therefore, the scope for *non-debt-creating flows* in the form of PFI is quite limited in the developing countries in some critical key areas, such as : rural roads and infrastructure, medium and major surface irrigation systems, drainage system, flood control, implementation of land reforms, achievement of *Millennium Development Goals* (MDGs)* like eradication of poverty, maternal illness, mal-nutrition, disease control, abolition of child labor, large gender gap, deep social divisions, universal primary education, ensuring environmental sustainability, and other development programmes, for, investment in such areas calls for huge outlays, which a developing country like India cannot generate in a foreseeable future, and PFI is proving to be shy for the discernible reasons like long gestation period, incommensurate returns, etc. "Evidently, such investments are crucial for sustaining the economic recovery and equipping the poor to participate in the growth process." (The World Bank, 1995a: p. 38).

(2) Debt-Creating Flows in the form of *External Commercial Borrowings, Foreign Remittances,* in general, and *Official Development Assistance (or Foreign Aid),* in particular, has also a

*Millennium Development Goals (1990-2015) have been adopted at September, 2000 'United Nations Millennium General Assembly' in New York by 189 countries and are to be achieved by year ending 2015 (www.developmentgoals.org).

significant role to play in supplementing the domestic financial resources and in developing the productive capacity of the recipient developing economies, in the above-mentioned areas, where PFI has a limited role. These flows are considered as debt-creating because these involve the repayment obligations in the form of amortization and interest payments, and hence create debt burden in the recipient countries.

External Commercial Borrowings (ECBs) refer to the loans procured from the private international commercial banks and financial institutions, such as : International Finance Corporation (Washington), Asian Development Bank, Asian Finance and Investment Corporation Ltd., etc.; securitized instruments like floating rate notes and fixed rate bonds, and loans from semi-government export credit agencies, like DEG Germany, CDC UK, Nordic Investment Bank ; and foreign currency convertible bonds, till these are converted into equity shares. These borrowings are usually taken by the developing countries at the market rate of interest for the purpose of meeting their BOP requirements. But these ECB accruals depend upon certain factors, such as international interest rates (particularly the US dollar denominated), demand of domestic industry for investment, expectation of exchange rate fluctuations, hedging costs and credit rating of the recipient country by the international credit rating agencies, like the Standard and Poor's Outlook, Moody's Investor Service, Duff and Phelps Credit Rating, and Japanese Credit Rating Agency, etc.

However, too much dependence on ECBs, in addition to a high cost method of raising resources, is fraught with serious risks. India's experience during the 1980-90 period provided an important lesson for developing countries. Even during 2003-04 ECBs recorded net outflows amounting to US $ 6.6 billion in the capital account for the third successive year, since 2001-02 (Govt. of India[b], 2004: p. 133). "This is simply that dependence on new money from commercial sources to finance current imports is likely to make the economy extremely vulnerable and complicate the task of balance of payments management during the periods of domestic economic, social or political difficulties. Banks are extremely susceptible to adverse developments in any sphere and can quickly withdraw support with or without adequate cause. In good times, international banks compete fiercely with each other for business. In hard times, they act in unison. The withdrawal of support by a single bank can trigger off a chain reaction among all other banks" (Jalan, 1992 : p. 184). Thus, it is not safe for a developing country to rely too much on ECBs, particularly for short-term credit.

The Foreign Remittances in the form of non-resident emigrant deposits has been another major but most vulnerable source of debt-creating external finance for the developing countries. Under this non-resident bank deposit schemes, expatriate nationals residing abroad are allowed to open bank accounts in the recipient country freely, out of the funds remitted from abroad or foreign exchange brought in from abroad or out of funds legitimately due to them. For instance : in India, RBI has granted general permission to the banks which are authorized to deal in foreign exchange, to open such accounts freely in the form of Foreign Currency Non-Resident (Bank) Accounts, Non-Resident (External) Rupee Accounts and Non-Resident (Non-Repatriable) Rupee Deposits, etc. However, like ECBs, foreign remittances in the form of non-resident emigrant deposits are also high cost method of raising external resources, for, these deposits mainly depend upon the interest rate differential between the domestic recipients and foreign countries. If the interest rate increases in the other foreign countries, larger external inflow in the form of foreign remittances may not be expected from the non-resident emigrant deposits. In other words, like ECBs, these deposits are also 'fair weather friends'. If conditions are favorable, the growing volume of such deposits underlines the expatriate investment community's increasing confidence in the recipient country and if conditions turn unfavorable for the country, large scale outflow from such deposits can plunge the recipient country into a serious crisis, as has happened in India in the early 1990s. Besides this, there are fiscal costs involved in terms of the interest outgo on these deposits which tend to increase along with the increase in the volume of the deposits. Hence, the past experience indicates that too much dependence on such deposits is also not a rational policy.

However, the *Official Development Assistance (ODA)* also known as *'foreign aid'*, in the form of the official flows from bilateral sources, like friendly countries, and multilateral sources, such as : the World Bank (including IBRD and IDA), Asian

Development Bank (ADB), International Fund for Agricultural Development (IFAD), etc., on concessional and non-concessional terms, is another major external debt-creating source used to supplement the domestic financial resources in the recipient developing countries. Though the term 'foreign aid' nevertheless remains fuzzy, but refers to the congeries of governmental programmes through which funds, goods and services, additional to those normally acquired are made available to the developing countries for the benefit and welfare of their citizens, in cash or kind, as outright grants or loans, on concessionary or non-concessionary terms including technical assistance in the form of technical equipment, know-how, expert human resources, and training to the local counterparts. It also includes the flow of "concessional and non-concessional financing for projects, and programmes, support for policy reforms, and assistance in building implementation capacity" (The World Bank, 1995c: p. 1).

The foreign aid can be used for improving productive capacity in certain key areas mentioned earlier, where PFI is unattractive. It can also be used in some other areas. First, as budgetary support for macroeconomic stabilization and structural reform measures in a developing country like India, particularly at a time, when "the world's economies move inexorably to embrace market-friendly policies, public sectors are reorienting themselves, and downsizing, 'less is better' has been the cry. But could this response go too far ? In many critical areas, there are essential public responsibilities—in developing human, institutional, and physical infrastructure—that government must continue to fulfil. In these areas less is not necessarily better but 'better is better'. One key to development is that government must do well those things that government must do." (The World Bank, 1998: p. 83). It is the foreign aid (both money and ideas) which mostly support the public sector. Second, despite progress 43.5 percent of South Asian; 24.3 percent Sub-Saharan African; and 23.2 percent East Asian and Pacific population has been living below poverty line (of US$ 1 per day) in 1998 (The World Bank, 2000: p. 4). Foreign aid is expected to attenuate the poverty by meeting critical needs in areas outside the private ambit, such as: primary health and education, urban infrastructure, rural and state roads, etc., and in many cases 'crowding in' private investment. Last, concessional external assistance is expected to provide stable inflows, long maturities, and low interest charges that support a continued low debt-service ratio, and the stable capital account. "Hence, if domestic savings are low, and the prospects for foreign investment or borrowings are bleak, then foreign aid should be given in order to achieve the desired rate of growth" (White, 1992: p. 169).

Therefore, continued high levels of support by the donor community will remain significant for a developing country like India, although PFI, particularly the FDI, has also been playing an increasing role, since 1990. Even though, in an ideal scenario, one may think of discontinuing foreign aid, if not immediately, at least over a period of time, but this may not be possible for a developing country like India, for, "India is home to 40 percent of the world's poor" (Brahmbhatt *et al.*, 1996: p. 47). Further, two-thirds of all Indian women and two-fifths of all Indian men are illiterate, 81 percent of all scheduled caste women and 54 percent of all scheduled caste men are illiterate (Zanini, 2001: p. 3), and India ranks 127th out of 177 countries in the Human Development Index (UNDP, 2004: p. 141). The constraints imposed on account of budgetary reasons, and also on account of the fact that benefits of international expertise and technology are required at least in certain critical areas. Therefore, foreign aid still has an important role to play in the economic development of a developing country like India.

Retrospect

Whether foreign aid should be regarded as a new phenomenon or not, depends on one's own point of view. "Going back into the history, sovereign lending (and the problems associated with it) has been a feature of international economic life, at least since the Medicis of Florence* started making loans to the English and Spanish monarchs in the fourteenth century" (Thirlwall, 1995: p. 303). The decline of Medici was followed by the rise of the South German bankers led by a German mercantile family and banking dynasty—the Fugger family. The Fugger bank owed its rise and descent to the royal German family—the Hapsburg family** which it financed, supported, and patronized

* *Medicis of Florence:* An Italian family of bankers, merchants, and rulers of Florence and Tuscany prominent in the Italian political and cultural history in the 14th, 15th, and 16th centuries.

***Hapsburg/Habsburg Family:* Royal German family, one of the principal sovereign dynasties of the Europe from 15th to 20th century. Its name is derived from ancestral castle Habsburg, in Aargau, Switzerland.

in the sixteenth and seventeenth centuries. Direct loans to monarchs, such as: Maximilian I and Charles V were made on a secured basis for one year maturity at 12 to 14 percent. Loans made for political purposes were common and losses were common also (Seiber, 1982: p. 20; The New Encyclopaedia Britannica, 1997, Vol. 5 : pp. 34 and 603). Foreign aid was also used as an instrument of national policy during the eighteenth century, when Frederick of the Great of Prussia subsidized certain allies to assure their military support and effectiveness. This practice continued intermittently in Europe during the nineteenth century (The New Encyclopaedia Britannica, 1997, Vol. 4 : p. 877). In other words, in the history of diplomacy, subsidies, tributes and loans were common, and wartime aid among allies was already given by the British during the eighteenth century, and Napoleonic wars. However, the idea of peacetime economic aid among governments is novel. During the nineteenth century, it has been a common practice for the governments to transfer money on concessional terms to the governments of their colonies under the label of 'grants-in-aid', 'budgetary subsidy' or some such term. The governments of Britain, France, Germany and the United States all gave 'infant colony subsidies' of this sort before 1914, but invariably on temporary basis, and without the slightest connotation of moral obligation or 'aid for development', a word which itself was not a part of the vocabulary of the time (Mosley, 1987: p. 21). During the nineteenth century, British capital also helped to develop the growing United States, which was a debtor country up to 1914. Also, it is true that English and French capital exports to the underdeveloped regions, just before the World War-I (1914-18), exceeded the present flow of capital to underdeveloped countries, and that colonial government in many respects served the end of economic development. Generally speaking, the West has been involved in the economic development of the rest of the world, since the time of discoveries (Ohlin, 1966: p. 9).

During the World War-I, the United States made substantial loans to its European allies that became, in effect, grants when the allies defaulted on their repayments at the outset of the Great Depression. Because of this experience, the US aid during World War-II (1939-45) was offered in the form of 'lend-lease'. The United States provided its allies with essential equipment and supplies, and in return the allies equipped and supplied US troops stationed abroad (The New Encyclopaedia Britannica, 1997, Vol. 4 : p. 877). After WW-I, the United States took over from Britain as the major source of new capital flows. "There were occasions when the US government found it to be in the national interest to assist other countries. During this period, the US lent more than US $ 10 billion to some 20 countries, and most of this money was not repaid. Negotiated funding agreements and the Hoover Moratorium* , in effect, cancelled a large proportion of these debts" (Black, 1968: pp. 3 and 4). However, during 1920s there was a boom in the private investment abroad through the sale of foreign securities in the richer countries. But, the Great Depression during 1930s ended the flow, and many of the securities went into default. The situation began to change during 1940s. Recognizing the virtual disappearance of PFI, and the urgent need for capital transfers, the Bretton Woods Conference in July, 1944 set-up the 'International Bank for Reconstruction and Development' (IBRD or the World Bank) using the backing provided by its members to obtain capital for relending to governments (Thorp, 1971: p. 46).

The World Bank (WB), which was the first and is still the most important vehicle for multilateral transfers of money from advanced to underdeveloped countries, had the dual function of promoting the reconstruction of war-ravaged countries, both developed and developing, and of promoting economic development in the underdeveloped countries. "The WB got-off to a slow start in making loans to the developing countries, in large part because of its conservative policies. In the first six fiscal years up to June 30, 1952 the Bank made development loans totalling only US$ 885 million of which US$ 329 million went to Latin America; US$ 129 million to Asia and the Middle East; US$ 125 million went to Africa; and the remainder went to Europe and Australia. The opinion of Eugene Black, President of the WB from 1949 to 1962, was that the function of foreign aid is to promote and marginally supplement the flow of private loans, and direct investment capital to the developing countries, and to

* The then US President Hoover was forced by circumstances to propose a one year moratorium on inter-government debt payments leading to the end of repatriation and war debt payments.

assist these countries in mobilizing their own resources for achieving their development goals" (Mikesell, 1983: p. 2).

However, the WW-II changed the political imperatives and power balance which became a major concern for the powerful nations. There were both political and economic needs for restructuring the countries ruined by the war. This led to the creation of American 'Marshall Plan' (named after George C. Marshall, the US Secretary of State from 1947 to 49), launched to bring about financial and economic recovery of war-ravaged Europe, "had both a wellspring and an objective. The wellspring was the generosity of people expressing their desire to help other nations in need. The objective was to build a Europe in which democracy would flourish and which consequently would be strong enough to resist communism" (Owens and Shaw, 1972: p. 1). As a result of Marshall's initiative, the US Foreign Assistance Act of 1948 was passed on April 3, 1948. The Act called for a plan of European recovery open to all the nations willing to cooperate. It authorized assistance by the United States to the countries participating in the Plan (US House of Representatives Committee on International Relations, 1976: p. 8).

In Europe, conference between Britain, France and the USSR (now Russia) broke down, when the Russians rejected the idea of receiving American economic assistance. But the sixteen countries of Western Europe led by Britain and France set-up the 'Organisation of European Economic Cooperation' (OEEC, now the OECD) in Paris. In the next few years, massive amounts of American capital assistance helped Europe to get back on its feet (Arnold, 1985: p. 2). In other words, the success of Marshall Plan in promoting the economic recovery of war-ravaged economies of Western Europe and the cold war situation in the immediate post-war period mainly contributed to the systematic continuation of foreign aid.

The 'Colombo Plan'—a Commonwealth scheme—for providing assistance to the underdeveloped countries of the South and South-East Asia, formulated by the seven Commonwealth countries (Australia, Britain, Canada, Ceylon, India, New Zealand and Pakistan) in January, 1950 in the capital city of Ceylon (now Sri Lanka), may be taken to be the real beginning of the modern foreign aid programme. Later on, the Plan was extended to include a much wider area stretching from

Iran to South Korea and from Fiji in Pacific to Maldives in Indian Ocean. The USA in 1951 and Japan in 1954 also joined the Plan as donor countries. The Plan, regarded as the pioneer of bilateral aid, acted to bring the two sides, donor and donee, together. Under the Plan, there was no central common fund; a developing member country after determining its requirements approached one of the donor members. Together they worked out the system to implement the programme. "The six donor countries (Australia, Britain, Canada, Japan, New Zealand and the USA) were the main sources of aid but the developing members also provided some technical assistance to each other" (*Ibid*., p. 4). In the early 1950s, the WB also switched its attention from reconstruction to development, and by the mid-1950s its task of lending for the repair of war damage in Europe and Japan was over. The Bank had become exclusively a development institution, lending largely to Asia and South America, at that stage. During the second half of the 1950s, the USSR (now Russia) became, for the first time, a substantial donor of aid to the developing countries and five countries (Afghanistan, Egypt, Indonesia, Iran and India) became the principal object of superpower competition. The obvious instrument of persuasion was development aid. India's first two FYPs, particularly the Second, were mainly influenced by the Soviet ideas of comprehensive planning with priority to heavy industry, and was concentrated on the expansion of iron and steel industry through the construction of three new plants: Rourkela (1954), Bhilai (1955) and Durgapur (1956) with assistance from West Germany, the USSR and the UK, respectively. Thus, foreign aid became both fashionable and politically significant during 1950s, whatever may be the reasons.

In late 1950s and early 1960s, the African colonies of both Britain and France became independent in quick succession. This led to a very rapid expansion of the aid programmes of these two countries. Some of the countries, notably Ghana, Nigeria, Kenya and Zambia, also became the object of competitive offers of aid from both the United States and the Soviet Union. It was also in the early 1960s that Japan, West Germany, Holland and the Scandinavian countries, none of whom had ever been colonial powers on any scale, became substantial donors of aid, for the first time. "The market for aid transfers had moved rather rapidly from virtual United States monopoly in early 1950s, to US-Soviet duopoly in selected countries in the late 1950s, to a situation of fairly free, actual or potential competition between donors by the early 1960s" (Mosley, 1987: p. 25).

However, 1960s was the period of substantial multi-lateralization of aid with the European Economic Community (EEC), the regional development banks and the WB (both IBRD and IDA) emerging as donors of aid. The Development Assistance Committee (DAC)* of the OECD was formed in 1962 to coordinate the efforts and policies of the western donor countries. Most strikingly, it was the period in which the largest bilateral donor—the US decided to give aid to the underdeveloped countries, not in order to contain the spread of communism, not because other countries were giving it, but because it was right. Thus, "in the two decades, which have elapsed since the end of WW-II, international financial aid for development has steadily expanded in volume and has increased in complexity. A considerable variety of new institutions have been created to carry out the policies which have evolved in this field" (Friedman *et al.*, 1966 : p. 4).

"There has been a steady rise in foreign aid from OECD countries during 1970s and 1980s, and ODA peaked at US $ 69 billion (at 1995 prices) in 1991. However, in 1990s three events have lowered the absolute and relative importance of foreign aid : fiscal problems in OECD countries; end of the cold war; and the dramatic growth in private capital flows to developing countries" (The World Bank, 1998: p. 7). In the recent years, OECD countries have been struggling to control their fiscal deficits and contain growth in government spending. Even though foreign aid is a tiny fraction of their budgets, it has been one of the first items for the ax. All major donors have reduced aid relative to their GNPs between 1991-97. The decline was especially sharp in the United States—aid was merely 0.08 percent of GNP in 1997. Sweden and other Nordic countries have

* DAC, one of the specialized committees of the OECD, was formed in 1962, to improve the effectiveness of resources made available to developing countries. The members of DAC are : Australia, Austria, Belgium, Canada, Denmark, Finland, France, Germany, Ireland, Italy, Japan, The Netherlands, New Zealand, Norway, Sweden, Switzerland, UK, USA and the Commission of the European communities.

traditionally been generous, giving almost one percent of their GNP. But among large countries, France is the only one that gave more than 0.45 percent. Collectively, OECD countries contributed just 0.22 percent of their GNP in 1997. The end of the cold war influenced some countries' decisions. The strategic importance of foreign aid has ebbed; as a result, it has risks of losing its broad support among the donor governments (*Ibid.*, p. 7).

At the same time, there has been a surge in the private capital flows to the developing countries. In the 1970s and 1980s, official finance, i.e., money from bilateral donors and multilateral institutions, constituted about half of all finance going from developed to developing countries. With private flows expanding to more than US $ 250 billion in 1996, however, official finance was only a quarter of all finance available to developing countries. Private capital flows were heavily concentrated in a few selected countries and in certain cases the flows were also volatile. A surge in the late 1970s receded after the onset of the debt crisis in 1982. Another big surge occurred in the mid-1990s, but with the financial crisis rocking East Asia in 1997, foreign investment dropped sharply. The flow of private money to developing world fell by US $ 80 billion between 1996 and 1997. In any event, private flows continued to go to a small number of (mostly) middle income countries. In 1996, 26 countries received 95 percent of private investment, the rest went to the other 140 developing countries. In a typical low-income country, foreign aid remained, by far, the primary source of external finance amounting to 7-8 percent of their GNP (*Ibid.*, pp. 8-9). The poorest of the less developed countries require concessional external resources on a significant scale (Singer *et al*, 1991: p. 9).

However, the recent changes in global politics due to Afghanistan and Iraq conflicts, efforts to reach the MDGs, and the rise of civil society are altering the landscape for official flows in important ways. Aid flows have risen in 2002, and in 2003. The United States announced an Emergency Plan for AIDs relief, while pledges by the European Union governments would raise the ODA to 0.44 percent of GNP by 2010, from 0.35 percent in 2002. Aid, thus, currently remained low relative to historical levels and well below levels required to meet the MDGs. Substantial increases in disbursements are required over the next few years to meet the pledges for higher aid made at the 2002

Monterrey Conference, held in Mexico. The failure of global community to reach agreement on reducing agricultural subsidies and trade barriers at the World Trade Organization talks in Cancun in September, 2003 placed even more pressure on finding additional sources of finance for the developing countries. Coherent aid and trade policies are vital in promoting development. Moreover, recipient countries have improved their policies, raising their capacity to absorb and use aid effectively—strengthening the call for more aid (The World Bank[b], 2004, Vol. I : p. 107).

Thus, the instrument of foreign aid is still useful, and significant for serving the multiplicity of objectives ranging from economic and humanitarian to political and strategic in the developing countries.

Like many developing countries of Asia and Africa, foreign aid to India has also been a post-WW-II phenomenon. India, following independence on August 15, 1947 decided that most rational and suitable approach to development would be through FYPs, and on April 1, 1951 the First FYP (1951-56) was initiated. "At that time per capita national income was estimated at US $ 55; the population growth rate was around 1.7 percent; industrial sector was relatively underdeveloped; and gold, and forex reserves stood at a little more than US $ 2 billion. A major goal of the planners was to raise per capita income to US $ 110 over a twenty-five-year period. This was equivalent to annual increases in per capita income of 3 percent. Even such a modest gain was recognized as a strain because of population increases." (Friedman *et al,* 1966: p. 217). The level of both savings and investment in 1950-51 was US $ 1.2 billion at 1960-61 prices, i.e., both savings and investment amounted to 5.7 percent of national income (Katz, 1968: p.18). Thus, the limited savings, forex reserves and varied but complex development requirements compelled India to seek larger amount of foreign aid.

On the eve of the launch of First FYP, Govt. of India (GOI) hardly had any foreign aid liability but the inception of planning process changed the scenario. India is an especially interesting country in this regard, for, it has been one of the largest aid recipients (in absolute terms) and has received aid from most aid-giving sources. On the average, India has received foreign aid to the tune of one billion US dollars annually in 1960s and early

1970s; two to three billion US dollars annually in the late 1970s; and four to five billion US dollars annually during 1980s and 1990s. During the year 2003-04, India received US $ 3826.7 million in the form of foreign aid (Govt. of India[b], 2005: p. S-96) from various countries and international financial institutions, which have been broadly grouped into three categories: (a) The WB coordinated consortium members (rechristened as 'India Development Forum'); (b) Russian Federation and East European Countries; and (c) others, like EEC, OPEC Fund, ADB, Switzerland, etc. But there are no outright grants from Russian Federation and East European Countries. Even the loans from this region were negligible and dwindled at a rapid pace, and since 1994-95 India did not receive anything, except for the year 1999-00, from this region. Both the loans and outright grants from the consortium members, and others were exhibiting a fluctuating trend. On the whole, there was not much increase in foreign aid during the post-reform period, albeit it has shown a declining trend recently during the year 2003-04, when authorized aid declined to US $ 3826.7 million (*Ibid.*, p. S-96). However, "only a few countries have received as much aid in absolute amounts from as wide a variety of sources and on such a variety of terms" as India has obtained (Gang and Khan, 1990: p. 432).

But, it must be noted that even in the peak aid years, per capita aid, and aid as percentage of GNP and GDP (i.e., relative aid) have been very low for India. Per capita aid in India peaked at US $ 8.1 in 1966; attenuated to US $ 1.9 in 1985; further declined to US $ 1.7 in 1993; and hit the lowest level at US $ 1.0 in 1999 (The World Bank, 2002c: p. 238). It increased to US $ 2.0 in the year 2001 (The World Bank, 2004: p. 260). However, aid as percentage of GDP of India peaked at 4.5 percent in 1966; declined to 1.25 percent in 1984 (Gang and Khan, 1990: p. 432); and touched the bottom level of 0.2 percent in the fiscal 1998-99 (RBI[c], 1999: p. X-21). Similarly, aid as percentage of economy's GNP peaked at 4.0 percent in 1966, and hit the bottom level of 0.4 percent in 1990 and is stable at this lowest level during the period 1998-2001. It was 0.4 percent of GNP in 2001 (The World Bank, 2004: p. 260).

These aid figures show that aid-donors have never been willing to provide the massive absolute sums of money required to render India's aid per person or as a proportion of GNP, comparable with that of other low income countries. This is, perhaps, due to certain reasons like 'large country effect', turbulent bilateral relations with the major donors, etc. This, 'large country effect' results partly from the geo-political motivations behind aid-giving. Most of the donors wish to appear to be generous in as many different countries as possible and can win friends in twenty medium-sized poor countries, each with 35-40 million people by economizing on aid to one large country like India. Apart from this 'large country effect', the amount of aid that India has received also depended on the state of its bilateral relations with major donors, particularly the United States, at least from 1960 to 1972. India's aid flows remained small compared with those of neighbouring (and similarly poor) Pakistan, reflecting both India's greater size, and its more distanced and at times turbulent political relations with the United States. "Thus, in macroeconomic context, aid resources have always played a much smaller role in India than in other Asian countries like Korea and Taiwan in the 1950s and 1960s, or in most African countries in the 1970s and early 1980s." (Lipton and Toye, 1990: p. 4).

Despite these much smaller and recently declining flows of aid, foreign aid is still considered as significant for India's economic development. Its advantages over the other types of market loans, such as : lower costs and longer maturity periods etc., are well known, and even the Indian planners and policy-makers have sought this type of resources for country's development. Though recently in September, 2004, GOI decided not to receive bilateral assistance from all other countries, except the G-8 countries : Japan, USA, Germany, UK, France, Italy, Canada and Russia along with the European Commission, yet the Tenth 'FYP' (2002-07) has expected net external assistance to be US $ 1572 million in its final year 2006-07 (Govt. of India, 2002, Vol. I : p. 112). Similarly, over the years, gross budgetary support for supporting State and Central plans has maintained a yearly aid component of about 20 percent on the average. In recent years, the State governments, in particular, are very keen for various reasons to have more of foreign-aided projects, especially in infrastructure and social sectors (Sarkar, 1999: p. 2). Hence, it becomes significant and essential to analyze the nature, extent, and impact of foreign aid on the Indian economy.

Foreign aid, which India has received from various friendly countries and multilateral financial institutions, is a complex mixture of outright grants, loans, sale of surplus products (food aid), and technical assistance, etc. Dominance of loans as compared to outright grants has been the most striking feature of foreign aid to India as the share of loans was more than 90 percent in 1960s and early 1970s; more than 80 percent in 1980s; again more than 90 percent in 1990s; and now 88 percent in the year 2003-04 (Govt. of India[b], 2005: p. S-95). However, the contribution of foreign aid, particularly in the form of loans, in the economic development of a recipient developing country like India, is not a matter of its quantum only, albeit it depends on the terms and conditions under which it is sanctioned by the donors, i.e., the real worth of loans depends on their terms and conditions like the rate of interest to be charged, grace period, and maturity period of the loans, etc. The loans are classified as concessional if their 'grant element' exceeds 25 percent and non-concessional otherwise (OECD, 1995: p. 123). Hence, it also becomes essential to estimate the 'grant element' of the loans in order to estimate their real worth and to analyze their effectiveness in Indian economy.

In the present study, an attempt has been made to estimate the loan-wise grant-element inherent in the various loans utilized by India from various friendly countries and multilateral financial institutions. Also, an effort has been made to evaluate the role, nature, extent, and effectiveness of foreign aid in the different sectors of the Indian economy, particularly after the liberalization and the changed global politico-economic environment.

Objectives of the Study

The specific objectives of the present study are:

1. to examine the various theoretical and empirical issues involved in the utilization of foreign aid;
2. to analyze the source-wise and purpose-wise nature, extent and utilization of foreign aid in India, and the changes there-in;
3. to analyze the loan-wise terms and conditions of foreign aid, particularly the loans utilized by India, both from

multilateral and bilateral sources, in order to estimate grant element inherent there-in;
4. to examine the effectiveness of foreign aid in India through its impact on the diverse sectors of the economy;
5. to review the policy of Govt. of India regarding accepting foreign aid; and
6. to identify the problems, especially in the authorization as well as utilization, of foreign aid in India and to suggest policy measures to override these problems.

Plan of the Study

The present study has been organized into 11 chapters including the present one, which introduces the topic. Chapter 2 explains the various concepts of foreign aid along with database and methodology applied in the study. Important theoretical issues involved in the major aspects of the flow of foreign aid to the developing countries have been discussed in Chapter 3. A brief review of the empirical studies relating to the foreign aid, particularly concerning India, has been made in Chapter 4. In Chapter 5, an attempt has been made to examine the source-wise and purpose-wise utilization of foreign aid in the Indian economy. Chapter 6 deals with the estimation of grant element inherent in the multilateral loans to India along with the role of multilateral agencies and private philanthropic organizations providing outright grants to India. In Chapter 7, measurement of grant element inherent in the bilateral loans to India has been undertaken. In Chapter 8, an endeavor has been made to examine the effectiveness of utilized foreign aid through its impact on the various sectors of the Indian economy. Chapter 9 reviews the policy of the Govt. of India regarding accepting foreign aid. Chapter 10 focuses upon the problems faced by India in obtaining, utilizing and repaying of foreign aid. Certain policy measures to overcome these problems, and for improving the effectiveness of foreign aid in India have been suggested in Chapter 11 which also summarizes the discussion and main findings of the study.

Foreign Aid : Concepts

In the present chapter, an endeavor has been made to discuss the basic terms, concepts and definitions relating to the 'foreign aid', and the data base and methodology applied in the study in two sections. Section I deals with the various concepts relating to foreign aid relevant for the discussion that would ensue in the following chapters, while Section II explains the data base and methodology applied in the present study.

Section I

MEANING OF FOREIGN AID

The term 'aid' is a fluid concept, for, like 'socialism' it means different things to different people. It has no universally acceptable definition, even after the passage of quite a few decades. In the *Oxford English Dictionary,* the word 'aid' is defined by the positive synonyms, like "help, assistance, support, succour and relief". However, it refers to a situation derived partly from the fact that there are two parties to any aid relationship. The donors' perception is totally different from that of the recipients'. Donors believe that aid is a transfer of goods and services that entails a cost to them. On the other side, recipients view aid as a transfer of goods and services that contributes to their economic development and welfare, and that would not otherwise have been available—at least not at affordable terms (Akbar, 1995: p. 358). Thus, "aid is an inflow of subsidised or gratis resources and in this sense it enriches the recipients. But unlike manna from heaven, it does not descend indiscriminately on everybody" (Roy, 1991: p. 5). It has important moral, political, economic and strategic considerations. It is called 'foreign' because it originates outside the national geographical boundaries of the recipient country. It is called 'aid' because such flows are not determined by the same principles that govern the normal flow of trade and capital (Hawkins, 1970: p. 17), i.e., "it refers only to those parts of capital inflow which normal market incentives do not provide" (Rosenstein-Rodan, 1961: p. 109). "It is the extension of welfare-state-style income transfer from the domestic to international level. Income is transferred, not from Citizen A to Citizen B, but from the government of Country A to the government of Country B. The common perception is that foreign aid is a means by which rich donor countries help poor people in foreign lands" (Krauss, 1997: p. 61). It should be kept in mind, however, that aid means more than the flow of financial resources, it also includes the transmission of ideas and policy experience. The effects of these contributions are extremely important but are much more difficult to measure and quantify (The World Bank, 1995c: p. V). Thus, the term 'foreign aid' consists of explicit transfer of real resources to the less developed countries on concessional terms. Unless the resource transfer involves to some degree more favorable terms than those available commercially, there is no 'gift' element involved (Bhagwati and Eckaus, 1970: p. 7). In other words, any flow of capital to less developed countries which meets two criteria: (a) its objective should be non-commercial from the point of view of the donor, and (b) it should be characterized by 'concessional' terms, that is, the interest rate and repayment period for borrowed capital should be 'softer' (less stringent) than commercial terms prevailing in the global capital, and labor markets. Even this definition can sometimes be inappropriate, since it could exclude military aid which is both non-commercial and concessional. Normally, however, military aid is excluded from the international measurements of foreign aid flows (Todaro and Smith, 2004: pp. 647-48). Properly speaking, "for the lack of a better term, 'foreign aid' is the expression, most frequently, used to describe the flow of financial and technical resources from the developed world to the underdeveloped world." (Black, 1968: p. 1). Outright grants of freely convertible currency constitute full-fledged aid in true sense as these do not generate a reverse flow of resources from the recipient country, while loans contain only some element of aid as they have to be repaid depending upon the rate of interest, length of maturity period and grace period, generally in the currency in which loan is granted, as the case may be. In this context another view is that the term foreign aid "should be reserved for outright grants and for a percentage of the face value of loans made on a more favorable terms than those prevailing in the commercial markets" (Zuvekas, 1979: p. 337), which means only the grant component of each resource inflow should be conceived as foreign aid in the real sense.

Any international inflow of capital, goods or services can be called 'foreign aid' if (a) it is different from the flow of goods and services that moves under normal trade agreements in search of profit; (b) the terms and conditions under which these flow takes place must be concessionary than the normal conditions prevailing in the global capital and labor markets. All the business transactions, private trade and capital movements are not foreign aid, since the resources so transferred are not provided on concessionary terms. Similarly, implicit transfer of resources occasioned by special import quotas and preferential tariffs accorded to the imports from developing countries—as advocated in the UNCTAD meetings, cannot be termed as foreign aid, even though such arrangements imply a definite addition to the purchasing power of the developing countries; and (c) military aid is generally excluded from the international measurements of foreign aid flows despite being both concessional and non-commercial.

It should also be noted here that outright grants and grant element inherent in the loans are not conceived as a part of debt-creating flows to the developing countries as these do not involve any repayment obligation. However, these are included in this category only as a part of foreign aid.

In brief, foreign aid is an international inflow of capital, goods and/or services for the welfare of developing countries, and their citizens; in cash or kind, either as outright grants or loans; on both concessionary, and non-concessionary terms including technical assistance and training usually in the form of expert human resources, technical know-how and equipment etc., from the relatively advanced industrialized countries or international organizations, directly or indirectly. It excludes, apart from private investments, short-term repayable loans, particularly those of the IMF.

CONCEPTS OF FOREIGN AID

There are five useful concepts of foreign aid. The first, as defined by the Development Assistance Committee (DAC) of the OECD is the *Official Development Assistance* (ODA) inclusive of grants and loans to the developing countries "which are: (a) undertaken by the official sector, (b) with the main objective of promotion of economic development and welfare of the recipient countries, and (c) at concessional terms (a loan having a grant element of at least 25 percent). In addition to financial flows, technical cooperation is also included in aid. Grants, loans and credits for military purposes are excluded" (OECD, 1995: pp. 122-23). "Foreign aid is usually associated with ODA and is normally targeted to the poorest countries" (The World Bank, 1998: p. 6). ODA is usually calculated net of amortization.

The second concept, *Effective Development Assistance* (EDA), espoused by the World Bank economists Charles C. Chang, Eduardo Fernandez-Arias and Luis Serven, is defined as "the sum of the grant equivalents of all development flows disbursed in a given period—grants tied to technical assistance are excluded from EDA" (Chang *et al.*, 1999: p. 6). EDA is also calculated on the basis of data from the DAC of OECD but lumps together the grant equivalents of loans (albeit their face value), including loans with a concessional element of less than 25 percent. This concept, unlike ODA, does not take into consideration debt adjustments, whether in the form of debt forgiveness or rescheduling. Only concessional flows from the IMF (such as : Structural Adjustment Facility and Enhanced Structural Adjustment Facility) are taken into account here.

The third concept, aggregate *Official Development Finance* (ODF), also calculated on the basis of data gathered by Chang *et al.* (1999), includes not only EDA (grants and grant element implicit in loans) but also the non-concessional element of loans, technical assistance grants and the IMF's non-concessional financing.

The fourth concept, gross *Total Official Flows* (TOF) from the public sector is calculated on the basis of data from OECD's DAC, includes gross ODA as well as other flows from the public sector. The latter, in the form of public credits for the exports, equity holdings, public sector portfolio investments, non-concessional IMF and the WB financing etc., are public sector interventions whose main aim is not development-related but are intended to foster development. These have a grant element less than 25 percent and are, ergo, excluded from the ODA category. However, both the ODF and TOF are conceptually equivalent, except for the debt adjustment issue, but they differ mainly in the statistical sources used.

The fifth concept, *Net Transfers* refers to the real contribution that aid flows are making to the domestic expenditure, as they deduct amortization and interest payments form the raw or gross amount. This concept is not only of macroeconomic significance but also represents for the government that portion of external contributions which helps to avoid the accumulation of external arrears.

Thus, it can be generalized that foreign aid (or ODA) is a generic term, which signifies the international transfer of financial, technical and human resources; in different forms, on non-commercial, concessional and softer terms; other than the loans available in the global capital market, from the advanced industrialized countries to the economically backward developing countries for the promotion of their economic development. In the present study, the term foreign aid is used in the strict sense of ODA.

However, the term foreign aid should be distinguished from the term PFI or capital, as the latter moves from one country to another only in response to the commercial considerations, i.e., the lure of profit and private expectations, whereas foreign aid is used to assist the developing countries in their development programme resulting from the policy decisions taken by the donor governments and institutions.

Similarly, foreign aid should also be distinguished from the term ODF. The first is a subset of the second and comprises grants plus concessional loans that have at least a 25 percent grant component. ODF is all financing that flows from the developed country governments and multilateral agencies to the developing countries. Some of this financing is at interest rates close to commercial rates (The World Bank, 1998 : p. 6).

COMPONENTS OF FOREIGN AID

The term foreign aid usually comprises four components viz : (1) Loans, (2) Grants-in-Aid, (3) Sale of Surplus products, and (4) Technical assistance.

1. Loans

Loans are that part of foreign aid which are furnished by the lender on the understanding that these will, in the due course of time, be paid for by the borrower, i.e., loans refer to the transfer of resources with repayment obligations, and involve debt servicing which impose monetary and transfer burden on the recipient. Repayment of loans are made either by the export of goods or by convertible or inconvertible currency. However, the loans can be of different types such as:

1.1 Term Loans

The loans sanctioned for a specific period of time with certain annual rate of interest are known as term loans. Such loans can be short-term, medium-term and long-term according to the period of time for which they are sanctioned. Short-term loans are generally repayable over a period of 10 years or less, while loans repayable between 11 to 20 years are considered as medium-term loans, and the loans repayable over 20 years or more are called as long-term loans.

1.2 Hard and Soft Loans

'Hard loans' are those loans which are repayable only in foreign currencies, have very little grace and maturity periods along with a very high rate of interest. These can be in 'hard' or 'dearer' foreign currencies, like US $, British £, Euros (€), etc.

On the flip side, 'soft loans' are those loans in which full or part repayment can be made in the borrower country's own local currency. These soft loans can be of many varieties such as : longer-term loans with more generous periods of grace of 50 years or more; loans repayable in foreign currencies at a very low rate of interest with a grace period of 10 years or more, etc.

1.3 Source-Tied Loans

Source-tied loan is the loan where recipient country, as a condition of loan, is obliged to use the loan money to buy goods and services from the donor country only, whatever the international market conditions and prices may be. However, in case loan is tied to both a specific project as well as purchases in donor country, this is conceived as double tying.

1.4 Currency-Tied Loans

Currency-tied loans are those loans in which repayments are strictly made in 'hard' or 'dearer' currencies, i.e., the recipient country is bound to repay the loan in the same currency in which loan has been received or in some hard currency. The recipient country is not allowed to repay in local currency or in the currency of any other third country.

2. Grants-in-Aid

Outright grants also known as 'something for nothing' refer to the transfer of resources without any obligation concerning their repayments. These can be commodities, services, funds in the form of US dollars or currencies other than US dollars. However, like loans, special conditions concerning receipt and use can be attached to the grants. The fundamental discrepancy between an outright grant and a loan seems too obvious to a belabor: an outright grant has not to be repaid, while a loan has to. An outright grant requires only a courteous acknowledgement, while repayment of a loan requires acts of saving, of discipline and of self-denial. But certain loans, for which repayment is not required in lender's currency, a category has been created, called as 'grant like contributions', usually included under the general heading of grants because these do not create an external indebtedness of recipient country payable in convertible currency.

3. Sale of Surplus Products

Sale of surplus products, both consumption and capital, for payments in local currency, like the US Public Law 480 and

Section 402 currencies. Local currency transactions involve the accumulation and disposition of foreign currencies that are either owned by the US Government as a result of its foreign economic operations or over which the US Government exercises some degree of control. For instance : the deposits acquired by the US Government in return for sale of surplus agricultural commodities pursuant to Title I of the Public Law 480 were used for the recipient country, mainly as loans and grants for economic development; as grants for military purposes; and for loans to private Americans and in certain cases foreign enterprises (known as Cooley amendment loans).

4. Technical Assistance

Technical assistance refers not only to the transfer of technical services but also of the technical know-how in the form of specialized modern sophisticated technical equipment, machinery, training facilities to local counterparts, and consultancy services of experts and technicians etc., intended to raise the level of output by changing the mode of production in the recipient developing countries. "Technical assistance, infact, covers two distinct areas—overseas training and employment of expatriates, the latter nearly always including an on-the-job training component for counterpart staff. Ideally speaking, expatriates are used where a genuine skill shortage exists and then be replaced by local personnel who became available through the two channels of training provided by technical assistance" (White and Luttick, 1994: p. 87).

SOURCES OF FOREIGN AID

Foreign aid can be obtained from three sources, mainly: (1) Bilateral, (2) Multilateral, and (3) Private Philanthropic Organizations.

1. Bilateral Aid

Bilateral aid refers to a programme in which one single donor country, normally a government, deals directly with one single recipient, also normally a government. It is generally administered by the official agencies of the donor countries, such as : Canadian International Development Agency (CIDA); Australian Agency for International Development (AUSAID); Japanese Overseas Economic Cooperation Fund (OECF); and United States Agency for International Development (USAID), etc. The term 'bilateral' is applied more to the source of aid than to the recipient.

But one major drawback of bilateral aid programme is that the allocation of aid is heavily influenced by the political considerations, historical links and the diplomatic relations, etc. For instance : bulk of the UK aid goes to the Commonwealth and a few remaining colonies; and bulk of the US aid goes to strategically important allies, like Israel, Pakistan, and Latin American countries. Another problem arises when bilateral aid is received from numerous donor countries, each with its own demands as to proper use of aid resources. These problems are compounded further when again as a characteristic of bilateral programs, aid is tied, by either donor country or by project or both.

2. Multilateral Aid

The surest way of avoiding the problems associated with bilateral aid program is the provision of multilateral aid. Major sources of multilateral aid are funds and contributions from rich, advanced, and industrialized countries administered by the prototype international agencies, like the World Bank (both IBRD and IDA), United Nations Development Programme (UNDP) and the various regional development banks such as : Asian Development Bank (ADB), African Development Bank, Inter-American Development Bank, and Arab Development Bank, etc. These multilateral aid sources tend to spread their aid more or less evenly—widely but thinly—over all their member-countries, for, there are strong pressures to do so (Singer and Ansari, 1978: p.164). However, transactions with the IMF are excluded as representing purchases of currency (or drawings), albeit, credit transactions in the usual sense. One might speculate about whether or not the issue of Special Drawing Rights (SDRs) is a form of assistance when given to developing countries as their share in a global transaction.

3. Private Philanthropic Organizations

The non-government organizations of the advanced industrialized countries, especially the US, such as : the Ford Foundation, the Rockefeller Foundation, etc., also forms a source of foreign aid for the developing countries. The assistance from such charitable institutions is only in the form of outright grants. But these Foundations provide a very small quantum of foreign aid as compared to the other sources.

TYPES OF FOREIGN AID

Foreign aid can take a variety of forms. The basic idea underlying it is simple, for, some terms have acquired special meanings and due to their speciality these are recognized in certain specific forms, such as:

1. Gross Aid *vs.* Net Aid

The term 'gross aid' is a broader one used to denote the total flow of external aid received by the donee country during a particular period of time, usually a fiscal year. On the other side, 'net aid' is a narrow term used to describe as the total external assistance received by the borrower country excluding amortization and interest payments during that particular fiscal year.

2. Economic Aid *vs.* Technical Aid

'Economic aid' is intended to raise the level of output by increasing the supply of capital in the recipient country, while the 'technical aid' is intended to raise the level of output by changing the methods of production, i.e., the difference between both rests not in form but in the purpose of aid. Technical assistance involves not only transfer of technical services but also of technical know-how, infact all types of aid, which provide for the acquisition and dissemination of know-how (Rao and Narain, 1963: pp. 6-7).

3. Economic Aid *vs.* Military Aid

As stated earlier, the 'economic aid' is intended to raise the level of output by increasing the supply of capital in the recipient country. Its main objective is to eradicate poverty and to promote long-term growth in the recipient developing country. On the flip side, 'military aid' neither helps in changing the mode of production nor increasing the percentage of investment directly, albeit, it makes the recipient country only militarily strong, like Israel, Pakistan, etc., with US military aid. The main objective of such aid is to build up military potential either for mutual defence or for aggressive expansion.

4. Development Aid *vs.* Maintenance Aid

The term 'development aid' is used to describe the quantum of foreign aid required to be utilizing for expanding the capital base of the recipient developing countries, while the 'maintenance aid' is used to denote the amount of aid which helps in utilizing the existing production capacity of the recipient economy. However, the latter depends upon the existing capital base of the economy as well as the additional capacity built during the process of development itself, which include the provision of raw materials, replacement of components and parts of the existing capital machinery, etc.

5. Authorized Aid *vs.* Utilized Aid

The term 'authorized aid' refers to the total amount of foreign aid which has been sanctioned by the donor country/ institution to the recipient country during a particular period of time, but not necessarily for release during that particular period. However, a part of it may remain unutilized due to administrative lags, procedural delays or other reasons. On the other hand, 'utilized aid' refers to that part of total authorized aid which has actually been utilized by the recipient developing country during a particular period of time. It depends upon the administrative efficiency, procedural implications, etc., of the recipient country.

6. Bilateral Aid *vs.* Multilateral Aid

The pure case of 'bilateral aid' is where one single donor, normally a government, deals directly with one single recipient, also normally a government. The pure case of 'multilateral aid' is represented by some global agency/institution dealing directly with a recipient government or group of governments (Singer and Ansari, 1978: p. 162), such as : the WB, ADB, IFAD, etc.

7. Tied Aid *vs.* Untied Aid

'Tied aid' also known as 'project aid' refers to that part of foreign aid which has been sanctioned for a separate specific project in the recipient country by the donor agency. However, under such category, aid is not tied to any particular currency. On the flip side, 'untied aid' or 'programme aid' refers to that type of foreign aid under which funds are provided for general purposes to the donee country and are not tied to any specific project, i.e., funds are permitted to flow into those sectors of the economy which really require them.

TERMS AND CONDITIONS OF FOREIGN AID : TERMINOLOGY

There is no denying the fact that the total magnitude of foreign aid is of great importance in facilitating and accelerating the process of development in the recipient developing countries, but it must be emphasized that the magnitude by itself is not a sufficient factor unless 'aid' of the right type may not produce the same satisfactory results that a smaller volume of an appropriate type of 'aid' may produce. The character of aid, i.e., the terms and conditions, under which aid is sanctioned are nevertheless and frequently more significant than the quantum of aid. The terms and conditions of foreign aid refer to the rates of interest charged on the sanctioned foreign loans; periods of grace and maturity accorded in these loans; modes of repayments, i.e., whether loans are repayable in local domestic currency or in foreign currencies; nature of these foreign loans, i.e., whether these loans are project-tied or source-tied or not; and commitment charges, etc., discussed below:

1. Grace and Maturity Periods

'Grace period' or 'moratorium' refers to the initial time period of a loan during which no repayment of principal amount (amortization) is required but only interest accrued is paid, while 'maturity period' denotes the period of time elapsing between the date of agreement of a loan and the date of the completion of total repayment of the overall loan amount.

2. Nominal or Face Value of the Loan

'Nominal' or 'Face' value of a loan are the terms used interchangeably to mean the value of the loan specified at the time of its sanctioning.

3. Rescheduling of the Loan

Rescheduling of the loan means increase in the maturity period of the loan, i.e., when maturity of loan is extended, it is acknowledged as rescheduling of the loan.

4. Refinancing

Refinancing refers to the raising of new loans to meet the obligations on outstanding loans.

5. Discounted Value

The term 'present value' or 'discounted value' of a loan repayments means the same thing and refers to the value of loan repayments discounted at an appropriate rate chosen to reflect the opportunity cost of capital.

6. Rate of Discount

Rate of discount is the rate of interest at which all the future repayments of a loan are discounted, i.e., the rate at which a loan could have been obtained from an alternative source under the similar terms and conditions.

7. Absorptive Capacity

Absorptive capacity refers to the .quantum of foreign aid which can be fruitfully and conveniently utilized in the recipient country.

8. Debt-Servicing

The repayments of principal amount of the loans (amortization) along with accrued interest on the outstanding loans by the borrowing country is known as debt-servicing.

9. Debt-Service Ratio

Payments of amortization along with accrued interest on the outstanding loans, as the ratio of country's forex reserves obtained by the export of goods and services in a given fiscal year, is known as debt-service ratio.

10. Grant Element

Grant element represents the portion of loan which at a given time is not expected to be repaid by the donee/

or recipient country, i.e., the amount of concessionality or subsidy (S) implicitly included in the loan relative to its face value, sensitive to an appropriate rate of discount. It is the discrepancy between the face value of a loan (L) and the present value (P) of all the future repayments (amortization and interest payments) discounted at an appropriate rate of interest. Symbolically, S = L—P, expressed as the percentage of the face value of the loan, i.e., Grant Element = S/L. It refers to "the value of aid as the combined nominal (or market) value of all forms of aid less the discounted present value of loan repayments, discounted at a rate of interest reflecting the alternative employment of long-term public capital" (Pincus, 1970: p. 169).

11. Commitment Charges

Grant element of a loan would be reduced by a small margin, in case commitment charges, wherever relevant, are paid. These charges are to be paid when withdrawls are less than the amount agreed to in the draw-down schedule of a loan agreement, i.e., these charges are levied on the discrepancy between the amount specified in the draw-down schedule and the amount actually withdrawn.

Section II

DATA BASE

The study entitled *'Foreign Aid in India : Effectiveness and Policy'*, being country specific, is primarily based upon the secondary data collected from the various reports published by the Ministry of Finance, Govt. of India; Reserve Bank of India; CMIE; the World Bank; the OECD; and the UNDP. The statistical data regarding source-wise and purpose-wise foreign aid, both authorized as well as utilized, have been collected from the *Economic Survey* (various issues: 1970-71 to 2004-05), published annually by the Economic Division, Ministry of Finance, Govt. of India; *Report on Currency and Finance, Vols. I and II* (various issues: 1950-51 to 1997-98), *Report on Currency and Finance* (various issues: 1998-99 to 2002-03), *Annual Report* (various issues: 1970-71 to 2003-04), and *Handbook of Statistics on The Indian Economy (2003-04)*, annual publications of the RBI; and the *External Assistance (2003-04)*, published annually by the Aid, Accounts and Audit Division of the Department of Economic Affairs, Ministry of Finance, Govt. of India. Reports of the 'Development Assistance Committee' of the OECD, the World Bank and the UNDP were also consulted. Statistical data regarding external debt burden were cross checked with figures reported in *India's External Debt: A Status Report* (various issues: 2000 to 2004), published annually by the Department of Economic Affairs, Ministry of Finance, Govt. of India.

For estimating source-wise and loan-wise 'grant element' inherent in the various foreign loans utilized by (committed to, in case of loans in pipeline) the India during the period 1980-81 to 2003-04, statistical information regarding source-wise and loan-wise terms and conditions, and exchange rate variations in Rupee *vis-a-vis* foreign currencies were obtained from the *External Assistance* (various issues: 1970-71 to 2003-04). Data regarding the domestic market sensitive discount rates used in the estimation of grant elements have been taken from the *Handbook of Statistics on The Indian Economy (2003-04)*. For the purpose of estimation of grant element *Global Development Finance* (Formerly, the *World Debt Tables*) *Vol. I and II* (various issues: 1990 to 2005) published annually by the World Bank have also been consulted.

For examining the effectiveness of utilized foreign aid in India through its impact on the various sectors of the economy, statistical data regarding various development indicators have been collected from the *Handbook of Statistics on The Indian Economy (2003-04)*; *Economic Survey* (various issues: 1970-71 to 2004-05); *National Accounts Statistics Back Series 1950-51 to 1992-93 (2001)*, and *National Accounts Statistics* (various issues: 1990 to 2004), published annually by the Central Statistical Organization, Ministry of Statistics and Programme Implementation, Govt. of India; and *Foreign Trade & Balance of Payments* (various issues: 2000 to 2004), one of the monthly publications of the Centre for Monitoring Indian Economy (CMIE).

For evaluating Govt. of India's policy regarding foreign aid, in addition to above, statistical information have also been obtained from the *Annual Report* (various issues: 1997-98 to 2003-04) published by the Ministry of Finance, Govt. of India; *Indian Public Finance Statistics (2003-04)*, yearly publication of the Economic Division, Department of Economic Affairs, Ministry of

Finance, Govt. of India; and various Drafts, Over-views and Mid-term Reviews of all the 'Five Year Plans' published from time to time by the Planning Commission, Govt. of India.

METHODOLOGY

In order to meet the specified objectives of the study, statistical techniques which applied to analyze the available data are discussed below:

1. Tabular Analysis

Simple as well as two-way tables along with ratios and percentages were mainly used to analyze the available data.

2. Linear Trend/Slope

The straight line trend/slope of the type

$$Y = \alpha + \beta t + \mu_t$$

was estimated to examine the trends in the different aspects of the utilized foreign aid in India during the period 1966-67 to 2003-04, which was further sub-divided into two sub-periods viz : (a) pre-eighty period (1966-67 to 1979-80), and (b) post-eighty period (1980-81 to 2003-04), to delineate the impact of economic reforms, mildly introduced since 1980.

3. Concept of Grant Element

The 'grant element' inherent in loans, basically, depends among other things upon the rate of interest to be charged, grace period and maturity of the loans, and an appropriate rate of discount. Of these, most important determinant of grant element is the choice of discount rate because the rate of interest, grace period and maturity of the loans are usually given already at the time of their commitment. The choice of discount rate is most important also because grant element varies with the variation in discount rate, given the other factors (Ohlin, 1966: pp. 111-12).

Choice of Discount Rate

Choice of discount rate, basically, depends upon the perspective of the estimation of grant element, that is, whether to estimate it from the angle of global market or from the angle of domestic local market for the recipient country. This indicate the alternative cost of borrowing the same amount on similar terms and conditions from the alternative source, which may be global market comprising multilateral development funding agencies, and bilateral arrangements on government to government level or domestic local market for the recipient country (India, in this case) comprising domestic financial institutions and sources.

In the present study, an attempt has been made to estimate grant element inherent in the foreign loans to India from the angle of alternative source of borrowing in the domestic economy. For this purpose, domestic market sensitive discount rates have been calculated as the weighted average of mean rates at which Govt. of India borrowed, and the average of the prime lending rates of the IDBI, ICICI and IFCI used as the proxy rates for financial institutions, at which these have supplied medium to long-term funds to the non-government borrowers in India. The lending financial institutions included have been IDBI, ICICI, IFCI, SIDBI, IRBI, SCICI, TDICI, TFCI, SFCs, SIDCs and LIC. These domestic market sensitive discount rates, calculated for the period 1980-81 to 2003-04, used in the present study to estimate grant element implicit in the foreign loans, have been given in Appendix 2.1. These have been mainly used here to estimate the alternative cost of borrowing foreign loans of the same amount on similar terms and conditions, from within the Indian economy, i.e., to test whether it has been fruitful to borrow from abroad or not, during the above mentioned period. For this purpose, the likely 'crowding out' effect of domestic borrowing for public investment on private investment has been ignored.

Aid tying (project, source or double tying) reduces the value of aid to the recipient country, it may also reflect in reduced grant element. As the effect of aid tying cannot be quantified, ignoring its effect may have upward bias in grant element. On the other hand, ignoring crowding out effect introduces downward bias in grant element. Thus, the two opposing effects may be assumed to cancel out.

Estimation of Grant Element

An endeavor has been made to estimate the 'approximate' grant element implicit in foreign loans by using the following conventional formula:

$$s=\left[1\frac{i}{q}\right]\left[1-\frac{e^{-qG}-e^{-qT}}{q(T-G)}\right]$$

where s = Grant element as percentage of face value of the loan,

i = Rate of interest to be charged on the loan,

q = Rate of discount,

G = Grace period of the loan, and

T = Maturity of the loan.

(Ohlin, 1966: p. 103; for more details see : pp. 102-04 and 111-12). Similar results are provided by a slightly modified formula presented by the WB economists Charles C. Chang *et al*, (1999: p. 15) mentioned below:

$$s=\left[1\frac{i}{q}\right]\left[1-\frac{\frac{1}{(1+q)^{G}}-\frac{1}{(1+q)^{T}}}{q(T-G)}\right]$$

Both these formulae are based on certain simplified assumptions mentioned as follows:

Assumption (i) The loan is disbursed in full at the time of commitment.*

Assumption (ii) The principal amount is repaid in T-G equal amortization payments starting in year G+1 and ending in year T (where $T > G \geq 0$).

Assumption (iii) The rate of interest to be charged on the loan remains fixed at 'i' throughout the life span of the loan.**

Assumption (iv) The rate of discount also remain fixed at 'q'.

* In the present study loan amount for grant element estimation is taken as amount utilized or the amount committed, net of cancellation, in case of loans in pipeline upto end-March, 2004, as reported in *External Assistance, 2003-04.*

** In case of variable interest rates, the rate applicable at the time of loan commitment is used for grant element estimation.

Assumption (v) The loan involves no charges other than interest and amortization, i.e., commitment fees, and other charges are ignored in the estimation.

These simplified expressions provide some useful insights. First, the sign of grant element depends only on the relation between the interest rate and the discount rate. If the discount rate equals interest rate, then the grant element will be zero, regardless of the moratorium and maturity period (this would not be the case if the loan involves any service charges in addition to the interest charges). Second, the lower the interest rate for a given discount rate, larger will be the grant element and *vice versa.* Third, for a given configuration of interest and discount rates, the absolute value of the grant element rises with rise in the grace and maturity periods, and reaches the maximum (equal to $a-\frac{i}{q}$) when both grace and maturity periods approach infinity, i.e., in the case of a consol.

Exchange Rate Variations

It is essential to analyze the impact of exchange rate variations in the domestic currency (Rupee) *vis-a-vis* foreign currencies, over the years, on the estimation of grant element implicit in foreign loans as these were given in foreign currencies on their own terms and conditions. In the present study, an attempt has been made to estimate the grant element, both without as well as with variations in the exchange rate of Rupee in relation to foreign currencies, during the period 1980-81 to 2003-04. The exchange rate variations in Rupee, i.e., average annual depreciation rate of Rupee *vis-a-vis* foreign currencies during the above-mentioned period has been estimated at their historical values between period 1 and n using the formula:

$$\text{Average Annual Depreciation Rate of Rupee} = \left[1-\exp\left\{\frac{(\log E_n - \log E_1)}{(n-1)}\right\}\right]$$

where E_1 and E_n are the exchange rates in period 1 and n respectively, n is the number of years in the period, and log is the natural logarithm.

The average annual rate of depreciation of Rupee in relation to foreign currencies given in Appendix 2.2, has been calculated for two sub-periods : (a) pre-reforms period (1980-81 to 1992-93), and (b) post-reforms period (1993-94 to 2003-04), because it has come down significantly in the post-reform years, after the devaluation and reform in the exchange rate regime in the early nineties. Moreover, exchange rate in post-reform years responded to market signals and was not administered like during the pre-reform years.

4. Annual Compound Growth Rate

Annual compound growth rates have been calculated by using exponential equation:

$$Y_t = \alpha\ \beta^t e^{\mu t}$$

for the period 1970-71 to 2003-04 along with three decades viz.: 1970-71 to 1979-80; 1980-81 to 1989-90; 1990-91 to 1999-2000; and 1990-91 to 2003-04, in case of variables for which time-series data have been available.

The percentage rate of growth (or decline) has been calculated as:

$$\text{Percentage rate of growth} = (\beta - 1) \times 100$$

In case of some social variables, where time-series data were not available, annual compound growth rates were calculated by using the following formula:

$$E_n = E_0\ (1+r)^t$$

where E_n = Value after nth year,
E_0 = Value in the initial year,
t = No of years/time period, and
r = Annual compound growth rate.

5. Index of Gross Aid Stock

Since most of the utilized foreign aid has been used for asset generation in the various sectors of the Indian economy, hence in the present study *'Index of Gross Aid Stock'* (IGAS) has been applied as a composite indicator of gross utilized foreign aid and has been used as an independent/explanatory variable. In order to construct time-series of gross foreign aid stock, Perpetual

Inventory Method, a most common method for making the estimates of written-down replacement cost for fixed capital stock, has been used, according to which "the cost of acquisition of each class (same type and same year of acquisition) of fixed assets is adjusted to current gross replacement cost by an index of the average change in prices from the year of acquisition to the date in question, and allowance, valued at current replacement cost for accumulated depreciation between the two dates is deducted in order to arrive at its written-down current replacement cost" (EPW Research Foundation, 2002 : p. 191). In the present study, value of foreign aid assets as on end-March, 1970 has been adjusted 1.5 times (weighted average of price index during the period 1951 to 1970) of the cumulative aid received since April 1, 1951 to end-March, 1970, the benchmark year, as a rough estimate of the replacement value of the fixed capital for constructing the IGAS. After obtaining the estimate of foreign aid stock for the benchmark year (1970-71), the following equation has been used for the estimation of gross foreign aid stock at current prices:

$$A_t = A_{t-1} + U_t + d\,A_{t-1}$$

where A_t = Gross utilized foreign aid at current prices by the end-year t,

U_t = Utilized gross foreign aid during the year t,

A_{t-1} = Gross utilized foreign aid at current prices during the year t–1, and

d = Annual rate of discard of capital assets.

Assuming 20 years as the average life of the foreign aid stock/assets, two percent annual rate of discard has been applied in the present study (Goldar, 1986 : p. 99).

After obtaining the time series of utilized gross foreign aid stock at current prices, the same have been converted into 1993-94 prices by utilizing 'spliced wholesale price Index' (1993-94=100) as deflator for constructing its index.

Selected Variables

In order to analyze the impact of utilized foreign aid on the various sectors of the Indian economy during the period 1970-71 to 2003-04, 23 socio-economic variables were selected, out of which 18 economic variables, whose time series data were available, were used as proxy growth/dependent variables representing various sectors on which foreign aid has been utilized. Time variable has been introduced as explanatory variable along with IGAS just to eliminate the trend component from the available time-series data in order to obtain trend-corrected variables (Gujarati, 1985: pp. 124-25). For analyzing the data, ratios and index numbers have been used. Wherever these were not available, quantity figures were converted into the same for use in the analysis. For preparing the index of variables, quantum figures at constant prices (1993-94 = 100) were used. Where these quantity figures were not available, figures at current prices were converted into constant prices by utilizing 'spliced wholesale price index' (1993-94 = 100) as deflator (Table 8.6) for the period 1970-71 to 2003-04. In case of the index of food grains (IFG) triennium base year ending 1981-82 = 100 was shifted to 1993-94 prices to make it comparable with other variables. Techniques like Correlation Analysis, Multiple Linear as well as Log-Linear Regression Analysis, and Multiple Lagged Linear Regression Analysis were applied in the study.

6. Correlation Analysis

In order to examine the inter-correlations amongst various selected indicators of development and the 'Index of Gross Aid Stock' (IGAS), correlation matrices were worked out using Karl Pearsonian coefficients of correlation. Significance of these correlation coefficients was tested by applying Student's 't-statistic' using formula :

$$t = r_{ij}\sqrt{\frac{n-2}{1-(r_{ij})^2}}$$

where 'n' is the number of paired observations (years), and r_{ij} is the coefficient of correlation between i^{th} and j^{th} variables. Calculated values of 't' have been compared with the tabulated values of 't' at (n–2) degrees of freedom, and results have been tested at 0.01 and 0.05 level of significance for two-tailed tests.

7. Multiple Regression Analysis

Multiple Linear as well as Log-Linear Regression equations were fitted by regressing the level of development, through each selected development indicator on the 'Index of Gross Aid Stock' (IGAS) and time variable (t) taken together, to estimate the impact of utilized foreign aid on growth by considering:

$$\text{Level of Development } Y_t = f(X_t, t)$$

where Y_t = Development indicator in year 't'
X_t = Index of Gross Aid Stock in year 't'.

Multiple Linear Regression Model was estimated as under :

$$Y_t = \alpha + \beta_1 (IGAS)_t + \beta_2 t + \mu_t$$

where 'Y' stands for the development indicator applied; IGAS represents the 'Index of Gross Aid Stock'; 't' refers to time variable, while α, β_1 and β_2 are the unknown parameters of the regression model to be estimated; and μ is the stochastic disturbance term.

The Log-Linear Multiple Regression Analysis was carried out in the following form:

$$Y_t = \alpha\,(IGAS)_t^{\beta}.e^{\mu t}$$

Taking log on both sides

$$\log Y_t = \log \alpha + \beta \log (IGAS)_t + \mu t$$

The statistical significance of the estimates α, β and μ have been examined by applying the t-test. The calculated value of 't' has been compared with the tabulated value of 't' at (N–K) degrees of freedom (where N stands for the number of observations and K for the total number of parameters to be estimated including the intercept term), and the results have been tested at 0.01 and 0.05 level of significance for two-tailed tests.

The overall significance of the estimated regression equations, i.e., significance of R^2—a measure of 'goodness of fit', was computed to see the percentage of variations in the dependent variable explained by both the independent/ explanatory variables taken together. 'Adjusted Coefficient of Determination' ($\bar{R}^2$) was calculated for each regression equation using:

$$(\bar{R}^2)=1-(1-R^2)\frac{N-1}{N-K}$$

where N is the number of observations and K is the total number of parameters to be estimated including the intercept term.

Significance of R^2 has also been checked by applying 'F statistic' estimated as under:

$$F_{\text{at }(K-1)\text{ and }(N-K)df} = \frac{R^2/(K-1)}{(1-R^2)/N-K)}$$

where K is the total number of parameters to be estimated including the intercept term, and N is the number of observations.

8. Lagged Multiple Regression Analysis

The impact of utilized foreign aid indicated by the explanatory variable the 'Index of Gross Aid Stock' (IGAS) during the current year 't' and the preceding years with a time lag up to five years, on the selected development indicators for the growth in the current year 't' has been estimated using the distributed–lag model of the following type:

$$Y_t = f(IGAS_t, IGAS_{t-1}, IGAS_{t-2}, \ldots\ldots\ldots IGAS_{1-5}), \text{ in the form of}$$
$$Y_t = \alpha + \beta_0 X_t + \beta_1 . X_{t-1} + \beta_2 . X_{t-2} + \ldots\ldots\ldots \beta_5 . X_{t-5} + \mu_t$$

where Y_t is the development indicator in the current year 't', and X_t, X_{t-1}, X_{t-2} . . . X_{t-5} represents 'Index of Gross Aid Stock' during the years t, t–1, t–2, . . . t–5, respectively. α, β_0, β_1, β_2, . . . , β_5 and μ_t are unknowns of the distributed lagged regression model of foreign aid.

The statistical significance of the estimates of α, β_0, β_1, β_2, . . . β_5 have been examined by applying 't-statistic'. The results have been tested at 0.01 and 0.05 level of significance for the two-tailed tests. R^2 has also been computed to know the proportion of variations in the dependent variable explained by the independent/explanatory variables. Significance of R^2 has also been checked by applying 'F-statistic' by duly making suitable adjustments in respect of the lagged regression model.

The results have been interpreted accordingly.

APPENDIX 2.1
Estimation of Domestic Market Sensitive Discount Rates (1980-81 to 2003-04)

Year	*Central Govt.*		*Financial Institutions*		*Weighted Average Discount Rate (Percent)*
	Rate (Percent)	*Amount (Rs. Crore)*	*Rate (Percent)*	*Amount (Rs. Crore)*	
1980-81	7.03	2871	14.00	1848	9.76
1981-82	7.29	3191	14.00	2352	10.14
1982-83	8.36	4166	14.00	2469	10.46
1983-84	9.29	4325	14.00	3138	11.27
1984-85	9.98	4591	14.00	3628	11.76
1985-86	11.08	5764	14.00	4940	12.43
1986-87	11.38	6351	14.00	5709	12.62
1987-88	11.25	7821	14.00	7061	12.56
1988-89	11.40	7725	14.00	7701	12.70
1989-90	11.49	8044	14.00	9640	12.86
1990-91	11.41	8989	14.50	12810	13.23
1991-92	11.78	8919	19.00	16260	16.44
1992-93	12.46	13885	18.00	23150	15.92
1993-94	12.63	50388	16.00	26624	13.80
1994-95	11.90	38108	15.75	33568	13.70
1995-96	13.75	40509	16.50	38650	15.09
1996-97	13.69	36152	16.65	42657	15.29
1997-98	12.01	59637	14.60	53648	13.24
1998-99	11.86	93953	13.92	58330	12.65
1999-00	11.77	99630	14.37	68594	12.83
2000-01	10.95	115183	13.17	75364	11.83
2001-02	9.44	133801	12.17	58735	10.27
2002-03	7.34	151126	11.35	26705	7.94
2003-04	5.71	147636	10.70	29526	6.54

N.B : (i) Central Govt. rates are weighted averages.

(ii) For financial institutions average of prime lending rates of IDBI, ICICI and IFCI have been used as a proxy. Where range of rates is given, the average of range has been used. This rate has been used as proxy for all the medium to long-term lending by the financial institutions to non-government borrowers. The lending institutions included are: IDBI, ICICI, IFCI, SIDBI, IRBI, SCICI, TDICI, TFCI, SFCs, SIDCs and LIC.

(iii) The likely 'crowding out' effect of the domestic borrowing for public investment on private investment has been ignored.

Source : RBI, *Handbook of Statistics on The Indian Economy, 2003-04*: pp. 110, 122, 170-71.

APPENDIX 2.2
Average Exchange Rates (Rs. Per unit of Foreign Currency : 1980-81 to 2003-04)

Creditor	Currency Unit	1980-81	1981-82	1982-83	1983-84	1984-85	1985-86	1986-87	1987-88	1988-89
(1)	(2)	(3)	(4)	(5)	(6)	(7)	(8)	(9)	(10)	(11)
Austria	Aus Sch.	0.60	0.55	0.57	0.57	0.57	0.65	0.90	1.06	1.15
Belgium	Bel. Franc	0.26	0.23	0.21	0.20	0.20	0.23	0.31	0.36	0.39
Canada	Can. $	6.78	7.48	7.86	8.40	9.07	8.96	9.37	9.97	12.04
Denmark	Dan. Kron	1.36	1.22	1.15	1.10	1.11	1.26	1.69	1.95	2.11
France	F. Franc	1.82	1.58	1.44	1.31	1.31	1.50	1.94	2.22	2.38
Germany	Deutsche Mark	4.22	3.89	3.99	3.97	4.01	4.59	6.34	7.44	8.13
Japan	Yen	0.10	0.04	0.04	0.04	0.05	0.06	0.08	0.09	0.11
Kuwait	Ku. Dinar	32.47	34.73	35.67	36.97	41.59	42.05	44.59	47.05	51.63
Netherlands	Guilder	3.87	3.52	3.62	3.53	3.56	4.07	5.62	6.61	7.19
Saudi-Arabia	Riyal	2.48	2.76	2.91	3.09	3.44	3.47	3.49	3.48	3.89
Switzerland	Swiss Franc	4.61	4.64	4.72	4.86	4.81	5.51	7.66	9.03	9.63
UK	British £	18.63	17.22	16.23	15.51	14.95	16.95	19.19	22.20	25.73
USA/IBRD ADB/OPEC	US $	7.96	9.03	9.72	10.41	11.96	12.31	12.86	13.04	14.56
*EEC	ECU/Euros	NA	NA	NA	NA	NA	NA	NA	NA	NA
IFAD/IDA	SDRs	10.18	10.49	10.80	11.55	12.78	14.13	16.72	17.16	19.34

(Contd.)

Appendix 2.2 (Contd.)

Creditor	*Currency Unit*	*1989-90*	*1990-91*	*1991-92*	*1992-93*	*1993-94*	*1994-95*	*1995-96*	*1996-97*	*1997-98*
(1)	(2)	(12)	(13)	(14)	(15)	(16)	(17)	(18)	(19)	(20)
Austria	Aus Sch.	1.31	1.61	2.09	2.78	2.65	2.84	3.31	3.25	2.97
Belgium	Bel. Franc	0.43	0.55	0.72	0.95	0.89	0.97	1.13	1.11	1.01
Canada	Can. $	14.08	15.39	21.46	24.89	23.88	22.64	24.49	26.03	26.4
Denmark	Dan. Kron	2.34	2.97	3.81	5.07	4.75	5.08	6.00	5.96	5.49
France	F. Franc	2.67	3.37	4.34	5.77	5.49	5.82	6.73	6.76	6.22
Germany	Deutsche Mark	9.07	11.37	14.75	19.55	18.67	20.03	23.32	22.91	20.92
Japan	Yen	0.12	0.13	0.19	0.25	0.29	0.32	0.35	0.32	0.30
Kuwait	Ku. Dinar	56.70	59.94	78.13	100.62	105.63	104.91	108.55	114.98	117.57
Netherlands	Guilder	8.04	10.10	13.09	17.37	16.63	17.84	20.83	20.46	18.58
Saudi-Arabia	Riyal	4.38	4.66	6.46	7.98	8.17	8.18	8.70	9.21	9.66
Switzerland	Swiss Franc	10.31	13.38	16.83	21.60	21.33	23.79	28.83	27.51	25.49
UK	British £	26.89	33.06	42.92	51.65	46.99	48.61	52.17	56.19	60.95
USA/IBRD ADB/OPEC	US $	16.63	17.86	24.77	30.60	31.25	31.29	33.33	35.52	37.10
*EEC	ECU/Euros	NA	NA	NA	39.35	36.05	38.11	43.03	43.70	41.15
IFAD/IDA	SDRs	22.33	24.91	33.43	36.94	43.89	45.82	50.50	50.88	50.68

(*Contd.*)

APPENDIX 2.2 (CONTD.)

Creditor	Currency Unit	1998-99	1999-2000	2000-01	2001-02	2002-03	2003-04	Average Depreciation of Rupee (Percent)	
								1980-81 to 1992-93	1993-94 to 2003-04
(1)	(2)	(21)	(22)	(23)	(24)	(25)	(26)	(27)	(28)
Austria	Aus Sch.	3.33	3.03	3.00	3.11	3.49	3.92	13.63	3.99
Belgium	Bel. Franc	1.14	1.03	1.02	1.06	1.19	1.34	11.40	4.18
Canada	Can. $	28.07	29.95	30.31	30.60	31.20	33.94	11.45	3.58
Denmark	Dan. Kron	6.17	5.61	5.53	5.74	6.45	7.25	11.59	4.32
France	F. Franc	6.99	6.36	6.30	6.52	NA	NA	10.09	—
Germany	Deutsche Mark	24.21	21.35	21.11	NA	NA	NA	13.63	—
Japan	Yen	0.36	0.41	0.41	0.37	0.40	0.41	8.03	3.42
Kuwait	Ku. Dinar	136.15	138.99	145.15	154.47	156.82	154.38	9.88	3.87
Netherlands	Guilder	20.81	18.94	18.74	19.39	NA	NA	13.33	—
Saudi-Arabia	Riyal	11.04	11.35	12.41	12.67	12.74	—	10.23	—
Switzerland	Swiss Franc	28.77	26.22	26.80	29.38	32.69	34.82	13.73	5.02
UK	British £	68.77	69.70	67.35	69.49	74.76	77.61	8.87	5.15
USA/IBRD ADB/OPEC	US $	42.33	43.56	45.59	48.73	48.39	45.94	11.87	3.93
*EEC	ECU/Euros	47.57	41.75	41.28	42.74	47.97	53.89	—	4.10
IFAD/IDA	SDRs	57.61	58.75	59.52	60.85	64.14	65.69	11.34	4.11

Source : Govt of India, *External Assistance*, (various issues), Ministry of Finance, Department of Economic Affairs; Aid, Accounts and Audit Division.

N.B. *Includes Germany, France and Netherlands.

3

Foreign Aid : Theoretical Issues

In order to examine the role, need, usefulness and effectiveness of foreign aid in the developing countries, in general, and India, in particular, certain theoretical issues need to be analyzed relating not only to its potentiality for contributing to the development process but also to a host of other aspects. The major issues are: (i) how the requirements and timing regarding foreign aid should be determined, and what kind of policies should be followed in the recipient developing countries for achieving a certain target rate of growth ?, (ii) whether foreign aid could be useful for the development process in the developing countries or not ?, and (iii) why is it conceived obligatory for the advanced industrialized rich countries to provide aid to the developing countries ?

An attempt has been made to examine each of the issue in this chapter. Accordingly, the chapter has been divided into three sections.

SECTION I

REQUIREMENTS, TIMING, AND POLICIES REGARDING FOREIGN AID : BASIC APPROACHES AND THEORIES

Basically, there exist three fundamental approaches for

determining foreign aid requirements of a developing country, either singly or in combination : (1) The Savings-Investment Gap Approach; (2) The Foreign Exchange Earnings-Expenditure Approach; and (3) The Capital-Absorptive Capacity Approach.

1. The Savings–Investment Gap Approach

The savings-investment gap approach in its simplest form employs a variation of the Harrod-Domar model and also follows the footsteps of Rosenstein-Rodan's theory of 'Big-Push' by assuming the numerical value of the 'marginal propensity to save' (MPS) greater than that of 'average propensity to save' (APS), i.e., MPS > APS. For any target rate of growth of GDP, (r), required foreign aid in the initial year (F_0) will be conditioned by the gap between the planned investment and domestic savings, as follows:

$$F_0 = I_0 - S_0$$

$$\text{or } F_0 = Y_0Kr - Y_0\, S_0^a$$

$$\text{or } F_0 = Y_0\,(Kr - S_0^a)$$

where Y_0 indicates the monetary GNP in the initial year; K reflects the incremental capital-output ratio; and S_0^a signifies APS in the initial year.

Following the same logic, foreign aid requirements of an economy in the year 't' will be equal to :

$$F_t = I_t - S_t$$

$$\text{or } F_t = Y_0Kr\,(1+r)^t - Y_0\, S_0^a - s'Y_0\,(1+r)^t + s'Y_0$$

If t = 1, in the second year, required foreign aid (F_1) will be as follows:

$$F_1 = I_1 - S_1$$

$$\text{or } F_1 = Y_0Kr\,(1+r) - Y_0\, S_0^a - s'Y_0\,(1+r) + s'Y_0$$

$$\text{or } F_1 = \left[Y_0Kr + Y_0Kr^{\,2}\right] - \left[Y_0\, S_0^a + Y_0\, s'\, r\right]$$

$$\text{or } F_1 = \left[Y_0\,Kr - Y_0\,S_0^a\right] + \left[Y_0\,Kr^2 - Y_0 S'r\right]$$

$$\text{or } F_1 = F_0 + Y_0 r\,[Kr - s'] \qquad \because F_0 = Y_0\,Kr - S_0^a$$

where s′ is the marginal savings ratio in the current year and S_0^a indicate the average gross domestic savings ratio in the year zero. Evidently, if the given economy has to become increasingly self-reliant then dependence on foreign aid has to reduce progressively over a period of time. F_1 must be less than F_0 (i.e., $F_1 < F_0$). For this, it is imperative that MPS (s′) must be greater than the product of the target rate of growth (r) and the incremental capital-output ratio (K), i.e., $s' > Kr$. [For further details see : D. Avramovic and Associates, 1964: pp. 188-89].

2. The Foreign Exchange Earnings-Expenditure Gap Approach

Another approach to determine the foreign aid requirements of a developing system finds expression in the form of foreign exchange earnings-expenditure gap approach to capital import requirements. The approach concentrates on the import capacity as the main constraint on domestic investment and growth. If the rate of change experienced by the export sector happens to be greater than the rate of change taking place in the import sector then the given economy will become increasingly self-reliant. Following this approach, the foreign aid requirements in the initial year (F_0) to fill the foreign exchange gap will be:

$$F_0 = M_0 - X_0$$

$$\text{or } F_0 = Y_0\,m_a - Y_0\,X_a$$

$$\text{or } F_0 = Y_0\,(m_a - x_a)$$

where Y_0 signifies the national output in the initial year, m_a and x_a reflects average import (average propensity to import) ratio and average export (average propensity to export) ratio, respectively, during the initial year.

Following the same logic, foreign aid requirements in the succeeding year (F_1) will be;

$$F_1 = (Y_0 m_a + Y_0 m'r) - (Y_0 x_a + Y_0 x'r)$$
$$\text{or } F_1 = (Y_0 m_a - Y_0 x_a) + (Y_0 m'r - Y_0 x'r)$$
$$\text{or } F_1 = Y_0 (m_a - x_a) + Y_0 r (m'-x')$$
$$\text{or } F_1 = F_0 + Y_0 r (m'-x') \qquad \because F_0 = Y_0 (m_a - x_a)$$

where m′ and x′ stands for marginal import ratio and marginal export ratio, respectively, and r is the target rate of growth. Thus, for foreign aid requirements to decline in the succeeding year and for the economy to become increasingly dependent upon its own legs, x′ must be in excess of m′ (i.e., $x' > m'$).

"However, in the formal sense, the savings-investment gap and the foreign exchange gap approaches to the determination of capital import requirements for achieving a target rate of growth are identical.

$$F = E - Y = I - S = M - X$$

where F indicates net capital imports; E signifies aggregate domestic expenditure; Y is suggestive of national output; I reflects domestic investment; S shows domestic savings; M represents imports; and X exports. Thus, the net capital imports or foreign aid requirements are equal to both the gap between imports and exports, and to that between domestic investment expenditure and domestic savings" (Mikesell, 1968: p. 76).

3. The Capital-Absorptive Capacity Approach

There are administrators, planners and economists who are not in sympathy with either of the approaches mentioned above. They display their confidence in another approach viz. : the capital-absorptive capacity approach, which signifies nothing but the ability of the domestic/recipient economy to absorb domestic and foreign capital productively in the sense that the rate of return available is sufficient to cover at least the cost of debt-servicing. One variant of this approach regards foreign capital as means of overcoming internal obstacles to growth, and as a catalyst for mobilizing domestic resources for increasing output and productivity (*Ibid*., p. 76). That is, the insertion of aid-funds into a recipient economy sets in motion a causal chain of positive influences in the following broad manner:

foreign aid ⇒ increase in the domestic investible resources ⇒ increase in domestic investment ⇒ more rapid rate of economic growth.

If this assertion is correct then, *prima facie*, one would expect increased aid flows to be positively associated with a rise in the domestic investment and more aid to lead to a higher rate of economic growth in the recipient country (Riddell, 1987: p. 103).

4. The Fiscal Gap

Recently, 'fiscal constraint' has been espoused as a possible 'third gap' limiting the growth prospects of the highly-indebted group of developing countries (Brazil being a conspicuous example) by some economists [See: Bacha (1990); Taylor (1994); and Iqbal (1995)] as an extended version of the 'two gap' model introduced by Chenery and Strout (1966). As debt crisis lingers on, there is an increasing feeling that the main cause of growth (and inflation) difficulties is the government budget limitations albeit the foreign exchange constraints or an overall savings restriction.

The fiscally constrained level of investment (I_T) has been given as:

$$I_T = (I + K^*) [f (p, h) + (T - G) + (F - J)]$$

where k* is the value of government investment; p is rate of inflation; h is the propensity to hoard; T is the government gross income; G is government consumption, i.e., T–G is the primary budget surplus in current account; F is the net capital inflows; and J is the net factor services to abroad, i.e., F–J represents net foreign transfers to the recipient government (Bacha, 1990: pp. 280-84).

The three-gap model has been criticized by the WB economists. They have developed their 'standard' three gap model known as the 'Revised Minimum Standards Model Extended'—(RMSM-X) used by the many WB country management units (for further details see: Ranaweera, 2003: pp. 6-7).

SOME FOREIGN AID THEORIES

Different economists and development analysts have presented various theories of foreign aid which can roughly be divided into theories about resource transfer, and theories about transaction in which it is embedded. Analysis of the resource transfer as such leads to the identification of other resources, such as: savings or foreign exchange earnings with which aid may be supposed to interact and to the formulation of theories concerning the relationship between them. Transfer theories can thus, in general, be characterized as economic theories. However, the analysis of aid as a transaction leads to the identification of the partners in this transaction, i.e., the users of aid, and to the formulation of theories concerning the interests of these users and how such interests will be pursued. Transaction theories can thus, in general, be characterized as political theories.

Economic theories, in turn, are of two main kinds. One kind of theories focuses on aid as a supplement to the recipient's own resources, and purports to trace a positive relationship between aid and the total value of resources available for the sorts of developmental purpose in which aid theorists are interested. Most such theories, infact, are rather more ambitious than that. Following this view, the opportunities created by the availability of aid make it worth the recipient's while to increase their own development efforts. Domestic or supplemental economic theories can thus, in general, be characterized as attributing positive effects to aid. However, there is another kind of economic theory which focuses on aid as supplant for recipient's own resources, which are switched from developmental to non-developmental expenditure, and purports to trace a negative relationship between aid and the proportion of domestic resources devoted to developmental expenditure such that the total volume of resources available for developmental purposes may well be reduced by aid, for instance, through imports of 'inappropriate' foreign technology leading to the claim that aid reduces the efficiency of developmental expenditure as well as its volume. External or displacement economic theories can thus, in general, be described as attributing negative effects to aid.

Political theories, similarly, are of two main kinds. One kind of theories focuses on the recipients as aid-users and are concerned with aid as an instrument of domestic policy, i.e., with the interests of the recipient government *vis-a-vis* competing groups within the national polity. Such recipient oriented theories, thus, form a part of the study of comparative politics. On the other hand, another kind of political theories focuses on the donors as aid-users and are concerned with aid as an instrument of foreign policy, i.e., with the interests of the donor country *vis-a-vis* recipient countries. Such donor-oriented theories, thus, form a part of the study of international relations (White, 1974: p. 105).

The brief classification of aid theories have been presented in Table 3.1.

TABLE 3.1
Four Types of Foreign Aid Theories

	Economic (transfer)	*Political (transaction)*
Domestic	Positive, i.e., supplemental theories	Recipient-oriented, i.e., comparative politics theories
External	Negative, i.e., displacement theories	Donor-oriented, i.e., international relations theories

Out of these four categories of theories, it is the first category that predominate most of the literature on aid. Indeed, it is only in this category that theories have been rigorously developed with the aim of constructing a general explanatory model of aid as such. The possibility of theories in other categories has been indicated mainly in passing references to aid (*Ibid.*, p. 106). These elegant, comprehensive and detailed theories have combined the three basic approaches: the savings-investment gap, the foreign exchange gap, and the capital absorptive capacity. Each theory has its own peculiar characteristics. But most of them have a number of important features in common : assuming 'self-sustaining growth' to be the only objective of foreign aid; abstracting from the socio-political aspects of development process; providing an analytical framework for determining how much aid a developing country will require; recommending the policies which such a country should follow in order to achieve a targeted rate of growth; implying a broad criterion for evaluating past aid programmes. The main theories are as follows:

1. McKinnon's Foreign Exchange Constraint Model

Stanford University economist Ronald I. McKinnon (1964) analyzed the nature of savings, trade and skill bottlenecks on the growth but gave more stress to the trade limitation. The model explained that "foreign aid could have a large favorable impact on the growth rate when such a bottleneck constraint is binding, even though these transfers are a small fraction of available domestic savings" (McKinnon, 1964: p. 388), particularly when these transfers are used to remove such bottlenecks by providing strategic goods and services not produced in the developing countries.

The model, which is based upon the Chenery and Bruno Model (1962), and is similar in many respects to the Chenery and Strout Model (1966), revealed that where the foreign exchange constraint is dominant, foreign aid will have a proportionately greater effect upon the growth rate than if the savings constraint holds because expenditure for imported capital goods constitutes only a fraction of domestic capital formation. Smaller the import component of investment expenditure, greater will be the impact of foreign aid on growth. The model emphasized the role of aid allocation of choosing a growth rate which will minimize the amount of foreign aid required to achieve a 'self-sustaining growth'. Given a very high marginal savings rate which permits domestic savings to rise rapidly, a higher target growth rate might actually require a smaller amount of total aid than a lower one, i.e., "the higher is $\bar{s}$ (marginal propensity to save), the higher will be the optimal growth rate ($\bar{w}$) that minimizes the foreign exchange transfers needed to double the national income" (*Ibid.*, pp. 399-400).

In analyzing the foreign exchange constraint, the model used two basic coefficients : e', the net marginal propensity to export over and above current account material needs; and β, a measure of the proportion of imported capital goods required for a unit of productive capacity (the higher the value of β, the smaller will be the requirements for foreign produced capital goods). For any value of β, "the larger the e', net marginal propensity to export, the smaller will be both t and $\frac{R}{Y_0}$, i.e., the time interval and the capital transfer" (*Ibid.*, p. 402) or amount of foreign aid required to maintain the given growth rate. The export coefficient, e, measures the increase in exports (over and above the current account material needs) as a function of output. The coefficient embody the capacity of a country, both to export and to generate import substitutes for current material needs, as output rises. In analyzing the nature of this variable, the model suggested that for developing countries whose exports consist largely of primary products, the sales of which are not readily expandable, the amount of such exports might be regarded as a constant and the export coefficient, e, would represent the ability of the economy to earn foreign exchange as the productive capacity increased. The model conceived net import substitution in the field of capital goods as being fairly limited since investment in import substituting capital goods will involve a larger proportion of imported capital and intermediate goods.

The possibility of a terminal date for capital imports for eliminating the foreign exchange constraint on 'self-sustaining growth' depends upon the existence of e', higher than the average propensity to export (e) by a critical amount. The oversimplified version of the model states that in order to support a growth rate ($\bar{w}$) starting at domestic output level P_0 (income level Y_0) with a capital coefficient σ, the initial foreign balance contribution will have to be $\frac{\bar{w}}{\sigma} P_0 = F_0 = I_0$ which is also the initial investment rate.

$\frac{\bar{w}}{\sigma} = s'$ is the average savings propensity that economy will have eventually to achieve growth rate ($\bar{w}$) to be self-supporting. In other words,

$$\bar{w} = \sigma \,.\, i$$

where, i, is the investment ratio which is equal to the savings ratio s'. σ/β is the fraction of total investment that must go for foreign produced capital goods so that

$$\frac{\sigma.i}{\beta} = \frac{\bar{w}}{\beta} = e$$

For 'self-sustained growth' at rate ($\bar{w}$) eventually to be achieved, the net marginal propensity to export (e') must be larger than (e) the average propensity to export, that is, e'> $\overline{w}/\beta$. To illustrate, the model supposed that a 'typical' growth rate $\overline{w}$ is 0.06 with an output-capital coefficient $\sigma = 0.3$ and $\beta = 1.2$ so that $\sigma/\beta = 0.25$, i.e., 25 percent of total investment must go for imported capital goods; and $\overline{w}/\beta = 0.05$ so that e' must exceed 0.05 (e'> 0.05) if the 6 percent growth rate is eventually to be self-sustaining. The extent to which e' exceeds 0.05 greatly affects the required aid transfer (*Ibid.*, p. 402). The larger the amount by which e' exceeds the critical ratio (0.05), the smaller will be the total amount of foreign aid and shorter will be the time required for 'self-sustained growth'. Unless a developing country is able to increase its exports beyond the critical rate, capital imports for avoiding the foreign exchange constraint can not be terminated without reducing the growth rate below the target level.

2. Fei and Paauw's Self-help Model

Another foreign assistance model, formulated by the USAID economists John C.H. Fei and Douglas S. Paauw (1965), constructed a revised Harrod-Domar prototype, and applied it to a group of thirty-one countries including India receiving bulk of the American development assistance. The model basically examined the implications of 'self-help', narrowly defined as "the mobilization of domestic savings which we take to be the essence of self-help problem" (Fei and Paauw, 1965: p. 251), as these affect (i) the relationship between foreign aid and domestic austerity efforts (i.e., savings); (ii) the assurance that a reasonable termination date be built into the assistance program; and (iii) the prospect that foreign aid will achieve its primary objectives of providing an adequate rate of growth of per capita income and consumption (*Ibid.*, p. 251).

The model assumed that "a savings function which postulates incremental per capita savings as a constant fraction, μ, of increments in per capita income referred to as the 'per capita marginal savings ratio' (PMSR)" (*Ibid.*, p. 257). In its open economy case, the model identified three categories of countries from the standpoint of the conditions favorable or unfavorable to the achievement of per capita growth rate in relation to the foreign aid objectives.

First, there has been the favorable case, where no foreign aid is necessary because the 'investment requirements' k(h+r) are less than the initial average savings rate [s(0)] owing to a low population growth or an unambitious target growth rate or some combination of the both. Symbolically,

$$\text{(i)} \quad h + r < \frac{s(0)}{k} \equiv \eta_0$$

$$\text{or} \quad k(h+r) < s(0) \equiv \eta_0$$

where 'h' is the target rate of growth in per capita GNP; r is the rate of population growth; s(0) is the initial average propensity to save; k is the capital-output ratio; and η_0 is the initial rate of growth of capital and GNP.

Second, there has been the intermediate case, where (h+r) is greater than the initial savings rate, s(0), but less than the long run growth rate of capital $\left(\frac{\mu}{k}\right)$, in which a developing country will require foreign assistance until some finite termination date, after which it will be able to export capital. Symbolically,

$$\text{(ii)} \quad \eta_0 < h + r < \frac{\mu}{k} \equiv \eta_\mu$$

where μ is the PMSR, and η_μ is the long-run rate of growth of capital and GNP.

And third, there has been the unfavorable case, where h+r exceeds the long run growth rate of capital in which need for foreign assistance is infinite because of a combination of high target and population growth rates. In symbols,

$$\text{(iii)} \quad \eta_\mu < h + r$$

In the intermediate case (ii), considered as 'gap filling' from the viewpoint of foreign aid policy, foreign assistance will be required at first but it will have a finite termination date, after this point is reached, the country will be able to export capital including repayment of loans contracted during the capital-import period. In this case PMSR divided by the capital-output ratio (defined as long-run growth rate of both capital and GNP) will be greater than the target per capita growth rate (h) plus the rate of population growth (r). However, in the unfavorable case (iii) where h+r is greater than the long-run growth rate of GNP as determined by the PMSR (μ), and the incremental capital-output ratio (k), foreign aid will be required indefinitely because of a combination of a high target (h) and high population growth rate (r). "The aid-income ratio will eventually approach a constant value implying that the absolute volume of foreign savings (aid) will grow at a constant rate, i.e., rate of the growth of GNP, h+r " (*Ibid.*, p. 256).

The model examined the conditions determining the aid termination date, governed by the growth target, the rate of population growth and the other parameters in the intermediate case (ii). Although in the normal case, aid termination date will vary directly with both the growth target and population growth rate, in cases where population pressure is quite heavy, so that the growth rate of population exceeds the initial growth rate of capital, increases in the target growth rate will lower the termination date within a limited range. As a matter of fact, only a large volume of assistance "enabling the country to maintain a rate of growth of per capita GNP high enough to mobilize savings through the effect of the PMSR will enable the country to escape the trap of a falling per capita GNP. In other words, the target must be sufficiently high so that per capita GNP increases will yield adequate savings to minimize the termination date" (*Ibid.*, p. 260).

Assuming reasonably realistic values for its parameters s(0), k, h, and r, the model suggested that a PMSR (μ) of about 35 percent is essential condition for self-sufficiency in development finance. "Roughly, this level of austerity (i.e., domestic savings) is required to qualify a country for 'gap-filling' assistance that more or less automatically complement the country's own self-help efforts" (*Ibid.*, pp. 261 and 263).

3. Chenery and Strout Model

Perhaps the most comprehensive of these theories, both in empirical and theoretical terms, is the one presented by Hollis B. Chenery with Alan M. Strout (1966). It is still considered as the core theory to which reference is made. In a World Bank publication (1979) this model was reprinted, indicating both its continued relevance and importance. This model gives us the classical theoretical justification for providing economic aid for development, i.e., for filling the savings-investment gap, the export-import gap and raising the capital-absorptive capacity. The basic objective of the model has been to help a developing country to achieve 'self-sustaining growth' in the Rostowian sense. Acknowledging their debt to Rostow and Lewis, Chenery and Strout stated that the aim of their model is to "investigate the process by which a poor, stagnant economy can be transformed into one whose normal condition is sustained growth" (Chenery and Strout, 1966: p. 680).

The model stated that foreign aid was not only able to accelerate the rate of investment during the 'take-off' stage but also facilitated the creation of basic requisites for the transition to 'self-sustained growth' such as: skills, the adoption of modern technology, change in the composition of output and employment, growth of new institutions, etc. The model analyzed the transitional process in terms of three phases each associated with a single bottleneck, designated as: (a) skills, (b) savings, and (c) foreign exchange. Foreign assistance, for which current payment is not required, can "contribute to the mobilization and allocation of all productive resources. Three types of resources should be distinguished : (a) the supply of skills and organizational ability; (b) the supply of domestic savings; and (c) the supply of imported commodities and services" (*Ibid.*, p. 681).

The 'skill limit', reflecting "the skill formation required of managers, skilled labor and civil servants in order to increase productive investment" (*Ibid.*, p. 686) during the Phase I of the model's description of the development process, does not permit a level of investment high enough for output to grow at the target rate. However, if investment can be increased at a rate which is higher than the target rate of growth, the rate of investment will eventually reach the level ($k.\bar{r}$) required to sustain the target growth rate of GNP, where k is incremental capital-output ratio and $\bar{r}$ is target rate of growth. Foreign assistance during Phase I will fill the gap between the increment in investment and increment in savings until the rate of investment is high enough to sustain the target rate of growth. Thus, if investment grows at the maximum rate β, the amount of investment in any given year 't' will be

$$I_t = I_0 + \beta k (v_t - v_0)$$

where v is GNP. The required amount of foreign aid in year 't' will be

$$F_t = I_t - S_t = F_0 + (\beta k - \alpha')(v_t - v_0)$$

where $F_0 = I_0 - S_0$ in the initial year, α' is marginal savings rate ($\Delta\bar{s}/\Delta v$). In this equation the increment of investment in each period is a constant ratio (βk) to the increment of domestic output. Thus, the increment of external capital ($F_t - F_0$) will finance the discrepancy between the increment of investment and increment of savings.

Chenery and Strout also proposed an investment criterion for Phase I to the effect that "the rate of growth of investment must be greater than the target growth rate ($i > \bar{r}$) of GNP. Thereafter, the investment rate must be adequate to sustain the target GNP growth rate ($I/v \geq k. \bar{r}$)" (*Ibid.*, p. 705).

Once the target growth rate and corresponding level of investment are attained, foreign assistance will be required to overcome the savings limit (Phase II), and foreign exchange bottleneck (characterized as Phase III). Phase II usually begins at the end of Phase I, when investment reaches the level required to sustain the target growth rate of GNP ($\bar{r}$), and ends when either: (a) savings are equal to investment, and hence the net flow of capital is reduced to zero or (b) when the foreign exchange bottleneck becomes more restrictive (Phase III). The basic performance criterion for Phase II in terms of progress towards self-sustained growth at the target rate is that the marginal savings rate must be greater than the target investment rate unless the average rate of savings is already above this level (*Ibid.*, p. 705).

Phase III, which has been defined as the condition in which foreign assistance required to meet minimum import requirements exceeds the amount needed during a particular year under the operation of Phase II condition. The foreign exchange bottleneck, also known as trade limitation, is mainly the result of limited flexibility of productive structure for expanding output for exports or import substitution. Although avoidance of foreign exchange bottleneck has been regarded as more amenable to policy measures, such as : the elimination of over-valued exchange rates, than the savings limit. But the experience of developing countries indicates that actually the trade gap is often 'structural' in the sense it can only be reduced over time without reducing the growth rate, by a redirection of investment. The model for the determination of the amount of foreign capital required to fill the balance of payments gap employs marginal import ratio (u'), which is the average of incremental ratios for different components of demand, and the growth rate of exports (e).

Assuming that Phase III starts in the year 0, GNP in the year 't' will be

$$v_t = v_o (1+r)^{t-0}$$

The volume of imports (M_t) required to sustain GNP in the year 't' will be

$$M_t \geq \bar{M}_t = \bar{M}_0 + u' (v_t - v_0)$$

Where M_t is import of goods and services, an $\bar{M}_t$ is required import of goods and services in the year 't'.

The growth rate of exports (e) will determine foreign exchange earnings as follows :

$$E_t = E_0 (1 + e)^{t-0}$$

Where E_t and E_0 are exports of goods and services in years 't' and '0', respectively. Both u' and e has been regarded as policy variables, with u' being determined in part by government measures affecting import substitution, and e by measures affecting exports. The need for foreign assistance (F) to overcome the trade limit in year 't' has been given by

$$F_t = M_t - E_t$$

or $$F_t = M_0 + u' (v_t - v_0) - E_0 (1 + e)^{t-0}$$

"For the trade gap to be eliminated, either the export growth rate (e) must exceed the target growth rate ($\bar{r}$) of GNP or the marginal import ratio (u') must be substantially less than the initial average import ratio" (*Ibid.*, p. 691). This condition establishes the trade criterion for progress toward a given rate of 'self-sustaining growth'.

The total capital required, according to the model assumptions, to complete the transition to 'self-sustaining growth' can be determined as the sum of capital requirements for each phase that the economy goes through. In Phases IA* and II, external capital is determined by the cumulative difference between investment, and savings. In Phases IB* and III, it is the cumulative difference between import requirements and exports.

In essence, the important implications of the model for development policy are: first, over the whole period of the transition to 'self-sustaining growth', the use that is made of the successive increments in the GNP is likely to be more important than the efficiency with which external assistance was utilized in the first instance (*Ibid*., p. 724); second, rapid achievement of a high growth rate, even if it must be supported by heavy capital inflows, is likely to make the most significant contribution to 'self-sustained growth'; third, the focus of public policy in aid-recipient countries should vary according to the principal limitations to growth, just as optimal counter-cyclical policy implies different responses in different phases of the business cycle, optimal growth policy requires different 'self-help' measures in different phases of the transition' (*Ibid*., p. 725); and last, with the increasing availability of reasonably reliable statistics, the project approach to aid-giving and aid assessment should give way to a programme approach based on the recipient's compliance with minimum standards of overall development performance.

Thus, these models highlight the role of foreign aid in the complex growth process. They identify a number of strategic growth factors, explore their implications for the effectiveness of foreign aid, and draw significant conclusions for the overall foreign aid policy because any gaps to be filled would arise from the time required for structural adjustment to take place. The main thrust of foreign aid programme should be the allurement of structural adjustments themselves.

---

* When trade gap determines capital inflow in Phase I, the model denoted corresponding set of restrictions as Phase IB. This combination does not seem to be of great significance empirically. The more common case in which ability to invest and the saving limit are controlling, has been renamed as Phase IA.

SECTION II

USEFULNESS OF FOREIGN AID FOR THE DEVELOPMENT PROCESS

The most significant and controversial issue involving foreign aid is, whether foreign aid is useful in the development process of a recipient developing country ? Using Myrdal's terminology (1957) two extreme effects of foreign aid are potential 'spread' and 'backwash' effects in the recipient countries. First,

FIG. 3.1
Channels Through which Foreign Aid Inflows May Affect the Recipient Developing Country

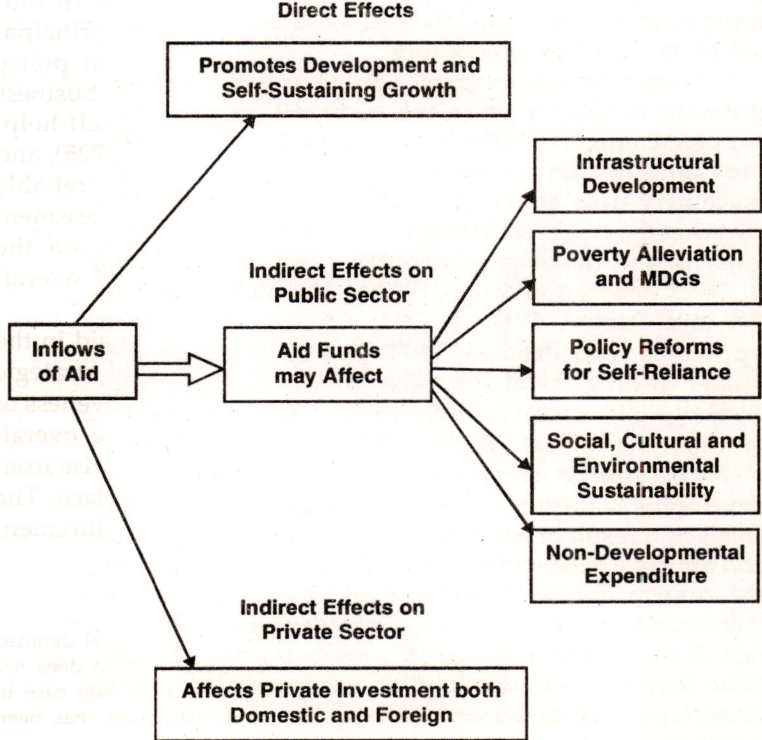

the direct effects of aid disbursement, that is, the effects which may be traced directly to the projects to which aid money is normally allocated, are mostly of the 'spread' type. Second, there are certain indirect effects on the recipient country's public and private sectors which may either be of the 'spread' or of the 'backwash' type (Mosley, 1987: p. 119). These effects are illustrated in the Figure 3.1.

Economists including primarily P.N. Rosenstein-Rodan (1961); Chenery and Bruno (1962); Ronald McKinnon (1964); Fei and Paauw (1965); Chenery and Strout (1966); William Thorp (1971); Gustav Papanek (1972); Paul Streeten (1983); Guy Arnold (1985); Anne Krueger (1991); Robert Cassen and Associates (1994); G.M. Meier (1995); Brian Opeskin (1996); and George Mavrotas (1998), etc., and the 'United Nations International Conference on Financing and Development' held in Monterrey (Mexico) on March 18-22, 2002 highlighted the spread effects of foreign aid, and presented their arguments in favour of providing aid to the developing countries.

Their first and foremost argument is that foreign aid will promote development in the recipient country not only by supplementing the domestic savings and investment but also by providing foreign exchange required to import material, and machinery from abroad, i.e., foreign aid is an effective way of covering the two basic savings-investment and foreign exchange gaps in the developing countries (Rosenstein-Rodan, 1961: p. 107; Chenery and Bruno, 1962: p. 102; McKinnon, 1964: p. 402; Fei and Paauw, 1965: p. 261; Chenery and Strout, 1966: pp. 687-91; and Papanek, 1972: p. 948). Similarly, a three gap model adding fiscal response to the savings, and foreign exchange gaps found a strong and positive impact of foreign aid on domestic savings (Bacha, 1990: pp. 280-84; Mavrotas, 1998: p. 26) because development is a long and slow process in which developing countries with larger populations; low productivity levels as a result of low levels of education and skills; and weak and almost absent socio-physical infrastructure, have to prepare the 'runway' for the future 'take off'. Foreign aid will help in the mobilization of resources, thus, accelerating thereby not only the rate of investment and overall growth but also for creating the basic requisites for transition to 'self-sustaining growth' in the developing countries, particularly at a time when forex reserves were hitting rock-bottom levels.

The basic requisite for transition to self-sustaining growth include investment in basic and key industries, like iron and steel, heavy engineering and electrical, etc., and socio-physical infrastructure in the form of uninterrupted regular power supply, quality highways and road network, rudimentary transport and communication, education, public health, water supply, housing and sanitation, etc. These are the basic elements of development strategy which are essential for the smooth and orderly functioning of primary, secondary and tertiary productive activities, and for the market economy and stability. Transport and communication infrastructure connect markets and people, both domestically as well as internationally. Better infrastructure reduces the effects of geography, costs to producers, and improve the reach of government and private services for consumers. These have to be financed from official sources as very little private funding is available from the market and user charges may not be appropriate in the early stages of development (Krueger, 1991: p. 52). However, the problem with increasing public expenditure or investment is that it may have to be financed by the governments either by raising taxes or by borrowing, both of which may have the effect of 'crowding out' private investment unless there is additional flow of resources from abroad in the form of foreign assistance. Increased tax revenues of the government will directly reduce the resources available to the private sector and the government borrowing will raise the interest rates with a given volume of domestic savings. To raise the public developmental expenditure without reducing private investment, government policy will have to be directed either at raising the domestic savings (the scope of which may be severely limited in the developing countries) or raising the inflow of foreign savings. Since such public expenditures are not guided by the market incentives but by the social objectives, hence increased foreign aid is conceived important both by the recipient countries who would like to increase the public expenditure for accelerating development, and by the donor governments who can influence the deployment of public expenditure in the recipient countries to maximise development (Sengupta, 2002: p. 1425).

Similarly, foreign aid in the form of technical know-how on project design, organization and management, provision of expert consultancy services, training to local counterparts, and establishment of research and training institutions etc., can also be of immense significance in many areas including agriculture and industry in the developing countries (For example: aid has obviously played a part in developing and disseminating high-yielding agricultural technologies, and promoting agricultural research in India, Mexico, Philippines and Pakistan). It is hard to imagine that this would have been achieved without massive investment by the World Bank and other assistance (Cassen and Associates, 1994 : p. 27; Meier, 1995 : p. 225). Thus, foreign aid can accelerate the overall growth of developing countries by transferring modern sophisticated and advanced technical know-how to them from the developed countries.

An argument on quite a different basis could be that economic development of developing countries will strengthen the world economy, in general, and the donor and recipient countries, in particular. "A small sacrifice by the donor country in the form of foreign aid may bestow a great benefit to the recipient country, in case substantial externalities and multiplier effects spring from the aid-financed projects or if aid given takes the form of deliveries from industries or firms in which excess capacity is above the average, in the economy as a whole. It may also be beneficial to the donors by stimulating domestic activity" (Streeten, 1983 : p. 382). This two-way self-interest is the best guarantee that aid relationship will work. The donors have capital and technical know-how, that is, their power to bargain, while the developing recipient countries have markets or resources which the donors seek. Aid must be seen as a bargain, for both the sides (Arnold, 1985 : p. 161; Ruttan, 1989 : p. 412). Thus, the poor developing countries will become better off emerging thereby as new and stronger trading partners to the benefit of both sides. Hence, foreign aid will prove mutually useful for the development of both the donor and donee countries.

However, as a consequence of cordial and cooperative relationship between the donor and recipient countries, developing countries can promote exports with the help of aid-funds after fulfilling their production targets set in their agricultural, and industrial sectors. With aid-funds, they can modernize their export-oriented industries by providing them latest technical know-how, basic infrastructure and quality control facilities. These countries can increase their bargaining power in the global market by exporting quality non-traditional goods, which are required in both the developed and developing countries. Consequently, "more productive activities in the rest of the world will increase the volume of trade in commodities and services between countries, not to mention the expanded sources of raw materials with a limited world supply. Foreign trade like all exchange is a means of obtaining greater return for the effort made on both sides" (Thorp, 1971: p. 326). Some countries that had been the major recipients of aid have now become successful exporters—partly because of aid, not despite it (such as : the Republic of Korea, Indonesia, etc.). "A study suggested that an increase of one percentage point in the rate of growth of exports adds on the average 0.15 to 0.27 points to the growth of a developing economy" (Cassen and Associates, 1994 : p. 28). But the developing countries are hampered by the real supply constraints that go with a lack of development. Therefore, development with foreign aid should be regarded as an engine for exports rather than exports being an engine of development, for the successful penetration in foreign markets which require extensive productive skills at home.

Foreign aid can also be useful in poverty alleviation in the developing countries, one of the prime 'Millennium Development Goals', (The World Bank, 2002a: p. 20; www.development goals.org) raising thereby the overall social welfare of the global society. This can be justified on a variety of philosophical grounds. Perhaps, the most common one is, the utilitarian argument that a dollar redistributed from a rich man to a poor man detracts less utility than it adds and ergo, increases the sum total of utility. Even if it were accepted that the sum total of global utility is a meaningful concept, the argument would require further elaboration, for, development aid is not aid from rich individuals in rich countries to the poor individuals in poor countries, but inter-governmental aid or aid from an agency to a government. It would, therefore, have to be ensured that either the aid reaches the poor in the developing countries or in the absence of tax-financed aid, tax relief would benefit the poor in the rich donor countries (Streeten, 1983: p. 380; Ruttan, 1989: pp. 416-17). Similarly, concessional aid can also be justified on Rawlsian grounds, i.e., the relief of the poorest people in the global community which are, perhaps, more appealing than utilitarian arguments because the relief of the absolute poorest is more widely accepted objective than the abstract utilitarianism (*Ibid.*, p. 380; *Ibid.* p. 417). Foreign aid, even on commercial terms subject to certain conditions would not reduce the social welfare, albeit, it would increase the same, if it encouraged improved policies or if private markets failed to supply capital, despite the higher real rates of return (Krueger, 1991: p. 50). Besides immediate relief from poverty in emergencies, aid can help to relieve poverty in five other ways also. First, by contributing to growth, it can create the conditions for raising the incomes and consumption of the poor. Second, it can achieve these results more directly through specific projects or sectoral activities. Third, it can improve the welfare of poor people through basic services such as : education, health, nutrition, housing or family planning programmes, etc. Fourth, it can assist the process of social change which gives assets, such as : surplus agricultural land to the poor landless laborers, etc. Last, it can support policy reforms which can benefit the poor (Cassen and Associates, 1994: p. 35). Thus, foreign aid can be used for such purposes which directly benefit the poor in the developing countries.

Besides poverty alleviation, foreign aid can also be useful for achieving the internationally agreed other Millennium Development Goals (1990-2015), such as : universal primary education; gender equality and empowerment of women; reduction by two-thirds the under-five mortality rate; reduction by three-quarters the maternal mortality ratio; fighting HIV/AIDS, malaria and other diseases; halve the proportion of people without access to potable water; significantly improve the lives of at least 100 million slum dwellers; expansion of market access; and to encourage debt sustainability, etc., in the developing countries (The World Bank, 2002a: p. 20).

Foreign aid can also be useful for 'crowding in' private foreign investment in the developing countries, which is largely bypassed by such private capital flows in a rapidly globalizing world. Majority of the developing countries will not be able to raise their rates of growth, if their investment remain constrained by domestic savings and foreign aid is not forthcoming. Despite the phenomenal growth of private capital flows internationally, private investors seeking highest marketable and reasonably low risk private returns will adopt a wait-and-see attitude towards these countries, and would rather move towards more advanced developing countries capable of offering larger returns. Hence, such private capital flows could be attracted to these countries by creating a good investment climate consisting of all the factors that most influence private sector decisions like macroeconomic stability and trade openness (known as 'Washington Consensus'); good governance and institutions including a good education system, effective legal institutions, and professional bureaucracy; vigorous competition and adequate infrastructure (The World Bank, 2002a: pp. 87-88); and by special programmes of risk-sharing or profit augmenting measures, possibly supported by foreign aid. Consequently, there would be net increase in the availability of resources or foreign savings in these countries. "Even if these private foreign capital flows cannot be used directly to finance public expenditures, they will relax the constraints of domestic savings by supplementing them with foreign savings. Hence, public expenditure can then be financed by the governments without 'crowding out' private investment because of larger part of available savings" (Sengupta, 2002 : p. 1425). Thus, developing countries would be able to attract the private foreign capital from international market easily.

Foreign aid can also be a useful means of initiating and/or speeding up serious policy reforms, both at macroeconomic level and in individual sectors, in the recipient developing countries (which is now, perhaps, the most important issue on their agenda). These policy reforms have crucial impact on the economic growth, development and effective use of aid in the recipient developing countries through the adoption of sound domestic policies, such as : transition from public sector-based socialism to private sector led market-based economic growth, strict fiscal discipline, empowerment to women, strengthening of panchayati raj institutions, and democratization of the economy, etc. The developing countries can be influenced in their choice of macroeconomic policies through 'policy dialogue' which can "take many forms: discussion and persuasion; information on policy effectiveness and techniques for reform; financial support for structural reform efforts; and 'conditionality', so that aid is given only if policies are changed" (Krueger, 1991: p. 52). Intangible and low cost efforts can promote policy reforms over the long-run, by disseminating development ideas, training the next generation of leaders, and stimulating policy debate in the civil society. Even the conditional loans can also be useful as signalling device to the private sector that the government is serious about the reforms and the new policy regime is likely to persist. Uncertainties about policy retard investment. In sound-policy countries, aid may be associated with higher private investment, while the combination of reform and foreign aid can boost investor's confidence (The World Bank, 1998: p. 54). Similarly, foreign aid through the donors' influence over the recipients' policies and their willingness to use it, have great potential to serve a purpose for which private capital markets seem ill-suited. Indeed one might imagine a situation where donor influence produced such improvements in global economic efficiency that they made large scale private investment on attractive proposition. In this light private capital might prove more complimentary to foreign aid than substitute.

Foreign aid, particularly at concessionary terms, promotes 'self-reliance' in the recipient developing countries in the long run, for, it enables the recipient countries to build up their own productive capacity in almost all the sectors including agriculture and industry so that they can finance their investments, and import requirements through normal commercial channels. As a result, 'graduation' will occur sooner and donors will have to furnish less total aid in order to achieve the development objectives than if terms had been harder. If the terms were not soft, either the poor recipient countries will be transferring back resources to the donor countries or as in the nature of compound interest, a rapidly mounting debt burden will be mortgaging the country's future. So, if the donor's objective is maximum development impact combined with the desire to wind up aid, soft terms are the appropriate instrument (Streeten, 1983: p. 384). Nevertheless, 'self-reliance' does not mean that the country would not accept any foreign aid in future but that its economic development would no longer be dependent on such aid. The country would compete in the global market on its own by importing latest technical know-how and modern sophisticated equipments; involve the foreign investment (MNCs) without any fear; strengthen the private sector and trust them; and limit the role of bureaucratic state R and D laboratories. The country would rather like to do without foreign aid, if it hinders country's politico-economic objectives. "Aid dependency is not an unchanging phenomenon" (Cassen and Associates, 1994: p. 26). Thus, foreign aid spurs self-sufficiency in the long-run, though it may have some negative effects on savings in the short run.

Foreign aid can also prove politically useful for the global economy, in general, and the recipient developing countries, in particular. There is one political argument which transcends all others : that aid may bring us closer to an appealing idea of 'single world society', especially if set against the background of endless global disputes (such as : Israel-Palestine; Indo-Pakistan; China-Taiwan, etc.), which trouble the mankind. Although it is an idealistic argument but it can not be considered as ignoble or unworthy due to the basic fact that world is shrinking, day-by-day, in terms of transport and communications. Foreign aid provides a regular means of contact between governments as well as individuals either side of the rich-poor divide. Such contacts have been especially important for the ex-colonial powers. "It is no accident that a high proportion of all British and all French aid goes to the countries which were their colonies" (Arnold, 1985: p. 157). In this way, the aims of helping allies and safeguarding their interests can regularly be sustained by means of foreign aid.

Foreign aid can also be socially, culturally and environmentally useful in protecting the global economy, in general, and richer countries, in particular, from the spill-over consequences of extreme poverty, hunger and deprivation in the form of crime, terrorism, illegal drugs and communicable diseases like AIDS, SARS, Malaria, Typhoid, Tuberculosis, etc. The Preamble of the US Foreign Assistance Act (1948) clearly states that "the freedom, security and prosperity of the United States are best sustained in a community of free, secure, and prospering nations. . . and ignorance, want, and despair breed extremism and violence which lead to aggression and subversion . . . . It is not only expressive of our sense of freedom, justice, and compassion but also important to our national security. . . . It is the policy of the United States to support the principles of increased economic cooperation and trade" (Thorp, 1971: pp. 321-22). Similarly, the historic global consensus which emerged at the United Nations International Conference on Financing and Development, held on March 18-22, 2002 in Monterrey, Mexico presented an approach based entirely on enlightened self-interest. This view recognizes that national borders and geographical barriers that once provided a buffer between rich and poor societies are increasingly becoming porous. Problem of crime, terrorism, illegal drugs and communicable diseases feed on the helplessness of extreme deprivation, yet their effects are confined to poor societies. James Wolfensohn, the President of the WB Group, in his keynote address at Woodrow Wilson International Center for Scholars, in Washington, D.C., on March 6, 2002 remarked, "there is no wall" separating rich from poor. Like it or not, events and trends in poor, and seemingly distant lands can have a direct impact on the lives of people in rich countries. From this angle development assistance serves a sort of preventive maintenance for richer countries (The World Bank, 2002a : p. 19).

On the flip side, some economists, both on the right and the left of the political spectrum, including primarily Milton Friedman (1958); Keith B. Griffin and J.L. Enos (1970); Teresa Hayter (1974 and 1982); Peter Bauer (1979, 1981, 1984 and 1993); Peter Bauer and Basil Yamey (1982); T.K. Mishra (1994); Melvyn Krauss (1997); Robert Lensink and Howard White (2001); Ales Bulir and Timothy Lane (2002), etc., have argued that spread effects of foreign aid are much less than its backwash effects due to various socio-politico-economic and administrative reasons. Therefore, foreign aid even at concessional terms may impose burden on the developing countries and virtually retard their growth. Consequently, the capital made available is likely to be dissipated as has happened in the Democratic Republic of Congo (formerly Zaire), Tanzania, Ethiopia, Somalia, Bangladesh, etc., during the recent past decades.

They have presented their arguments highlighting the backwash effects of foreign aid. Foreign aid is likely to retard the economic growth and development of the developing countries because it hampers the working of free market mechanism by encouraging government intervention, protectionism, excessive money creation, and state-created distortions, like political intervention, corruption, bureaucratic procedural delays, etc. "What is required (for development) is rather an atmosphere of freedom, of maximum opportunity for individuals to experiment and of incentive for them to do so in an environment in which there are objective tests of success and failure—in short, a vigorous, free capitalistic market" (Friedman, 1958: p. 71). Free market without central planning and government intervention has been most effective route to economic development, and for the well-being of the masses. Bauer, perhaps the strongest critic of foreign aid, has also supported this argument. "External donations have never been necessary for the development of any society anywhere" (Bauer, 1984: p. 44). This economic objection is also basically an argument for private enterprise that development will be best served by giving free rein to the forces of market, albeit by a system of hand outs. Similarly, foreign aid may retard long-run economic growth by altering the composition of investment to the disadvantage of recipient countries, in case a large proportion of publicly sponsored foreign assistance is channelled into activities which are either not directly productive or have long gestation periods (Griffin and Enos, 1970: p. 323). Thus, "foreign aid is plainly not indispensable to economic progress and is indeed likely to obstruct it" (Bauer, 1979: p. 95).

Though foreign aid increases the resources of the recipient countries but it does not follow that it will accelerate the rate of development because the results depend on the expenditure of aid-funds, and also on the repercussions of the flow of aid on the basic determinants of material progress, particularly attitudes, policies and institutions. "Some of these effects and repercussions are adverse, and can easily outweigh any favorable result of the inflow of resources" (Bauer, 1979: p. 99). Sometimes, recipients mostly intentionally divert the aid funds to spending on items which donors did not wish to support, i.e., aid can be 'fungible' to the policy officials in the Finance Ministry of the recipient countries, in case they treat aid funds like any other category of revenue, and allocate these according to their own priorities and preferences. Though the malicious intent is not necessary, yet the diversion of aid funds can delay the completion of projects and hence, adversely affect the growth policies. So, "what is required in the developing countries is the release of the energies of millions of able, active and vigorous people—(who) require only a favorable economic environment to transform the face of their countries" (Friedman, 1958: p. 71), and not foreign aid. Hence, in the long-run, foreign aid "will almost surely retard economic development and promote the triumph of communism" (*Ibid*., p. 64).

Foreign aid can also hamper the growth of recipient countries in case it is 'tied' either to source or to a project. In such a situation, recipient countries can not buy the most suitable product in the cheapest market taking into consideration other relevant circumstances like the availability of installation, repair and maintenance services, etc., but are forced to accept, what the donors provide. That is, "aid has never been an unconditional transfer of financial resources. Usually, the conditions attached to aid are clearly and directly intended to serve the interests of the governments providing it. For example, aid must generally be used to buy goods and services from its provider" (Hayter, 1974: p. 15). As a consequence, recipient countries are encumbered with costly operation from the beginning with the purchases of expensive machinery, plants and equipments (Griffin and Enos, 1970: p. 324). Hence, recipients have to bear the burden of tied aid. How heavy this burden is, will depend among other things, on the degree of project tying, on the range of goods which the donor country can offer and their prices relative to other sources of supply, and on the advantage which the firms of donor country are willing and able to take of the fact that the tying of aid has placed them in a monopoly position as far as tendering for the aided projects is concerned. "The evidence seems to suggest that tied aid may be worth about 20 percent or so less to the recipients than untied aid" (Singer and Ansari, 1978: p. 171). This tied aid indirectly represents disguised subsidy for the exporters of the donor countries (Griffin and Enos, 1970: p. 324).

Similarly, the arguments that foreign aid is mutually useful to both the donors and recipients may also be invalid. The idea that the donor countries benefit from the aid simply ignores the cost of resources given away. Enterprises do not prosper by giving away money, even if the recipients use some or all of the aid funds to buy products from these enterprises. Such aid money is also not sufficient for the economic development of developing countries (Bauer, 1993 : p. 12). Albeit, foreign aid can be dangerous as it spreads, and perpetuates the animosities between the donor and recipient countries because assistance is usually given to gain favors in the recipient countries. Favors granted are favors asked for, the favor to a lender is often disfavor to the lender's opponent (Griffin and Enos, 1970 : p. 317). Similarly, aid ostensibly given in friendship seems inevitably leading to enmity in case agreements break between the lender and borrowers, no matter which one instigates the act. Just as assistance has not created obligations, so default will not promote concord. "When ingratitude barbs the dart of injury, the wound has double danger in it" (*Ibid.*, p. 327).

Foreign aid is far from being necessary to rescue the developing countries from a 'vicious circle of poverty', but is more likely to keep them in the same state. There is different model behind the hypothesis of vicious circle : the growth of income depends on investment; investment depends on savings; and savings on income. The model pivots on the notion that the low level of income itself prevents the investment required to raise it and hence, leading to a zero or negligible rate of economic growth. However, the model is refuted by the obvious reality of the existence of developed countries, all of which started poor and developed without foreign aid. God did not create the world in two parts: one developed and the other underdeveloped. If a hypothesis conflicts with empirical evidence, especially if it does so conspicuously, as in this case, this means either that the variables specified are insignificant or that they do not interact, in the manner postulated. Both of these defects apply in this instance (Bauer, 1993: p. 10).

Similarly, foreign aid may not be necessary for the developing countries for emergence from backwardness and poverty, albeit it can—and often does—prolong and exacerbate the poverty. Alleviation of poverty depends upon people's own efforts, motivations, mores, arrangements, institutions, and policies of their rulers. It is indeed unwarranted to argue that the people of the Third World, unlike those of West, cannot achieve material progress without assistance from abroad. "In reality, throughout the world and throughout the history, countless individuals, families, groups, communities, and countries have emerged from poverty to prosperity without donations, and often did so within a few years or decades. Immigrant communities in South-East Asia and North America are familiar examples" (*Ibid.*, p. 9).

Most of the aid-funds received by the donor countries may be dissipated lavishly on non-developmental purposes either in the form of building huge, expensive and sophisticated military arsenal, and weaponry; on the prestigious projects like airports, hotels, urban sewerage, etc., all satisfying prestige needs of the urbanized privileged class or for depositing in the Swiss bank accounts by their corrupt rulers, etc. Bauer (1993) quoted numerous such examples as "Western aid has often been given simultaneously to the governments at war with each other" (*Ibid*., p. 5); (for example: India and Pakistan, Iran and Iraq, Uganda and Tanzania); lavish expenditure on the construction from scratch of brand new capitals [such as : Brasilia (in Brazil) and Dodoma (in Tanzania)]; and on the operation of international airlines in countries (such as : Burundi and Laos), where vast majority of people do not even use them and local people cannot operate them (*Ibid*., p. 8). Similarly, rather then going to the poor people in real need, food aid often ended up being used by the governments in poor countries to subsidize the politically powerful their middle class support base just to keep themselves in power as has happened in Ethiopia, Bangladesh and Somalia during the '80s. Its "dirty little secret is that US foreign-aid dollars often wind up in numbered Swiss bank accounts and palatial estates of Third World tyrants—not in the pockets of the poor" (Krauss, 1997: p. 62). Thus, foreign aid is not necessary for the economic development of developing countries.

Foreign aid may also make it easier for the developing countries to restrict the inflow of foreign commercial capital, particularly the equity capital. The developing countries usually pay only lip service to inward foreign equity investment but practically many severely restrict it. They often restrict the expansion and sometimes, even the current operation of the foreign enterprises. Many of these enterprises are not allowed to expand, even if they are prepared to finance their expansion from their own resources and even when they are prepared to bring in forex necessary for this purpose. They do so because these restrictions suit their political purposes and commercial interests of their supporters. These restrictions are plainly anomalous when shortage of capital is used as the basic argument for aid-funds. "Inflow of equity capital together with commercial, administrative and technical skills that accompany it, have been the prime instrument of the economic advance of many developing countries. The restrictions are, therefore, correspondingly damaging" (Bauer, 1979: pp. 107-08; Bauer, 1993: pp. 14-15).

Foreign aid can also be used as a weapon, in the armoury of developed countries, to influence the policy reforms in the recipient developing countries, particularly the smaller ones, to ensure that they should remain politically and economically loyal to the donor countries, for, 'a beggar cannot be a chooser'. Donors can "use their power to withhold or increase aid as a means of influencing the general economic policies of developing countries in specific direction" (Hayter, 1974: p. 17). They can use aid to foster their strategic, political, cultural or economic interests, etc., in the developing countries (Griffin and Enos, 1970: p. 315). For instance, "the concept of Third World or the South and the policy of official aid are inseparable. They are the two sides of the same coin. The Third World is the creation of foreign aid; without foreign aid there is no Third World" (Bauer, 1981: p. 87). Foreign aid often delays the implementation of much needed reforms in the recipient developing countries, while suspending or reducing aid leads to more rapid implementation (Krauss, 1997: pp. 74-75), (Russia is a recent case in point. The West has given Boris Yeltsin administration hundreds of millions of dollars in aid. But instead of accelerating the pace of needed economic reforms in Russia the pace has slackened). Similarly, aid may be used to build up social and economic systems considered to be durable, and resistant to revolutionary changes according to the desires of donor countries, i.e., maintaining the status quo, enabling the borrowing countries to postpone institutional changes.

Foreign aid perpetuates an ultimately destructive sense of dependency on others and perverts the genuine attempts to achieve self-reliance in the recipient countries, i.e., "it may help to create and sustain within Third World countries, a class which is dependent on the continued existence of aid and foreign private investment, and which, therefore, becomes an ally of imperialism" (Hayter, 1974: p. 9; Krauss, 1997: p. 68). For example, the African countries received the highest levels of aid per capita yet they remained poor. In some African countries aid accounted for half of their budget and in some half of their GDP. But many are ravaged by civil war and tribal strife which made any economic development difficult. Thus, "it seems that while aid stimulated in small doses, it acted as drug when given in larger doses, converting the recipients into aid junkies" (Mishra, 1994: p. 7). Similarly, foreign aid can reinforce the belief that economic development depends on the outside forces albeit domestic efforts. The prospect of foreign aid encourages the recipient governments to seek it through beggary or blackmail rather than to consider the potentialities of change at home. Such attitudes and conduct can spread from the government to other sectors of the population (Arnold, 1985: p. 165; Bauer, 1993: p. 13). Thus, it pauperizes the country making it increasingly dependant on foreign aid.

Sometimes, foreign aid can prove 'illusionary', particularly when the over optimistic recipient developing countries base their spending plans to some extent on the donor's commitments of aid funds, which practically do not materialize. In such a situation, the country can continue to spend at the level originally envisaged, running down the available precious scarce forex reserves and expanding domestic credit to make up for the aid that do not arrive. Though this approach reduces the risk that the country has to curtail its planned spending instantly or maintain this spending only by relying heavily on the domestic financing, yet persistent aid shortfalls can introduce a lack of transparency into macroeconomic programmes, by making fiscal policies and targets for international reserves appearing more conservative than they are (Bulir and Lane, 2002: p. 29).

Moreover, foreign aid can not be considered as an ideal palliative, for, aid receipts can be uncertain, volatile and less reliable than the other sources of revenue. Its disbursements usually are subject to the vagaries of donor countries' budgetary processes, in which aid has to compete with their domestic priorities and conditions imposed by the donors regarding its uses, which may not be in tune with the views and requirements of the recipient country. Though some conditions may be required to ensure the kind of environment in which aid can be effective in boosting growth but the interruptions in aid flows associated with conditionality introduce greater uncertainty into the recipient country's fiscal plans (*Ibid.*, pp. 29-30). It is likely to go to sectors and areas which are accorded priority by the donor institutions albeit by the recipient countries. It is, thus, necessary to avoid an excessive dependence on foreign aid in the development process (Gilles, 2003 : pp. 34-35).

Perhaps, the greatest objection to foreign aid is that it is provided for political reasons albeit to promote development. It has helped to sustain those governments in the developing countries, whose policies have proved so damaging that only aid has enabled them to remain in power and continue on their destructive course. It enables those in power to evade and avoid fundamental reforms; it does little more than patch plaster on the deteriorating social edifice (Griffin and Enos, 1970: p. 325). Such circumstances encourage or even compel people to divert their attention, energy and resources from productive economic activities to concern with the outcome of political and administrative decisions. Politicization of life often provokes tensions and conflicts, especially in countries with heterogeneous ethnic and cultural groups including most of the Third World, and Eastern Europe. Extensive politicization of life has been a major factor behind these ubiquitous conflicts, often armed on the contemporary scene. In Asia and Africa, groups and communities that have lived together peacefully for generations have been set against each other by the politicization promoted by foreign aid (Bauer and Yamey, 1982: p. 57; Bauer, 1993: p. 14). For instance: in Lebanon, Christians and Muslims; in Malaysia, Malay's and Chinese; in Sri Lanka, Singhalese and Tamils; in Nigeria, Ibo and Hausa. Nothing beats national security as a justification of and rationalization for foreign aid. Before the collapse of communism, the Right justified foreign aid because of the need to fight the spread of communism in poor countries. In the post-cold war era, it is the Left who argues for foreign aid on national security grounds—allegedly to fight the resurrection of communism and fascism in the former Soviet Union (Krauss, 1997: p. 69). Thus, aid props up reform resisting oligarchies, and conservative and feudal social systems, and perpetuate system which makes it necessary.

Similarly, moral arguments for providing foreign aid to the developing countries seem illogical and baseless, for, "charity should begin at home first", i.e., the donors should first use their aid-funds for domestic poverty alleviation, instead of providing these to other developing countries. For instance: countries like India, on the one hand, receive billions of rupees as foreign aid and, on the flip side, give millions of rupees as foreign aid to the neighbouring countries every year, just to keep hold on them.

Also, it is argued that there are many rich people in the various aid recipient countries, where there is no domestic income redistribution in favor of poor. For example: "in 1980s, Nigerians were significant operators at the top end of real estate market in London" (Bauer, 1993: p. 5), while Nigeria progressively became more dependent on the WB loans, despite having ample crude oil income. Thus, it is obvious that there is no moral obligation on the rich advanced countries to provide assistance to all the developing countries from their tax payer's money collected compulsorily.

Hence, foreign aid is neither necessary nor a sufficient condition for the overall economic development of all the developing countries.

AID AND GROWTH RELATIONSHIP—AN ESTIMATE

Though nothing conclusively can be said: whether foreign aid promotes or prohibits economic growth in the developing countries, yet "some rough calculations can help to indicate the contribution of foreign aid to growth. Assume that, for developing countries, the investment-income ratio lies between 15 and 25 percent. Let the incremental capital-output ratio lie within a range of 3.0 to 5.0. If aid adds 20 percent to the level of investment, it will raise the investment-income ratio by 3 to 5 percent. A one percent rise in that ratio will in turn raise the growth rate of output between 0.3 and 0.2 percent. Assuming that population growth is exogenous in the medium run, aid will also raise the per capita output by a similar amount. In other words, given a reasonable volume of aid that is used reasonably efficiently, the annual growth rate with aid would be higher, between 0.6 percent and 1.5 percent. These are the significant increases on plausible assumptions" (Cassen and Associates, 1994: pp. 20-21).

SECTION III

WHY SHOULD DONORS PROVIDE AID ?

Another important issue involving foreign aid is to sort out the main motives of the donor rich countries for providing aid to the developing countries. As a matter of fact, donor countries provide aid for the reasons of self-interest—might be economic, commercial, strategic, political or otherwise and for ethical humanitarian or moral reasons, etc. The donor's self-interest may play a relatively larger role in bilateral assistance, while recipient's need may play a larger role in multilateral assistance (Maizels and Nissanke, 1984: p. 891; Burnside and Dollar, 2000: p. 848).

One of the most important self-interest reason for providing aid is to foster, protect, and proliferate the economic interests including trade and commercial interests of the donor countries in the recipient countries because as the infrastructure develops in these developing countries, demand for new and replacement equipment compatible with aid-funded investment, transport and communication network, etc., is expected to widen the sale opportunities. Injections of aid, particularly tied to the purchase of goods and services from the donor countries, reinforces such business trade objectives. Similarly, if aid is effective in contributing to the economic growth of developing countries, the effect will be on expansion of demand for the developed countries' goods and services that are characterized by high import demand elasticities. For example, "agricultural producers in the United States are urged not to become overly concerned about loss of oilseed markets to Malaysia and Brazil because, as incomes rise, growth in demand for animal proteins will generate demand for US feedgrains. Loss of exports by the mature industrial sectors will be more than compensated for by the capital goods and high technology exports" (Ruttan, 1989: p. 412). Foreign aid is also used to "keep the rivals away from the recipient countries to protect and safeguard the donor investments. It can also be used to persuade the recipients to accept further investment from donor countries" (Arnold, 1985: p. 102).

Then comes political and strategic interests. Since foreign aid is a part of hard-headed political bargain, hence is always used by the donor countries as the major principle for providing aid to the developing countries. Donors possess certain surpluses of capital and trained people which they are willing to make available to the donee countries, at a price in the form of allies and friends, their vote and support in the UN Security Council, and other international bodies. For example, the US directs larger proportion of its aid to its allies like Israel, Pakistan, Afghanistan, etc., that it considered strategic, earlier against Soviet communism, now against global terrorism. Similarly, most of the British aid goes to the Commonwealth countries, French aid to Francophone countries, Arab aid to Islamic countries etc. Such choices are a matter of preference which are made in order to maintain or increase solidarity with the natural allies. The primary rationale, therefore, of aid is to strengthen the political commitment of aid recipients to the donor country or to the West . . . has been a consistent and at times dominant theme in the motivation for development assistance (Streeten, 1983: p. 385; Maizels and Nissanke, 1984: p. 885; Ruttan, 1989: p. 413).

However, there is an inherent contradiction in both the economic and the security self-interest arguments. "The danger is that donor countries might pursue their self-interest under the rubric of aid even if it harms the recipient country. If the donor self-interest argument is used as a primary rationale for development assistance it imposes, on donors, some obligation to demonstrate that their assistance does not harm the recipient" (Ruttan, 1989: p. 414).

Donors, particularly bilateral donors, also provide aid to the developing countries to reward or punish them: to reward them (by giving concessionary aid) in case they follow their policies, support them in the UN or provide them strategic advantages; and punish them (by withdrawing aid) in case they do not follow their polices. For instance: the USA and its allies provided rewards in the form of renewed aid to Pakistan and Afghanistan for throwing away Taliban regime and Al-Qaida terrorists in the year 2001, and to Iraq after dethroning President Saddam Hussain in the year 2003, after the September 11 attack on the World Trade Centre in New York in 2001. Foreign aid can also be used as a punitive measure as has happened against India and Pakistan, in the year 1998, when both conducted nuclear test explosions. This led to economic sanctions against and suspension of foreign aid to India, total loss of foreign exchange was estimated by the RBI at US $ 2.8 billion as a combined total of such aid from all donor sources (Wadhva, 1998: p. 1604).

Similarly, there has been an extended argument that it is the humanitarian moral obligation of the rich countries to assist the poor developing countries in reducing poverty, and over-coming their problems, over and above any consideration of self-interest. This view takes various forms like accepting the persistence of desperate poverty—that is, to do nothing to change a world where 1.2 billion people subsist on less than a dollar a day, where 120 million children do not attend school, and where tens of millions of people die annually from the combined effects of poor nutrition and diseases that could easily have been prevented or treated—is morally untenable (The World Bank, 2002a: p. 18). Sometimes, there is an element of guilt included on the part of donors that they (as colonialists, for example) exploited them in the past, now they must make amends (Opeskin, 1996: pp. 26-27) or trans-national corporations are exploiting them today, so the balance has to be redressed (Arnold, 1985: p. 102). Similarly, the obligations of humanity urge individuals and states to be guided by some principles such as: individuals in the developed countries must have regard for the welfare of individuals beyond their geographical borders, for, 'every citizen is a brother to fellow citizens and nothing at all to others' (Opeskin, 1996: p. 39), it is a notion that is central to all the major religions of the world; it is a concept of goodness that was founded in the philosophies of classical civilizations; and it is a part of our understanding of being a decent citizen of the world. So, the developed countries as moral agents for their inhabitants should utilize their taxation system to generate an appropriate level of revenue without compromising the basic needs of the worst-off in their own societies; a sufficient portion of the revenue so raised should be expended on aid to developing countries; the aid should be given in such a way as to secure maximum benefits for individuals in these countries, such as: by making the transfer conditional on its just-distribution among the population of the recipient country; and finally, where a developed country fails to take the necessary action, obligations of humanity impel people fortunate enough to be born into the richer countries to share their good fortunes with the poor in the developing countries. However, whatever may be the driving force behind the humanitarian, ethical or guilt arguments, by and large, these are advanced by the aid lobbies which do so to placate their own supporters, either as an expression of public relations or their wish to give an appearance of being humane themselves, while pursuing other more hard-headed objectives. But, as a matter of fact, donor governments are not overly concerned with humanitarian or ethical arguments.

Then comes entitlement arguments, frequently put forth during the 'New Economic Order' dialogue of the 1970s, that there should be compensation by the rich advanced industrialized countries to the poor developing countries "for the unequal distribution of world's natural resources among states, to which all the mankind may be thought to have an equal right of access" (Streeten, 1983: p. 381; Mitra, 1990b: p. 260) for the violation of human rights such as: excluding poor people from entry into the rich countries or as compensation for capital flights or for erecting barriers to imports. "It has been argued that natural resources are a part of our global heritage and that those areas that are favorably endowed have an obligation to share rents from differential resource endowments with those areas that are less favorably endowed" (Ruttan, 1989: p. 415). Perhaps, the area in which the natural resources distribution issue is of greatest contemporary significance is the debate about the management and distribution of the potential rents associated with the exploitation of the global commons—the ocean and space resources (*Ibid.*, p. 416). Though, the natural resource endowment differentials and violation of human rights do not represent a very powerful factor in explaining differential growth rates among either developed or developing countries, but are a cause for providing concessionary assistance to the developing countries. It has been rightly remarked, "if social services are justified within Britain or the USA, why not also between the rich and poor countries ? The argument is a logical one" (Arnold, 1985: p. 160).

There is another argument of longer-term nature which does carry some weight: that a world divided between 'haves' and 'have-nots' is a dangerous world that may one day erupt in violence to the detriment of everyone, especially of the more advanced countries, since they have the most to lose in the form of terrorism, crime, illegal drugs, and communicable diseases, etc., fed on the hopelessness of the extreme deprivation. Therefore, the argument runs, it is better to ameliorate the lot of the poor now, in order to avert such a calamity in the future. But that too is an argument of enlightened self-interest, although one which clearly recognizes the force of humanitarian concern. Not to care is to build up trouble for the future (Arnold, 1985: p. 102; The World Bank, 2002a: p. 19).

Lastly, there is an idea of a better world for providing aid to the developing countries. It proceeds from the question, what kind of world would we like to live in and to pass on to our children ? Most of us would picturize a global scenario in which people behave in a collaborative and supportive manner, and where differences are celebrated and valued, as opposed to a world in which people are combative, undermine one another, and are fearful of differences. "To create the first kind of world, we must begin by behaving in a manner that brings people together—a manner we would like to see in others. We must work to eliminate widespread deprivation, if we want everyone to live in the kind of world we desire for our children. Further, the very act of working together to build a better world helps make this better world a reality" (The World Bank, 2002a: pp. 18-19). All this requires that the rich countries should provide concessionary aid to the needy developing countries.

Thus, in essence, without an aid program, rich, advanced and industrialized countries would be greatly handicapped in conducting their foreign affairs—might be economic, commercial, political or otherwise. Hence, it becomes obligatory for them to provide aid to the developing countries, if they want to play the role of 'superman' in the global affairs.

Overall, despite the arguments highlighting both the 'spread' and 'backwash' effects of foreign aid, the fact is, donors are continuously offering it, and the recipients are taking it. Both the donors and recipients are doing, what they are willing to do. They could stop but they do not choose to do so, due to the complex array of goals ranging from political and strategic to economic and humanitarian. The variety of experience suggest that blanket criticism of aid is not convincing. Foreign aid has played a significant role in many developing countries, especially in the recent difficult international conditions, though empirical evidence varies depending upon the country groupings and the time period chosen. "Their evidence is more selective but in some ways stronger. They show that aid has raised growth when it is maintained for sometime and combined with sensible development policies" (Cassen and Associates, 1994: p. 16), "and that its poverty reduction impact also increased overtime" (The

World Bank, 2002a: p. 117). Even the developing countries "have not done badly compared either to the developed countries or (more pertinently) to their pre-aid programme growth rates and there are as many examples of successful aid absorption by the recipients as there are horror stories of aid wastage on specific projects" (Bhagwati and Eckaus, 1970: p. 8). However, it should not be used as 'dependent approach'. The main effort must come from within the recipient country itself. Rosenstein-Rodan has aptly remarked, "The function of outside capital in a development program is not directly to raise the standards of living in the recipient countries but to permit them to make transition from economic stagnation to 'self-sustaining growth'. The principal element in this transition must be the efforts that the citizens of recipient countries themselves make to bring it about. Without these efforts, outside capital will be wasted" (Rosenstein-Rodan, 1961: p. 107).

To sum up, it can be generalized that foreign aid is still a useful economic instrument having more 'spread effects' which can be geared to serve the multiplicity of objectives in the developing countries, despite having certain 'backwash effects'. That is why, the significance of foreign aid as a distinct sub-discipline of 'International Finance and Economics' grew considerably, over the years. At the same time, with the end of cold war, donors have become less interested in using aid to achieve geo-political goals and more interested in using aid for poverty reduction. Large scale financial assistance is being increasingly allocated to countries that have reasonably good policies and institutions—that is, the countries that can best use aid for poverty reduction. With this, poverty reduction effectiveness of Official Development Assistance has been tripled during the 1990s (The World Bank, 2002a: pp. 92-93).

4

Foreign Aid : Review of Empirical Studies

Foreign aid in different times and at different places has played a different role. No blanket statement to the effect that foreign aid 'does good' or 'does harm' to growth in recipient countries can be given. It has been proved highly effective, totally ineffective and everything in between. It has, at times, been a spectacular success. Botswana and the Republic of Korea in the 1960s; Indonesia in the 1970s; Bolivia, China and Ghana in the late 1980s; and Uganda and Vietnam in the 1990s are all good examples of countries that have gone from crisis to rapid development. Foreign aid has played a significant role in each transformation contributing ideas about development, training for public policy-makers, and finance to support reforms and an expansion of public services. On the flip side, foreign aid has also been, at times, an unmitigated failure. Democratic Republic of Congo (formerly Zaire), Tanzania and Nigeria are some of the instances where a steady flow of foreign aid has ignored, if not encouraged, incompetence, corruption and misguided policies. "Perhaps all that is to be expected in a complex endeavor that has spanned half a century, with scores of countries as donors, a hundred countries as recipients, tens of thousands of specific activities and nearly $1 trillion in finance. But hindsight is valuable only if it produces insight." (The World Bank, 1998: p. 2).

In the present chapter, an attempt has been made to review the empirical studies related to the different aspects of the effectiveness of foreign aid, particularly with reference to India. The review of these studies provide a wide spectrum of the empirical research done in this area and basis for the formulation of a suitable methodology for the present study. Though it is not an exhaustive review of the extensive research done in this area yet the aim is to highlight, in a general way, the type of work done in this direction. Some of the important studies are briefly reviewed here in a chronological order in two sections. Section-I reviews the general studies on foreign aid, while Section-II covers the studies relating to some specific aspect/purpose of the utilization of foreign aid.

Section I

Rao and Narain (1963) analyzed the character, magnitude and organization of foreign aid, and the impact it made on the Indian economy during the period April 1, 1951 to December 31, 1961. The study revealed that bulk of the aid was bilateral and economic in character; the rate of investment increased considerably from an annual level of 5 percent of the national Income (at current prices) in 1951-52 to 11 percent in 1960-61 under the impact of foreign aid; and most of the foreign aid was utilized to strengthen the public sector and country's productive capacity not only in respect of infrastructure but also in respect of producer goods. The study also evaluated the administrative machinery involved in the formulation of aid; channels through which aid was given and received; administration of aid including alteration, evaluation and follow up; and the machinery for the repayment of aid. The study also highlighted certain problems raised by the foreign aid, some for the recipient country and some for donor country, such as : fear of interference; influence and strings accompanying aid in respect of bilateral aid; attitude of donor governments towards offering aid at governmental level; uncertainty of the magnitude of and purpose for which aid was available; administration and supervision of aid receiving projects by the several ministries of the recipient government, etc.

Mishra (1965) presented the details of foreign aid to India from various sources for diverse purposes for the period 1951-1964. The study explained that India received foreign aid from three sources, mainly: (a) international institutions like the World Bank; (b) foreign governments, particularly USA, USSR (now Russia), West Germany, etc.; and (c) private foundations like the Ford Foundation and the Rockefeller Foundation. The study revealed that most of the aid was in the form of loans (74 percent up to December 1963). The study also highlighted certain defects in the working of international institutions and their aid giving procedures, such as : many of the institutions were only propaganda forums; active only in technical assistance on a very small scale; were much influenced by the political scenario of the world; and did not supervise the proper utilization of aid in the recipient countries, etc. The study suggested that advanced countries should help generously and raise their share by 50 percent; attempt should be made by all to increase the number of trained personnel in underdeveloped countries; all loans and aid should be given through the UNO or any of its specialized agency to avoid 'political attachment'; encouragement to private investment for more check and control, etc. The study also suggested to reduce the dependence of India on foreign aid by all means, as far as possible.

Katz (1968) examined the contribution made by the external assistance to the development of Indian economy during the period 1951-61. The study revealed that the Indian economy received a strong support from the investible resources provided in the form of external assistance during the decade of First and Second Five Year Plans. Aid accounted for US $ 1 of every US $ 11 invested during the decade. Without external assistance, total investment would have been nine percent short of the volume actually realized. Agricultural commodities made up à larger contribution to the volume of aid received and used. It was observed that 95 percent of the total aid received was from the western countries and institutions, with the United States alone accounting for almost three-fifth of the total. It covered a broad range of Indian needs, like it filled current income and production gap, and saving gap, the two functional gaps reflected by India's BOP deficit. The study also analyzed the theoretical model of Indian development, particularly the two sector Mahalanobis model, used in the Second Plan. It, like Harrod–Domar model, made investment the key variable but did not consider investment as homogenous. The study distinguished between the investment coefficient for capital-producing and consumable-producing industries dividing thereby the economy into the two sectors.

Streeten and Hill (1971) assessed the utilization of foreign aid and its impact, in general, and of food aid from the USA, in particular, to India during the period 1951-66. The study outlined certain causes of the slow utilization of foreign aid in India, such as : faulty project preparations, programming and scheduling; faults in complementing actions, like failure of supplies of raw-materials, components and services including transport and electricity; and failures in aggregate planning due to the non-availability of rupee resources, inadequate aggregate demand, wrong choice of top personnel and project-tied aid, etc. Despite all these problems, the study found that added foreign exchange shortages would have led to even more severe cuts in the Second and Third Five Year Plans, even if domestic savings had been available, i.e., additional foreign aid enabled India to mobilize a multiple of the resources provided by aid.

Banerjee (1977) analyzed the role, forms, agencies, objectives and problems involving the US aid to India for the period 1951-73. The study showed that the US aid to India had been supplied through the three main agencies viz : (a) The United States Agency for International Development (USAID) ; (b) The US Export-Import Bank; and (c) The Public Law 480, a temporary 'Food for Peace Programme' enacted in 1954 and extended a couple of times. The study also revealed that bulk of the US aid had been in the form of farm supplies, like wheat and cotton, which the US could not keep with itself for the fear of crash in prices of these, and other agricultural commodities. The US offered aid to India for multipurpose uses to achieve various objectives, such as : humanitarian—relieving somebody of poverty and disease; manipulative—attempting to influence the outcome of an election; ephemeral—concern over the tenor of remarks of UN General Assembly; and long-run investment in a country's capacity to maintain growth without external aid. The study also analyzed the purpose, terms and uses of the 'Cooley Loan Programme' involving US $ 1.25 billion, which supported more than 60 different Indian companies of the US subsidiaries for India's industrial development. The study found that the US aid to India was a constructive cooperation and development of Indo-US economic relations as, among others, eight agricultural universities, 12 river valley projects, five fertilizer plants, five Indian Institutes of Technology, many engineering colleges including the National Productivity Council were established, and several thousands of Indian scientists, engineers, teachers, etc., were trained in the USA. However, the study further revealed that this 22 years US economic assistance programme was unilaterally put back in the pipeline in June, 1973 owing to various reasons and developments like : dependence on the Soviet Union for political, technical and military aid; unfavorable BOP for India, which forced her to devalue its rupee in the spring season of 1966 at the instance of the US; spending of a larger share of the US aid on American consultants, and their logistic support, most of whom were ruthless and arrogant; India's triumphant entry into the nuclear club; and the US nuclear provocations and menacingly entry into the Bay of Bengal during the Bangladesh war of independence in December 1971, etc.

Tiwari (1982) also attempted to analyze the macroeconomic contribution of foreign aid in India, particularly received from the USA during the period 1951-75, both in qualitative and quantitative terms. The study revealed that though the US aid has been offered for multipurpose uses, such as: building infrastructure and strategies required to supply agricultural inputs, transportation and electricity; establishment of universities for encouraging research in agriculture; expansion of social sectors like health, education and family planning programmes ; and improving technical know-how of the Indian economy, etc., yet the negative aspects of PL-480 program had severe effects on India's wheat production. Most of the US aid to India was tied in nature and was given on hard terms, which even also led to the devaluation of Indian rupee in 1966 under the US pressure. However, despite such limitations, US aid proved to be a stimulant to expansion in the Indian economy and helped her to achieve political stability in the country. The study also highlighted efforts of the State Trading Corporation of India, Indo-American Chamber of Commerce and the United Nations Industrial Development Organization in encouraging Indian exports, and contribution of the US aid in the improvement of Indo-US trade relations.

Sanghvi (1985) evaluated the role of bilateral foreign aid, in general, and the World Bank (WB) aid, in particular, in the Indian economic planning in the background of the outcome of 'Aid India Consortium' meeting held in June, 1985. The article revealed that the consortium meeting was neither encouraging nor depressing because US $ 4000 million, the total consortium pledge for the fiscal year 1985-86, was maintained at the previous year's level in real terms, in an atmosphere where the global outlook for ODA was not so cheerful. Decline in the interest rates, both in the donor countries as well for WB credits, made the terms of aid little less harsh. The study feared that the share of India in the concessional loans from IDA, the soft loan affiliate of the WB, which dropped from 40 percent in 1980 to 28 percent in 1984, would further decline, with China claiming its share for the first time from IDA funds. The study also found that of the total aid commitment for the year 1985-86, US $ 2400 million were contributed by the WB and the balance US $ 1600 million were bilateral aid extended by the donor countries. So far the WB assistance was concerned, US $ 1700 million came from IBRD and the remaining US $ 700 million from IDA. The study revealed further that the role of bilateral aid was shrinking, while the role of multilateral WB aid was steadily rising, since the beginning of Fourth Plan, as the share of WB aid in India's total aid had gradually expanded from 18 percent in Fourth Plan to almost 55 percent in Sixth Plan.

Patil (1987) examined the trends and issues in the resource flows to the less developed countries during the period 1950-85. The paper revealed that the level of total resource flows to these countries increased from an annual average of US $ 15.89 billion during 1950-55 to US $ 63.9 billion in 1973, while the share of ODA declined from about one-half (52.6 percent) to almost one-third (34.54 percent) of these resources during the same period. The 'Development Assistance Committee' countries were gradually becoming relatively less significant as suppliers of ODA with their share in total development assistance declining to 56 percent in 1973 from almost 100 percent during 1950-55. The study further revealed that a steep rise in the oil prices by the end of 1973 and during 1978-79 resulted in a massive shift in the level, direction, and composition of global resource flows. These high oil prices turned the surplus BOP position of the most of advanced countries into larger BOP deficits; huge BOP surpluses for some of the oil exporting countries; led to the sharp growth of Euro currency markets and international banking, a substantial portion of the funds of which were directed to the developing countries, during this short span of time. The growth in the volume of total resource flows during the decade (1973-83) was as much as 85 percent; resource flows peaked to US $ 118.26 billion in 1983; the share of ODA in total resource flows declined sharply to 28.6 percent; and the share of DAC countries remained steady around 55 percent. However, there was a sharp rise in the non-concessional flows to US $ 82.12 billion in 1983 from US $ 37.41 billion in 1973. Similarly, assistance from the multilateral sources like the WB and other regional development banks increased consistently from US $ 2.4 billion in 1973 to US $ 7.57 billion in 1983. But these total resource flows continued to decline during the last three years of the study up to 1985, primarily due to the sharp decline in international bank lending from US $ 49.6 billion in 1981 to US $ 13.5 billion in 1985.

Hill (1988) resorted to examine the quantitative impact of foreign aid on the Bangladesh economy by using a linear macroeconomic model for the period 1960-79. The study used twenty three linear equations, two stage least square model involving the use of instrumental variables, to analyze the role of aid in relieving constraints on production, which included the availability of food as well as of fertilizer, capital and other imports. Allowance was also made for a possible negative effect of aid on government revenue collection efforts and its positive effect on government development expenditure. The study estimated that with 95 percent level of confidence, the cumulative impact of halving of aid inflows over the 1960-79 period would have been a drop between 5.9 and 11.8 percent in GDP. The probability that no fall in national output would occur was less than 0.001 percent. The study revealed that aid financed most of the government capital expenditure and provided foreign exchange which financed majority of imports. The study also separated the effects of food aid from those of non-food aid and found that food aid was more closely linked to foodgrains requirements during the previous year than the current year. Food aid was found to have a negative but statistically insignificant effect on the price of rice. The study also revealed that an undeflated government revenue equation provided an estimate of the negative effect of aid inflows on revenue collection efforts. Though this negative incentive effect was substantial, however, it was out-weighed by revenue accruing to the government from import duties on goods financed by aid. The study estimated a rising revenue as aid fell, under the assumption that other taxes would be substituted for import duties and a model simulation with this version of the government revenue function was also tested. Nevertheless, even in this case, the additional revenues generated were not sufficient to offset the loss of external financing for the development budget.

Mittal (1988) studied the impact of foreign aid on India's economic development in terms of national income, investment, employment and foreign trade for the period 1950-51 to 1979-80. The study revealed that the impact of foreign aid on national income was not very satisfactory as the growth rate remained less than four percent per annum despite rapid industrial growth, due to the inflationary trends, low agricultural growth and slow utilization of foreign aid. Employment showed an increasing trend as working population increased from 139.5 million in 1951 to 180.3 million in 1971. However, the cost of aid in the form of debt-servicing as percentage of national income went up from 1.31 percent in 1970-71 to 2 percent in 1979-80, for, aid has been used to finance the excess of imports over exports. The study also highlighted various political, economic and technical problems involved in the utilization of foreign aid, like varying political objectives of the donors, shortage of skill formation, less exportable capacity, tying of aid and absorption of foreign sophisticated techniques, etc. The study further opined that trade is not a perfect substitute for aid, although it has some aid characteristics in it. The study also explained Govt. of India's favorable policy towards foreign aid and capital. Reasonable facilities were extended to the foreigners for the remittance of profits and repatriation of capital consistently with forex position of the country from time to time. But it was certainly not the policy to throw open the doors for unrestricted foreign investment.

Narain (1988) attempted to evaluate the contribution of the United States' financial assistance to India's economic growth covering the activities of USAID and its predecessor agencies during the period 1951-71. The US financial aid covered 41 percent of the total official flows and 43.7 percent of the ODA to India during this period. The study pointed out that outright grants formed only 12.8 percent of the total aid received from the United States and were replaced gradually with loans during the above-mentioned period. The terms and conditions of loans were also made gradually harder, and mode of repayment was changed from rupees to dollars, since the establishment of USAID in 1961. The aid was also tied to source since 1959. The study also estimated 'grant element' in the loans received from the USAID and its predecessor agencies at four different discount rates, and found that it varied with discount rate chosen. The grant element on USAID dollar repayable loans varied from 55.9 percent (at 6 percent discount rate) to 76 percent (at 10 percent discount rate). The study also revealed that though the US aid supplanted domestic savings in India yet its contribution to the macroeconomic variables, like national income, savings and investment was not very significant. Its contribution to national income and savings was less than one percent each, and its share in investment stood at around 4.5 percent of total investment during the study period.

Lipton and Toye (1990) examined the effectiveness of aid in India for the period 1966-86, which is a country with long history of receiving aid in large absolute amounts, although it becomes quite smaller in per head amounts if her huge population is taken into consideration. The study revealed that different attempts to find the link between aid and economic performance by econometric methods have been diverse, and have produced conflicting results. But, as a whole, aid almost certainly raised India's ratio of total savings (both domestic and foreign) to GNP. However, alongside this rise, India suffered an almost offsetting fall in the utilization and/or productivity of capital. Hence, its growth rate showed little or no secular rise. The study revealed further that the concentration of aid was mainly in the public sector industries, like steel, heavy electricals, etc., up to the year 1970 and aid certainly contributed to these. While in the years since 1970, more emphasis was placed on aid to large scale development programmes focused on the aspects of agricultural extension, irrigation and credit, forestry, draining, family planning and health, etc., which were less capital-intensive and were more of rural emphasis. Later on, aid was channelled to new industrial investment, which proved less effective due to the persuasive inefficiencies detected in the Indian public sector. The study also disclosed that India's overall growth performance, by comparison with its own past or with other developing countries, has been consistent and above all improving, despite increasingly difficult circumstances of 1973-86. However, in spite of real policy efforts, income distribution worsened and poverty did not become less prevalent during 1961-86. The study expressed the fear that India was likely to be 'punished' by the aid donors for a relatively good aid performance through the redistribution of aid towards Sub-Saharan Africa.

Iqbal (1991) evaluated the trends in Japanese ODA to the different parts of the world with special reference to the Asia region—the largest recipient region of Japanese ODA, during the period 1980-90. The study revealed that Japan has become the second largest aid giver in the world after the United States with ODA of US $ 10 billion in the year 1990. The major share of Japanese ODA has been in the form of loans (55.2 percent) instead of grants (28.6 percent) and technical assistance (16.2 percent) in the year 1989. The study revealed further that Japanese ODA policy has not depended on the needs of the developing countries but on their own selfish considerations and interests, that is why global disparities have been the glaring feature of Japanese ODA policy. In Asia, its ODA concentrated mainly in Indonesia (12.7 percent), China (11.8 percent), the Philippines (8 percent) and Thailand (6.8 percent), which offered a big market to the Japanese goods. India received only 3.9 percent of Japan's ODA in 1989. The study concluded that Japan, being the largest surplus nation in the world, could play the role of *'Masiha'* for the poorest nations of the world.

White (1992) analyzed the macroeconomic impact of development aid by critically reviewing the different theoretical perspectives, such as : the dual gap, the savings debate, recipient's fiscal response, aid as 'Dutch disease', and the empirical debates on aid, savings and growth. The study found that the dual gap model of aid has been a bottleneck theory in which deficiency of capital has been a critical constraint on growth. The study used Harrod-Domar model to show how this shortage of capital could make its impact felt in one of the two ways: through the savings gap or through the foreign exchange gap. The study reported the radicals' position in the savings debate that aid supplants domestic savings, lessening thereby the impact on growth, did not provide adequate answer as to why aid has not increased growth in a way suggested by the Harrod-Domar model. This argument has two main theoretical problems: first, there were certain conditions under which aid simply would not be fungible in the way suggested by the radicals. Second, an aid multiplier of greater than unity implied that income would not rise by more than the value of aid inflow, resulting in circumstances under which aid could increase current consumption with no diminution of domestic savings. The study revealed further that the empirical literature on aid-growth relationship has also been almost entirely based on a single equation Harrod-Domar model of the recipient economy, the results of which were empirically as well as theoretically ambiguous, due to the limited knowledge about non-economic and even the economic factors that affect the growth. The study also revealed that there was no macro-micro paradox of aid because the study was not in a position to say, what aid did at macro-level. However, the study found two other areas in the recent literature which were the promising developments: first of which analyzed aid from a trade theoretic perspective and suggested that aid would have similar effects to the Dutch disease, caused by a commodity boom, basically an increase in the price of non-traded goods relative to traded goods, i.e., an appreciation of the real exchange rate, which reduced the recipient's export competitiveness, making it more dependent on aid as a source of foreign exchange. When the impact of aid on real exchange rate was significant, this analysis provided a theoretical explanation for a negative effect of aid on the growth. Second, the revival of debate about the possible inflationary consequences of counterpart funds. It has been shown theoretically that the impact might actually be deflationary and experience showed the effect to be insignificant in most of the cases.

Sharma (1994) investigated the role of private resource flows, such as : international bank lending, foreign direct investment, bonds and grants from the non-government organizations to the developing countries. The study revealed that total net resource flows to the developing countries increased by 21 percent to a record US $ 159 billion in 1992 from US $ 133 billion in 1991, mainly due to the performance of private flows as international bank lending rose from US $ 11 billion to US $ 38 billion and other private flows expanded by 60 percent to US $ 10.5 billion. However, almost all of the recent expansion of private flows has been attracted by only a few developing countries, like China, Indonesia and India. In contrast, poorer countries are lagging behind due to unattractiveness prevailing there. The author is of the opinion that in the face of a fragile world economic outlook and tight aid budgets, the recent upsurge in the private flows to the developing countries needs to be encouraged further.

Somanathan (1994) attempted to analyze the WB aid to Indian sub-continent (South-Asia), dominated by India, for the period 1985-94, which declined from an average US $ 3939 million (22 percent of the WB total lending) in 1985-89 to US $ 2370 million (11 percent) in 1994. The study revealed that the WB aid has been skewed against South-Asian countries as the funding decisions were mainly influenced by Western politics albeit development economics. The study predicted difficult external debt situation for India because decline in multilateral aid have to be made up by commercial borrowing at higher costs. The drop in the WB lending coincided with India's new market-oriented economic policies, hence its influence in country's policy making has reached an all time high. The WB seemed to be compensating India for reduced financial aid by a blitzkrieg policy of advice and the weight given to its advice was likely to be proportional to the cash it gave.

The World Bank (1998) in a study 'Assessing Aid' explained how aid could be made more effective. Two key themes emerged in the report : first, effective aid required the right timing, and second, it required the right mix of money and ideas. The right timing of assistance was crucial in helping the countries to improve their policies and institutions. When countries reform their policies, well timed assistance could increase the benefits of reforms and maintain popular support for them. On the mix of activities, the findings revealed that money has a larger impact only in the low-income countries with sound economic management. The main findings of the report were : that financial aid worked in a good policy environment; three way partnership is necessary among the recipient countries, aid agencies and the donor countries to reduce the global poverty through equitable and sustainable development; foreign aid did not replace private initiative albeit effective aid complemented private investment; knowledge supported by aid led to improvements in particular sectors, while financial part of aid expanded the public services, in general; and an active civil society improved public services and aid nurtured reforms even in the most distorted environment. To make aid more effective in global poverty reduction, the report advised some policy reforms like financial assistance be targeted more effectively to low-income countries with sound economic management; policy-based aid should be provided to nurture policy reforms in the credible reformers; the mix of aid activities should be tailored to country and sector conditions; projects need to be focus on creating and transmitting knowledge and capacity; and aid agencies need to find alternative approaches to helping highly distorted countries as traditional methods have failed in these cases. The report also analyzed the four case studies of aid under different conditions : first, adjustment without adjustment lending in Vietnam; second, support to education decentralization in El Salvador, Pakistan and Brazil; third, a health financing innovation in Cameroon; and fourth, the Africa's road maintenance initiative. The report also aimed at persuading developed countries to continue to give aid, and take an active interest in the development and development cooperation, particularly at a time when aid is poised to be most effective but the volume of it was declining and was at its lowest level ever.

Dawson and Tiffen (1999) examined the long-run relationship between ODA and economic growth, as measured by per capita GDP in India, using annual data for 1961-92 by applying unit root tests. They found that ODA was stationary, while GDP has a unit root. Hence, long-run relationship cannot exist. Thus, aid neither promoted economic growth and hence development at macro-level nor adversely affected it. A corollary was that aid was not responsive to the changes in India's income.

Herbst and Soludo (2001) discussed the relationship between the poor economic performance, foreign assistance and debt rescheduling in Nigeria during the period 1970-98. The study revealed that in 1985, Gen. Ibrahim Babangida government attempted, for the first time, to address the complex economic crisis faced by the country but failed to implement a coherent programme because of the logic of austerity, and economic reform was anathema to the clientelistic system of country's politics. The study revealed further that Nigeria received much less aid than the other African countries, mainly, due to the fact that country has ample crude oil wealth which caused many donors to assume that country did not require aid. Whatsoever aid Nigeria received, most part of it was received from the WB loans, throughout the period of study. However, in an odd manner, the study explained that foreign assistance though less, was both inadequate and too much for Nigeria, by presenting various arguments and incidents. The study found that Nigerian reform program did not fail because of the lack of ideas, albeit, it failed because of the lack of government's commitment to the reform package.

Holmgren et al. (2001) assessed the implementation of market- based reforms and the positive effect of foreign aid on one of the most successful Sub-Saharan African countries–Uganda, particularly since the late 1980s. The study revealed that the real take off in terms of aid volume occurred since 1986, when the reform programme started. The period 1986-98 was divided into three phases: 1986 when the present government under the Presidentship of Mr. Yoweri Museveni assumed power and initially rejected the market-based reforms; 1987-92 when it reluctantly implemented the reforms; and from 1992-onwards characterized by full government ownership of reform program. The study revealed further that foreign aid in diverse forms supported and supplemented the reforms during all the three phases. Consequently, the average annual growth rate increased to 6.5 percent during 1986-98; annual rate of inflation declined to 8 percent in 1996 from 190 percent in 1987; private sector investment increased to 13 percent in 1998-99 from 9 percent of the GDP in 1991-92; agricultural output grew by 62 percent between 1986-98 benefiting small and marginal farmers, mainly; and manufacturing sector grew by 12.74 percent per annum during 1989-99. However, since 1992 despite full government ownership of reform programme, the aid/GDP ratio started to decline. Thus, the study found that foreign aid proved pivotal in generating, implementing and cementing the reforms, particularly during the period 1987-92.

Guillaumont and Chauvet (2001) compared and contrasted the two diverse visions of aid effectiveness and allocation in the recipient developing countries: first, corresponding to the new aid paradigm argued that aid is effective only if the domestic policies are appropriate and sound; and second, in contrast argued that aid effectiveness depended upon the external and climatic environment. The worst this environment, greater will be the effectiveness of aid, i.e., aid seemed to have accelerated growth only in the more vulnerable developing countries. Cross-sectional econometric tests related to GDP growth on two 12-year pooled periods clearly favored the second view. The study revealed that these two diverse views could be reconciled through the principle of performance-based aid allocation, where performance is defined as outcomes adjusted for the impact of environmental factors. Performance-based aid allocation might increase both aid effectiveness and provide developing countries with the incentive to promote better policies on their own, which means the countries will receive more aid when they face a difficult environment, and when they implement policies leading to better performance, whatever be the chosen instruments.

Lensink and White (2001) tested the assumption of the WB report 'Assessing Aid' (1998) that an inflow of foreign aid, over and above a certain level, have negative effects on the recipient developing countries. The regression results of the study provided some support for this notion of negative returns at high levels of aid inflows. However, the results seemed to be quite sensitive to the countries included in the sample and model specification. Moreover, the turning point above which aid started to have negative effect on growth seemed to be higher than assumed in the background calculations for the WB study which were used to determine a poverty efficient allocation of aid.

Mavrotas (2002) examined the impact of foreign aid on the growth in India, using disaggregated aid data (project, programme, technical and food aid) for the period 1970-92 constructed by the OECD office in Paris. The study employed modern time-series econometric technique to estimate a reduced-form growth equation based on general-to-specific modelling. The study revealed that the composition of foreign aid partly mattered for its effectiveness. Both programme and project assistance series seemed to have exerted a rather negative influence on growth in India during the period under examination. But due to the serious estimation problems, the inclusion of a set of policy variables in the model, with or without uncertainty variables, did not shed much light on aid's growth impact in the presence of policies.

SECTION II

The studies, which have been carried out to highlight some specific aspect/purpose of the utilization of foreign aid in the recipient developing countries, particularly India, are briefly reviewed in this Section which has been further divided into two parts. Part-A deals with the various studies highlighting one or the other aspect of the utilization of foreign aid, while Part-B covers those studies which brought out certain specific problems faced by India in the utilization of foreign aid.

PART-A

The studies highlighting some specific aspect of the utilization of foreign aid are reviewed in this part:

Fei and Paauw (1965) applied their foreign assistance model to a group of selected 31 developing countries including India, receiving over 70 percent of the American development assistance, in order to examine the implications of 'self help' (i.e., domestic savings) to estimate the aid-termination dates on the basis of recent past of the study. The model estimated the values of its five primary parameters pertaining to these selected countries together with their initial population and GNP estimates in terms of three types of cases. The model revealed that out of the 31 countries, 22 including Brazil, India and Turkey, to which a large proportion of US aid has gone, were in the unfavorable region having aid termination dates of infinity. Only Yugoslavia was in favorable region requiring no foreign aid, while eight countries (Columbia, Greece, Mexico, Pakistan,

Philippines, Taiwan, Thailand and Tunisia) were found in the intermediate region with a finite termination date for foreign aid.

Sharma (1977) made an attempt to estimate the real value of foreign aid in India by taking into account its terms and conditions during the period 1950-51 to 1974-75. The study found these terms and conditions very hard. As a result, the real value of aid received was much less than it appeared to be. The share of grants in the overall assistance declined progressively, while the share of loans expanded gradually. The proportion of loans with longer maturity was fairly high. The larger proportion of aid was either source-tied or project-tied in nature. The study also showed that foreign aid created the external debt-servicing problem of a severe nature, which had not allowed India to reap all the benefits of foreign aid as the indicators of debt-servicing burden such as : the ratic of debt-service to national income, savings, government tax revenue, exports, etc., increased considerably in the recent past of the study.

Streeten (1983) presented five sets of arguments for extending loans on concessional terms to the low income countries. First, the set of distribution arguments justified on a variety of philosophical grounds, like the most common utilitarian argument that a dollar redistributed from a rich country to a poor country detracts less utility than it adds and hence increases the sum total of utility, provided that aid reaches the poor in the poor countries. The second set of arguments compared the general costs and benefits to both the borrower as well as lender countries, and argued that a small cost to the donor can bestow a great benefit to the recipient in case substantial externalities and multiplier effects spring from the aid-financed project or if the aid given takes the form of deliveries from industries or firms in which excess capacity is above the average in the economy as a whole, and therefore, imposes a small burden on the donor. The third set of arguments related to the constraints on servicing debt at fully commercial rates and suggested that if the rate of return on borrowed money exceeded commercial rate of interest, the project should be carried out; otherwise should be abrogated. The interest rate imposed discipline which was necessary in project selection. It also created correct incentives and signals in economizing the use of capital. The fourth set of arguments explained that since development was a long and slow process in the poor countries with larger populations, and low productivity levels, hence soft loans with longer maturities were the appropriate instruments. The fifth set of arguments stated that the grant element in the loans was intended to buy non-commercial benefits, like votes in the UNO or democracy or peace or stability or strategic advantages. The greater grant element in loans increased the right of the donor to exercise control and imposed conditions on the recipients.

Helleiner (1984) examined the neglect of least developed low income countries, under the emerging international monetary system, in the distribution of aid and liquidity, during the initial years of 1980s. The study found that international development assistance in terms of multilaterally agreed targets has been scandalously inadequate. It fell in every year from 1980 to 1983. Against the 0.7 percent of GNP target, OECD members remained only at 0.36 percent in 1983 and indications were there that it would soon decline further, placing heaviest resultant burden upon the poorest countries. The article revealed that some new sources of international liquidity, in the form of resurrection of international commercial bank finance for the 'credit worthy' countries; bilateral swap agreements among central banks; credit proffered by the Bank for International Settlement; special bilateral credits, etc., despite their dominance over the traditional sources, fell far short of the aspirations of the architects of the IMF, in terms of both predictability and its inter-country distribution. The study suggested certain measures in order to evolve an expanded role for the IMF relative to commercial banks or major governments such as : orderly arrangement for continuing increases in the IMF quotas in line with the overall global needs; resumption of issues of Special Drawing Rights; allocation of funds in accordance with needs albeit quotas, etc., while for the WB's 'Structural Adjustment Lending Programme' to play a role in the low income countries, IDA must be replenished at more satisfactory levels. The study also suggested some measures to both the IMF and the WB which should be taken into account while lending to the poor countries, like longer periods of adjustment, contingency provisions, etc., so that the risk of unexpected exogenous shocks should not be borne exclusively by the borrowing poor countries.

Menon (1988) analyzed the impact of Dutch development and technical assistance amounting Rs. 16 crore to supplement the Ganga Action Plan, since January 1986, confined to the two projects, viz: the Integrated Sanitation Project at Kanpur, and the Low-cost Treatment and Conveyance System at Mirzapur in U.P. The main thrust of the scheme was immediate reduction of pollution load on the river Ganga and the establishment of financially self-sustained treatment system. However, the paper showed that Dutch aid had no positive additive and connecting effect on the Indian economy, albeit, it was likely to have certain negative effects, as better indigenous alternatives were ignored without proper technical assessment, especially by putting forward the Dutch alternative which was a pre-treatment as a full treatment facility.

Gang and Khan (1990) estimated the magnitude, composition and determinants of the levels of foreign aid to India during the period 1960-85 using factor analysis technique. The authors found that latent motivations classified the donor countries into four convenient groups, each with different political and economic motivations. Group-I was a major source of foreign aid to India as it accounted for 32.4 percent of country's foreign aid. In this group, the United States was most significant donor to India. The study found that latent variables capturing the motivations of the United States, Western European countries as well as trade balance, previous year's aid and GDP growth were the main determinants of foreign aid to India. But authors were of the view that GDP growth rate was not a significant determinant of foreign aid to India as compared to the others.

Mitra (1990a) made an attempt to analyze the donor country's perspectives on foreign aid. The study considered foreign aid as an international public good aimed at achieving certain socio-economic objectives, like : equity, self-reliance, political stability, growth and viability of international accounts in the developing Third World countries. The study explained that aid allocation by the donor countries depend, besides the creation of a strong public opinion within donor countries in respect of foreign aid, on a number of macroeconomic crucial criteria such as : per capita income, rate of growth of income per capita, average saving ratio, repayable capacity and self-help on the part of the recipient countries. However, the appropriate criteria for foreign aid, as judged by the people of donor countries, determined their perspectives on aid programmes and influenced the amount of aid to be allocated annually in the budget. The study explained further that in reality foreign aid, in general, and ODA, in particular, was allocated not strictly on the basis of these socio-economic criteria, albeit, the substantial proportion of aid allocation was influenced by the political, strategic, commercial interests and traditional ties, and even this deserved recognition. However, some donors such as : Denmark, Norway, Sweden, Holland, and multilateral agencies, in general, as well as the unofficial institutions donated aid funds solely on the socio-economic and humanitarian grounds. The study expected that the heterogeneity of objectives, governing the flow of foreign aid stemming from the divergent interests of donors, should give way to the increased flow of foreign aid, in real terms, consistent with the development objectives.

Mitra (1990b) examined the perspectives of foreign aid from the standpoint of the recipients, and attempted to evaluate some of the issues in respect of its past and future role in the arena of socio-economic development of the developing countries. The study considered foreign aid as a supplement to the international trade and capital flows to bring about a structural change in the developing countries in such a way as to provide a sustained stimulus for their expansion, and income growth, i.e., to fill up their income gap, saving-investment gap as well as foreign trade gap. The study argued that foreign aid involving transfer of resources and technology, in the face of sluggish prospects of trade with developing countries, as a means to reduce poverty and inequality in these countries, is a moral obligation for the developed countries due to the basic principle of justice and equity. The study explained further that the quantitative and qualitative changes in the foreign aid program in light of the recipient's perspectives, left much to be desired in spite of the high proportion of grant element (around 90 percent from mid-seventies to mid-eighties) in foreign aid. However, not much headway has been made in case of multilateral aid, the proportion of which increased from just 18.05 percent to 23 percent only during the ten years period 1975-85. Similarly, the proportion of program aid remained below 25 percent of the total aid. The study suggested that substantial quantitative and qualitative improvement in foreign aid program would help the developing countries to change the structure of their economies ensuring better allocation of resources, and viable program of self-reliance contributing to the growth of global trade so that their objective of obtaining aid to end aid be fulfilled.

Clark (1991) assessed, and compared the degrees of Generalized System of Preferences (GSP) trade and foreign aid concentration among the beneficiaries under schemes proffered by the two leading donor countries viz: Japan and the United States for which data were available. The study revealed that the US long believed trade albeit foreign aid as the most equitable way to allure economic development in the developing countries, while Japan demonstrated increased commitment to foreign aid and by 1989 emerged as the leading aid donor. The study used Surt's index to quantify concentration of GSP trade and foreign aid which involved the ranking of beneficiaries in ascending order by per capita GNP marked off in deciles. The study found that GSP trade of both the donors was extremely concentrated among higher income countries, like Korea, Taiwan, Singapore, Brazil, and Israel, etc., because these were better suited to export GSP eligible products than the poor beneficiaries. The study revealed further that among the higher income beneficiaries, Japanese GSP trade was considerably less concentrated than the US GSP imports. On the other hand, Japanese ODA was found to be concentrated among the lower income beneficiaries such as : China, Philippines, Thailand, Bangladesh, Burma (Now Myanmar) and India, respectively, as they received 54 percent of Japanese ODA disbursement, while the US ODA pattern exhibited the well known 'middle income' bias. The top six US aid recipient middle income countries were : Israel, Egypt, Philippines, El Salvador, Pakistan and Honduras—which received 66 percent of the US ODA disbursement. The study also showed that each donor's overall ODA disbursement demonstrated a more equitable distribution among the beneficiaries than their GSP trade showed.

Khan and Hoshino (1992) examined the impact of foreign aid on the fiscal behaviour of the five South and South-East Asian less developed countries : India, Pakistan, Bangladesh, Sri Lanka and Malaysia, using regression model for the combined pooled time-series and cross-sectional data for the period 1955-76. The study confirmed that foreign aid affected both expenditure and revenue sides of the budgets of the recipient governments. On consumption side, foreign aid treated as an increase in income, led to increase in consumption, given the positive income elasticity of demand in the government sector. Since the marginal propensity to consume out of foreign aid turned out to be less than unity, therefore some public investment was also financed out of aid money. However, the study did not find any discrepancy between the aid given by multilateral and bilateral sources. It found significant differences between the two components of aid: loans and grants, with regard to how they were utilized. The study revealed that both loans and grants were used for consumption as well as investment purposes. The study revealed further that 85 percent of the loans received were utilized for investment as compared to 32 percent of grants. Hence, by making loans to the recipient LDC governments, purpose of generating investment could be served much better than by giving grants. Similarly, aid also affected the tax effort of these LDC governments—grants reduced the tax burden, while loans increased it. At the same time, comparison of welfare effects of grants versus loans was not straight forward. Since grants have not to be repaid, the reduction of taxes seemed to be more welfare enhancing than the effects of loans.

Sengupta (1993) explained the objectives of aid and development policies in the altered new world of 1990s such as : helping the developing countries to integrate them into global mainstream as well as to serve their traditional goals of supporting long-term development programmes of building infrastructure, and financing projects of substantial social benefits. The paper stated that the confidence of donors, in the ability of aid-receiving countries to make most effective use of funds received, would be increased if the programmes were implemented within the framework of discipline of international donor agencies like the IMF, the WB and other regional development banks. This would also facilitate increase in the flow of funds to these countries, particularly at times when these funds were necessary for financing the requirements of development programmes. However, in order to provide such assurance, the study suggested that advanced countries must accept the 'principle of reciprocal obligation' of helping these developing countries through aid, BOP finance, improved market access, and flows of investment and technology. But the study doubted that this 'principle of reciprocal obligation' would not be accepted easily by all the countries. For this, the study revealed that it would be necessary to work out a mechanism like 'Development Compact', i.e., an agreement between a developing country undertaking programmes of adjustment and a group of industrial countries providing necessary assurance to help the implementation of the programme, to give a concrete shape to the 'principle of reciprocal obligation'. The study also made an attempt to identify potential savings in the rich countries. The study revealed further that if only 10 percent of the amount of negligible additional utility yielded in the rich countries was transferred to the developing countries as aid, it would generate US $ 170 billion or about four times of the current level of aid. The study suggested that the rich countries should not reject the 'principle of reciprocal obligation' of the 'Development Compacts' proposed in the study on the ground of the paucity of resources.

McGillivrey and Ahmad (1994) resorted to examine the aid, savings and investment relationship in the South Asian countries of Bangladesh, India, Nepal, Pakistan and Sri Lanka using time-series data for the period 1969-91 by fitting a partial (or stock) adjustment investment ratio model. The study revealed that in only the minority of cases, foreign aid inflows significantly influenced domestic investment ratios and domestic savings ratios.

White and Luttick (1994) examined three main approaches: (i) before versus after ; (ii) control group (simple and modified); and (iii) modelling, to analyze the macroeconomic effects of aid money and aid-supported policy reforms in the structural adjustment, and stabilization programmes of an economy. The study found that the macroeconomic impact of aid inflows can best be understood within the context of an accounting framework, relied almost entirely on modelling. But much of the work has used single equations, due to which many potentially important relationships, particularly aid's effect on output and income were excluded from the analysis. Even the simultaneous models used were mostly partial, not general, equilibrium models—which made the findings doubtful, i.e., much of the empirical work suffered from methodological shortcomings. The study stressed the need for research on how aid affected the private sector macroeconomically because more was known about how to analyze the public sector's response to aid inflows. The study favored a country specific modelling approach because it allowed the separate analysis of policies and money as well as the separate analysis of different policies. It could capture local factors that might be omitted from cross-country analysis. The study argued that counterfactual analysis using econometric general equilibrium model might be the most legitimate approach to analyze the relationship between poverty and economic reforms. Modelling has yielded results quite different from the common view about the social impact of reform policies but the existing models failed to incorporate aid as an important macroeconomic variable. The study revealed too, that the macroeconomic repercussions of the different forms of aid such as : project aid, commodity (mainly food) aid and technical aid would also be different. Thus, the literature on the macroeconomic impact of aid is in search of better models, while at the same time the modelling of the impact of reforms inadequately accounted for the role of foreign savings. The study suggested that a marriage of the two is obviously in everyone's mutual interest.

Sudarshan (1995) analyzed certain reasons for advocating the cessation of international aid to the developing countries by the politicians in rich Western countries, like general malaise of having abandoned virtue as an integral part of governance responsible for scandals abound, both in the history of international aid as much as in the misuse of domestic public funds; failure of visiting expert economists as advisors in the developing countries; limited absorptive capacity, both for capital and technical assistance; technical fixes without much regard for social and cultural factors; etc. The study submitted that philosophical foundations of sympathetic West's critique of international aid were firmly rooted in an age where Aristotlean and New Testament conceptions of virtuous conduct have given way to utilitarian calculus. The study emphasized that the entire edifice of attitude informing both the donors and recipients of international aid need radical changes—radical in the sense of recovering a legacy of the classical past which once informed virtues that needed to be practiced by those who give, and those who receive.

Gounder (1996) empirically examined the foreign aid motivations of Australia's bilateral ODA, and the regional economic development of the rapidly growing South-East Asian and South Pacific countries with stress on the two competing models of 'Recipient Need' (RN) and 'Donor Interest' (DI) for the period of six years 1988-89 to 1993-94. The study discussed the political economy of aid and evaluated the various aid motivations like : humanitarian, political and strategic interest, investment and export interest, etc. However, the study revealed that Australia's aid objective has been greatly influenced by the foreign policy and commercial interests. The regional focus of Australian bilateral aid indicated the geographical focus of aid program mainly to 'near neighbor' countries in South-East Asia and the South Pacific under country program, and multilateral organizations. The econometric results of RN model based on the growth rates in GDP, using OLS multiple regression, indicated that Australia has concerns for recipient need and supported the view that these fore-said were important regions for Australia. Whereas the empirical results of DI model highlighted various categories of interests like : economic, political and security, development and performance, etc., which also supported the model, and indicated that Australia's aid program had concern for aid motivation as well. The overall empirical results of the study revealed that Australia's bilateral aid program was characterized by both the RN and DI concerns. Both motivations could be said to have succeeded and foreign aid impacted on these countries. Thus, the study found these regions of strategic and commercial interests to Australia.

Opeskin (1996) argued that developed countries contributed very little—on an average 0.33 percent of their annual GNP as foreign aid to the underdeveloped countries, well short of the target of 0.7 percent of GNP set for developed countries in the United Nations. Only five developed countries: Denmark, Finland, Netherlands, Norway and Sweden met or exceeded the target. The author further argued that foreign aid to underdeveloped countries was neither morally bad nor morally good, albeit it has been the moral obligation based on humanity and corrective justice for the developed countries to provide assistance as they were the colonial powers with a history of exploitation. These obligations necessitate a substantial revision of the attitude of those in the West to those in developing states, for, 'every citizen is a brother to fellow citizens and nothing at all to others'.

Rao (1997) employed a modified combined index of equity and scale, using data published by the OECD and the WB, for the period 1970-93, to rank and compare both the quality, and quantity of aid given by the donor countries. The quality of aid was measured by the extent of an aid donor's allocation conformed to the revealed need of the aid recipients, while the need was measured in terms of realized per capita income. The study revealed that scores and rankings for both the indices for the two 12 year sub-periods of 1970-81 and 1982-93 were not perfectly stable. On equity index Austria, Australia and Canada fell significantly, while Germany, Italy, and the Netherlands all improved their ranks. However, the USA not only remained at the bottom of the rankings but also had the largest drop in both the indices. The study revealed further that leaving aside IDA and IBRD, for which the combined index could not be computed, the correlation between the mean scores and rankings on both the indices was also high, and statistically significant for both the sub-periods, which implied that generous donors also tended to be fair donors. The results also showed that there was a high degree of temporal stability in the donor performance both absolute and relative, and high level of concordance between equity and scale measures of donor performance. The study also advocated, to some extent, the hypothesis that generosity and equity in aid giving are negatively related to the degree of domestic inequality within the donor countries, although the correlation was not statistically significant. The study expected that improvements in the distribution within the donor countries would improve the international distribution of income.

McGillivrey and Morrissey (1998) assessed the relationship between aid and trade in one of the most dynamic regions of the global economy—the East-Asian economies, and the two major donor countries of the region viz : Japan and Australia, for the period 1980-95. The study outlined various arguments to show relationship between aid and trade flows, both for causality from aid to trade, and from trade to aid. The study revealed that there was indeed a relationship between aid and trade but the specific nature of this relationship clearly varied between different donor-recipient pairs. The study also demonstrated that there was a notable concentration of Australian aid on Pacific islands, which were close economic partners, and dynamic Asian economies where the allocation of aid reflected trade potential albeit development needs. Similarly, Japan, a major donor and trading partner on a global scale, also concentrated its aid on the more dynamic Asian economies supporting the argument that Japanese aid flows were more related to economic cooperation albeit to need-based development cooperation. The evidence that aid flows within the region reflected or followed trade flows was plausible. The study too analyzed certain implications for donor-recipient relations. One implication of this was that aid and trade flows within the region have played a role in sustaining, if not actually promoting, the economic dynamism within the region. Another implication was that the tendency of aid to 'follow' trade might imply that aid was attracted away from more deserving needy poor countries, both in and outside the region, toward countries with stronger economic performance and hence larger markets for trade. Because of the significance of trade links, it might be the case that much aid has gone to the countries that needed it the least. This might have been a benefit to the dynamic economies of East Asia but at a cost to less dynamic developing countries throughout the world.

Azam et al. (1999) examined the controversy that whether foreign aid supplemented domestic resources by filling the fiscal-gap or it created dependence. The diversity of actual experience indicated that neither gap-filling view nor the dependency view provided an adequate account of the dynamics of aid and development. The study captured some of the features of both the view points, and revealed that one equilibrium outcome could be high aid and weak institutions, even when the donors and recipients fully anticipated aid's effects on institutional development, but did not take the drastic steps required to put the country on the path to independence. Another equilibrium outcome could be low aid and strong institutions. The study encompassed such diverse aid profiles as those of Tanzania and the Republic of Korea. When the donor community ignored aid's effect on institutions, the outcome largely depended on initial conditions. Where institutions were initially weak, as in many Sub-Saharan African countries, since their independence, institutional capacity collapsed, and foreign aid eventually financed the whole public budget, locking thereby the donors and recipients into a permanent situation of high aid and low institutional capacity. Where these were initially stronger, the result could be close to the institutions-sensitive equilibrium. The study suggested that even for countries with similar per capita incomes, the foreign aid strategy should be designed to suit the country's institutional capacity. In some cases, a short-term reduction in aid might increase a country's chances of graduating from aid.

Chang et al. (1999) attempted to examine the methodological shortcomings of conventional OECD's measure of Net ODA, such as : lumping together of the net increase in loans, which entailed future interest and repayment obligations, with grants that did not; inclusion of certain loans at full face value and total exclusion of others; and calculation of grant element of loans using an arbitrary rate of discount set at 10 percent. The study proposed a new approach, based on the use of overall grant equivalents of the official disbursements as the key measure of aid, labelled as 'Effective Development Assistance' (EDA), which corrected most of these fore-mentioned shortcomings. The use of grant equivalents, as the basic aid measure, has the virtue of allowing comparability between aid flows implicit in grants as well as loans with different degrees of concessionality. Most significantly, EDA has been based on adjusted grant equivalents constructed using discount rates sensitive to market conditions along several dimensions—timing, currency and maturity of loans. The study revealed that this new approach has been implemented empirically using detailed data on some 40,000 official loans from the World Bank's DRS data-base to the 133 developing countries, included in the DRS system. The numerical results underscored certain important points : first, the conventional approach led to a systematic over-estimation of concessionality of official loans, particularly since mid-1980s. Conventional approach showed a rising trend, while the new approach showed the opposite. Second, as a consequence of these results, Net ODA increasingly overstated the true aid content of official flows, although the divergence between two approaches was somewhat muted by the relative importance of grants over loans in total official flows. The study also found certain caveats in the new approach, like the use of ex-ante perspective in order to capture donor's effort instead of ex-post approach, and the neglect of the default risk in the calculation of loan concessionality.

Jha and Swaroop (1999) discussed the fungibility of foreign aid, and analyzed its influence on the level and composition of public spending in India at central government level by using annual time-series data from 1970 to 1995. In addition the paper constructed a panel data base for the period 1980 to 1992 on 14 'general category states' to look at the fungibility at inter-governmental level. The study explained that aid could be fully fungible in case the recipient country treated the entire aid amount as a pure supplement to its domestic resources used to finance some other expenditure or tax reduction of the government. The study found no evidence that foreign aid led to a reduction in the tax revenue of the central government. The aid money, instead of being spent on the purposes intended by the donors, was used to finance non-developmental activities in the country. The article also found no discernible relationship between foreign aid and interest spending. Similarly, no such link existed with the principal payments on loans. Together these two items accounted for nearly 42 percent of non-developmental spending. The study revealed that out of every additional rupee of aid given to India, about 75 paise were used to finance its administrative and general service expenditures. The paper revealed further that in passing foreign aid earmarked for the states, the central government made a reduction in transfers, it would have otherwise made to the states. A rupee increase in central government transfers on account of foreign aid was associated with a reduction of Rs. 1.62 in other transfers to the states. Thus, the states which were able to procure foreign aid, ultimately ended up having less assistance from the central government.

Burnside and Dollar (2000) assessed the relationship among foreign aid, economic policies and growth of per-capita GDP in a cross country analysis using a panel of 56 countries, and 6 four-year time periods from 1970-73 until 1990-93. The study found that on the average aid has little impact on growth, although a robust finding has been that it has had a more positive impact on growth in good policy environment, but there has been no significant tendency for total aid or bilateral aid favoring good policy, while multilateral aid (about one-third of total) has favored good policy environment. The study also found that climate for effective aid has been improving in poor recipient countries but the quantum of aid has been diminishing.

O'Connell and Soludo (2001) estimated the intensity of aid flows to the seven Sub-Saharan African (SSA) countries viz: Botswana, Burkina Faso, Cameroon, Mali, Mozambique, Uganda and Zambia for the period 1965-98 in a cross-country inter-temporal perspective. The term 'aid intensity' referred to the size of aid flows relative to the categories of economic activity they were designed to support. While measuring aid relative to GNP, population, imports, investment and government spending, the study compared regional medians, and ranked the case study countries relative to the full sample. The study revealed that roughly half of the SSA countries and five of the seven case study countries fell in the upper quartile of aid intensity in the 1990s. The study identified them as 'highly aid intensive' countries. The study also observed that a country's aid ratio could be high in an absolute sense, but low relative to what would have been expected, given the country's structural characteristics. The study also revealed that Africa's high aid intensity became unremarkable once the study controlled for low real incomes, relatively small populations and other widely accepted determinants of aid over the entire period of study. What emerged, instead, was that aid to Africa had risen more rapidly over the time than was readily attributable to changes in these structural determinants. The study also distinguished between the resource intensity of aid flows and their transactions intensity. The study found SSA's interface with global financial markets was overwhelmingly with official rather than private creditors. The study decomposed debt service due and found that although Africa's external debt had a median grant element of over twice that of the typical developing country. African countries had been paying, by far, the smallest share of what was due including arrears.

Sengupta (2002) highlighted that the ODA has increasingly came to incorporate the human rights approach to development process, particularly due to the two reasons. First, many of the objectives of development could be given concrete form in terms of socio-economic rights, such as : to food, health, education, housing, and social security, as were spelt out in the convention of economic, social and cultural rights which had a large support base in most of the advanced industrialized countries. Second, in all international human rights agreements it has been accepted that the international community has an obligation to cooperate with the developing countries trying to realize these human rights. The study argued that the articles 55 and 56 of the UN Charter which has the authority of an international treaty; adoption of the Declaration on the Right to Development in 1986 at the United Nations; and then through inter-governmental conferences and agreements culminating in the Vienna Declaration of 1993, the human rights approach to development has gained almost universal acceptance in the advanced industrialized countries.

Gilles (2003) analyzed and evaluated the Government of India's policies regarding foreign aid, for the period August 1947-January 1966, and revealed that India has drawn wide benefits from the aid granted by the two superpowers of the time: the USA and the Soviet Union, by following the policy of non-alignment. Both gave assistance to India, less as a result of a wide identity of political and economic views or ideological affinities than in order to prevent her from falling into the sphere of influence of the enemy camp, either as the result of economic contingency or because of military threat. Though sometimes, the USA showed some irritation at India's policy of non-alignment or reapproachment with the Soviet Union and castigated her for its leniency *vis-a-vis* the Soviet Union, yet such differences never caused a disruption in the flow of American aid to India due to her importance as a pluralist regime and geo-strategic pivot. The USA remained largest donor to India with 59.9 percent share in her utilized aid as against the 6.4 percent share of the Soviet Union between 1951 and 1966. The Soviet Union opted for a policy of aid to India with aiming at preventing her dependence for development programme exclusively on Western aid and for forging closer relations with non-communist Asian states in order to safeguard its security threatened by the Chinese hegemonic aspirations. However, the official stand of India was that it preferred to give up aid, whatever be the consequences, instead of making concessions that would compromise its national interests. Nevertheless, the Indian government, sometimes, had to come to the terms with the donor country. Even then the ability of India to obtain aid from both the superpowers, since 1951, constituted a remarkable trump card in the face of her growing dependence on foreign aid. Apart from a few accommodations, India did not allow itself to be dictated to on its fundamentals and continued to pursue its policy goals without unduly jeopardizing its national development.

PART–B

The studies which highlighted the various problems in the effective utilization of foreign aid faced by India are briefly reviewed in this part.

Arun (1991) brought out the gross under-utilization of foreign aid to India in 1980s. The study revealed that utilization of aid was 91.3 percent in 1973-74, which dropped gradually to the lowest level of 41 percent in 1988-89. In other words, Rs. 22,271 crore worth of foreign exchange that was offered to India, during the latter half of 1980s, was not availed of. Consequently, a significant portion of non-official debt incurred by the nation during the Seventh Plan (1985-90) could most certainly have been avoided by means of better utilization of official aid. The study identified some factors responsible for and suggested two types of measures to effectively utilize it. Firstly, India should influence the developed countries' aid policy in concert with other Third World countries organized in bodies, like Non-Aligned Movement etc., so that donor's delay in establishing credit lines be reduced. Secondly, being the result of purely indigenous maladroitness, their remedy lies within domestic grasp. Hence, working out and implementing speedy procedures for executing externally aided projects should be undertaken as a matter of national priority. Legal wrangles in land acquisition should be solved by means of special tribunals or otherwise. A 'revolving fund' should be created or special overdraft facilities with RBI should be provided to help the cash-strapped state governments to avoid the delay in the execution of externally aided projects. Similarly, rigorous planning, strict earmarking of funds, and vigorous scrutiny, before and after submission of projects for foreign assistance, could help to effectively utilize external official aid, and to avoid a large part of it to lapse like in the past.

Shirali and Chatterjee (1993) examined the various factors responsible for the mind-boggling problem of unutilized foreign aid amounting about US $ 20 billion, (Rs. 65,940 crore) in December 1992, in which the WB's share was US $ 11 billion, on which India has paid yearly commitment fee of 0.75 percent or whopping US $ 82.5 million for not using the sanctioned money, like, the delays which took place between aid committed to the centre and then transferring it to the states; cumbersome tendering procedures with several layers of bureaucracy both at the centre and the state level; delays in the procedural formalities; and non-compliance with negotiated conditionalities; etc. The study also highlighted the concern expressed by the donor agencies such as : the WB, ADB, 'Aid India Consortium' member countries. Even the WB officials had threatened to link the future loan pacts with the disbursement of already committed credits. Some bilateral donors like the US, Germany, the Netherlands, France and Denmark had already reduced their aid commitments to India during 1992-93. The study too evaluated certain measures announced by the Finance Ministry under the WB pressure such as : setting up of a new project management unit in the Finance Ministry to monitor the disbursement of aid funds; another committee to streamline the present aid procurement system; permission to state and central undertakings to directly borrow from foreign donors on the terms mutually agreed upon; etc.

Vaidyanathan (1993) analyzed foreign aid receipts and the consequent debt-service payments of Indian economy for the period 1979-80 to 1992-93. The study showed that the share of grants in total external assistance had come down sharply to 6.9 percent in 1992-93 from 22.5 percent in the year 1979-80, the base year for the Sixth Plan, while the share of loans had increased to 93.1 percent from 77.5 percent during the same period. As a result, in 1992-93, almost four-fifths (79 percent) of the gross aid receipts flown back from the country to the very donors: 43.5 percent for amortization, i.e., in writing down outstanding stock of debts and the balance 35.5 percent for meeting current payments on interest obligations. The net resource transfer constituted barely one-fifth (21 percent) of the gross aid receipts for the year, while in mid-eighties, i.e., in 1985-86 less than half of the gross aid receipts flowed out of the country by way of the debt-service payments.

Kausaliya, et al. (1995) examined the problem of poor utilization of aid in India owing to the bottlenecks, like budgetary constraints of Central Government, tying of loans, procedural delays and cost escalation, etc. Low capacity utilization in power sector had a significant influence on the utilization of aid and as such a large portion of unutilized aid was in the power sector. Dealing with dual ownership projects of centre and state was another area of difficulty. As a result, the stock of unutilized aid assumed proportions which were disquieting, and was seen as a reflection of country's poor ability to absorb foreign aid and utilize it efficiently. Such an image can adversely affect the size of annual fresh commitments.

Sundari (1996) analyzed the utilization rate of foreign loans (aid) in India, which was showing a downward trend, since the Fourth Five Year Plan. The highest ever utilization rate was 99 percent during the three annual plans (1966-69) period, while the lowest utilization rate of 48.7 percent was recorded during the Seventh Five Year Plan (1985-90). Sector-wise—agriculture, industry, transport and communications—showed a satisfactory performance regarding the utilization of foreign loans, but power sector recorded a poor disbursement. Major portion of foreign loans was utilized for the industrial development. The main reasons for the under-utilization of external loans were: undue delay in the implementation of projects, hasty drafting of project proposals, submission of project proposals to foreign agencies without evaluating their feasibility and above all most of the loans were tied. The falling utilization rate and recent diversion of foreign loans for debt-servicing were termed as a matter of concern for India.

Sarkar (1999) highlighted some critical issues, involved at macro and micro-level, responsible for low aid disbursement ratio in India during the period 1992-96. The study revealed that a disbursement ratio of 20 percent per year is considered as a good indicator of portfolio performance, but in India aid disbursement ratio had declined from 17.32 percent in 1992-93 to 15.87 percent in 1995-96 and then slightly improved to 17.96 percent in 1996-97. The study highlighted that this disbursement ratio was well below the internationally accepted benchmarks due to certain macro-level issues such as : inadequate domestic fund provisioning for externally aided projects; limitations on the quick inflow of funds; *adhoc* release of funds to the projects against advance additional central assistance to the states; etc. At micro-level, issues, like start-up delays due to inadequate preparation; long delays in the award of contracts due to lingering bid procedures; reluctance on the part of international contractors to participate in bids due to the packaging of the size of contract into smaller units by the project authorities; unmanageable large number of smaller contracts; high turnover of staff in the project implementation cell resulting in loss of expertise; and some project specific issues in the form of land acquisition, land alienation, various clearances, shifting of utilities and staff, etc., impeded aid utilization to the expected level in the country.

The above review has acted as a base for the present study and helped in formulating it.

5

Foreign Aid to India : Source-wise and Purpose-wise Utilization

"The coming in of foreign aid has coincided with the starting of economic planning in India; and this has been most fortunate from the point of view of evolving some kind of rationality and order in formulating requests for foreign aid" (Rao and Narain, 1963: 16). On April 1, 1951 when the First 'Five Year Plan' (FYP) commenced, Govt. of India (GOI) hardly had any foreign aid liability. Even during the First Plan (1951-56) need for foreign aid was not much larger because it was limited in its objectives and modest in its expenditure targets. The Plan, which laid greater emphasis on the development of agriculture, has actual outlay amounted to Rs. 3360 crore including public sector plan outlay of Rs. 1960 crore as against the target of Rs. 3760 crore (Govt. of India, 2001b: p. 30). The utilization of external assistance was of the order of Rs. 201.7 crore (Govt. of India, 1981: p. 14) which financed only six percent of the aggregate investment and 10.3 percent of public sector plan outlay during the First Plan. Though the first ever loan to India was sanctioned by the IBRD on September 18, 1949 for the expansion and modernization of Indian Railways, yet the foreign aid started flowing to her through the 'Colombo Plan' formed in 1950, by India and six other Commonwealth countries.

However, a radically different strategy was introduced in the Second 'FYP' (1956-61) in which the total plan outlay was increased to Rs. 7772 crore. But the actual outlay worked out Rs. 6831 crore, including public sector plan outlay of Rs. 4672 crore (Govt. of India, 2004a: p. 50), more than doubled as compared to the First Plan outlay. The emphasis of public sector investment shifted from agriculture to heavy industries, like steel, cement, machine-building, fuel and power, chemicals, etc. Consequently, there was a substantial increase in the forex requirements due to the import of capital goods necessary for these basic and heavy industries. The balance of payment deficit increased to Rs. 1725 crore, of which Rs. 1430.4 crore, i.e., 30.6 percent of the public sector plan outlay of Rs. 4672 crore, (Govt. of India, 1981: p. 14) and 20.9 percent of actual total plan outlay of Rs. 6831 crore, was financed through foreign aid.

Accordingly, the foreign aid requirements increased correspondingly on a massive scale in magnitude as the successive FYPs became more and more ambitious. Limited savings and forex reserves, alongwith varied but complex economic development requirements compelled India to seek larger amount of foreign aid. It remained a major factor responsible for raising investment level during the successive plans, particularly up to the early seventies, although bulk of the resources required for development have been generated indigenously.

Since 1951, India received foreign aid from a wide variety of sources including bilateral arrangements, multilateral financial institutions, and private philanthropic organizations for her development plans and programmes. It consisted of outright grants on the one extreme and hard loans of strictly commercial nature, on the other. In between there were soft loans, also loans repayable in domestic currency and in foreign currency; commodity aid in the form of agricultural products; and loans for rescheduling the existing ones, etc.; has been utilized for varied purposes. Accordingly, the chapter has been divided into three sections. Section-I explains the trends in authorization as well as utilization of aggregate foreign aid to India during the period 1966-67 to 2003-04. The analysis has been made for the overall time period along with two sub-periods to delineate the impact of liberalization mildly introduced since 1980, i.e., (1) the pre-eighty period (1966-67 to 1979-80), and (2) the post-eighty period (1980-81 to 2003-04). It also examines the details of gross as well as net utilized aid. Section-II provide details of the major donors of India, while in Section-III, an attempt has been made to examine the purpose-wise utilization of aid in India during the same period.

SECTION I

The year-wise total amount of foreign aid comprising loans and outright grants, both authorized to as well as utilized by India ending March, 2004 has been given in Tables 5.1 and 5.2.

AUTHORIZATION OF FOREIGN AID

Table 5.1 delineates the aggregate foreign aid authorized to India which presented a fluctuating trend during the overall period of 1966-67 to 2003-04. Authorization of aggregate aid dropped sharply from Rs. 1506.5 crore in 1966-67 to the lowest level of Rs. 634.3 crore in 1969-70 and then with fluctuations rose to Rs. 3847 crore in 1980-81, touched the highest level of Rs. 25,095 crore in 2001-02 before declining to Rs. 17,105.1 crore in 2003-04. The linear slope (trend) of the loans during the pre-eighty period (1966-67 to 1979-80); post-eighty period (1980-81 to 2003-04); and the overall period (1966-67 to 2003-04) have been found positive and significant at one percent level. Similarly, the trend values of outright grants for the corresponding periods were also positive and significant at one percent level. The trend values for aggregate authorized aid during the fore-mentioned periods were also found to be positive and significant at one percent level. However, loans under the US Public law 480/665 presented a downward trend from Rs. 392.7 crore in 1966-67 to Rs. 22.8 crore in 1977-78. Thereafter, no such loan was authorized to India. Thus, the authorized loans, outright grants and the overall authorized aid to India increased at significant rate, especially during the overall period.

TABLE 5.1
Aggregate Authorized External Assistance

(Rs. Crore)

Period/Year	*Loans*	*Outright Grants*	*PL-480/665 Assistance etc.*	*Total Assistance*
(1)	*(2)*	*(3)*	*(4)*	*(5)=(2+3+4)*
Up to end of Third Plan	3808.8	392.0	1510.8	5711.6
1966-67	1034.1	79.7	392.7	1506.5
1967-68	398.5	16.8	303.5	718.8
1968-69	753.1	68.4	125.3	946.8
1969-70	421.8	26.0	186.5	634.3
1970-71	705.4	56.5	—	761.9
1971-72	774.5	36.0	118.7	929.2
1972-73	639.6	36.6	—	676.2
1973-74	1129.5	41.1	—	1170.6
1974-75	1481.4	189.8	—	1671.2
1975-76	2192.8	440.7	20.0	2653.5
1976-77	806.7	386.1	93.6	1286.4
1977-78	1536.6	337.6	22.8	1897.0
1978-79	1894.6	441.1	—	2335.7
1979-80	1295.1	564.4	—	1859.5
1980-81	3771.2	75.8	—	3847.0
1981-82	2766.5	207.4	—	2973.9
1982-83	2549.4	423.3	—	2972.7
1983-84	1700.8	386.9	—	2087.7
1984-85	4409.3	470.7	—	4880.0
1985-86	5337.0	313.4	—	5650.4
1986-87	5730.0	429.5	—	6159.5

(Contd.)

TABLE 5.1 (Contd.)

(1)		(2)	(3)	(4)	(5)=(2+3+4)
1987-88		8203.1	1062.2	—	9265.3
1988-89		12855.6	214.2	—	13069.8
1989-90		10105.8	720.2	—	10826.0
1990-91		7601.3	522.1	—	8123.4
1991-92		11805.8	901.8	—	12707.6
1992-93		13082.1	1011.7	—	14093.8
1993-94		11618.8	2415.1	—	14033.9
1994-95		12384.3	1075.8	—	13460.1
1995-96		10833.2	1330.0	—	12163.2
1996-97		14208.8	2932.6	—	17141.4
1997-98		14865.0	2101.0	—	16966.0
1998-99		8320.8	209.8	—	8530.6
1999-00		17703.7	2615.3	—	20319.0
2000-01		17184.1	940.6	—	18124.7
2001-02		21630.0	3465.0	—	25095.0
2002-03		19875.7	1161.0	—	21036.7
2003-04		14754.4	2350.7	—	17105.1
Up to end-March 2004		272169.2 (89.12)	30448.9 (9.97)	2773.9 (0.91)	305392 (100.00)
Linear Slope (T-Value)	1966-67 to 1979-80	87.12856** (3.14005)	40.21714** (5.8465)	—	104.7688** (3.189935)
Linear Slope (T-Value)	1980-81 to 2003-04	713.46110** (9.474905)	96.07535** (4.535037)	—	809.53640** (9.540482)
Linear Slope (T-Value)	1966-67 to 2003-04	532.35900** (14.177110)	60.91238** (6.748150)	—	588.83030** (13.767860)

N.B. : (i) Figures in brackets represent percentage to total authorized aid.
(ii) ** Significant at 0.01 level.
* Significant at 0.05 level.

Sources : (i) Govt. of India, *Economic Survey*, 2004-05, p. S-98 and other issues.
(ii) Linear Slope (T-values) have been computed.

TABLE 5.2
Overall Utilized External Assistance

(Rs. Crore)

Period/Year	Loans	Outright Grants	PL-480/665 Assistance etc.	Total Assistance	Utilization Rate (%)
(1)	(2)	(3)	(4)	(5)=(2+3+4)	(6)
Up to end of Third Plan	2768.7 (61.41)	336.9 (7.47)	1403.2 (31.12)	4508.8	78.94
1966-67	674.7 (59.64)	97.1 (8.58)	359.6 (31.78)	1131.4	75.10
1967-68	793.2 (66.34)	60.7 (5.08)	341.7 (28.58)	1195.6	166.33
1968-69	679.8 (75.32)	65.2 (7.22)	157.6 (17.46)	902.6	95.33
1969-70	660.7 (77.15)	26.1 (3.05)	169.5 (19.80)	856.3	135.0
1970-71	658.9 (83.26)	43.5 (5.50)	89.0 (11.24)	791.4	103.87
1971-72	671.7 (80.53)	50.5 (6.05)	111.9 (13.42)	834.1	89.77

(Contd.)

TABLE 5.2 (Contd.)

(1)	(2)	(3)	(4)	(5)=(2+3+4)	(6)
1972-73	649.9 (97.55)	12.0 (1.80)	4.3 (0.65)	666.2	98.52
1973-74	1015 (98.00)	20.7 (2.00)	—	1035.7	88.48
1974-75	1220.4 (92.86)	93.9 (7.14)	—	1314.3	78.64
1975-76	1464.9 (79.59)	283.3 (15.39)	92.3 (5.02)	1840.5	69.36
1976-77	1285.3 (80.39)	245.8 (15.37)	67.8 (4.24)	1598.9	124.29
1977-78	1007.5 (78.10)	260.6 (20.20)	21.9 (1.70)	1290.0	68.00
1978-79	942.3 (77.52)	273.3 (22.48)	—	1215.6	52.04
1979-80	1048.6 (77.50)	304.5 (22.50)	—	1353.1	72.77
1980-81	1765.3 (81.66)	396.5 (18.34)	—	2161.8	56.19
1981-82	1519.4 (81.47)	345.5 (18.53)	—	1864.9	62.71

1982-83	1909.2 (84.78)	342.8 (15.22)	—	2252.0	75.76
1983-84	1962.4 (86.61)	303.4 (13.39)	—	2265.8	108.53
1984-85	1962.2 (83.17)	397.2 (16.83)	—	2359.4	48.35
1985-86	2493.1 (84.92)	442.9 (15.08)	—	2936.0	51.96
1986-87	3175.7 (88.09)	429.3 (11.91)	—	3605.0	58.53
1987-88	4574.4 (90.55)	477.5 (9.45)	—	5051.9	54.53
1988-89	4738.6 (89.33)	565.8 (10.67)	—	5304.4	40.59
1989-90	5137.8 (88.55)	664.7 (11.45)	—	5802.5	53.60
1990-91	6170.0 (92.03)	534.3 (7.97)	—	6704.3	82.53
1991-92	10695.9 (92.09)	919.1 (7.91)	—	11615.0	91.40
1992-93	10102.2 (91.99)	879.6 (8.01)	—	10981.8	77.92

(Contd.)

TABLE 5.2 (Contd.)

(1)	(2)	(3)	(4)	(5)=(2+3+4)	(6)
1993-94	10895.4 (92.48)	885.6 (7.52)	—	11781.0	83.95
1994-95	9964.5 (91.58)	916.0 (8.42)	—	10880.5	80.84
1995-96	9958.6 (90.35)	1063.6 (9.65)	—	11022.2	90.62
1996-97	10892.9 (90.94)	1085.6 (9.06)	—	11978.5	69.88
1997-98	10823.4 (92.16)	921.3 (7.84)	—	11744.7	69.22
1998-99	12343.4 (93.24)	895.5 (6.76)	—	13238.9	155.19
1999-00	13330.7 (92.55)	1073.9 (7.45)	—	14404.6	70.89
2000-01	13527.1 (94.90)	727.2 (5.10)	—	14254.3	78.65
2001-02	16111.7 (91.76)	1447.6 (8.24)	—	17559.3	69.97
2002-03	13999.2 (88.40)	1836.7 (11.60)	—	15835.9	75.28

2003-04		15271 (88.05)	2073.4 (11.95)	—	17344.4	101.40
Up to end-March 2004		208865.7 (89.45)	21799.1 (9.34)	2818.8 (1.21)	233483.6 (100)	76.45
Linear Slope (T-Value)	1966-67 to 1979-80	43.65604** (3.151447)	21.25099** (4.3875)	—	41.41208* (2.15804)	—
Linear Slope (T-Value)	1980-81 to 2003-04	675.21000** (19.410650)	56.84974** (8.296364)	—	732.05980** (20.111840)	—
Linear Slope (T-Value)	1966-67 to 2003-04	434.71210** (17.719980)	40.60409** (12.61373)	—	470.42900** (14.717890)	—

N.B. : (i) Figures in brackets represent percentage to total utilized aid.
(ii) Utilization rate (as percentage of aggregate authorized aid).
(iii) ** Significant at 0.01 level.
* Significant at 0.05 level.

Sourçes : (i) Govt. of India, *Economic Survey,* 2004-05, p. S-102 and other issues.
(ii) Linear Slope (T-values) have been computed.

UTILIZATION OF FOREIGN AID

The study of the quantum of foreign aid utilized by India out of the aggregate authorized aid, as presented in Table 5.2, shows that the utilization of overall aid was maximum in 1967-68 (166.33 percent of the aggregate authorized aid), also presented a fluctuating behaviour. After touching the lowest level (40.59 percent of authorized aid) in 1988-89 utilized foreign aid rose to the level of 101.40 percent of the authorized aid (due to the utilization of previously sanctioned aid) in 2003-04. However, the linear trend of the overall utilized aid worked out to be positive and significant at five percent level during the pre-eighty period (1966-67 to 1979-80), while during the post-eighty period (1980-81 to 2003-04) as well as during the overall period (1966-67 to 2003-04) it was found positive and significant at one percent level.

1. Loans vs. Grants

Table 5.2 further outlined that the share of loans in the overall utilized aid always remained dominant as compared to the outright grants. During the pre-eighty period, the maximum share of loans (98.2 percent), taken together of loans and PL-480 loans, was found in 1972-73, while the share of outright grants (1.80 percent) was at its lowest level. Since then the share of loans ranged between 77.50 percent in 1979-80 and 98 percent in 1973-74, while in case of outright grants the share dwindled between 22.50 percent and 2.0 percent, respectively, during these corresponding years. During the post-eighty period, the share of outright grants reduced to 5.1 percent in 2000-01 and then increased to 11.95 percent in 2003-04. However, the trend values of both the loans and outright grants, taken individually, for the pre-eighty period; post-eighty period; and the overall period were all found to be positive and significant at one percent level. Thus, like aggregate authorized aid, utilization of aid demonstrated an almost similar trend during all the three above-mentioned periods.

2. Cumulative Assistance

Cumulative foreign aid at historical exchange rates (at the time of sanction) authorized to India up to end-March 2004, totalled Rs. 3,05,392 crore, of which 89.12 percent were in the form of loans; 9.97 percent in the form of outright grants; and remaining 0.91 percent in the form of US Public Law 480/665 aid and third country currency assistance (Table 5.1). The utilized cumulative assistance up to the same time amounted to Rs. 2,33,483.6 crore, i.e., 76.45 percent of the overall cumulative authorized assistance which comprised 89.45 percent loans; 9.34 percent outright grants; and the remaining 1.21 percent US Public Law 480/665 and the third country currency assistance (Table 5.2).

3. Aid-GDP Ratio

There has been a widespread impression that India received large sums of foreign aid. This, of course, is true in absolute terms but is not, if the large size of country and its huge population are taken into consideration. Gross utilized aid as ratio of country's GDP at 1993-94 prices remained quite low and declined with fluctuations from the peak level of 3.98 percent in 1966-67 to the lowest level of 0.72 percent in 2002-03 as has been shown in Table 5.3.

4. Gross vs. Net Aid

The details of gross utilized aid, and net utilized aid along with debt service payments in the form of amortization and interest payments have been amplified in Table 5.4, which show that despite there being nominal increase in the gross utilized aid over the years, net assistance has declined significantly owing to the rising cost of debt servicing. The net assistance declined to its lowest level of Rs. (–)17,872 crore in 2002-03 which indicated that instead of providing budgetary support to the domestic resources, it has become a liability as the country is repaying its servicing costs from its own precious forex reserves. Even the linear slope for the net external assistance for the pre-eighty period (1966-67 to 1979-80) has been worked out as negative (–7.14066) though non-significant, while the trend value of gross utilized aid has been positive and significant at five percent level during the same period. However, during the overall period (1966-67 to 2003-04) gross utilization of aid recorded positive trend which was significant at one percent level, while the net utilization presented negative values and declining trend. The fall in net

TABLE 5.3

Gross Utilized Aid As Percentage of GDP_{FC} (At 1993-94 Prices)

Year	*Gross Utilized Aid (Rs. Crore)*		*GDP at 1993-94 Prices (Rs. Crore)*	*Aid/GDP Ratio (Percent)*
	At Current Prices	*At 1993-94 Prices*		
(1)	*(2)*	*(3)*	*(4)*	*(5)*
1966-67	1131.4	9507.56	238710	3.98
1967-68	1195.6	9057.58	258137	3.51
1968-69	902.6	6890.08	264873	2.60
1969-70	856.3	6296.32	282134	2.23
1970-71	791.4	5534.27	296278	1.87
1971-72	834.1	5523.84	299269	1.85
1972-73	666.2	3989.22	298316	1.34
1973-74	1035.7	5152.74	311894	1.65
1974-75	1314.3	5236.26	315514	1.66
1975-76	1840.5	7421.37	343924	2.16
1976-77	1598.9	6319.76	348223	1.82
1977-78	1290.0	4831.46	374235	1.29
1978-79	1215.6	4552.81	394828	1.15
1979-80	1353.1	4336.86	374291	1.16
1980-81	2161.8	5858.54	401128	1.46
1981-82	1864.9	4627.54	425073	1.09
1982-83	2252.0	5323.88	438079	1.22
1983-84	2265.8	4979.78	471742	1.06
1984-85	2359.4	4864.74	492077	0.99
1985-86	2936.0	5802.37	513990	1.13
1986-87	3605.0	6738.32	536257	1.26
1987-88	5051.9	8725.22	556778	1.57
1988-89	5304.4	8527.97	615098	1.39
1989-90	5802.5	8673.39	656331	1.32

TABLE 5.3 (Contd.)

(1)	(2)	(3)	(4)	(5)
1990-91	6704.3	9096.74	692871	1.31
1991-92	11615.0	13843.86	701863	1.97
1992-93	10981.8	11897.94	737792	1.61
1993-94	11781.0	11781.00	781345	1.51
1994-95	10880.5	9671.56	838031	1.15
1995-96	11022.2	9064.31	899563	1.01
1996-97	11978.5	9417.06	970082	0.97
1997-98	11744.7	8843.90	1016595	0.87
1998-99	13238.9	9409.31	1082748	0.87
1999-00	14404.6	9913.70	1148368	0.86
2000-01	14254.3	9154.98	1198592	0.76
2001-02	17559.3	10886.11	(P)1267833	0.86
2002-03	15835.9	9488.26	(QE)1318321	0.72
2003-04	18697.4	10629.56	(RE)1426701	0.75

N.B. : Gross Utilized Foreign Aid has been converted into 1993-94 prices by using Spliced Wholesale Price Index (1993-94=100) as deflator.

Sources : (i) Govt. of India, *Economic Survey;* 2004-05, p. S-102 and other issues.

(ii) RBI, *Handbook of Statistics on The Indian Economy,* 2003-04, p. 5.

inflow from abroad has also been attributed to international sanctions following Pokhran nuclear tests and inadequate provisions for counterpart funding for externally aided projects through domestic resources (Govt. of India, 2002, Vol. I : p. 77).

SECTION II

SOURCE-WISE UTILIZED AID

India received foreign aid mainly from the multilateral financial institutions as well as through the bilateral arrangements. The main sources of multilateral assistance to India included the World Bank (both IBRD and IDA); Asian

TABLE 5.4
Gross and Net Inflow of External Assistance

(Rs. Crore)

Year	*Gross Disbursement/ Utilization*	*Amortization*	*Interest Payments*	*Debt Service Payments*	*Net Inflow of Aid*
(1)	(2)	(3)	(4)	(5)=(3+4)	(6)=(2-5)
Up to end of Third Plan	4509	371	315	686	3833
1966-67	1131	159	115	274	857
1967-68	1196	211	122	333	863
1968-69	903	236	139	375	528
1969-70	856	268	144	412	444
1970-71	791	290	160	450	341
1971-72	834	299	180	479	355
1972-73	666	327	180	507	159
1973-74	1036	400	196	596	440
1974-75	1314	411	215	626	688
1975-76	1841	463	224	687	1154

1976-77	1599	508	247	755	844
1977-78	1290	561	260	821	469
1978-79	1216	596	286	882	334
1979-80	1353	570	314	884	469
1980-81	2162	518	287	805	1357
1981-82	1865	538	311	849	1016
1982-83	2252	587	360	947	1305
1983-84	2266	615	417	1032	1234
1984-85	2359	647	529	1176	1183
1985-86	2936	776	591	1367	1569
1986-87	3605	1176	853	2029	1576
1987-88	5052	1581	1043	2624	2428
1988-89	5304	1646	1301	2947	2357
1989-90	5803	1987	1699	3686	2117
1990-91	6704	2329	1954	4283	2421
1991-92	11615	3650	3006	6656	4959

(Contd.)

TABLE 5.4 (Contd.)

(1)	(2)	(3)	(4)	(5)=(3+4)	(6)=(2-5)
1992-93	10982	4788	3961	8749	2233
1993-94	11781	5352	4199	9551	2230
1994-95	10881	5791	4635	10426	455
1995-96	11022	7566	5082	12648	-1626
1996-97	11979	7070	4870	11940	39
1997-98	11745	7550	4795	12345	-600
1998-99	13239	8860	5192	14072	-833
1999-00	14405	9686	5480	15166	-761
2000-01	14254	11662	5429	17091	-2837
2001-02	17559	10705	5256	15961	1598
2002-03	15710	28976	4606	33582	-17872
2003-04	17313	27752	3560	31312	-13999

Linear Slope (T-Value)	1966-67 to 1979-80	41.42857* (2.15794)	33.97143** (23.46234)	14.59780** (23.19233)	48.56923** (31.010870)	-7.14066^{NS} (-0.379838)
Linear Slope (T-Value)	1980-81 to 2003-04	730.59700** (20.014000)	884.55650** (6.606298)	262.79220** (10.622850)	1147.46200** (9.575925)	Trend cannot be estimated due to negative values.
Linear Slope (T-Value)	1966-67 to 2003-04	469.82170** (14.722930)	442.94490** (6.475018)	165.89560** (11.651720)	608.89950** (8.500494)	

N.B. :
1. Gross Disbursement of aid take into account debt relief inclusive of debt rescheduling/postponements etc.
2. Figures of both authorization and utilization include loans and grants of both Govt. and Non-Govt. accounts.
3. **Significant at 0.01 level,
   * Significant at 0.05 level, and
   ^{NS} indicates non-significant.

Sources : (i) Govt. of India, *Economic Survey*, 1981-82, p. 147 and other issues.
(ii) RBI, *Handbook of Statistics on The Indian Economy*, 2003-04, p. 236.
(iii) Linear slope (T-values) have been computed.

Development Bank; the OPEC Fund; European Commission; the IMF Trust Fund; the International Fund for Agricultural Development (IFAD); the International Sugar Organization (ISO); and the United Nations Development Programme (inclusive of UNICEF, WHO and World Food Programme), etc. The contribution of these multinational institutions taken together was 62.2 percent of the total utilized assistance up to the end-March 2004. The World Bank (both IBRD and IDA) has been the largest source with a share of 48.5 percent amounting Rs. 1,07,658.27 crore up to the above mentioned period. The source-wise details of aggregate utilized external assistance up to the end-march 2004 have been presented in Table 5.5. Individually, Japan has been the largest contributor among all the bilateral donor countries with a share of 17.4 percent followed by Germany, UK, USA, and Russia with respective shares of 4.7, 4.2, 3.2 and 1.8 percent during the above-mentioned period. The contribution of other sources, taken individually, has been marginal (i.e., less than 2 percent). Thus, from the stand point of their relative shares only eight sources were worth-mentioning viz.: IDA, IBRD, ADB, Japan, Germany, UK, USA and Russia as their contribution in total utilized aid, taken together, has been more than 90 percent up to the end-March 2004. The relative share of other sources has been marginal.

SOURCE-WISE UN-DISBURSED AID

Authorized aid amounting to Rs. 81,122.93 crore has been remained un-utilized up to end-March, 2004 (Table 5.6) out of which Rs. 33,438.12 crore (41.22 percent) has been sanctioned by the WB (both IBRD and IDA); Rs. 13,591.76 crore (16.76 percent) by the ADB; Rs. 11,277.11 crore (13.90 percent) by Japan; and Rs. 10,375.35 crore (12.79 percent) by Russia.

MULTILATERAL *Vs.* BILATERAL AUTHORIZED AID

The major share of total authorized aid to India until 1973-74 was of bilateral nature, an indication of willingness on the part of donor countries to give up control over their aid-funded projects and programmes. The main reason was that such type of aid has been tied to purchases from donor countries and was an adjunct of foreign policy which can be used to serve the various

Table 5.5
Aggregate External Assistance Utilized up to end-March 2004

(Rs. Crore)

Institution/ Country	Loans	Grants	PL-480/665 Third Country Currency Assistance	Total Utilized Assistance	
(1)	(2)	(3)	(4)	(5)=(2+3+4)	
1. IBRD	49039.67	125.74	—	49165.41	(22.1)
2. IDA	58320.61	172.25	—	58492.86	(26.4)
3. ADB	24196.66	120.30	—	24316.96	(11.0)
4. EEC	42.00	3002.26	—	3044.26	(1.4)
5. OPEC*	2098.50	112.36	—	2210.86	(1.0)
6. IFAD	680.79	18.17	—	698.96	(0.3)
7. Japan	37617.70	1130.15	—	38747.85	(17.4)
8. Germany	9728.66	823.38	—	10552.04	(4.7)
9. UK	1292.00	7983.40	—	9275.40	(4.2)
10. USA	3460.00	820.18	2819.00	7099.18	(3.2)

(Contd.)

Table 5.5 (Contd.)

(1)	(2)	(3)	(4)	(5)=(2+3+4)
11. Russia	3985.40	8.00	—	3993.40 (1.8)
12. France	3475.07	72.86	—	3547.93 (1.6)
13. Netherlands	1288.07	2197.77	—	3485.84 (1.6)
14. Sweden	798.00	1164.50	—	1962.50 (0.9)
15. Canada	716.00	725.08	—	1441.08 (0.6)
16. Others	1626.48	2271.11	—	3897.59 (1.8)
Total	198,365.61 (89.4)	20,747.51 (9.3)	2819.00 (1.3)	2,21,932.12 (100.0)

* Comprises Iran, Iraq, Kuwait, Abu-dhabi, Saudi-Arabia and OPEC Special Fund.

N.B. : (i) Figures are exclusive of suppliers' credits for the period 1978-79 to 1996-97.

(ii) Figures are also exclusive of food grants for the period 1997-98 to 2003-04.

(iii) Figures in Parentheses represent percentage to the total.

Sources : (i) RBI, *Report on Currency and Finance, Vol. II*, 1997-98, Statement 209, pp. 268-69 (up to 1996-97).

(ii) Govt. of India, *External Assistance*, 2003-04, pp. 302-6 and 313, Statement 13, 16 and 21 (1997-98 to 2003-04).

TABLE 5.6

Source-wise Details of Cumulative Un-disbursed Aid up to end-March 2004

(*Rs. Crore*)

Source	*Loans*	*Grants*	*Total Amount*	*Percentage of Grand Total*
(1)	*(2)*	*(3)*	*(4) = (2+3)*	*(5)*
1. IBRD	16976.37	347.57	17323.94	21.36
2. IDA	15911.37	202.81	16114.18	19.86
3. ADB	13480.01	111.75	13591.76	16.76
4. IFAD	654.34	25.85	680.19	0.84
5. EEC	—	2505.90	2505.90	3.09
6. UN Agencies	—	316.09	316.09	0.39
7. Global Fund	—	148.39	148.39	0.18
8. Japan	11248.38	28.73	11277.11	13.90
9. Germany	1612.76	698.96	2311.72	2.85
10. France	65.19	2.73	67.92	0.08
11. Russia	10375.35	—	10375.35	12.79
12. UK	—	4016.88	4016.88	4.95
13. USA	—	1037.18	1037.18	1.28
14. Netherlands	—	640.01	640.01	0.79
15. Denmark	—	413.11	413.11	0.51
16. Switzerland	21.76	92.42	114.18	0.14
17. Canada	—	82.51	82.51	0.10
18. Norway	43.38	7.86	51.24	0.06
19. Italy	25.39	—	25.39	0.03
20. Sweden	—	29.88	29.88	0.04
Grand Total	70414.30	10708.63	81122.93	100.00

Source : Govt. of India, *External Assistance, 2003-04,* Ministry of Finance, Department of Economic Affairs; Aid, Accounts and Audit Division; pp. 299-300.

objectives of donor countries, such as: (i) national security, (ii) humanitarian, and (iii) national economic benefit (Mikesell, 1968: p. 5). However, as a matter of fact, the objectives of foreign aid vary from donor to donor ranging from political and strategic to economic and humanitarian. Since 1974-75, the major share of aggregate authorized aid to India remained of multilateral character for most of the time, with a few exceptions. It has been untied in nature giving recipient the freedom to buy in the cheapest global market or in the market appropriate to its economic policy and thereby in turn did not cause any distortion in its authorized aid. The details of total authorized aid in terms of multilateral and bilateral share has been outlined in Table 5.7 which showed that India received maximum share of multilateral assistance 91.6 percent amounting to Rs. 16,609.4 crore in

TABLE 5.7

Division of Authorized Assistance into Bilateral and Multilateral Assistance

(Rs. Crore)

Period/Year	*Bilateral Aid*	*Multilateral Aid*	*Total Authorized Aid*
(1)	(2)	(3)	(4) = (2+3)
Up to end of Third Plan	4987.0 (87.3)	724.6 (12.7)	5711.6
1966-67	1275.7 (84.7)	230.8 (16.3)	1506.5
1967-68	688.7 (95.8)	30.0 (4.2)	718.8
1968-69	841.7 (88.9)	105.1 (11.1)	946.8
1969-70	500.8 (79.0)	133.5 (21.0)	634.3
1970-71	594.7 (78.1)	167.2 (21.9)	761.9
1971-72	549.7 (59.2)	379.5 (40.8)	929.2
1972-73	476.7 (70.5)	199.5 (29.5)	676.2
1973-74	679.3 (58.0)	491.3 (42.0)	1170.6
1974-75	709.9 (42.5)	961.3 (57.5)	1671.2
1975-76	767.3 (28.9)	1886.2 (71.1)	2653.5
1976-77	822.5 (63.9)	463.9 (36.1)	1286.4
1977-78	987.5 (52.1)	909.5 (47.9)	1897.0
1978-79	820.9 (35.1)	1514.8 (64.9)	2335.7
1979-80	1008.8 (54.3)	850.7 (45.7)	1859.5
1980-81	1358.4 (35.3)	2488.6 (64.7)	3847.0
1981-82	974.3 (32.8)	1999.6 (67.2)	2973.9
1982-83	1022.8 (34.4)	1949.9 (65.6)	2972.7

TABLE 5.7 (Contd.)

(1)		*(2)*	*(3)*	*(4) = (2+3)*
1983-84		859.4 (41.2)	1228.3 (58.8)	2087.7
1984-85		1338.2 (27.4)	3541.8 (72.6)	4880.0
1985-86		2193.9 (38.8)	3456.5 (61.2)	5650.4
1986-87		3555.0 (57.7)	2604.5 (42.3)	6159.5
1987-88		4003.8 (43.2)	5261.5 (56.8)	9265.3
1988-89		8269.2 (63.3)	4800.6 (36.7)	13069.8
1989-90		4096.5 (37.8)	6729.5 (62.2)	10826.0
1990-91		3392.5 (41.8)	4730.9 (58.2)	8123.4
1991-92		4054.3 (31.9)	8653.3 (68.1)	12707.6
1992-93		4865.9 (34.5)	9227.9 (65.5)	14093.8
1993-94		7468.7 (53.2)	6565.2 (46.8)	14033.9
1994-95		5484.3 (40.7)	7975.8 (59.3)	13460.1
1995-96		6353.8 (52.2)	5809.4 (47.8)	12163.2
1996-97		8588.0 (50.1)	8553.4 (49.9)	17141.4
1997-98		5951.6 (35.1)	11014.4 (64.9)	16966.0
1998-99		938.7 (11.0)	7591.9 (89.0)	8530.6
1999-2000		14126.1 (69.5)	6192.9 (30.5)	20319.0
2000-01		1515.3 (8.4)	16609.4 (91.6)	18124.7
2001-02		4868.0 (19.4)	20227.0 (80.6)	25095.0
2002-03		5775.8 (27.5)	15260.9 (72.5)	21036.7
2003-04		6857.8 (40.1)	10247.3 (59.9)	17105.1
Linear Slope (T-Value)	1966-67 to 1979-80	6.8017590^{NS} (0.4528002)	97.9694500** (3.6686820)	104.7688** (3.1899350)
Linear Slope (T-Value)	1980-81 to 2003-04	244.00850** (3.019952)	565.52800** (6.935170)	809.53640** (9.540482)
Linear Slope (T-Value)	1966-67 to 2003-04	198.89550** (6.071370)	389.93520** (10.410570)	588.83030** (13.767860)

N.B. : (i) Figures in parentheses represent percentage share in total authorized aid.
(ii) ** Significant at 0.01 level.
^{NS} Indicate non-significant.

Sources : (i) Govt. of India, *Economic Survey, 2004-05*, pp. S-97 and 98, and other issues.
(ii) Linear slope (T-values) have been computed.

2000-01, and the lowest share of 4.2 percent to the tune of Rs. 30 crore in 1967-68. The trend values of multilateral authorized aid during the pre-eighty period (1966-67 to 1979-80); post-eighty period (1980-81 to 2003-04); and the overall period (1966-67 to 2003-04) were found to be positive and significant at one percent level. But the trend value of the bilateral assistance authorized to India during the pre-eighty period worked out to be non-significant, while the same during the post-eighty period and for the overall period found significant at one percent level. Thus, in brief, the multilateral authorized aid proved more dominant and significant as contrasted to the bilateral assistance in the Indian economy.

MULTILATERAL *Vs.* BILATERAL UTILIZED AID

The details of total utilized aid in terms of multilateral and bilateral share, delineated in Table 5.8, show that India utilized

TABLE 5.8
Division of Utilized Aid into Bilateral and Multilateral Assistance

(*Rs. Crore*)

Period/Year	*Bilateral Aid*	*Multilateral Aid*	*Total Utilized Aid*
(1)	(2)	(3)	(4) = (2+3)
Up to end of Third Plan	3928.2 (87.12)	580.6 (12.88)	4508.8
1966-67	970.9 (85.81)	160.5 (14.19)	1131.4
1967-68	999.1 (83.57)	196.5 (16.43)	1195.6
1968-69	814.6 (90.25)	88.0 (9.75)	902.6
1969-70	736.7 (86.03)	119.6 (13.97)	856.3
1970-71	705.2 (89.11)	86.2 (10.89)	791.4
1971-72	725.5 (86.98)	108.6 (13.02)	834.1
1972-73	499.3 (74.95)	166.9 (25.05)	666.2
1973-74	716.6 (69.19)	319.1 (30.81)	1035.7
1974-75	751.6 (57.19)	562.7 (42.81)	1314.3
1975-76	1290.6 (70.12)	549.9 (29.88)	1840.5
1976-77	1050.7 (65.71)	548.2 (34.29)	1598.9
1977-78	821.3 (63.67)	468.7 (36.33)	1290.0

TABLE 5.8 (*Contd.*)

(1)	*(2)*	*(3)*	*(4) = (2+3)*
1978-79	767.5 (63.14)	448.1 (36.86)	1215.6
1979-80	722.8 (53.42)	630.3 (46.58)	1353.1
1980-81	870.1 (40.25)	1291.7 (59.75)	2161.8
1981-82	699.7 (37.52)	1165.2 (62.48)	1864.9
1982-83	727.7 (32.31)	1524.3 (67.69)	2252.0
1983-84	774.7 (34.19)	1491.1 (65.81)	2265.8
1984-85	940.4 (39.86)	1419.0 (60.14)	2359.4
1985-86	1161.0 (39.54)	1775.0 (60.46)	2936.0
1986-87	1686.1 (46.77)	1918.9 (53.23)	3605.0
1987-88	1973.0 (39.05)	3078.9 (60.95)	5051.9
1988-89	1518.0 (28.62)	3786.4 (71.38)	5304.4
1989-90	2041.1 (35.18)	3761.4 (64.82)	5802.5
1990-91	2631.6 (39.25)	4072.7 (60.75)	6704.3
1991-92	4317.3 (37.17)	7297.7 (62.83)	11615.0
1992-93	3845.4 (35.02)	7136.4 (64.98)	10981.8
1993-94	4927.1 (41.82)	6853.9 (58.18)	11781.0
1994-95	3600.6 (33.09)	7279.9 (66.91)	10880.5
1995-96	4491.6 (40.75)	6530.6 (59.25)	11022.2
1996-97	3501.9 (29.23)	8476.6 (70.77)	11978.5
1997-98	3929.3 (33.46)	7815.6 (66.54)	11744.9
1998-99	4341.9 (32.80)	8897.0 (67.20)	13238.9
1999-00	4864.5 (33.77)	9540.1 (66.23)	14404.6
2000-01	3829.7 (26.87)	10424.6 (73.13)	14254.3
2001-02	5964.7 (33.97)	11594.6 (66.03)	17559.3
2002-03	5245.1 (33.12)	10590.8 (66.88)	15835.9
2003-04	6060.8 (34.94)	11283.6 (65.06)	17344.4
Linear Slope 1966-67 to	-0.64176^{NS}	42.05384**	41.41208*
(T-value) 1979-80	(-0.047984)	(5.60433)	(2.15804)
Linear Slope 1980-81 to	234.76230**	497.29840**	732.06070**
(T-value) 2003-04	(12.384900)	(21.168660)	(20.112000)
Linear Slope 1966-67 to	141.93350**	328.49610**	470.42950**
(T-value) 2003-04	(11.323860)	(15.838700)	(14.717910)

N.B. : (i) Figures in parentheses represent percentage share in total utilized aid.

(ii) ** Significant at 0.01 level,
* Significant at 0.05 level, and
^{NS} indicates non-significant.

Sources : (i) Govt. of India, *Economic Survey*, 2004-05, p. S-101 and 102, and other issues.

(ii) Linear slope (T-values) have been computed.

the maximum share of multilateral assistance of 73.13 percent in 2000-01 and the lowest share of 9.75 percent in 1968-69. The table indicates that until 1979-80, most of the utilized assistance was from bilateral sources, while since then it has been multilateral in nature. The trend values of multilateral assistance during the pre-eighty period, post-eighty period and during the overall period has been found positive and significant at one percent level. However, the trend value of the bilateral assistance during the pre-eighty period worked out to be negative and non-significant, while the trend value of the same during the post-eighty period as well as during the overall period has been positive and significant at one percent level. Thus, country has been utilizing more multilateral assistance as compared to the bilateral assistance, since 1980-81. Multilateral assistance is preferred, perhaps, due to the three reasons. First, information gathering has a public-good character, i.e., multilateral agencies are better equipped at global level to assess the political situation for the potential recipients or choice of projects to support as these employ many specialists to watch closely the evolution of economic situation both in the developed and developing world. Second, in case of multilateral aid, rent-seeking behaviour either by the donor or the recipient or other political problems can sometimes be avoided. Third, multilateral aid can be conditional and might be a signal of the recipient's prudent economic policies (Brakman and Van Marrewijk, 1998: pp. 119-20).

Section III

PURPOSE-WISE UTILIZED AID

The analysis of purpose-wise distribution of utilized foreign aid in India is important for examining and evaluating its role in the development of different sectors of the economy, such as: agriculture, industry, transport and communications, power projects, water resources management, social and urban development, etc., and in raising the overall productive capacity of the Indian economy. However, the classification of purposes for which aid has been utilized in India changed after 1985. As it was difficult to reconcile the purposes, therefore, the evaluation of purpose-wise utilized aid has been carried out for two periods in view of the comparability of purposes: (1) April 1, 1951 to March 31, 1985 and (2) April 1, 1985 to March 31, 2004.

1. Pre-1985 Period

During 1951-85, foreign aid was utilized mainly for the purposes mentioned in Table 5.9, such as : industrial development; steel and steel projects; iron ore projects; agricultural development; transport and communications; food grains; oil and petroleum products, etc. A perusal of Table 5.9 indicates that during the First Plan, 71.4 percent (Rs. 90.3 crore) of the total aid was utilized on the import of food grains to meet the acute food shortages in the country, while 12.4 percent (Rs. 15.6 crore), and 9.6 percent (Rs. 12.1 crore) were spent on the development of transport and communications, and the power projects, respectively. The share of food-aid declined sharply to the lowest level of 0.03 percent (Rs. 2.91 crore) during the Sixth Plan, while the maximum of 36.3 percent (Rs. 3106.88 crore) of the total utilized aid was spent on the development of agricultural sector, followed by 27 percent (Rs. 2312.05 crore) on industrial development and 19.7 percent (Rs.1684.07 crore) on the development of power projects during the Sixth Plan.

However, during the overall (1951-85) period on the average maximum, i.e., 42.3 percent (Rs. 9519.54 crore) of the total foreign aid was utilized for the development of industries followed by 20.3 percent (Rs. 4563.06 crore) on agricultural development; 11.3 percent (Rs. 2543.79 crore) on the development of power and power projects; 9.3 percent (Rs. 2089.81 crore) on the development of transport and communications; and 4.3 percent (Rs. 970.67 crore) on the steel and steel projects. Thus, evidently, most of the foreign aid during 1951-85 was either utilized for building social overhead capital or for the development of directly productive activities, although initially larger aid was used to meet the food shortages in the country.

2. Post-1985 Period

Since April 1, 1985 a new classification of purposes for the utilization of external assistance was made, incorporating certain new areas/objectives, like water resources management, social sector, urban development, structural adjustment, environment and forestry etc., and deleting certain (now) less significant activities such as : food aid, iron ore, steel and steel projects, etc.

Table 5.9
Purpose-wise Utilization of Overall Net External Assistance up to end-March 1985

(Rs. Crore)

Purpose	First Plan (1951-56)	Second Plan (1956-61)	Third Plan (1961-66)	Annual Plans (1966-69)	Fourth Plan (1969-74)	Fifth Plan (1974-79)	(1979-80)	Sixth Plan (1980-85)	Total Utilized Aid up to end March 1985
I. Transport and Communication	15.6 (12.4)	152.2 (21.3)	291.4 (15.3)	166.23 (7.5)	371.65 (10.5)	344.30 (7.5)	46.33 (5.5)	702.10 (8.2)	2089.81 (9.3)
II. Power and Power Projects	12.1 (9.6)	29.3 (4.1)	152.6 (8.0)	145.38 (6.6)	105.12 (3.0)	261.63 (5.7)	153.59 (18.0)	1684.07 (19.7)	2543.79 (11 3)
III. Steel & Steel Projects	2.7 (2.1)	254.1 (35.6)	94.2 (4.9)	118.76 (5.4)	109.78 (3.1)	195.97 (4.3)	3.06 (0.4)	192.10 (2.2)	970.67 (4.3)
IV. Iron Ore Projects	—	—	10.4 (0.5)	1.33 (0.1)	—	191.38 (4.2)	—	—	203.11 (0.9)
V. Industrial Development	2.3 (1.8)	255.4 (35.8)	1270.4 (66.6)	1510.84 (68.7)	2197.82 (62.4)	1744.09 (37.8)	226.64 (26.7)	2312.05 (27.0)	9519.54 (42.3)
VI. Agricultural Development	3.4 (2.7)	—	22.5 (1.2)	70.83 (3.2)	175.02 (5.0)	840.17 (18.2)	344.26 (40.5)	3106.88 (36.3)	4563.06 (20.3)
VII. Food Aid	90.3 (71.4)	15.7 (2.2)	—	109.23 (5.0)	312.44 (8.9)	276.40 (6.0)	—	2.91 (0.03)	806.98 (3.6)

VIII. Oil & Petroleum Products	—	—	—	—	—	433.26 (9.4)	12.98 (1.5)	18.16 (0.2)	464.40 (2.1)
IX. Debt Relief	—	—	—	77.24 (3.5)	244.93 (6.9)	208.04 (4.5)	—	—	530.21 (2.4)
X. Miscellaneous	—	6.8 (1.0)	66.8 (3.5)	0.64 (0.0)	7.06 (0.2)	111.34 (2.4)	63.18 (7.4)	546.31 (6.4)	802.13 (3.5)
Grand Total (I to X)	126.4 (100)	713.5 (100)	1908.3 (100)	2200.48 (100)	3523.82 (100)	4606.58 (100)	850.04 (100)	8564.58 (100)	22493.7 (100)

Source : RBI, *Report on Currency and Finance, Vol. II*, 1988-89 and other issues.

Purpose-wise distribution of utilized aid during 1985-2004 has been amplified in Table 5.10, which showed that during the Seventh Plan (1985-90) maximum, i.e., 35.2 percent (Rs. 3779.40 crore) of the total utilized aid amounting to Rs. 10,736.04 crore was spent on the development of total energy sector, of which a major share of 25.4 percent (Rs. 2720.49 crore) was incurred on the development of power sector only. This was followed by 15.5 percent (Rs. 1669.02 crore) of the total utilized aid used for the development of total infrastructure sector inclusive of railways, road network, telecom, ports and others having share of 5.7, 0.6, 4.6, 3.2, and 1.4 percent, respectively.

The share of total utilized aid spent on the social sector increased to 23.3 percent (Rs. 13,332.82 crore) during the Ninth Plan (1997-02) period from 6.3 percent (Rs. 674.13 crore) during the Seventh Plan period. This has been followed by 22.98 percent (Rs. 13,145.42 crore) of the total utilized aid spent on the development of total energy sector inclusive of power, coal, and oil sectors. The share of industrial sector, fertilizer sector and infrastructure sector declined to 1.52 percent (Rs. 868.18 crore); 0.64 percent (Rs. 367.50 crore); and 12.8 percent (Rs. 7319.82 crore), respectively, during the Ninth Plan. However, the share of newly incorporated water resources management, urban development, environment and forestry sectors increased from 3.7, 2.6, and zero percent, respectively, during Seventh Plan to 9.88, 4.76, and 5.81 percent, respectively, during the Ninth Plan.

On the whole, during 1985-2004, total energy sector accounted for the maximum, i.e., 28.65 percent (Rs. 46,039.28 crore) and individually the power sector absorbed the maximum, i.e., 24.6 percent (Rs. 39,526.97 crore) of the total utilized foreign aid, followed by social sector with 15.49 percent (Rs. 24,888.39 crore); total infrastructure sector with 10.97 percent (Rs.17,614.30 crore); and structural adjustment with 10.44 percent (Rs. 16,771.67 crore). The lowest proportion of 1.43 percent (Rs. 2303.32 crore) was spent for the development of fertilizers sector. Thus, the significance of energy, particularly the power sector; water resources management; social and urban development sector; and environment and forestry has increased, while the importance of agricultural, industrial, fertilizers and infrastructure sectors has declined in terms of foreign aid utilization during the post-1985 period, although it has been utilized in almost all the strategic sectors of the Indian economy.

TABLE 5.10

Purpose-wise Utilization of Overall Net External Assistance during the Period 1985-2004

(Rs. Crore)

Purpose/Sector	Seventh Plan 1985-90	Eighth Plan 1990-95	1995-97	Ninth Plan 1997-02	Tenth Plan 2002-04	Total Utilization during 1985-04
(1)	(2)	(3)	(4)	(5)	(6)	(7)
I. Agricultural Sector	1228.37	3261.57	1648.71	3517.33	2160.49	11816.47
	(11.40)	(7.50)	(8.17)	(6.15)	(7.41)	(7.35)
II. Total Energy Sector	3779.4	16196.07	7849.78	13145.42	5068.61	46039.28
	(35.20)	(37.30)	(38.90)	(22.98)	(17.39)	(28.65)
(a) Total Energy (General)	—	98.31	30.74	428.79	71.11	628.95
		(0.20)	(0.15)	(0.75)	(0.24)	(0.39)
(b) Total Energy (Coal)	176.19	492.66	87.39	278.39	4.32	1038.95
	(1.60)	(1.10)	(0.43)	(0.49)	(0.02)	(0.65)
(c) Total Energy (Power)	2720.49	12583.06	6924.98	12305.26	4993.18	39526.97
	(25.40)	(29.00)	(34.30)	(21.50)	(17.13)	(24.60)
(d) Total Energy (Oil)	882.72	3022.04	806.67	132.98	—	4844.41
	(8.20)	(7.00)	(4.00)	(0.23)		(3.01)

(Contd.)

Table 5.10 (Contd.)

(1)	(2)	(3)	(4)	(5)	(6)	(7)
III. Fertilizer Sector	908.95	431.21	550.41	367.5	45.25	2303.32
	(8.50)	(1.00)	(2.73)	(0.64)	(0.15)	(1.43)
IV. Industry Sector	1449.55	5873.66	1195.25	868.18	49.91	9436.55
	(13.50)	(13.50)	(5.92)	(1.52)	(0.17)	(5.87)
V. Total Infrastructure Sector	1669.02	2873.3	2373.75	7319.82	3378.41	17614.3
	(15.50)	(6.60)	(11.76)	(12.80)	(11.59)	(10.97)
(a) Infrastructure (General)	—	11.19	89.58	1598.93	142.83	1842.53
		(0.03)	(0.44)	(2.79)	(0.49)	(1.15)
(b) Infrastructure (Railway)	611.35	409.77	631.35	993.98	3.99	2650.44
	(5.70)	(0.90)	(3.13)	(1.74)	(0.01)	(1.65)
(c) Infrastructure (Roads)	68.63	1529.7	1099.56	4583.69	3155.86	10437.44
	(0.60)	(3.50)	(5.45)	(8.01)	(10.83)	(6.50)
(d) Infrastructure (Telecom)	496.47	426.14	195.94	19.26	76.24	1214.05
	(4.60)	(1.00)	(0.97)	(0.03)	(0.26)	(0.76)
(e) Infrastructure (Ports)	340.7	377.36	192.21	123.96	-0.51	1033.72
	(3.20)	(0.90)	(0.95)	(0.22)	(—)	(0.64)
(f) Infrastructure (Others)	151.87	119.14	165.11			436.12
	(1.40)	(0.27)	(0.82)	—	—	(0.27)

VI. Water Resources Management Sector	402.15 (3.70)	2475.87 (5.70)	1271.24 (6.30)	5653.19 (9.88)	2516.99 (8.64)	12319.44 (7.67)
VII. Social Sector	674.13 (6.30)	2305.44 (5.60)	2156.38 (10.69)	13332.82 (23.30)	6419.62 (22.03)	24888.39 (15.49)
VIII. Urban Development	275.25 (2.60)	1676.61 (3.80)	1159.75 (5.75)	2723.16 (4.76)	4137.87 (14.20)	9972.64 (6.21)
IX. Structural Adjustment	—	6934.91 (16.00)	1916.7 (9.50)	5263.4 (9.20)	2656.66 (9.12)	16771.67 (10.44)
X. Environment and Forestry	—	—	—	3323.86 (5.81)	954.09 (3.27)	4277.95 (2.66)
XI. Others	349.22 (3.30)	1390.28 (3.20)	53.08 (0.26)	1685.6 (2.95)	1753.92 (6.02)	5232.1 (3.26)
Grand Total (I to XI)	10736.04 (100)	43418.92 (100)	20175.05 (100)	57200.28 (100)	29141.82 (100)	160672.11 (100)

N.B. : (i) Figures 1997 onwards include only Govt. loans and grants.
(ii) Figures in parentheses represent percentage of total.

Sources : (i) RBI, *Report on Currency and Finance, Vol. II*, 1997-98, pp. 275-95.
(ii) Govt. of India, *External Assistance, 2003-04*, p. 319.

1. PURPOSE-WISE UTILIZATION OF THE WORLD BANK AID

The WB, comprising IBRD and its 'soft lending window'—IDA, has been the largest source of foreign aid to India, which contributed cumulatively 47.7 percent (Rs. 61,677 crore) of the total utilized aid amounting Rs. 1,29,352 crore having 22.9 percent share of IBRD and 24.8 percent share of IDA up to the end-March 1998 (RBI[b], 1998, Vol. II : p. 274).

The purpose-wise distribution of utilized IBRD aid has been given in Table 5.11, a cursory glance at which showed that 49.39

TABLE 5.11
Purpose-wise Distribution of Utilized IBRD Aid in India

Purpose/Sector	*Utilized Aid up to end-March 1998 (Rs. Crore)*	*Percentage of Total*
I. Agriculture Sector	1565.77	5.86
II. Total Energy Sector	13189.73	49.39
(a) Total Energy (General)	Nil	Nil
(b) Total Energy (Coal)	251.03	0.94
(c) Total Energy (Power)	10326.98	38.67
(d) Total Energy (Oil)	2611.72	9.78
III. Fertilizer Sector	690.15	2.59
IV. Industry Sector	6503.27	24.35
V. Steel and Steel Projects	88.36	0.33
VI. Infrastructure Sector	2672.11	10.01
(a) Transport and Telecom	431.15	1.62
(b) Infrastructure (Railways)	791.13	2.96
(c) Infrastructure (Roads)	854.88	3.20
(d) Infrastructure (Telecom)	267.14	1.00
(e) Infrastructure (Ports)	327.81	1.23
(f) Infrastructure (Others)	Nil	Nil
VII. Water Resources Management	193.43	0.72
VIII. Urban Development	162.45	0.61
IX. Structural Adjustment	1625.95	6.09
X. Miscellaneous/Others	12.53	0.05
# Total Utilized Aid (I to X)	26703.75	100.00

Source : Compiled from RBI, *Report on Currency and Finance, Vol. II*, 1997-98 and other issues.

percent (Rs. 13,189.73 crore) of the total IBRD utilized aid during the fore-said period, has been spent on the total energy sector, most of which, i.e., 38.67 percent (Rs. 10,326.98 crore) of the total IBRD aid has been incurred on the power sector only. This has been followed by the industrial sector with share of 24.35 percent (Rs. 6503.27 crore); total infrastructure sector inclusive of railways, roads, ports, telecom, etc., with proportion of 10.01 percent (Rs. 2672.11 crore); and the structural adjustment program with share of 6.09 percent (Rs. 1625.95 crore) of the total IBRD utilized assistance. Thus, almost 90 percent of the IBRD aid up to end-March 1998 in India has been used for the development of energy, especially power; industry and infrastructural sectors; and for the structural adjustment programme.

The purpose-wise distribution of utilized IDA aid in India up to the end-March 1998 has been presented in Table 5.12, which showed that the maximum 27.91 percent (Rs. 8099.98 crore) of the utilized aid has been used for the development of agricultural sector followed by the social sector with share of 20.04 percent (Rs. 5815.83 crore); water resources management

TABLE 5.12
Purpose-wise Distribution of Utilized IDA Aid in India

Purpose/Sector	*Utilized Aid up to end-March 1998 (Rs. Crore)*	*Percentage of Total*
I. Agriculture Sector	8099.98	27.91
II. Total Energy Sector	2203.12	7.59
(a) Total Energy (General)	46.97	0.16
(b) Total Energy (Power)	2156.15	7.43
III. Industry Sector	1634.89	5.63
IV. Infrastructure Sector	1597.03	5.50
(a) Transport & Communication	1071.86	3.69
(b) Infrastructure (Roads)	525.17	1.81
V. Water Resources Management	4495.71	15.49
VI. Social Sector	5815.83	20.04
VII. Urban Development	2241.30	7.72
VIII. Structural Adjustment	2293.42	7.90
IX. Miscellaneous/Others	640.93	2.22
# Total Utilized Aid (I to IX)	29022.21	100.00

Source : Compiled from RBI, *Report on Currency and Finance, Vol. II,* 1997-98 and other issues.

with proportion of 15.49 percent (Rs. 4495.71 crore); structural adjustment programme with share of 7.90 percent (Rs. 2293.42 crore); and urban development sector with share of 7.72 percent (Rs. 2241.30 crore). Thus, most of the IDA assistance has been utilized for the development of agriculture, social sector, water resources management, structural adjustment program, urban development and total energy sector, especially power sector of the Indian economy.

2. PURPOSE-WISE UTILIZATION OF ADB ASSISTANCE

The Asian Development Bank, a major regional financial institution, has been providing assistance to India, since 1986. The purpose-wise distribution of utilized ADB aid up to the end-March 1998 has been shown in Table 5.13, which highlighted

TABLE 5.13
Purpose-wise Distribution of Utilized ADB Aid in India

Purpose/Sector	*Utilized Aid up to end-March 1998 (Rs. Crore)*	*Percentage of Total*
I. Agriculture Sector	Nil	Nil
II. Total Energy Sector	4604.84	38.45
(a) Total Energy (Power)	2446.26	20.43
(b) Total Energy (Oil)	2158.58	18.02
III. Fertilizer Sector	Nil	Nil
IV. Industry Sector	1089.81	9.10
V. Infrastructure Sector	4337.09	36.22
(a) Infrastructure (General)	380.85	3.18
(b) Infrastructure (Railways)	854.99	7.14
(c) Infrastructure (Roads)	1823.92	15.23
(d) Infrastructure (Telecom)	529.29	4.42
(e) Infrastructure (Ports)	579.65	4.84
(f) Infrastructure (Others)	168.39	1.41
VI. Water Resources Management	Nil	Nil
VII. Social Sector	Nil	Nil
VIII. Urban Development	333.48	2.78
IX. Structural Adjustment	1610.51	13.45
X. Miscellaneous/Others	Nil	Nil
# Total Utilized Aid (I to X)	11975.73	100.00

Source : Compiled from RBI, *Report on Currency and Finance, Vol. II*, 1997-98 and other issues.

that the maximum 38.45 percent (Rs. 4604.84 crore) share was used for the total energy sector, of which major share was spent on power sector (20.43 percent of the total ADB aid) and oil sector (18.02 percent of the total ADB aid). This was followed by the infrastructure sector with share of 36.22 percent (Rs. 4337.09 crore) and structural adjustment sector with proportion of 13.45 percent (Rs. 1610.51 crore). In brief, 97.22 percent of the total utilized ADB assistance up to the end-March 1998 has been spent on the development of energy sector comprising power and oil sectors; infrastructure sector consisting of roads, railways, ports, telecom, etc.; structural adjustment sector; and industry sector of the body economic of India.

3. PURPOSE-WISE UTILIZATION OF JAPANESE AID

Japan has been the single largest contributor of bilateral assistance to India which has provided Rs. 18,642.73 crore in the form of utilized assistance to her up to the end-March 1998. The sector-wise distribution of utilized Japanese aid has been indicated in Table 5.14, a perusal of which depicted that the

TABLE 5.14
Purpose-wise Distribution of Utilized Japanese Aid in India

Purpose/Sector	*Utilized Aid up to end-March 1998 (Rs. Crore)*	*Percentage of Total*
(1)	(2)	(3)
I. Agriculture Sector	666.99	3.58
II. Total Energy Sector	9491.04	50.91
(a) Total Energy (Power)	9366.18	50.24
(b) Total Energy (Oil)	124.86	0.67
III. Fertilizer Sector	634.15	3.40
IV. Industry Sector	2357.23	12.64
V. Infrastructure Sector	569.46	3.06
(a) Transport & Communication	137.32	0.74
(b) Infrastructure (Roads)	69.17	0.37
(c) Infrastructure (Telecom)	152.36	0.82
(d) Infrastructure (Ports)	27.38	0.15
(e) Infrastructure (Others)	183.23	0.98

(Contd.)

TABLE 5.14 (Contd.)

(1)	(2)	(3)
VI. Water Resources Management	174.89	0.94
VII. Social Sector	351.97	1.89
VIII. Urban Development	796.73	4.27
IX. Structural Adjustment	3232.71	17.34
X. Miscellaneous/Others	367.56	1.97
# Total Utilized Aid (I to X)	18642.73	100.00

Source : Compiled from RBI, *Report on Currency and Finance, Vol. II,* 1997-98 and other issues.

largest share of 50.91 percent amounting Rs. 9491.04 crore were expended on the total energy sector comprising mainly power sector with share of 50.24 percent of total utilized Japanese assistance. This has been followed by structural adjustment sector with a share of 17.34 percent (Rs. 3232.71 crore); industry sector with a proportion of 12.64 percent (Rs. 2357.23 crore); and urban development sector with 4.27 percent (Rs. 796.73 crore). In essence, almost 85 percent of the total Japanese aid has been spent on the development of power generation, structural adjustment, industry and urban development sectors of the Indian economy.

4. PURPOSE-WISE UTILIZATION OF GERMAN AID

Germany has been the second largest source of bilateral assistance up to the end-March 1998, which made available Rs. 7451.65 crore to India, since 1955 with the credit agreement signed for the construction of Rourkela Steel Plant. The sector-wise distribution of utilized German aid to India can be seen from Table 5.15, a cursory glance of which showed that the largest share of assistance 31.89 percent (Rs. 2376.17 crore) has been spent on industrial sector, followed by total energy sector with proportion of 29.96 percent (Rs. 2232.54 crore); other miscellaneous sectors with share of 10.29 percent (Rs. 767.06 crore); and agricultural sector with 4.32 percent (Rs. 321.71 crore). In other words, most of the German aid has been used for the development of Indian industries; energy sector, mainly the

TABLE 5.15

Purpose-wise Distribution of Utilized German Aid in India

Purpose/Sector	*Utilized Aid up to end-March 1998 (Rs. Crore)*	*Percentage of Total*
I. Agriculture Sector	321.71	4.32
II. Total Energy Sector	2232.54	29.96
(a) Total Energy (Coal)	351.06	4.71
(b) Total Energy (Power)	1881.48	25.25
III. Fertilizer Sector	595.81	8.00
IV. Industry Sector	2376.17	31.89
V. Steel and Steel Projects	157.65	2.12
VI. Infrastructure Sector	145.94	1.96
(a) Transport & Communication	55.88	0.75
(b) Infrastructure (Railways)	75.27	1.01
(c) Infrastructure (Telecom)	14.79	0.20
VII. Water Resources Management	132.20	1.77
VIII. Social Sector	79.79	1.07
IX. Urban Development	286.80	3.85
X. Debt Relief	266.96	3.58
XI. Structural Adjustment	89.02	1.19
XII. Miscellaneous/Others	767.06	10.29
# Total Utilized Aid (I to XII)	7451.65	100.00

Source : Compiled from RBI, *Report on Currency and Finance, Vol. II*, 1997-98 and other issues.

power sector; agriculture, urban development, debt relief and other miscellaneous sectors.

5. PURPOSE-WISE UTILIZATION OF THE US AID

The American economic assistance to India has also been one of the major source of bilateral arrangement which started in 1951. The assistance mainly comprised development assistance, food and technical assistance. Initially, the main thrust of US assistance to India was on projects that were designed to key institutions, and transfer of resources for infrastructure programmes in agriculture and social forestry. Since mid-1980, the priority has been diversified to include science and technology, health and family welfare areas. On the whole, purpose-wise distribution of utilized US assistance to India up to end-March 1998 has been mentioned in Table 5.16. A perusal of the table demonstrates that largest chunk of US assistance, 49.47 percent (Rs. 1803.06 crore) has been spent on the industrial sector, followed by food aid with a share of 15.9 percent (Rs. 579.43 crore); agricultural sector with a proportion of 10.57 percent

TABLE 5.16

Purpose-wise Distribution of Utilized US Aid in India

Purpose/Sector	*Utilized Aid up to end-March 1998 (Rs. Crore)*	*Percentage of Total*
I. Agriculture Sector	385.32	10.57
II. Total Energy Sector	255.30	7.01
(a) Total Energy (Power)	255.30	7.01
(b) Total Energy (Coal)	Nil	Nil
III. Industry Sector	1803.06	49.47
IV. Steel and Steel Projects	40.11	1.10
V. Iron ore	8.87	0.24
VI. Infrastructure Sector (Transport & Communication)	292.45	8.02
VII. Food Aid	579.43	15.90
VIII. Debt Relief	77.61	2.13
IX. Water Resources Management	148.95	4.09
X. Miscellaneous/Others	53.44	1.47
# Total Utilized Aid (I to X)	3644.54	100.00

Source : Compiled from RBI, *Report on Currency and Finance, Vol. II*, 1997-98 and other issues.

(Rs. 385.32 crore); and infrastructure (mainly transport and communications) with 8.02 percent (Rs. 292.45 crore). Thus, the main thrust of American assistance to India has been the development of basic infrastructure.

6. PURPOSE-WISE UTILIZATION OF BRITISH AID

Though UK exploited the Indian economy during its 190 years (1757-1947) colonial rule, yet its economic assistance after independence has been much below expectations. The total utilized UK assistance to India up to the end-March 1998 amounting Rs. 1274.22 crore has been used only in the five sectors of the economy. The largest share of 79.06 percent (Rs. 1007.45 crore) was utilized in the industrial sector, followed by 11.12 percent (Rs. 141.72 crore) for debt relief; and 5.87 percent (Rs. 74.75 crore) for the steel and steel projects, while other sectors got negligible share. This has been evident from Table 5.17.

TABLE 5.17
Purpose-wise Distribution of Utilized British Aid in India

Purpose/Sector	*Utilized Aid up to end-March 1998 (Rs. Crore)*	*Percentage of Total*
I. Agriculture Sector	14.86	1.17
II. Industry Sector	1007.45	79.06
III. Steel and Steel Projects	74.75	5.87
IV. Debt Relief	141.72	11.12
V. Miscellaneous/Others	35.44	2.78
# Total Utilized Aid (I to V)	1274.22	100.00

Source : Compiled from RBI, *Report on Currency and Finance, Vol. II,* 1997-98 and other issues.

In sum, most of the donors gave larger part of their aid for the development of basic infrastructure in the Indian economy and that too mostly for the public sector.

6

Foreign Aid to India : Grant Element in Multilateral Assistance

Recipient countries like India received foreign aid from various multilateral financial institutions as well as from friendly foreign countries on a wide variety of terms and conditions which differ from source to source, loan to loan, and even from purpose to purpose. The effectiveness of foreign aid in such countries depends, among other things, on its own 'real worth' which in turn is determined by five factors: outright grant to loan ratio; the maturity or repayment period of the loan component; the duration of grace period, i.e., the initial period during which no repayment of principal is required; the rate of interest to be charged; and the extent to which it is tied. All these factors determine 'grant element' inherent in the foreign loans which can be worked out by using a suitable discount rate, i.e., a rate which reflect the cost of raising the same loan on almost similar terms and conditions from a relevant alternative source. Basically, grant element arises because of the discrepancy between the rate of interest at which the loan component is serviced, and rate of interest (discount rate) at which it could have been obtained from an alternative source under the similar terms and conditions. The concept of grant element was developed in the early 1960s by John Pincus, whose work had been subsequently taken further by Goran Ohlin (Ohlin, 1966: pp. 101-03) and has been incorporated in the OECD publications from 1967 onwards. The concept is quite useful in converting the loan components obtained on heterogeneous terms and conditions (i.e., grace period, maturity period, rate of interest) into a single scale of comparison. It also permits aggregation of different loan streams into a single weighted measure of grant element.

The concept can be illustrated with an example: suppose one needs to borrow Rs. 1000 for a year from a commercial bank at 10 percent just because he can make a profit of 10 percent with that money, that is, Rs. 1100 in a year's time is worth same to him as is Rs. 1000 now. If this is so, he is discounting the future costs and benefits at the rate of 10 percent (discount rate). Suppose further, at this time some family friend of him comes and offer him Rs. 1000 for a year without charging any interest. He will, in fact, giving him Rs. 100 in year's time comprising grant element of the loan.

Thus, to estimate grant element implicit in loan components, one takes the schedule of annual repayments of principal and interest, discounts these repayments by the number of years before each instalment falls due, at one's chosen discount rate, and subtracts the sum of these discounted amounts from the face value. If the discount rate is 10 percent, any loan bearing interest rate less than 10 percent will have at least some grant element.

However, the choice of discount rate is a difficult problem, over which there has been much discussion among the economists. Earlier, the rate of 10 percent, adopted by the OECD, was used to estimate grant element. The main justification for this rate was that it was thought to be the rate at which developing countries would have to repay at that time, if they borrowed in the open market. Subsequently, the market rate of interest rose, which meant that the discount rate of 10 percent became too low, i.e., it understated the value of concessional terms to the recipients (White, 1974: p. 159). As a result, the OECD started using market-based discount rates to estimate grant element implicit in loans, since 1983.

As a matter of fact, choice of discount rate also depends upon the perspective of the estimation of grant element, that is, whether to estimate grant element from the angle of global market or from the angle of domestic local market for the recipient countries. In the former case, interest rate and the discount rate should be in the foreign currency terms, while in the latter case, the amount of loan and the stream of debt-service including the discount rate should be in local (Rupee, in case of India) denomination. For instance, in India, grant element inherent in foreign loans can be estimated from the global market angle by using the global market-based discount rates/Commercial Interest Reference Rates (CIRRs) notified by the Department of Economic Affairs, Ministry of Finance, Govt. of India. These rates are based on the OECD announcements and represent averages of CIRRs of different currencies during the preceding six months in a year. Similarly, grant element implicit in foreign loans can also be estimated by using the domestic market-based discount rates by constructing domestic market sensitive discount rates, which should reflect the alternative cost of borrowing an equivalent amount on similar terms and conditions from within the domestic economy.

In the present study, an endeavor has been made to estimate grant element inherent in the foreign loans utilized by India during the period 1980-81 to 2003-04, by using domestic market sensitive discount rates (given in Appendix 2.1) in view of the alternative cost of borrowing the same amount on similar terms and conditions from within the Indian economy, i.e., to verify whether it has been useful to borrow from abroad or not ? An attempt has also been made to analyze the impact of exchange rate variations on the estimation of grant element, i.e., grant element has been estimated both with and without incorporating average depreciation of Rupee against the foreign currencies in which loans have been sanctioned/utilized. Depreciation of Rupee *vis-a-vis* foreign currencies plays a crucial role in determining grant element inherent in foreign loans. Average rates of depreciation of Rupee in relation to foreign currencies during the fore-mentioned time period (given in Appendix 2.2) indicate the average increase in the interest payments on these foreign loans, during the said-period, sanctioned in foreign terms and conditions owing to the depreciation of local Rupee *vis-a-vis* foreign currencies. Hence, average rate of depreciation is added to the rate of interest to estimate the implicit grant element in local Rupee terms. Grant element may become negative if the sum of interest rate and average rate of depreciation along with their product term exceeds the discount rate.

The chapter has been divided into three sections. Section-I explains the estimation of grant element inherent in the multilateral loans utilized, during the above mentioned period, in India, while Section-II deals with the multilateral agencies, such as : the UNDP, UNICEF, WFP, WHO, Global Fund Organization and European Commission, etc., which have provided foreign aid in the form of outright grants to India during the said-period. In Section-III, outright grants obtained from the US-based two private philanthropic organizations have been discussed.

SECTION I

The results of estimated grant element implicit in the multilateral loans utilized (committed to, in case of loans not yet fully utilized) by India, from the multilateral agencies, such as : the WB (both IBRD and IDA), Asian Development Bank (ADB), International Fund for Agricultural Development (IFAD), the OPEC Fund, and the IMF Trust Fund during the period 1980-81 to 2003-04 have been discussed source-wise as follows:

1. GRANT ELEMENT IN THE WORLD BANK LOANS

The term 'The WB' and 'The Bank' refer to IBRD and IDA only. These have been the two 'windows' through which the WB makes loans to the developing countries. Legally these are two separate organizations, though in practice, both share a common staff, management structure, policies and rules.

1.1 IBRD Loans

IBRD, a parent body of 'the WB Group', established in December, 1945 started its program of economic assistance in June, 1946 extended loans on a near market rates of interest to the governments of middle-income countries and credit worthy low-income countries, using funds borrowed at commercial rates in the global capital markets. India has been a major and regular client of IBRD, since September 18, 1949 when it sanctioned a loan for the modernization and development of Indian Railways. So far, it has financed 195 development projects in India. Most of its assistance has been in the form of loans, of which more than 80 percent has been given to the public sector and the remainder to the private sector in India, as has been shown in Table 6.1. It has also given assistance to India in the form of outright grants amounting Swiss Francs 16.454 million (fully utilized) up to the end-March, 2004. It has also authorized Japanese Yen 2184.336 million; SDRs 3.8 million; and US $ 130.80 million in the form of outright grants, out of which Yen 1622.839 million (74.3 percent); SDRs 0.79 million (20.8 percent); and US $ 78.176 million (59.8 percent) have been utilized during the same period (Govt. of India[c], 2004: pp. 229-30). Besides this, IBRD has also been playing the role of coordinator of external assistance to India through the 'India Development Forum' (IDF), formerly known as 'Aid India Consortium', which meet annually to discuss and determine aid commitments by the multilateral development funding agencies and the bilateral donors. The WB (IDF) has given assistance in the form of outright grants amounting US $ 5.542 million and SDRs 13.9 million up to the end-March 2004, out of which US $ 4.463 million (80.5 percent) and SDRs 12.032 million (86.6 percent) have been utilized during the same period (*Ibid.*, p. 232).

During the period 1980-81 to 2003-04, IBRD has provided 163 semi-concessional loans to India which have been repayable over 20 years period (maturity) inclusive of a five year grace period at interest rates slightly higher than those 'the Bank' paid to borrow funds. The rate of interest on IBRD loans ranged between 8.25 to 11.6 percent per annum during the period 1980-85; 7.59 to 10.8 percent during the period 1985-90; 7.71 to 7.75 percent during 1990-95; 6.03 to 7.40 percent during the period 1995-2000; and 1.71 to 4.00 percent per annum during 2000-04. Recently (March, 2004), the rate of interest on IBRD loans was 1.59 percent per annum. India borrowed under single currency loans (in US $) on variable spread basis only (*Ibid.*, p. 75). These interest rates have been variable after every six months, since 1994.

The results of year-wise estimated grant element inherent in IBRD loans to India, both without and with depreciation of Rupee *vis-a-vis* US $, have been presented in Table 6.2. A perusal

TABLE 6.1

IBRD Loans to India (Million US$)

Period	*Public Sector*	*Private Sector*	*Total*
First Five Year Plan (1951-56)	67.23	52.91	120.14
Second Five Year Plan (1956-61)	335.71	211.26	546.97
Third Five Year Plan (1961-66)	142.76	130.62	273.38
Yearly Plans (1966-69)	—	25.64	25.64
Fourth Five Year Plan (1969-74)	38.95	158.08	197.03
Fifth Five Year Plan (1974-78)	515.84	408.82	924.66
Yearly Plans (1978-80)	162.77	—	162.77
Sixth Five Year Plan (1980-85)	3431.47	377.97	3809.44
Seventh Five Year Plan (1985-90)	5758.41	773.99	6532.40
Yearly Plan (1990-91)	675.84	243.44	919.28
Yearly Plan (1991-92)	733.97	644.99	1378.96
Eighth Five Year Plan (1992-97)	1417.47	877.71	2295.18
Ninth Five Year Plan (1997-02)	4037.01	775.73	4812.74
Tenth Five Year Plan (2002-04)	1904.00	—	1904.00
Grand Total	19221.43 (80.42%)	4681.16 (19.58%)	23902.59 (100%)

Source : Govt. of India, *External Assistance, 2003-04*, Ministry of Finance, Department of Economic Affairs; Aid, Accounts and Audit Division, pp. 187-97 and 267-72.

of the table indicates that grant element in IBRD loans remained positive for all the years except for 1981-82 and 1982-83, if depreciation of Rupee in relation to US $ is ignored. It ranged between the lowest level of 5.06 percent in 1980-81 to the maximum level of 60.7 percent in 2002-03, and on the whole, average grant element worked out to 39.42 percent without depreciation of Rupee. However, if depreciation of Rupee is incorporated, the overall average grant element in IBRD loans worked out to (–)3.27 percent during the period 1980-81 to 2003-04. It remained negative during the period 1980-81 to 1992-93. It ranged between 26.45 percent in 2001-02 to (–)88.99 percent in 1982-83. Thus, the results indicate that IBRD loans proved highly costly and did not constitute 'aid' if 25 percent grant element criteria of OECD definition of 'aid' is applied, when depreciation

Table 6.2
Grant Element in IBRD Loans

Year	*No. of Loans*	*Without Depreciation of Rupee against US $*		*With Depreciation of Rupee Against US $*		*Loan Amount*
		Percent	*Rs. Crore*	*Percent*	*Rs. Crore*	*Rs. Crore*
(1)	(2)	(3)	(4)	(5)	(6)	(7)
1980-81	4	5.06	21.53	-75.52	-321.32	425.48
1981-82	4	-7.49	-48.35	-85.66	-553.08	645.69
1982-83	6	-4.10	-40.57	-88.99	-879.67	988.50
1983-84	5	5.15	9.26	-71.26	-128.11	179.78
1984-85	8	10.74	176.01	-67.08	-1099.35	1638.87
1985-86	9	15.67	231.26	-56.94	-840.33	1475.81
1986-87	7	16.77	283.25	-55.07	-930.16	1689.05
1987-88	11	29.14	601.34	-42.67	-880.55	2063.63
1988-89	9	30.88	558.57	-40.86	-739.10	1808.85
1989-90	16	31.07	617.58	-40.00	-795.08	1987.70
1990-91	14	32.15	471.63	-37.44	-549.24	1466.98
1991-92	9	44.30*	1019.35	-16.09*	-370.23	2301.02

1992-93	4	43.48	725.75	-18.28	-305.12	1669.15
1993-94	5	34.79	709.05	12.34	251.50	2038.09
1994-95	8	34.37	531.87	11.82	182.91	1547.50
1995-96	4	43.74	337.49	22.54	173.92	771.59
1996-97	7	44.43	586.20	23.42	309.00	1319.39
1997-98	5	40.32	1202.63	17.29	515.71	2982.71
1998-99	4	39.87	1161.13	16.20	471.79	2912.30
1999-00	5	32.43	277.58	8.96	76.69	855.95
2000-01	7	47.70	3208.19	23.08	1552.30	6725.76
2001-02	6	53.04	4262.07	26.45	2125.41	8035.58
2002-03	3	60.70	3542.35	15.83	923.81	5835.83
2003-04	3	33.23	1065.56	0.75	24.05	3206.61
Overall Average for 163 Loans		39.42	21510.73	-3.27	-1784.25	54571.82

N.B. : (i) *Indicate one loan which has been excluded whose grant element is undefined.
(ii) Weighted average of grant element has been computed in years in which terms and conditions were different.
(iii) Grant element of loans since 1993-94 has been based on general terms and conditions.

Source : *(Basic Data):* Govt of India, *External Assistance,* (2003-04 and other issues); Ministry of Finance, Department of Economic Affairs; Aid, Accounts and Audit Division.

of Rupee is accounted for. These loans also proved costly than if the same could have been raised within the country on similar terms and conditions (ignoring negative effect on private investment).

1.2 IDA Loans

International Development Association established in 1960, as an affiliate of the WB, makes concessionary long-term loans to the governments of the world's poorest countries, though some small countries—mostly island countries, with somewhat higher income levels may also qualify. IDA, also known as 'soft lending agency' of 'the Bank', lends without charging interest (interest free loans) using funds provided entirely by the contributions by the member-countries, with a grace period of 10 years and principal repayments stretching thereafter over 20-30 years depending upon the situation. However, the borrower has to pay three-fourth of one-percent as service charge to IDA, which the WB uses to cover its administrative charges. There is no grace period for the service charge obligations, like interest payments.

IDA assistance to India began in June, 1961 and since then, has been an important component of her external assistance program. It has financed 269 development projects and the consolidated loan assistance amounted to US $ 26,047.35 million up to the end-March, 2004 (Govt. of India[c], 2004: pp. 75-77). This includes assistance in the form of non-project credits for industrial imports and credits for various sectors, like irrigation, agriculture, health and family welfare, and rural development, etc.

IDA credits to India up to end-June, 1987 were repayable in 50 years (maturity) inclusive of a grace period of 10 years and those approved from July 1, 1987 onwards were repayable in 35 years (maturity) including a moratorium of 10 years. Though IDA credits carried commitment charges of 0.5 percent per annum on the un-disbursed balance, yet these have been waived off by 'the Bank' from 1989-90 onwards (*Ibid.*, p. 75). The estimated grant element in 201 IDA loans committed/utilized during 1980-81 to 2003-04, both with and without average depreciation rate of Rupee in relation to SDRs, and US $ are amplified in Table 6.3. The table shows that grant element inherent in IDA loans remained positive throughout the period under consideration, if

TABLE 6.3

Grant Element in IDA Loans

Year	No. of Loans	Without Depreciation of Rupee against SDRs and US $		With Depreciation of Rupee against SDRs and US $		Loan Amount
		Percent	Rs. Crore	Percent	Rs. Crore	Rs. Crore
(1)	(2)	(3)	(4)	(5)	(6)	(7)
1980-81	19	83.59	1254.17	-24.82	-372.39	1500.38
1981-82	10	84.46	1020.66	-17.54	-211.96	1208.46
1982-83	9	85.15	623.76	-14.29	-104.68	732.54
1983-84	7	86.70	416.06	-6.76	-32.44	479.88
1984-85	11	87.54	745.83	-2.62	-22.32	851.99
1985-86	10	88.55	913.97	2.58	26.63	1032.15
1986-87	3	88.82	287.71	3.97	12.86	323.93
1987-88	8	88.73	1053.33	3.49	41.43	1187.12
1988-89	4	86.11	676.69	4.39	34.50	785.85
1989-90	6	86.40	964.60	5.50	61.40	1116.44
1990-91	8	87.01	1283.48	7.93	116.97	1475.10
1991-92	11	91.03	2547.74	25.27	707.25	2798.79

(Contd.)

Table 6.3 (Contd.)

(1)	(2)	(3)	(4)	(5)	(6)	(7)
1992-93	10	90.51	2963.78	22.85	748.23	3274.53
1993-94	9	87.88	1764.83	60.21	1209.15	2008.23
1994-95	7	87.75	3053.58	59.89	2084.09	3479.86
1995-96	7	89.59	2712.08	63.91	1934.69	3027.21
1996-97	9	89.82	3183.17	64.42	2283.01	3539.50
1997-98	8	87.03	2796.96	58.39	1876.53	3213.79
1998-99	8	86.03	3032.32	56.32	1985.13	3524.73
1999-00	5	86.34	3020.76	56.95	1992.50	3498.68
2000-01	10	84.46	3487.78	53.11	2193.18	4129.50
2001-02	10	80.76	3481.26	45.90	1978.57	4303.31
2002-03	7	72.76	3875.80	31.17	1660.37	5326.83
2003-04	5	65.86	2165.77	19.11	628.42	3288.44
Overall Average for 201 Loans		84.35	47326.09	37.13	20831.12	56107.24

N.B. : Weighted average of grant element has been taken in years in which terms and conditions of loans were different.

Source : *(Basic Data)*: Govt of India, *External Assistance*, (2003-04 and other issues); Ministry of Finance, Department of Economic Affairs; Aid, Accounts and Audit Division.

depreciation of Rupee *vis-a-vis* SDRs and US $ is ignored, and ranged between the lowest level of 65.86 percent in 2003-04 and the highest level of 91.03 percent in 1991-92. The overall average grant element during the period 1980-2004 has been worked out as 84.35 percent. However, if average rate of depreciation of Rupee is added to the interest rate (service charges) on IDA loans, grant element became negative during the period 1980-81 to 1984-85, but was positive for the remaining years up to 2003-04. This grant element ranged between the lowest level of (–)24.82 percent in 1980-81 to the highest proportion of 64.42 percent in 1996-97. Even the overall average grant element during the period 1980-2004 worked out to 37.13 percent. This indicates that IDA loans to India proved quite concessional during the above-mentioned period. Besides these loans, IDA has also given assistance in the form of outright grants amounting to Swiss Francs 6 million; Japanese Yen 144.477 million; Dutch Guilder 0.8 million; US $ 53.428 million; and SDRs 18.5 million to India up to end-March 2004, out of which Swiss Francs 3.76 million (62.6 percent); Japanese Yen 133.167 million (92.2 percent); Dutch Guilder 0.08 million (100 percent); US $ 32.510 million (60.8 percent); and SDRs 2.771 (15 percent) have been utilized during the same period (*Ibid*., pp. 230-31).

Thus, IDA loans proved highly concessional in contrast to IBRD loans, mainly due to the soft terms and conditions. IDA loans were almost interest free (except 0.75 percent per annum service charges) and that is why it is called as the 'soft loan window' of the WB, while IBRD charge near market rate of interest and is consequently known as the 'hard loan window' of the WB.

2. GRANT ELEMENT IN ADB LOANS

Asian Development Bank, headquartered in Manila, the Philippines, is another multilateral development funding institution established in December, 1966. Its stock is owned by 58 members, 42 of which are from the Asia and Pacific region. India is one of its founder members, and her subscription to its capital stock is the fourth largest of all the member-countries after Japan, USA and China.

Although eligible to borrow under the criteria laid down by ADB, India voluntarily refrained from borrowing initially.

However, in order to broad base country's resources, India decided to borrow from ADB in 1986. The first ever ADB loan to India was sanctioned on May 2, 1986 to the ICICI amounting to US $ 98.788 million. Since then, ADB has approved 78 loans (for the public sector projects) amounting to US $ 12.911 billion, of which four were cancelled without signing, two were cancelled before effectiveness, three were discontinued after signing, 42 have been closed and 27 were going on. The ongoing loans have a net loan amount of US $ 5.433 billion. ADB has also approved technical assistance of US $ 102 million to India as on December 31, 2003 (Govt. of India[c], 2004: p. 83). Besides this, ADB has also authorized outright grants amounting to US $ 50 million to India up to end-March 2004, out of which US $ 25 million (50 percent) have been utilized during the same period (*Ibid*., p. 222).

During the period 1986-87 to 2003-04, India utilized 64 ADB committed loans, which have been repayable over a period ranging between 24 to 25 years (maturity) including a moratorium of four to five years. Only a single loan with a maturity of 23 years inclusive of a grace period of three years was sanctioned in 1987-88. However, since 2002, maturity of loans has been reduced to the period ranging between 12 to 20 years including a grace period of three to five years. The rate of interest on ADB loans committed for/utilized on the public sector projects ranged between 6.53 to 6.58 percent and for private sector projects between 9.5 to 9.65 percent per annum during the period 1986-93. Since 1993, it ranged between 5.69 to 6.875 percent per annum for all the projects and was variable after every six months. The estimated grant element inherent in these 64 ADB loans, both without and with average depreciation of Rupee *vis-a-vis* US $, has been given in Table 6.4. The table shows that grant element remained positive during the above-mentioned period and fluctuatingly declined from 28.59 percent in 1986-87 to 6.79 percent in 2003-04, if depreciation of Rupee in relation to US $ is ignored. It ranged between the maximum level of 52.26 percent in 1991-92 to the lowest level of 6.79 percent in 2003-04 and the overall average for the above period has been worked out 32.64 percent. However, if average rate of depreciation of Rupee is incorporated, grant element for most of the years as well as the overall average (–)0.81 became negative for the period 1986-2004. Grant element ranged between the lowest level of (–)43.66 percent

Table 6.4
Grant Element in ADB Loans

Year	No. of Loans	Without Depreciation of Rupee against US $		With Depreciation of Rupee Against US $		Loan Amount
		Percent	Rs. Crore	Percent	Rs. Crore	Rs. Crore
(1)	(2)	(3)	(4)	(5)	(6)	(7)
1986-87	2	28.59	76.91	-43.66	-117.44	269.00
1987-88	3	36.63	152.23	-40.20	-167.07	415.60
1988-89	4	38.33	254.33	-35.42	-235.02	663.52
1989-90	2	38.21	179.63	-32.70	-153.73	470.12
1990-91	3	37.38	213.70	-34.15	-195.23	571.70
1991-92	2	52.26*	485.43	-10.66*	-99.02	928.87
1992-93	4	50.70	1284.18	-13.73	-347.77	2532.90
1993-94	1	43.71	329.24	20.08	151.25	753.23
1994-95	3	43.23	729.56	19.58	330.44	1687.62
1995-96	1	51.31	427.54	29.13	242.73	833.25
1996-97	4	51.94	1110.59	29.97	640.82	2138.22

(Contd.)

TABLE 6.4 (Contd.)

(1)	(2)	(3)	(4)	(5)	(6)	(7)
1997-98	6	39.37	894.63	15.06	342.22	2272.37
1998-99	3	39.13	242.03	14.87	91.97	618.52
1999-00	2	38.53	839.18	14.49	315.59	2178.00
2000-01	7	33.01	1647.89	7.72	385.39	4992.10
2001-02	7	28.30	1738.17	Zero	Zero	6141.93
2002-03	6	12.07	461.41	-17.03	-651.02	3822.81
2003-04	4	6.79	224.59	-24.62	-814.35	3307.68
Overall Average for 64 Loans		32.64	11291.24	-0.81	-280.24	34597.44

N.B. : (i) * Two loans whose grant element is undefined are not included.
(ii) Weighted average of grant element has been calculated where terms and conditions of loans were different in a year.
(iii) Average of terms and conditions is used where these have been given in the form of range.

Source : *(Basic Data):* Govt of India, *External Assistance,* (2003-04 and other issues); Ministry of Finance, Department of Economic Affairs; Aid, Accounts and Audit Division.

in 1986-87 to the highest level of 29.97 percent in 1996-97. It was zero in the year 2001-02. Thus, ADB loans like IBRD loans also proved costly to India during the above-mentioned period, owing mainly to the exchange rate depreciation of Rupee, than if the same could have been raised domestically within India.

3. GRANT ELEMENT IN IFAD LOANS

International Fund For Agricultural Development came into existence on December 2, 1977 on the recommendation of the 'World Food Conference' which advocated the setting up of an institution to finance agricultural development projects, primarily for the expansion of food production, in the developing countries. The recommendation was endorsed by the UN General Assembly and the Fund was set-up as the 13th specialized agency of the UN, with headquarters in Rome. Presently, 163 countries are members of the Fund which are grouped into three lists. List-A comprises developed countries; List-B Oil producing countries; and List-C developing countries. Within List-C, sub-list C-I comprises Africa; C-II Europe, Asia and the Pacific; and C-III Latin America and the Caribbean. India has been one of the original members of the Fund and is the largest contributor with an amount of US $ 26 million towards its resources.

IFAD loans are repayable over a period of 50 years (maturity) including a moratorium of 10 years and carry no interest charges. However, a service charge at the rate of three-fourths of one percent (0.75%) per annum is levied on loan amount withdrawn and outstanding. Up to end-March 2004, 10 projects with assistance from the Fund amounting to US $288.16 million have been implemented and presently, eight projects with a total assistance of US $169.81 million are under implementation (Govt of India[c], 2004: p. 79). IFAD has also provided outright grants amounting to US $7.29 million to India for two projects up to the end-March 2004, out of which US $1.506 million (20.7 percent) have been utilized during the same period (*Ibid.*, 232).

The estimated grant element of 16 IFAD loans committed to/ utilized by India during the period 1980-81 to 2003-04 has been outlined in Table 6.5. A glance at the table indicates that IFAD loans proved highly concessional having the overall average grant element of 84.26 percent, if depreciation of Rupee *vis-a-vis* SDRs and US $ is neglected. These also proved, on the whole, quite concessional with average grant element of 41.27 percent, if

TABLE 6.5
Grant Element in IFAD Loans

Year	No. of Loans	Without Depreciation of Rupee against SDRs and US $		With Depreciation of Rupee against SDRs and US $		Loan Amount
		Percent	Rs. Crore	Percent	Rs. Crore	Rs. Crore
(1)	(2)	(3)	(4)	(5)	(6)	(7)
1980-81	1	81.26	11.04	-23.90	-3.25	13.59
1982-83	1	82.96	19.62	-16.48	-3.90	23.65
1983-84	1	84.65	26.67	-8.82	-2.78	31.51
1987-88	1	86.86	13.78	1.65	0.26	15.87
1989-90	1	87.30	25.21	3.82	1.10	28.88
1991-92	1	91.16	39.50	24.21	10.49	43.33
1994-95	1	88.42	76.77	59.81	51.93	86.83
1995-96	2	89.96	130.03	63.59	91.91	144.54
1996-97	1	90.16	61.01	64.25	43.48	67.67
1997-98	1	87.83	73.66	58.33	48.92	83.87
1999-00	1	89.09	88.72	58.77	58.52	99.58
2001-02	2	84.75	144.40	48.18	82.09	170.38
2003-04	2	72.22	168.71	22.19	51.84	233.60
Overall Average	for 16 Loans	84.26	879.12	41.27	430.61	1043.30

N.B. : Weighted average of grant element has been taken where terms and conditions of loans were different in a year.
Source : *(Basic Data)*: Govt of India, *External Assistance*, (2003-04 and other issues); Ministry of Finance, Department of Economic Affairs; Aid, Accounts and Audit Division.

depreciation of Rupee is accounted for, though in the initial years grant element was negative. Thus, IFAD loans like IDA loans proved quite concessional to India despite depreciation of Rupee in relation to SDRs and US $ during the above-mentioned period.

4. GRANT ELEMENT IN THE OPEC FUND LOANS

'The OPEC Fund for International Development' (earlier known as the 'OPEC Special Fund') is another multilateral agency for financial cooperation and assistance, which has provided assistance to India in the form of loans only, during the period 1980-81 to 2003-04. It has been established by the OPEC member-countries and endowed by them within international legal personality. The main objective of the fund is to reinforce financial cooperation between the OPEC member countries and the other developing countries by providing financial support to assist them in their socio-economic developmental efforts. The Fund does this by providing loans for the BOP support, and for the implementation of developmental projects and programs. The Fund also provides finance for technical assistance activities.

The Fund loans, during the above mentioned period, have been repayable over a period ranging between 14 to 22 years (maturity) including a grace period ranging between four to five years, carrying interest rate charges between 0.75 percent to four percent per annum. So far, the Fund has extended 14 loans to India amounting US $ 218.80 million till the end-March 2003, out of which US $ 206.592 million have been utilized up to end-March, 2004. The first ever OPEC Fund loan to India was for BOP support in 1977 amounting to US $ 21.80 million and the subsequent 13 loans for various development projects. Last loan of US $ 10 million was sanctioned for Shimla sewerage project on August 21, 1997 (Govt. of India[c], 2004: pp. 53 and 161).

The worked out grant element in 11 OPEC Fund loans utilized by India during the above-mentioned period, both without and with average depreciation rate of Rupee *vis-a-vis* US $, are given in Table 6.6. The table shows that these grant elements have been positive in all the years, if depreciation of Rupee is ignored. The overall average grant element worked out to be 61.64 percent, i.e., the loans seems to be highly concessional. However, if average depreciation of Rupee is included in the interest rate charged on the utilized loans, the overall average grant element becomes slightly negative (–0.28 percent). It has

Table 6.6
Grant Element in OPEC Fund Loans

Year	*No. of Loans*	*Without Depreciation of Rupee against US $*		*With Depreciation of Rupee Against US $*		*Loan Amount*
		Percent	*Rs. Crore*	*Percent*	*Rs. Crore*	*Rs. Crore*
(1)	(2)	(3)	(4)	(5)	(6)	(7)
1980-81	2	59.51	23.68	-18.89	-7.52	39.80
1982-83	1	65.06	18.38	-14.47	-4.09	28.25
1983-84	1	39.85	9.33	-25.21	-5.90	23.42
1987-88	2	65.55	11.41	-8.13	-1.41	17.41
1988-89	1	67.07	9.76	-0.97	-0.14	14.56
1990-91	1	68.53	7.22	2.02	0.21	10.54
1991-92	2	70.98	17.54	12.63	3.12	24.71
1997-98	1	62.96	23.36	40.94	15.19	37.10
Overall Average for 11 Loans		61.64	120.68	-0.28	-0.54	195.79

Source : *(Basic Data)*: Govt of India, *External Assistance*, (2003-04 and other issues); Ministry of Finance, Department of Economic Affairs; Aid, Accounts and Audit Division.

also been negative for most of the years, and ranged between the lowest level of (–)25.21 percent in 1983-84 and the maximum of 40.94 percent in 1997-98. Thus, on the whole, the 11 loans extended by the OPEC Fund also proved non-concessional to India when the exchange rate depreciation of Rupee is incorporated.

5. GRANT ELEMENT IN THE IMF TRUST FUND LOAN

'The Trust Fund', administered by the IMF Washington, had extended only a single loan to India in 1980 in US $ equivalent to SDRs 529.009 million to provide BOP assistance. The loan which was repayable in ten equal semi-annual instalments, beginning not later than the end of the first six months of the sixth year, has already been repaid in full. Interest on the outstanding loan shall be paid semi-annually at the rate of one half of the one percent per annum on 30th June and 31st December, each year.

The grant element implicit in single Trust Fund loan, both without and with exchange rate depreciation of Rupee in relation to SDRs, is given in Table 6.7. The Table 6.7 shows that this single loan extended by the IMF Trust Fund proved concessional (grant element 48.79 percent) if depreciation of Rupee *vis-a-vis* SDRs is ignored and proved non-concessional (grant element –13.75 percent) otherwise.

On the whole, multilateral loans extended by the IBRD, ADB, OPEC Fund and the IMF Trust Fund proved non-concessional, if exchange rate variations in Rupee *vis-a-vis* foreign currencies are incorporated, during the period 1980-81 to 2003-04, as their overall average grant element worked out to be negative, which means the loans extended by these institutions proved quite costlier. However, the loans given by the IDA and IFAD proved quite concessional despite the exchange rate depreciation of Rupee during the same period.

Section II

1. UNITED NATIONS DEVELOPMENT PROGRAMME

UNDP is the largest multilateral source of development cooperation under the UN system with the overall mission of

Table 6.7
Grant Element in IMF Trust Fund Loan

Year	*No. of Loans*	*Without Depreciation of Rupee against SDRs and US $*		*With Depreciation of Rupee against SDRs and US $*		*Loan Amount*
		Percent	*Rs. Crore*	*Percent*	*Rs. Crore*	*Rs. Crore*
(1)	*(2)*	*(3)*	*(4)*	*(5)*	*(6)*	*(7)*
1980-81	1	48.79	262.75	-13.75	-74.05	538.53

Source : *(Basic Data)*: Govt. of India, *External Assistance*, (2003-04 and other issues); Ministry of Finance, Department of Economic Affairs; Aid, Accounts and Audit Division.

sustainable human development with high priority to poverty alleviation, gender equity and women's empowerment, and environmental protection. The programme has been funded by the voluntary contributions from the various donor countries. The genesis of UNDP dates back to 1949 when the 'Expanded Programme to Technical Assistance' (EPTA) was established as a channel for the transfer of technical knowledge and skills to the newly emerging countries. Subsequently, in 1958 the UN General Assembly instituted the 'Special Fund' (SF) which took up larger and more complex projects for the transfer of technology. In 1965, EPTA and SF were merged, and subsequently UNDP came into being on January 1, 1966. India has been the largest single contributor to its core resources from amongst the developing countries.

UNDP used to follow a global 'Indicative Planning Figure' (IPF) cycle for the purpose of allocating precise and exact quantum of assistance to the recipient countries. An IPF is nothing but a magnitude of resources expected to be made available from UNDP to a given country during a prescribed period of five calendar years. India's IPF for the various cycles have been given in Table 6.8.

TABLE 6.8
IPF Cycles of India from UNDP

IPF Cycle	*Assistance (US $ million)*
I. 1972-76	50.0
II. 1977-81	97.0
III. 1982-86	138.6
IV. 1987-91	156.1
V. 1992-96	109.3
VI. 1997-2002	135.0

Source : Govt of India, *External Assistance*, 1998-99; Ministry of Finance, Department of Economic Affairs; Aid, Accounts and Audit Division, p. 59.

India has been the third largest beneficiary of UNDP assistance after China and Bangladesh during the Vth programme cycle (Govt. of India[c], 2003: p.55). However, now its approach has been shifted, as per the new UN mandate, to 'sustainable human development' and from projects to programmes. Instead of several scattered projects across the country, it now concentrates on a few programmes. It now canalizes its development assistance through the five year 'Country Cooperation Framework' (CCF). The first CCF ran from 1997-2002 in synchronization with India's 'Ninth Five Year Plan'. The main thematic areas of the CCF-I were: (a) employment and sustainable livelihoods, (b) access to basic services, (c) management of development, and (d) sustainable development. Under CCF-I, 16 mutually reinforcing programmes were sanctioned in the said thematic areas involving revised allocation of US $ 93.394 million (Govt. of India[c], 2004: p. 55).

The Second CCF synchronized with India's 'Tenth Five Year Plan' (2002-07) have two cross-cutting themes of gender equality and strengthening of decentralization. The main thematic areas of CCF-II were: (a) promoting human development and gender equality, (b) capacity building for decentralization, (c) poverty eradication and sustainable livelihoods, and (d) vulnerability reduction and environmental sustainability. The total resource base of this programme was around US $ 200 million. Presently (2004), there are 10 on-going projects with UNDP assistance for various development activities in the North-Eastern Region, such as: Cane and Bamboo, Community Based Solar Energy, Non-Mulberry Silk, Integrated Development of Spice Industry, National Bio-Diversity and Action, Capacity Building for Panchayati Raj Institutions, Preparation of State Level Human Development Reports, and Sector Based Initiatives in Khadi, Village and Small Industries.

UNDP has authorized outright grants amounting Rs. 43.83 crore (fully utilized) and US $ 75.084 million up to end-March 2004, out of which US $ 42.653 million (56.8 percent) have been utilized by India during the same period (*Ibid.*, pp. 239-40).

1.1 United Nations International Children's Emergency Fund

UNICEF is a special organization of the UN created to help the children all over the world, after WW-II. In India, since 1949, it has supported programmes for improvement of the status of women and children. The major themes of its cooperation with Govt. of India have been health, education, safe drinking water and nutrition. The specific projects which received special attention were integrated child development services, immunization, oral dehydration therapy and safe drinking water.

UNICEF's current programme cycle for India covers the period 2003-07 with a budget allocation of US $ 400,394 from its own regular resources and other resources subject to the availability of funds, to support the activities in the following areas:

(i) early child development through a focus on children below three years of age, and with special attention to early learning and care, low birth weight and malnutrition, sanitation and hygiene, routine immunization and safe motherhood interventions;
(ii) promotion of universal elementary education, particularly for girls, by concentrating on girls from difficult backgrounds including scheduled castes and tribes by mobilizing community involvement in schools;
(iii) protection of children vulnerable to labor, trafficking and sexual exploitation as well as promoting an enabling environment for addressing protection issues;
(iv) prevention of HIV/AIDS among children through imparting life skills to young people, scaling up national efforts in the prevention of mother-to-child transmission and advocating community-based actions to respond to those affected by HIV/AIDS; and
(v) emergency preparedness and response to reduce vulnerabilities, and support the continuity of sector interventions.

During the calendar year 2003, UNICEF provided assistance totalling US $ 94.7 million to the Country Programme of Cooperation as against US $ 80 million in 2002. UNICEF is also actively working with the Govt. of India and other partners, such as : WHO and Rotary, to eradicate polio, with special focus on UP and Bihar. In 2004, UNICEF continued to support the Govt. of India's Polio Eradication Programme through the procurement of 1.4 billion doses of oral polio vaccine, at an anticipated cost of

US $ 149.4 million (Govt. of India[c], 2004: p. 57). UNICEF authorized US $ 0.364 million in the form of outright grants up to end-March 2004 to India, out of which US $ 0.329 million (90.4 percent) have been utilized during the same period (*Ibid.*, p. 241).

1.2 World Food Programme

WFP assisted the Govt. of India, through the donation of food aid, in the socio-economic development projects such as : supplementary nutrition, reclamation of land and resettlement of communities, canal construction, forestry and rural development, etc. The sale of WFP food at concessional rates to the workers in a wide range of development projects increases their real wages and the food available to them, while generating additional funds for the development of socio-economic infrastructure in the project areas. The Programme also provided assistance to natural calamities such as : floods in Assam and Madhya Pradesh, super cyclone in Orissa, and earthquake in Gujarat.

Under WFP, since the inception of its first project in India in the year 1963, over a billion US $ have been provided to the country in the form of food and developmental assistance. The WFP-India implements its projects through five year Country Programme (CP) cycle keeping the inputs of the Five Year Plan of the Govt. of India. The current CP (2003-08), consistent with the Tenth Five Year Plan, focuses on assisting the Govt. to improve its food-based programme by creating replicable models to overcome the issue of food insecurity within the country, nutrition, and education for girls along with asset creation in the regions with high levels of food insecurity and low levels of human development. The current CP has two major goals:

(i) to play a catalytic role in the country's efforts to reduce vulnerability, and eliminate hunger and food insecurity among the targeted hungry poor, especially the children and women, and
(ii) to promote, and demonstrate models that provide immediate and longer-term food security in the most food insecure districts in the least developed states of the country.

The activities under the current CP include improving the nutritional status of children and women (support to the Integrated Child Development Services); investing in the human development with special emphasis on girls (food for education); and improving food security through disaster mitigation, and the preservation and creation of assets (food for work). The WFP has authorized Rs. 0.141 crore to India in the form of outright grants up to end-March 2004, out of which Rs. 0.113 crore (80.14 percent) have been utilized during the same period (Govt. of India[c], 2004: p. 245).

1.3 World Health Organization

WHO, also an important part of the UN family, has made significant inputs in providing technical assistance to the Govt. of India in its implementation of National Health Programmes to consolidate the gains in health development. A lot of ground has been covered and the country is marching steadily towards its goal of 'health for all' with renewed commitment to fulfil the aspirations of the people for a healthier and better life. WHO has mobilized considerable resources in support of health development activities in India. During 2002-03, US $ 58.60 million comprising US $ 47.2 million from extra budgetary sources, and US $ 11.4 million from regular budget has been received and disbursed (Govt. of India[c], 2004: p. 61) for the various projects and programmes such as : National Polio Surveillance Project; Revised National Tuberculosis Control Programme; Leprosy Elimination; Roll Back Malaria; Tobacco Free Initiative; Lymphatic Filariasis; Health Internet Work; and National Surveillance Programme for Communicable Diseases, etc.

Significant achievements have been made for capacity strengthening at all levels for disease surveillance and response, especially in the areas of epidemic prone diseases, vector borne diseases (dengue, JE), water borne diseases (Cholera, ADD), zoonotic diseases (Plague), and diseases nearing eradication (Leprosy, Kala Azar, Lymphatic filariasis and yaws) thereby reducing the mortality and morbidity due to these diseases. Similarly, surveillance for common risk factors is being piloted in five regions of the country for non-communicable diseases, like cancer, cardiovascular diseases, diabetic mellitus and chronic lung diseases, etc. WHO has authorized Rs. 0.06 crore to India as outright grants up to end-March 2004, out of which Rs. 0.015 crore (25 percent) have been utilized during the same period (*Ibid.*, p. 245).

2. GLOBAL FUND ORGANIZATION

'The Global Fund to fight AIDS, Tuberculosis and Malaria', having secretariat in Geneva (Switzerland), is an independent public-private partnership organization to provide funds in the form of outright grants to fight these diseases in various countries in need. Its grants are managed by the WB as its trustee, which makes disbursement from the Trust Fund upon written instructions of the Fund. The Fund has sanctioned US $ 53.67 million to India in the form of four grant agreements during the year 2003-04 for the prevention and treatment of above mentioned diseases (Govt. of India[c], 2004 : p. 79), out of which India has utilized nothing up to end-March, 2004 (*Ibid.*, p. 228).

3. EUROPEAN COMMISSION

The EC has been providing economic assistance to India since 1976, entirely in the form of outright grants, which has been used to finance both the Rupee as well as foreign exchange costs of the identified projects in the sectors like : watershed management, irrigation, forestry, health and education. Presently (2004), there are two ongoing sector development programmes: one in the health sector (Sector Investment Programme) with a total contribution of € 240 million (approximately Rs. 1250 crore) and the other in the education sector (Sarva Shiksha Abhiyan) with total contribution of € 200 million (approximately Rs. 1040 crore), (Govt. of India[c], 2004: p. 51). The EC has authorized outright grants amounting to € 1380.145 million up to end-March 2004 to India, out of which € 918.315 million (66.54 percent) have been utilized during the same period (*Ibid.*, pp. 225-26). Currently EC is also in the process of shifting its development strategy from project-based and sector-wise approach towards a 'partnership' with two Indian states viz: Chhattisgarh and Rajasthan, chosen with the concurrence of Govt. of India, covering the sectors of health, education and environment. For this purpose, an Indo-EC memorandum of understanding has been signed in February, 2004 under the 'National Indicative Programme for India 2004-2006' for an outright grant of € 160 million. This amount is an indicative financial envelope from EC for the project (*Ibid.*, p. 51).

4. INTERNATIONAL DEVELOPMENT RESEARCH CENTRE

IDRC of Canada also extends outright grant assistance to various government and non-government organizations for projects in the field of agriculture, food, health and family welfare, etc. It has cleared 36 proposals involving grant assistance of CAN $ 16.562 million to India up to end-March 2004 (Govt. of India[a], 2004: p. 43).

Besides these above mentioned organizations, some other UN agencies like : UN-FAO, UN Development Fund for Women, Universal Postal Union etc., have also provided assistance to India in the form of outright grants, although the amount has been quite nominal, up to the period ending-March 2004.

SECTION III

1. THE FORD FOUNDATION

The US-based philanthropic foundation was established in 1936, in the state of Michigan, as a private, non-profit charitable, and tax exempt institution with gifts and bequests from Henry Ford, an automobile manufacturer, and his son Edsel B. Ford. It is a private independent agency with no political and commercial purpose, and is not affiliated with any religious group. Its chief concerns have been international affairs (particularly population control and alleviation of the food shortages); improving communications (especially, public television); humanities and the arts; and in the later years, resources and the environment (The New Encyclopaedia Britannica, 1997, Vol. 4 : p. 877). The main objective has been to receive and administer funds for scientific, educational, and charitable purposes, all for the public welfare. Normally, it does not assist purely personal or local needs, the routine operating costs of an institution or maintenance or construction of buildings. It has been providing assistance to the developing countries in South and South-East

Asia, Africa, Middle-East, Latin America and the Caribbean region. India was the first country, outside the USA, to invite and receive Foundation's assistance in the early autumn of 1951.

The Foundation accepted the invitation of the Govt. of India, and the first grant in 'Overseas Development Programme' was made to the Ministry of Food and Agriculture, in December 1951. Since then, it has provided cash grants on a generous scale, from year to year, for a wide range of development programmes both in the public and private sectors of the Indian economy. It has concentrated largely on assisting the public sector projects with financial assistance, nearly all of which were a part of or closely related to India's Five Year Plans. The assistance was given, generally, to finance the services of foreign experts, specialists and consultants, import of tools, equipment, and literature, etc. The Foundation has also given substantial outright grants to the various departments of the Union and State Governments, public and semi-public institutions including social and educational establishments, for a number of welfare programmes, mainly confined to the development of rural areas with special emphasis on the training of rural workers, industrial training and development, management training, education and culture, economic and social research, urban planning, family planning, and strengthening of public administration, etc.

The total institutional assistance received from the Ford Foundation, since its inception in India, up to end-March 1983 was US $ 142.89 million, when its activities were ceased (Govt. of India[c], 1999: p. 79). However, the Foundation has restarted its activities again, in the year 1998-99, by providing an outright grant amounting to US $ 0.073 million as support for participation in the International Film Festival and related seminars (*Ibid.*, p. 79). The Foundation has, since then, provided outright grants to India amounting to US $ 0.267 million which have been fully utilized up to the end-March, 2004, the details of which have been given in Table 6.9.

Similarly, 90 project proposals involving total grants of US $ 12.52 million have been cleared in 2003-04 (up to end-March 2004) as compared to 119 proposals involving total grant of US $ 17.77 million in 2002-03 (Govt. of India[a], 2004: p. 43).

TABLE 6.9

Ford Foundation's Authorized (and Utilized) Assistance to India up to end-March 2004

Government Grant	*Amount US $ (million)*
(i) Citizens charter, and Post Forums in Delhi and Pune	0.050
(ii) Film Festival of India	0.144
(iii) Film Festival of India–I	0.073
Total	0.267

Source : Govt of India, *External Assistance,* 2003-04; Ministry of Finance, Department of Economic Affairs; Aid, Accounts and Audit Division, p. 226.

In brief, the Ford Foundation has contributed towards building up number of major scientific and technical institutes, such as : University of Agricultural Sciences, Bangalore; Birla Institute of Technology, Pilani; Indian Institute of Science, Bangalore; Planning Commission, New Delhi; Universities of Rajasthan, Kerala, and Delhi etc. All the Foundation's grants were meant for training, teaching and research.

2. THE ROCKEFELLER FOUNDATION

Another US-based private philanthropic institution has been established by John Davison Rockefeller, Jr. (1874-1960) in association with his father John D. Rockefeller Sr. (1839-1937), for promoting the welfare of mankind throughout the global universe, in 1913 in the New York city (The New Encyclopaedia Britannica, 1997, Vol. 10 : p. 123). Its valuable assistance programme has been mainly concerned with the extension and application of knowledge in certain specific areas of medical education, public health, agriculture, humanities and social sciences, generally in the form of post-doctoral fellowships and travel grants to the training personnel, and grants-in-aid to the institutions.

The Rockefeller Foundation began its operating activities in India in 1920 with hook-worm studies and control measures in

Madras Presidency (now Tamilnadu). Specific projects have been assisted from time to time for the study, and control of hook-worm and malaria, development of rural health, and research in various diseases and population studies, besides giving grants-in-aid to various medical colleges. It also contributed towards the building and equipment of All India Institute of Hygiene, Calcutta; Virus Research Centre at Poona; and Indian Agricultural Institute at New Delhi. Books and equipment valued at US $ 1,25,000 (about Rs. 6 lakh) were supplied to the Central Rice Research Station at Poona during 1960-63. The Foundation also helped the All India Institute of Medical Sciences, New Delhi in the acquisition of teaching and research equipment for pre-clinical and clinical departments, and the India International Centre, New Delhi for meeting the capital costs and recurring operative costs, etc. Moreover, the Foundation rendered active support in setting up the Indian Council for Medical Research at Bangalore and Agricultural Development Programme in the country.

However, the activities of the Rockefeller Foundation in India were terminated by the Govt. of India with effect from end-March, 1976. The total amount of outright grants made available by the Foundation, up to the above mentioned period, in various fields was US $ 21.49 million (Govt. of India[c], 1999: p. 79). The Foundation has again been allowed to operate in India in the year 1998-99, when 16 project proposals involving a total grant of US $ 0.62 million were cleared, while during 1999-2000, nine project proposals worth US $ 1.980 million were cleared by the Govt. of India (Govt. of India[a], 2001: p. 49).

Thus, the foreign aid given by these two Foundations in the form of outright grants has been proved of considerable significance to the Indian economy in various fields.

7

Foreign Aid to India : Grant Element in Bilateral Assistance

India also received development assistance from the various friendly donor countries under bilateral arrangements. In this chapter, an attempt has been made to estimate the 'grant element' inherent in these bilateral loans sanctioned to India, since 1980. The chapter has been divided into three sections. Section-I deals with the estimation of grant element implicit in the loans obtained from such major donor G-8 countries from which India decided to continue accepting bilateral assistance after the revised bilateral development cooperation policy of September, 2004. Grant element inherent in the loans granted by the other bilateral sources from which India has decided not to accept any further bilateral development assistance at government to government level, since February 2003, have been explained in Section-II. In Section-III, a comparison of grant element inherent in loans received from all the sources, both bilateral as well as multilateral, has been made.

Section I

The G-8 countries from which India would continue accepting bilateral assistance at government to government level under the revised bilateral development cooperation policy of September, 2004 include: Japan, Germany, USA, UK, France, Italy, Canada and Russian Federation. Grant element in case of the assistance received from these countries has been discussed below:

1. GRANT ELEMENT IN JAPANESE AID

Japanese aid has become the primary external source of funds for development in the developing countries, especially in Asia and Africa, since it overtook the US in 1989 (Iqbal, 1991: p. 5). It has been, by far, the single largest contributor to India among all the bilateral sources. Japanese aid to India started in a modest way in 1951, when Govt. of India entered into discussion with the Japanese mission on the possibilities of developing small scale industries in India. Japanese Govt. agreed to provide technical assistance to this vital Indian sector (Sharma, 1977: p. 51). However, Japanese financial assistance of Indian development programme has been coming since February 2, 1958 when it sanctioned loans to the Govt. of India and Shipping Corporation of India. Initially, it was channalized through government owned 'Export-Import Bank of Japan' (J-EXIM). During 1975-76, it was channeled through 'Overseas Economic Cooperation Fund' (OECF) of Japan. From 1976-77 onwards, both the project and commodity aid was being channalized through the OECF. Since October 1, 1999 J-EXIM and OECF have been merged, and a new agency 'Japan Bank for International Cooperation' (JBIC) has been established as a channel for both the ODA operations as well as the international economic operations of the Govt. of Japan.

The cumulative Japanese ODA loan to India reached Yen 2035.81 billion (i.e., about Rs. 85,504 crore at current exchange rate of 100 Yen = Rs. 42) on commitment basis up to end-March 2004, out of which Yen 1849.67 billion (90.86 percent) have been given through the Govt. of India budget for public sector projects and the remaining Yen 186.140 billion for non-government projects (Govt. of India[c], 2004: pp. 153 and 261).

Japanese aid has mainly been provided in terms of soft loans with repayment spread over 30 years (maturity) including a moratorium of 10 years, carrying an interest rate ranging between 2.5 to 4.5 percent per annum during the period 1980-90; 2.5 to 2.6 percent per annum during 1990-98; and 0.75 to 1.8 percent per annum during 1999-2004. The estimated grant element in 149 loans committed to in case of loans in pipeline/ utilized by India, since 1980, both without and with exchange rate depreciation of Rupee *vis-a-vis* Japanese Yen, have been presented in Table 7.1.

The table shows that Japanese aid to India has proved quite concessional, despite depreciation of Rupee in relation to Yen, during the period 1980-81 to 2003-04. With depreciation of Rupee, grant element inherent in Japanese loans was negative during the years 1980-81, 81-82 and 82-83. However, afterwards it became positive and increased from 4.35 percent in 1984-85 to 57.14 percent in 1996-97, though later on it declined to 23.83 in 2003-04. On the whole, average grant element worked out to be 40.43 percent during the above-mentioned period, exceeding the 25 percent proportion fixed by the OECD for qualifying it to be considered as 'aid' in real terms. The concessionality element, on the whole, worked out to 72.91 percent during the above-mentioned period, when depreciation of Rupee as compared to Yen is ignored.

Apart from Yen loans from the JBIC, Japan also provided outright grants to the Govt. of India amounting to Yen 81.745 billion, out of which India utilized Yen 81.063 billon (99.2 percent) up to end-March 2004 (Govt. of India[c], 2004: p. 234) through the 'Japanese International Cooperation Agency' (JICA) which also facilitated the implementation of technical assistance programmes like, project-type technical cooperation, development study, dispatch of experts, training to Indian officials in Japan, etc. JICA provided approximately Rs. 35-40 crore to India during a fiscal year by way of technical cooperation (*Ibid.*, p. 27). Besides these, Govt. of Japan also provided technical assistance under its 'Green Aid Plan' through its Ministry of Economy, Trade and Industry, to support the self-help efforts of Indian industries to cope with the issues in the area of energy and environment. Thus, Japanese aid proved quite concessional to India during the above-mentioned period.

TABLE 7.1
Grant Element in Japanese Loans

Year	No. of Loans	Without Depreciation of Rupee against Yen		With Depreciation of Rupee against Yen		Loan Amount
		Percent	Rs. Crore	Percent	Rs. Crore	Rs. Crore
(1)	(2)	(3)	(4)	(5)	(6)	(7)
1980-81	3	59.93	83.30	-8.72	-12.12	139.00
1981-82	9	64.23	151.85	-5.96	-14.07	236.41
1982-83	6	64.15	42.20	-2.66	-1.75	65.79
1984-85	8	64.53	242.13	4.35	16.32	375.22
1985-86	5	66.00	125.70	8.27	15.75	190.46
1986-87	6	64.65	341.16	5.67	29.92	527.70
1987-88	8	68.34	546.14	12.42	99.25	799.15
1988-89	8	72.14	593.54	15.35	126.29	822.76
1989-90	5	72.48	212.73	16.24	47.66	293.50
1990-91	7	73.31	1004.49	18.29	250.61	1370.20
1991-92	8	79.70	1750.35	33.64	738.79	2196.18
1992-93	6	79.13	1780.61	31.78	715.12	2250.23

1993-94	7	74.89	2989.08	52.22	2084.26	3991.30
1994-95	13	74.66	2340.71	51.86	1625.89	3135.16
1995-96	9	77.62	3343.05	56.53	2434.72	4306.95
1996-97	12	78.00	3621.53	57.14	2653.00	4642.99
1997-98	9	73.54	2588.77	50.13	1764.69	3520.22
1998-99	1	76.97	317.90	52.67	217.54	413.02
2000-01	2	74.83	586.32	49.31	386.36	783.54
2001-02	2	69.93	1436.66	41.72	857.11	2054.43
2002-03	9	67.45	3233.83	32.84	1574.48	4794.41
2003-04	6	62.74	2604.12	23.83	989.10	4150.66
Overall Average for 149 Loans		72.91	29936.17	40.43	16598.92	41059.28

N.B. : (i) Weighted average of grant element has been computed in years in which terms and conditions of loans were different.

(ii) Average of terms and conditions is taken where these have been given in the form of range.

Source : (*Basic Data*): Govt of India, *External Assistance*, (2003-04 and other issues); Ministry of Finance, Department of Economic Affairs; Aid, Accounts and Audit Division.

2. GRANT ELEMENT IN GERMAN ASSISTANCE

The German Government has been providing development assistance, both financial as well as technical, since February, 1958 under the bilateral development cooperation programme for the priority areas such as : energy, health and family welfare, environmental protection, sustainable utilization of natural resources, implementation of economic reforms, development and strengthening of market system, and the private sector potential, etc. Madhya Pradesh, Himachal Pradesh, Karnataka, Maharashtra, Rajasthan, West Bengal and Orissa have been the regional priorities in case of the state sector projects. Recently (2004), Germans also indicated their readiness to support the development projects of North-Eastern, and newly created states of Chhattisgarh and Jharkhand consistent with their comparative advantages.

The German financial assistance has been provided in the form of soft loans, commercial credit and outright grants. The soft loans has been provided at an interest rate of 0.75 percent per annum with a repayment period of 50 years up to end-March 1989 and 40 to 50 years afterwards up to end-March 2003 including a grace period of 10 years, while the commercial credit, also known as loan under 'second window', has been provided at prevailing market rate of interest ranging between 8 to 13 percent per annum up to end-March 1991 and 6.13 to 7.5 percent per annum afterwards up to end-March 2003 with a maturity of 10 to 13 years including a moratorium of zero to seven years. These German loans also carried a commitment charges of 0.25 percent on un-disbursed amount. For a particular project in areas like ports, power, coal and railways commercial credit has been provided as a mix of both the soft and commercial loans in the form of composite financial cooperation loan.

Grant element implicit in 127 Germen loans utilized by India during the period 1980-81 to 2002-03 has been estimated, both without as well as with deprecation of Rupee *vis-a-vis* Deutsche Mark (up to end-March 1993) and Euros (afterwards up to end-March 2004), and are amplified in Table 7.2. A perusal of the table shows that, on the whole, Germen loans proved concessional to India in both ways, i.e., without as well as with exchange rate variations. Although grant element was found to

TABLE 7.2
Grant Element in German Loans

Year	No. of Loans	Without Depreciation of Rupee against Deu. Mark and Euros		With Depreciation of Rupee against Deu. Mark and Euros		Loan Amount
		Percent	Rs. Crore	Percent	Rs. Crore	Rs. Crore
(1)	(2)	(3)	(4)	(5)	(6)	(7)
1980-81	8	83.58	87.11	-42.86	-44.67	104.23
1981-82	5	84.46	47.25	-38.14	-21.33	55.94
1982-83	8	80.48	128.30	-39.05	-62.25	159.42
1983-84	3	86.71	21.34	-25.63	-6.31	24.61
1984-85	11	55.85	109.23	-52.52	-102.72	195.58
1985-86	7	81.78	108.86	-14.17	-18.86	133.11
1986-87	6	88.82	372.79	-13.17	-55.28	419.71
1987-88	14	84.14	259.02	-15.66	-48.21	307.85
1988-89	6	89.84	284.63	-12.65	-40.08	316.82
1989-90	5	88.11	108.05	-11.06	-13.56	122.63
1990-91	5	86.30	963.85	-7.95	-88.79	1116.86

(Contd.)

TABLE 7.2 (Contd.)

(1)	(2)	(3)	(4)	(5)	(6)	(7)
1991-92	4	90.30	135.50	9.59	14.39	150.06
1992-93	6	92.33	918.29	9.37	93.19	994.57
1993-94	4	88.91	205.50	60.98	140.94	231.13
1994-95	4	88.78	314.85	60.67	215.16	354.64
1995-96	12	74.58	190.49	50.85	129.88	255.41
1996-97	7	74.91	895.79	51.43	615.01	1195.82
1997-98	3	49.75	251.21	26.80	135.33	504.95
1998-99	1	71.65	121.98	45.34	77.19	170.25
1999-00	2	73.39	188.00	46.19	118.32	256.16
2000-01	2	70.86	132.95	42.39	79.54	187.63
2001-02	3	66.68	422.57	35.15	222.76	633.73
2002-03	1	74.96	55.16	32.21	23.70	73.58
Overall Average for 127 Loans		79.38	6322.72	17.12	1363.35	7964.69

N.B. : (i) Weighted average of grant element has been computed in years in which terms and conditions of loans were different.

(ii) Average of terms and conditions is taken where these have been given in the form of range.

Source (Basic Data): Govt. of India, *External Assistance*, (2003-04 and other issues); Ministry of Finance, Department of Economic Affairs; Aid, Accounts and Audit Division.

be negative in the initial years, if exchange rate changes are incorporated, ranging between (–)42.86 percent in 1980-81 to (–)7.95 percent in 1990-91, yet later on it rose to the maximum level of 60.98 percent in 1993-94, thereafter fluctuatingly declined to 32.21 percent in 2002-03. The overall average grant element has been worked out as 17.12 percent with the incorporation of Rupee depreciation. However, these loans seemed highly concessional, with overall average grant element of 79.38 percent, when depreciation of Rupee is ignored.

Besides loans, German assistance including technical assistance has also been available in the form of outright grants amounting to Deutsche Mark 445.052 million (fully utilized), € 327.427 million and US $ 0.750 million, out of which € 199.033 million (60.8 percent) and US $ 0.234 million (31.2 percent) have been utilized by India up to the end-March, 2004 (Govt. of India[c], 2004: pp. 227-28).

3. GRANT ELEMENT IN THE US ASSISTANCE

The American development assistance has been coming to India since 1951, except during the years 1972-78, in the form of project and non-project loans, commodity assistance under US PL-480, and outright grants mainly through the 'United States Agency for International Development' (USAID) which was established on November 3, 1961. Initially, the main thrust of US bilateral assistance to India was on projects that were designed to strengthen the key institutions, and transfer of resources for infrastructure programs in agriculture and social forestry. However, since mid-1980, the priorities have been diversified to include science and technology dimension focusing specifically on the commercialization of technology. Health and family welfare, and disaster management were also among the top priority areas. Since mid-1980, assistance extended by the USAID has been in the form of outright grants only. During the preceding five financial years (1999-2004), US $ 524.234 million has been utilized in the form of outright grants including food aid/ agricultural commodities given through the US NGOs like 'Cooperative for American Relief Everywhere' and 'Catholic Relief Services' etc. (Govt. of India[c], 2004: p. 45). US $ 1128.195 million were authorized to India in the form of outright grants up to the end-March 2004, out of which US $ 896.161 million (79.4 percent) were utilized during the same period (*Ibid*., p. 245). This also included technical assistance grants amounting to US $ 461.21 million provided under the 'Technical Cooperation Mission' until end-March 1999.

The US assistance to India in the form of loans was available only up to end-March 1986. During the period 1980-81 to 1985-86, India utilized 25 US loans which were available at an interest rate ranging between two to five percent per annum with a repayment period of 40 years (maturity) including a moratorium of nine to ten years for the public sector government account loans. The only single loan outside government account, during this period utilized by the Indian Airlines, was available at an interest rate of 8.368 percent per annum with a maturity of 10 years including a grace period of seven years. (Govt. of India[c], 1993 : 202).

The details of estimated grant element inherent in these 25 US loans, both without and with exchange rate variations, have been presented in Table 7.3, which show that these loans proved quite non-concessional with an overall average grant component of (–)30.25 percent, if depreciation of Rupee *vis-a-vis* US $ is accounted for, and proved quite concessionary, otherwise with an overall average grant element of 52.76 percent, when exchange rate variations are neglected, during the above-mentioned period.

4. GRANT ELEMENT IN BRITISH ASSISTANCE

The Govt. of UK has been providing bilateral development assistance to India, since 1958. The assistance was in the form of loans up to 1975 and thereafter in the form of outright grants only. Presently, UK is the largest bilateral development partner of India in terms of outright grants which are distributed through the 'Department for International Development' (DFID), Govt. of UK. These outright grants, by the way of financial cooperation, are routed through the Annual Budget of the Govt. of India, while the same for technical cooperation including direct payments by the DFID for consultancy services, experts, training fellowships, and ancillary equipment for scientific research and allied purposes in the fields of science and technology, industry, agriculture, power, health education, and environment etc., are

TABLE 7.3
Grant Element in the US Loans

Year	No. of Loans	Without Depreciation of Rupee against US $		With Depreciation of Rupee against US $		Loan Amount
		Percent	Rs. Crore	Percent	Rs. Crore	Rs. Crore
(1)	(2)	(3)	(4)	(5)	(6)	(7)
1980-81	7	21.84	30.66	-40.79	-57.26	140.39
1981-82	3	44.93	6.79	-58.83	-8.89	15.11
1982-83	1	46.61	8.42	-54.72	-9.89	18.07
1983-84	6	74.64	77.04	-20.93	-21.60	103.22
1984-85	5	68.17	45.71	-24.20	-16.23	67.05
1985-86	3	74.03	44.57	-13.85	-8.34	60.20
Overall Average for 25 Loans		52.76	213.19	-30.25	-122.21	404.04

N.B. : Weighted average of grant element has been computed in years in which terms and conditions of loans were different.

Source (Basic Data) : Govt of India, *External Assistance,* (2003-04 and other issues).

not routed through the Annual Budget, Govt. of India. The total value of British assistance authorized to India in the form of outright grants up to end-March 2004 has been British £ 2822.794 million, out of which £ 2326.332 million (82.4 percent) has been utilized during the same period (Govt. of India[c], 2004: p. 243).

During the period 1980-81 to 2003-04, UK extended only a single fast disbursing interest free loan to India, amounting to British £ 10 million, to tide over the BOP crisis in the year 1991-92, having a repayment period of 0.6 years without any moratorium. The loan proved concessionary to India with a grant element of 4.77 percent, both without as well as with exchange rate depreciation of Rupee *vis-a-vis* British £ (because it was an interest free loan), as has been shown in Table 7.4.

5. GRANT ELEMENT IN FRENCH ASSISTANCE

The French Government started extending development assistance to India in 1967, mostly in the form of loans, and that too on hard terms and conditions. The French assistance has been tied to the import of goods and services from France. The French Government made commitments only against specific projects, where contracts have been won by the French companies and where substantial value of French products/services have to be imported. France did not give pure soft loans albeit a mix of soft loan, (treasury loan) and a commercial loan (bank credit), in the ratio of 50:50 which varied up to 55:45 under 1994 protocol, have been provided. The terms and conditions of French loans to India varied from loan to loan, which have been provided in Swiss Francs, Deutsche Marks, French Francs and lately in Euros. The rate of interest on soft loans ranged between 2.0 to 3.7 percent per annum during the period 1980-93 with a repayment period (maturity) of 28 to 33 years including a grace period of 10 years, while commercial loans were availed at an interest rate ranging between 3.7 to 8.35 percent per annum with a maturity period of 13 to 31.5 years including a moratorium of 3.0 to 3.5 years during the same period. The rate of interest on soft loans ranged between 0.47 percent to 2.8 percent per annum during the period 1993-2003 with a maturity period of 22 to 33 years including a grace period of 10 years, while commercial loans have been committed to/utilized at the interest rate ranging between 6.34 to 10.75 percent (variable every six monthly) with a maturity period of 10

Table 7.4
Grant Element in British Loan

Year	No. of Loans	Without Depreciation of Rupee against £		With Depreciation of Rupee against £		Loan Amount
		Percent	Rs. Crore	Percent	Rs. Crore	Rs. Crore
(1)	(2)	(3)	(4)	(5)	(6)	(7)
1991-92	1	4.77	2.05	4.77	2.05	42.92

Source (Basic Data) : Govt. of India, *External Assistance,* (2003-04 and other issues).

years without having any moratorium, during the same period. The total aid committed by France up to end-March 2004 amounted to French Francs 15,443.669 million and € 15.201 million inclusive of both loans as well as outright grants (Govt. of India[c], 2004: p. 13)

The grant element inherent in 72 French loans utilized by India during the period 1980-81 to 2002-03 have been calculated, both without and with incorporating exchange rate variations in Rupee *vis-a-vis* French loan currencies: Swiss Francs, Deutsche Mark and French Francs (up to end-March 1993), and Euros (afterwards up to end-March 2004). The results have been outlined in Table 7.5, which show that French loans were found to be non-concessional with overall average grant element of (–)0.44 percent during the above mentioned period, if exchange rate depreciation of Rupee is accounted for. Grant element fluctuated between the lowest level of (–)41.75 percent in 1982-83 to the highest level of 33.62 percent in 1998-99. However, like other sources, French loans also proved quite concessional with overall average grant component of 55.57 percent during the above-mentioned period, when exchange rate depreciation of Rupee is ignored.

The French outright grants have been restricted to a few small value technical cooperation projects. India has fully utilized the French grants authorized in French Francs amounting to 251.495 million, while utilized only 38.2 percent in Euros amounting to 0.311 million, out of the authorized amount of € 0.815 million, up to end-March 2004 (*Ibid*., pp. 226-27).

6. GRANT ELEMENT IN ITALIAN ASSISTANCE

Italian assistance to India began in the year 1966 and mainly came in the form of either government credits or suppliers' credits. The amount of suppliers' credit offered up to 1981 was US $ 401 million, against which the utilization up to end-September 1982 was US $ 328 million (81.8 percent) and since then the facility is no more operational. In February, 1981 an inter-governmental agreement was concluded for technical cooperation under which Italy agreed to provide expert services and related equipment on outright grant basis for specific approved projects. But, during the Indo-Italian cooperation meeting held in June, 1995 Italy informed that technical

TABLE 7.5
Grant Element in French Loans

Year	No. of Loans	Without Depreciation of Rupee against Fr. Francs, Deu. Marks and Euros		With Depreciation of Rupee against Fr. Francs, Deu. Marks and Euros		Loan Amount
		Percent	Rs. Crore	Percent	Rs. Crore	Rs. Crore
(1)	(2)	(3)	(4)	(5)	(6)	(7)
1980-81	2	56.97	92.74	-28.06	-45.68	162.79
1981-82	4	52.92	58.90	-30.77	-34.25	111.31
1982-83	3	26.21	63.01	-41.75	-100.37	240.41
1983-84	3	45.26	11.68	-16.31	-4.21	25.81
1984-85	2	40.22	35.40	-10.13	-8.19	88.01
1985-86	2	70.69	101.04	-1.14	-1.63	142.93
1986-87	1	42.28	98.43	-23.55	-54.82	232.80
1988-89	1	65.76	165.01	3.75	9.41	250.93
1989-90	3	76.97	279.72	5.46	19.84	363.41
1990-91	1	77.81	0.91	7.90	0.09	1.17
1991-92	1	80.00	53.50	22.09	14.77	66.88

(Contd.)

TABLE 7.5 (Contd.)

(1)	(2)	(3)	(4)	(5)	(6)	(7)
1992-93	1	75.71	57.80	18.79	14.34	76.34
1993-94	9	51.29	114.08	30.21	67.20	222.43
1994-95	7	51.84	8.54	30.52	5.03	16.47
1995-96	3	47.65	16.49	28.33	9.80	34.60
1996-97	4	48.10	41.51	28.95	24.98	86.30
1997-98	13	43.10	49.74	22.01	25.40	115.40
1998-99	7	55.35	46.28	33.62	28.11	83.62
1999-00	1	54.09	12.19	32.55	7.34	22.54
2001-02	3	52.15	23.72	23.53	10.70	45.48
2002-03	1	42.44	9.28	9.86	2.16	21.87
Overall Average for 72 Loans		55.57	1339.97	-0.44	-10.70	2411.50

N.B. : (i) Weighted average of grant element has been computed in years in which terms and conditions of loans were different.

(ii) Average of terms and conditions is taken where these have been given in the form of range.

Source (Basic Data) : Govt. of India, *External Assistance,* (2003-04 and other issues).

cooperation grant projects would not be considered any more. However, Italian Government agreed to provide loans on soft terms in 1981-82. Since then US $ 161.2 million and Deutsche Marks 144.2 million as soft credit at an interest rate ranging between 1.5 to 2.5 percent per annum, repayable over 13.6 to 30 years including a moratorium of 2.6 to 10 years, have been committed to/utilized by India in the form of 12 loans through the Govt. of India budget. The only single loan amounting to € 5.165 million at an interest rate of 1.5 percent per annum, with maturity of 30 years including a grace period of 10 years, has been provided outside the Govt. of India budget.

Grant element inherent in these 13 Italian loans utilized by India during the period 1980-81 to 2000-01 have been estimated, both without as well as with depreciation of Rupee *vis-a-vis* Italian loan currencies: Deutsche Mark and US $ (up to end-March 1993), and Euros (afterwards up to end-March 2004). The results have been shown in Table 7.6, which indicate that Italian loans proved non-concessional with an overall average grant element of (–)6.23 percent during the period 1983-84 to 2000-01, if exchange rate changes are incorporated. Grant element worked out to 46.48 percent only for a single Euro loan given in 2000-01, despite depreciation of Rupee in relation to Euros. These 13 Italian loans found highly concessional with overall average grant element of 68.22 percent, when exchange rate variations are excluded, while estimating implicit grant element.

7. GRANT ELEMENT IN CANADIAN ASSISTANCE

Canadian bilateral development assistance comprising economic, food and technical assistance to India began in 1951. It has been channeled through the 'Canadian International Development Agency' (CIDA) in the form of outright grants for food and non-food items; non-project loans for the purchase of industrial commodities, fertilizers and miscellaneous capital goods; and project loans for meeting the import requirements of specific projects. Canada has provided nine interest free loans to India during the period 1980-81 to 1984-85 with a maturity period of 50 years including a moratorium of 10 years. Grant element implicit in these nine loans have been calculated, both without and with incorporating exchange rate depreciation of Rupee *vis-a-vis* CAN $, and results have been presented in

Table 7.6
Grant Element in Italian Loans

Year	*No. of Loans*	*Without Depreciation of Rupee against US $, Deu. Marks and Euros*		*With Depreciation of Rupee against US $, Deu. Marks and Euros*		*Loan Amount*
		Percent	*Rs. Crore*	*Percent*	*Rs. Crore*	*Rs. Crore*
(1)	*(2)*	*(3)*	*(4)*	*(5)*	*(6)*	*(7)*
1983-84	1	45.82	3.68	-14.48	-1.16	8.04
1984-85	3	52.17	12.73	-12.95	-3.16	24.40
1985-86	3	63.58	49.16	-9.10	-7.04	77.32
1986-87	2	78.92	38.81	-5.33	-2.62	49.18
1987-88	2	66.71	74.01	-15.18	-16.84	110.94
1990-91	1	75.56	39.40	-0.90	-0.47	52.14
2000-01	1	77.07	16.43	46.48	9.91	21.32
Overall Average for 13 Loans		68.22	234.22	-6.23	-21.38	343.34

N.B. : Weighted average of grant element has been computed in years in which terms and conditions of loans were different.

Source (Basic Data) : Govt. of India, *External Assistance*, (2003-04 and other issues).

TABLE 7.7
Grant Element in Canadian Loans

Year	No. of Loans	Without Depreciation of Rupee against CAN.$		With Depreciation of Rupee against CAN.$		Loan Amount
		Percent	Rs. Crore	Percent	Rs. Crore	Rs. Crore
(1)	(2)	(3)	(4)	(5)	(6)	(7)
1980-81	3	90.54	45.74	90.54	45.74	50.52
1981-82	4	91.21	95.31	91.21	95.31	104.50
1983-84	1	92.89	7.90	92.89	7.90	8.51
1984-85	1	93.50	38.29	93.50	38.29	40.95
Overall Average	for 9 Loans	91.57	187.24	91.57	187.24	204.48

Source (Basic Data) : Govt. of India, *External Assistance,* (2003-04 and other issues).

Table 7.7. The results show that nine Canadian loans utilized during the above-mentioned period proved highly concessional, both without and with exchange rate variations in Rupee in relation to CAN $, having overall average grant element of 91.57 percent as all these were interest free loans.

Since April 1, 1986 CIDA has been extending assistance to India in the form of outright grants only, for the purposes of promoting economic and social reforms; environmentally sound development; and building a strong economic relationship between the private sectors of both the countries. The assistance through the Govt. of India budget is quite negligible. Canada is assisting NGO's outside the bilateral programme. Till December, 2002 the total Canadian aid has been around CAN $ 2.7 billion (Govt. of India[c], 2004: p. 5) including loans and outright grants. India utilized outright Canadian grants amounting to CAN$ 1324.078 million (98.2 percent) out of the total authorized amount of CAN $ 1348.649 million up to end-March 2004 (*Ibid.*, pp. 223-24).

However, in February 2003, Govt. of India decided to discontinue taking development assistance from the bilateral partners including Canada at government to government level. Consequently, CIDA was notified to phase out their current bilateral aid programme by 2007. Govt. of India has also pre-paid the entire outstanding Canadian credit amounting CAN$ 419.94 million against the loans taken by it during 1966-84 in October, 2003 (*Ibid.*, p. 9). But in September 2004, Govt. of India reviewed her policy decision regarding accepting foreign aid and decided to continue accepting foreign aid in future from all the G-8 countries including Canada at government to government level.

8. GRANT ELEMENT IN RUSSIAN ASSISTANCE

The former USSR had extended financial and economic assistance to India from 1955 to 1989 in the form of state credits amounting to Roubles 9966.60 million. These were utilized mainly for the public sector projects in basic and heavy industries, such as : Bhilai and Bokaro Steel Plants; Heavy Machine Building Plant at Ranchi; Bharat Heavy Electricals Limited, Hardwar; oil refineries at Barauni, Koyali and Mathura; power plants at Korba, Neyveli, Singrauli, Bhakhra, and Lower

Sileru, etc.; and for other development projects included in the Five Year Plans.

However, following the disintegration of the USSR, bilateral arrangements were entered between India and Russia in 1993 to address the issue of Rupee-Rouble exchange rate. The agreed arrangements provided for the principal amount of Rouble denominated debt as on April 1, 1992 being converted from Roubles to Rupees using the exchange rate on April 1, 1990 as determined by the old 1978 Protocol (Rouble 1= Rs. 19.9169). The amount of the principal debt as on April 1, 1992 was also converted from Roubles to Rupees using exchange rate on April, 1, 1992 determined by the 1978 protocol (Rouble 1= Rs. 31.7514). The discrepancy between the two Rupee amounts as calculated above was rescheduled to be repaid in annual instalments over a period of 45 years including a grace period of one year. This rescheduled portion carried no interest. It had no protection against any fluctuation in the value of the Rupee for a period of five years. Thereafter, it was to be indexed to the SDR if the average annual depreciation of the Rupee exceeded three percent over this five-year period. Similar review was to be conducted at the end of every five-year period. The non-rescheduled portion of the debt was the amount in Rupees corresponding to the conversion of the Rouble debt at the exchange rate as on January I, 1990. This amount is now denominated in Rupees, and repayment of the principal and interest on this portion of the debt are being effected by India in accordance with the schedule in force for each of the relevant inter-government credit agreements. The Rupee payments in respect of principal and interest of this non-rescheduled portion of the debt are, however, protected by adjusting the Rupee amounts in line with the changes in the Rupee value of the SDR basket of five currencies. The Rupee debt is being repaid through the export of goods and services from India to Russia (Govt. of India[c], 2004: p. 43).

Besides three non-rescheduled and one rescheduled loans, Russia extended another loan amounting to US $ 2600 million in June, 1998. All these loans have been carrying interest rate ranging between zero to 6.1 percent per annum, with a repayment period of 20 years including a moratorium of three years. The rescheduled loan has been interest-free and repayable over 45

TABLE 7.8
Grant Element in Russian Loans

Year	*No. of Loans*	*Without Depreciation of Rupee against US $*		*With Depreciation of Rupee against US $*		*Loan Amount*
		Percent	*Rs. Crore*	*Percent*	*Rs. Crore*	*Rs. Crore*
(1)	(2)	(3)	(4)	(5)	(6)	(7)
1992-93	4	74.48	2325.83	74.48	2325.83	3122.76
1998-99	1	57.68	6348.14	35.35	3890.55	11005.80
Overall Average for 5 Loans		61.39	8673.97	44.00	6216.38	14128.56

Source (Basic Data) : Govt. of India, *External Assistance*, (2003-04 and other issues).

years including one year of moratorium. Grant element implicit in these five Russian loans committed to/utilized by India have been calculated and are presented in Table 7.8, which shows that a single loan given in US $ proved quite concessional to India, both without and with depreciation of Rupee against US $, during the period 1992-93 to 2003-04. Grant element have been worked out same (74.78 percent) for the one rescheduled and three non-rescheduled loans as these have been repayable in Indian Rupees. The overall average grant element have been 44 percent, if exchange rate variations are incorporated, and 61.39 percent otherwise, when depreciation of Rupee *vis-a-vis* US $ is ignored. Apart from these loans, India has also totally utilized Rs. 9.63 crore sanctioned in the form of Russian outright grants up to the period ending-March 2004 (*Ibid*., p. 237).

In February 2003, Govt. of India decided to discontinue taking any further development assistance from all the bilateral sources other than Japan, USA, UK, Germany and Russia as well as the European Commission. It was also decided not to accept 'tied aid' any longer. However, on September 20, 2004 Govt. of India again reviewed the existing bilateral development cooperation policy and decided to accept bilateral development assistance only from all the G-8 countries namely: Japan, USA, UK, Germany, France, Italy, Canada and Russia (discussed earlier) as well as the European Commission (discussed in Chapter 6). The assistance from countries of the European Commission outside the G-8, which would provide a minimum bilateral aid package of US $ 25 million per annum to India, has also been welcomed under this reviewed policy. The other countries not covered by this policy were advised to provide their development assistance to India either through the NGOs, autonomous organizations and universities etc., or through the multilateral financial agencies (Govt. of India, 2004: p. PIB-15), while the development assistance for the ongoing projects would continue till their completion depending upon the case.

SECTION II

1. GRANT ELEMENT IN AUSTRALIAN ASSISTANCE

Development assistance from Australia to India began in 1951 and has been channeled through the 'Australian Agency for

International Development' (AUSAID), mostly in the form of outright grants, and that too in the form of technical assistance, equipment and supply. India utilized the cent percent Australian outright grants authorized to her amounting Australian $ 166.16 million up to end-March 2004 (Govt. of India[c], 2004: p. 222). India also fully utilized the two Australian loans sanctioned to her in 1992-93 at an interest rate of 1.625 percent per annum, with a repayment period of 12 years including a moratorium of four years. Grant element implicit in these two loans have been calculated both without as well as with incorporating depreciation of Rupee *vis-a-vis* US $. Both these loans proved concessional with average grant element of 10.67 percent, despite incorporating exchange rate depreciation of Rupee, and of 62.93 percent, otherwise when these exchange rate variations are ignored, as have been shown in Table 7.9.

2. GRANT ELEMENT IN AUSTRIAN ASSISTANCE

Austria has been extending bilateral development assistance to India, since November 1962, through the Government and other credits, mainly for financing the import of capital goods, machinery, components, raw materials and services of Austrian origin. The total bilateral development assistance given by Austria to India up to end-March 2003 amounted to Austrian Schillings 1680.89 million (Govt. of India[c], 2004: p. 5), out of which six loans amounting to Austrian Schillings 510.50 million have been utilized by India during 1980-81 to 2003-04. These loans were repayable over a period of 28 to 40 years (maturity) including a grace period of 10 years, carrying an interest rate of two percent per annum. Grant element inherent in these six Austrian loans have been calculated and are amplified in Table 7.10. The results show that out of these six loans, five proved quite non-concessional, if exchange rate depreciation is accounted for. On the whole, average grant element of these six Austrian loans has been found to be (–)13.52 percent if depreciation of Rupee is added to the rate of interest, but proved quite concessional with average grant element of 78.12 percent when exchange rate changes are dispensed with. Besides these loans, India has also fully utilized Austrian outright grants amounting to Austrian Schillings 55.96 million up to end-March 2004 (*Ibid.*, p. 222).

TABLE 7.9
Grant Element in Australian Loans

Year	No. of Loans	Without Depreciation of Rupee against US $		With Depreciation of Rupee against US $		Loan Amount
		Percent	Rs. Crore	Percent	Rs. Crore	Rs. Crore
(1)	(2)	(3)	(4)	(5)	(6)	(7)
1992-93	2	62.93	24.90	10.67	4.22	39.57

Source (Basic Data) : Govt. of India, *External Assistance,* (2003-04 and other issues).

TABLE 7.10
Grant Element in Austrian Loans

Year	*No. of Loans*	*Without Depreciation of Rupee against Aust. Schillings*		*With Depreciation of Rupee against Aust. Schillings*		*Loan Amount*
		Percent	*Rs. Crore*	*Percent*	*Rs. Crore*	*Rs. Crore*
(1)	(2)	(3)	(4)	(5)	(6)	(7)
1980-81	1	66.34	1.10	-50.06	-0.83	1.66
1981-82	1	67.80	1.96	-45.73	-1.32	2.89
1983-84	1	70.84	3.97	-33.32	-1.87	5.61
1986-87	1	75.47	6.79	-21.39	-1.92	9.00
1989-90	1	76.07	11.96	-19.40	-3.05	15.72
1991-92	1	84.38	19.74	4.73	1.11	23.39
Overall Average for 6 Loans		78.12	45.52	-13.52	-7.88	58.27

Source (Basic Data) : Govt. of India, *External Assistance*, (2003-04 and other issues).

3. GRANT ELEMENT IN BELGIAN ASSISTANCE

The Govt. of Belgium has been extending bilateral development assistance to India, since 1962, in the form of suppliers' credits up to 1965-66, and since 1966-67 government to government credits in the form of project and non-project assistance for the import of capital goods, mainly. The aggregate bilateral development assistance committed by the Belgian Government, mostly in the form of loans, up to end-March 2003 amounted to Belgian Francs 5212.486 million (Govt. of India[c], 2003: p. 5). Currently (2004), there is no on-going project in India under the Indo-Belgian Bilateral Development Cooperation Programme.

During the period 1980-81 to 2003-04 Belgium provided five interest free loans and one loan at an interest rate of one percent per annum (in 1992-93) to India, which were repayable over a period of 30 years (maturity) including a moratorium of 10 years. Grant element implicit in these six loans have been calculated and the results have been presented in Table 7.11, which show that on the average six Belgian loans proved highly concessional, both without as well as with incorporating exchange rate variations. With depreciation of Rupee *vis-a-vis* Belgian Francs, grant element, on the average, has been 59.62 percent and without depreciation 86.87 percent.

Besides these six loans, outright grants in the form of food grants amounting to Belgian Francs 46.95 million have also been fully utilized by India up to end-March 2003 (*Ibid.*, p.199).

4. GRANT ELEMENT IN DENMARK ASSISTANCE

Denmark has been giving bilateral development assistance to India, since 1963, in the form of soft loans as well as outright grants through the 'Danish International Development Agency' (DANIDA). Tied grants were meant for large value projects, while untied ones for local cost projects. The total assistance committed by Denmark to India, up to end-March 2004, amounted to Danish Kroner 5250.07 million and US $ 15 million, which also included grants outside the Govt. of India account (Govt. of India[c], 2004: p. 11). During the period 1980-81 to 2003-04, Denmark provided

TABLE 7.11

Grant Element in Belgian Loans

Year	No. of Loans	Without Depreciation of Rupee against Bel. Francs		With Depreciation of Rupee against Bel. Francs		Loan Amount
		Percent	Rs. Crore	Percent	Rs. Crore	Rs. Crore
(1)	(2)	(3)	(4)	(5)	(6)	(7)
1981-82	2	84.46	13.60	84.46	13.60	16.10
1982-83	1	85.28	6.19	85.28	6.19	7.26
1983-84	1	87.13	6.10	87.13	6.10	7.00
1989-90	1	90.07	6.20	90.07	6.20	6.88
1992-93	1	87.98	20.89	17.98	4.27	23.75
Overall Average for 6 Loans		86.87	52.98	59.62	36.36	60.99

Source (Basic Data) : Govt. of India, *External Assistance*, (2003-04 and other issues).

six interest free loans to India with a repayment period of 35 years (maturity) including a grace period of 10 years. Grant element inherent in these six loans, calculated both without and with incorporating depreciation of Rupee against Danish Kroners, during the above-mentioned period indicate that all these loans proved highly concessional with overall average grant element of 89.72 percent; both ways, as has been outlined in Table 7.12 because these have been interest free loans.

Denmark has also authorized outright grants amounting to Danish Kroners 2796.355 million, out of which Danish Kroners 2228.895 million (79.7 percent) have been utilized by India up to end-March 2004 (*Ibid.*, p. 224).

5. GRANT ELEMENT IN KUWAITI ASSISTANCE

The 'Kuwait Fund for Arab Economic Development' was established in 1961 as the main agency of the State of Kuwait for providing loans and technical assistance to Arab countries for implementation of their development programme. Later on, its scope of operation was extended to cover all the developing countries. The Fund is a Kuwait public corporation with independent legal personality, and financial and administrative autonomy. India has been receiving Kuwaiti assistance from this Fund, since 1976. Since then, out of the total commitment of Kuwaiti Dinar 91.84 million up to end-March 2002, Kuwaiti Dinar 82.353 million (89.7 percent) have been utilized. The entire outstanding debts of Kuwait have also been pre-paid during 2003-04 (Govt. of India[c], 2004; p. 31). During the period 1980-81 to 2003-04, Kuwait has sanctioned six loans at an interest rate ranging between 4.0 to 4.5 percent per annum, repayable over a period ranging between 19 to 25 years including a moratorium of four to six years. These loans proved quite non-concessionary with overall average grant element of (–)22.19 percent, when depreciation of Rupee *vis-a-vis* Kuwaiti Dinar is accounted for and were found quite concessionary with overall average grant element of 45.88 percent, if exchange rate variations are ignored as has been shown in Table 7.13.

Kuwait has also provided outright grants to India amounting to Rs. 12.03 crore up to end-March 2004, which have been wholly utilized during the same period (*Ibid.*, p. 235).

TABLE 7.12
Grant Element in Danish Loans

Year	*No. of Loans*	*Without Depreciation of Rupee against Dan. Kroners and US $*		*With Depreciation of Rupee against Dan. Kroners and US $*		*Loan Amount*
		Percent	*Rs. Crore*	*Percent*	*Rs. Crore*	*Rs. Crore*
(1)	*(2)*	*(3)*	*(4)*	*(5)*	*(6)*	*(7)*
1981-82	1	86.82	15.89	86.82	15.89	18.30
1982-83	1	87.55	15.10	87.55	15.10	17.25
1983-84	1	89.19	19.62	89.19	19.62	22.00
1984-85	1	90.06	23.66	90.06	23.66	26.27
1986-87	1	91.41	18.56	91.41	18.56	20.31
1995-96	1	94.27	12.24	94.27	12.24	12.98
Overall Average for 6 Loans		89.72	105.07	89.72	105.07	117.11

Source (Basic Data) : Govt. of India, *External Assistance*, (2003-04 and other issues).

TABLE 7.13

Grant Element in Kuwaiti Loans

Year	*No. of Loans*	*Without Depreciation of Rupee against Kuwaiti Dinar*		*With Depreciation of Rupee against Kuwaiti Dinar*		*Loan Amount*
		Percent	*Rs. Crore*	*Percent*	*Rs. Crore*	*Rs. Crore*
(1)	(2)	(3)	(4)	(5)	(6)	(7)
1981-82	2	44.93	39.01	-27.37	-23.76	86.83
1982-83	1	46.42	23.68	-24.58	-12.54	51.01
1983-84	1	44.68	19.19	-16.04	-6.89	42.94
1985-86	1	49.46	13.47	-12.16	-3.31	27.24
1988-89	1	49.28	1.37	-10.10	-0.28	2.78
Overall Average for 6 Loans		45.88	96.72	-22.19	-46.78	210.80

Source (Basic Data) : Govt. of India, *External Assistance,* (2003-04 and other issues).

6. GRANT ELEMENT IN DUTCH ASSISTANCE

The Netherlands has been extending bilateral development assistance to India, since 1962-63, mainly in the form of general purpose credits, debt relief assistance and suppliers' credits. Till December, 1991 Dutch assistance comprised both loans and outright grants on roughly 50:50 basis, and was mainly in the form of local cost financing. The 16 loans which have been utilized by India during the period 1980-81 to 2003-04 carried an interest rate of 2.5 percent per annum, repayable over 30 years (maturity) including a grace period of eight years. Grant element inherent in these 16 loans have been calculated, both without as well as with incorporating depreciation of Rupee *vis-a-vis* Dutch Guilder (up to end-March 1993) and Euros (afterwards up to end-March 2004). The results are outlined in Table 7.14, which show that these Dutch loans proved non-concessional with an overall average grant element of (–)16.72 percent, if exchange rate variations in Rupee are incorporated. Grant element ranged between the lowest level of (–)50.85 percent in 1980-81 and the maximum level of 45.85 percent in 1997-98. However, like most of the other sources, these loans were found to be highly concessional (overall average grant element 69.91 percent) during the same period when exchange rate depreciation of Rupee is ignored.

Since 1997, the Dutch assistance has been completely in the form of outright grants including technical assistance grants for expert services, project appraisal and training. The technical assistance is not reflected in the Annual Budget of the Govt. of India. Netherlands has authorized Dutch Guilder 1584.129 million; € 290.047 million; and Rs. 55.081 crore in the form of outright grants to India up to end-March 2004, out of which Guilder 1584.129 million (100 percent); € 182.168 million (62.8 percent); and Rs. 0.446 crore (0.8 percent) have been utilized by her during the same period (Govt. of India[c], 2004: pp. 235-36).

However, Dutch assistance has been completely withdrawn w.e.f. April 1, 2004 in accordance with the Govt. of India's latest policy regarding bilateral development assistance announced in February, 2003.

Table 7.14
Grant Element in Dutch Loans

Year	No. of Loans	Without Depreciation of Rupee against Dutch Guilder and Euros		With Depreciation of Rupee against Dutch Guilder and Euros		Loan Amount
		Percent	Rs. Crore	Percent	Rs. Crore	Rs. Crore
(1)	(2)	(3)	(4)	(5)	(6)	(7)
1980-81	1	60.82	41.19	-50.85	-34.44	67.73
1981-82	1	62.39	36.24	-46.46	-26.98	58.08
1982-83	1	63.64	20.50	-42.93	-13.83	32.22
1983-84	1	66.54	22.55	-34.60	-11.73	33.89
1984-85	1	68.14	13.83	-29.95	-6.08	20.29
1985-86	1	70.14	3.42	-24.01	-1.17	4.88
1986-87	1	72.65	26.95	-23.05	-8.55	37.09
1987-88	3	70.15	116.22	-22.77	-37.72	165.67
1988-89	2	70.90	4.30	-21.76	-1.32	6.07
1989-90	1	70.98	59.92	-20.34	-17.17	84.42
1990-91	1	74.14	74.88	-17.96	-18.14	101.00
1991-92	1	80.21	20.37	3.51	0.89	25.40
1997-98	1	74.17	82.74	45.85	51.15	111.55
Overall Average for 16 Loans		69.91	523.11	-16.72	-125.09	748.29

Source (Basic Data) : Govt. of India, *External Assistance*, (2003-04 and other issues).

7. GRANT ELEMENT IN SAUDI-ARABIAN ASSISTANCE

The Saudi-Arabian Government set-up in September, 1974, under a royal decree, the 'Saudi Fund For Development' as an autonomous organization with their own legal entity and autonomous financial status with the objective of financing by way of loans for development projects in the developing countries. India received bilateral assistance in the form of loans only and that too through the Annual Budgets of the Govt. of India from Saudi-Arabia, since June 1977. Since then, total commitments made by the Saudi-Fund up to end-March 2002 aggregated to Saudi Riyals 766.64 million, out of which Saudi Riyals 626.179 million (81.7 percent) have been utilized up to end-March 2004 (Govt. of India[c], 2004: pp. 37 and 167). Saudi-Arabia has sanctioned only three loans in the year 1983-84, 1985-86 and 1987-88 to India repayable over a period of 20 years including a moratorium of five years, carrying an interest rate ranging between three to four percent per annum, during the period 1980-81 to 2003-04. Grant element calculated in these three Saudi loans, on the average, indicated the loans to be non-concessional (overall average grant element –8.88 percent) if the depreciation of Rupee *vis-a-vis* Saudi Riyals is incorporated and found concessional (overall average grant element 54.10 percent) when exchange rate variations in Rupee are dispensed with, as has been shown in Table 7.15.

8. GRANT ELEMENT IN SWEDISH ASSISTANCE

India has been a recipient of Swedish bilateral development assistance, since 1964, although Sweden joined the 'Aid India Consortium' (presently, 'India Development Forum') as a full member only in 1969. Swedish assistance has been channeled through the 'Swedish International Development Agency' (SIDA) in the form of soft loans and outright grants. Since 1995, it has been in the form of outright grants only. India has utilized Swedish outright grants amounted to Swedish Kroners 5184.623 million (99 percent) out of the total authorized grants amounting to Swedish Kroners 5235.696 million (Govt. of India[c], 2004: p. 238).

TABLE 7.15
Grant Element in Saudi-Arabian Loans

Year	No. of Loans	Without Depreciation of Rupee against Saudi Riyals		With Depreciation of Rupee against Saudi Riyals		Loan Amount
		Percent	Rs. Crore	Percent	Rs. Crore	Rs. Crore
(1)	(2)	(3)	(4)	(5)	(6)	(7)
1983-84	1	53.23	12.07	-12.61	-2.86	22.67
1985-86	1	57.40	18.68	-4.87	-1.58	32.54
1987-88	1	51.78	19.56	-10.10	-3.82	37.78
Overall Average for 3 Loans		54.10	50.31	-8.88	-8.26	92.99

Source (Basic Data) : Govt. of India, *External Assistance,* (2003-04 and other issues).

During the period 1980-81 to 2003-04, Sweden has extended only three loans to India: two in the year 1989-90 at an interest rate of 1.5 percent per annum, repayable over 10.5 years including a grace period of 2.5 years; and one in 1993-94 at an interest rate of two percent per annum, with maturity of 16 years including a moratorium of one year. Grant element worked out in these three loans, both without and with incorporating exchange rate depreciation in Rupee *vis-a-vis* Swiss Francs and US $, have been shown in Table 7.16, which indicated that two Swiss Franc loans given in 1989-90 proved non-concessional, and the one US $ loan authorized in 1993-94 proved concessional if depreciation of Rupee is accounted for. On the whole, all the three loans proved concessional both without (grant element 50.67 percent) and with (grant element 8.80 percent) incorporating exchange rate variations.

However, in accordance with the new policy regarding bilateral development assistance, announced in February 2003, the entire outstanding Swedish debt has been pre-paid during 2003-04.

9. GRANT ELEMENT IN SWISS ASSISTANCE

India has been receiving bilateral development assistance from the Switzerland Government channeled through the 'Swiss Agency for Development and Cooperation' (SDC), since 1960, in the form of both soft loans as well as outright grants. However, since 1993 it has been completely in the form of outright grants only. The total Swiss bilateral development assistance excluding grants given up to end-March 2004 has been of the order of Swiss Francs 282.638 million, while the outright grants utilized during the same period amounted to Swiss Francs 408.049 million (93.9 percent) out of the authorized amount of Swiss Francs 434.521 million, and Rs. 26.267 crore (100 percent) given in local currency (Govt. of India[c], 2004: pp. 37 and 239).

India utilized the two Swiss authorized loans: one each in the year 1983-84 and 1991-92, during the study period 1980-2004, repayable over a period of 18 and 15 years, respectively, each including a grace period of three years, carrying an interest rate of 1.5 percent per annum. Grant element of these loans worked out, on the average, as (–)3.28 percent if exchange rate

TABLE 7.16
Grant Element in Swedish Loans

Year	No. of Loans	Without Depreciation of Rupee against Swiss Francs and US $		With Depreciation of Rupee against Swiss Francs and US $		Loan Amount
		Percent	Rs. Crore	Percent	Rs. Crore	Rs. Crore
(1)	(2)	(3)	(4)	(5)	(6)	(7)
1989-90	2	48.43	162.58	-10.08	-33.91	336.39
1993-94	1	54.06	125.93	36.06	84.00	232.95
Overall Average for 3 Loans		50.67	288.51	8.80	50.09	569.34

Source (Basic Data) : Govt. of India, *External Assistance,* (2003-04 and other issues).

depreciation of Rupee compared to Swiss Francs is incorporated. One loan sanctioned in 1983-84 proved non-concessional (grant element –23.05 percent), while the other authorized in 1991-92 found to be concessional (grant element 5.40 percent). Both these loans, separately as well as jointly, proved highly concessional (average grant element 63.68 percent) when exchange rate variations are not included, as has been shown in Table 7.17.

Though India decided to discontinue taking development assistance from Switzerland since February 2003, yet the same for ongoing projects have been continuing till their completion.

10. GRANT ELEMENT IN SPANISH ASSISTANCE

India received only a single loan from the Spanish Government under Indo-Spanish Bilateral Development Programme in June, 1989. Currently (2004), there is no on-going project under the above-said programme in India. The only soft loan India received from Spain had 20 years maturity with a grace period of nine years at an interest rate of two percent per annum, which covered the 40 percent of the total project import cost. The balance 60 percent was met by the buyers' credit. Grant element implicit in this single Spanish loan has been worked out in Table 7.18, both without as well as with incorporating exchange rate depreciation of Rupee against the US $. The results show that this single Spanish loan proved non-concessional with grant element (–)6.53 percent when depreciation of Rupee is added and found, otherwise, highly concessional with grant element 70.24 percent if exchange rate depreciation is ignored.

Following the recent policy guidelines regarding foreign aid, the entire outstanding Spanish debt have also been pre-paid during 2003-04.

Besides these, during the study period 1980-2004, Govt. of Norway also extended a single loan amounting to US $ 10 million to India outside the Annual Budget of the Govt. of India in 1997-98, which is the only on going Indo-Norwegian development assistance project. Grant element inherent in this single Norwegian loan could not be estimated as its terms and conditions were not available. Although, Norway has sanctioned outright grants amounting to Kroners 1366.478 million up to the period ending-March 2004, out of which India has utilized

TABLE 7.17

Grant Element in Swiss Loans

Year	No. of Loans	Without Depreciation of Rupee against Swiss Francs		With Depreciation of Rupee against Swiss Francs		Loan Amount
		Percent	Rs. Crore	Percent	Rs. Crore	Rs. Crore
(1)	(2)	(3)	(4)	(5)	(6)	(7)
1983-84	1	56.87	16.51	-23.05	-6.69	29.03
1991-92	1	66.66	44.02	5.40	3.57	66.03
Overall Average for 2 Loans		63.68	60.53	-3.28	-3.12	95.06

Source (*Basic Data*) : Govt. of India, *External Assistance*, (2003-04 and other issues).

Table 7.18
Grant Element in Spanish Loan

Year	*No. of Loans*	*Without Depreciation of Rupee against US $*		*With Depreciation of Rupee against US $*		*Loan Amount*
		Percent	*Rs. Crore*	*Percent*	*Rs. Crore*	*Rs. Crore*
(1)	(2)	(3)	(4)	(5)	(6)	(7)
1989-90	1	70.24	53.73	-6.53	-4.99	76.50

Source (Basic Data) : Govt. of India, *External Assistance,* (2003-04 and other issues).

Norwegian Kroners 1354.116 million (99 percent) during the same period (Govt. of India[c], 2004: p. 237).

SECTION III

GRANT ELEMENT IN LOANS : AN OVERALL COMPARATIVE ANALYSIS

In this section, an attempt has been made to compare and contrast the calculated grant element implicit in various loans, both without as well as with incorporating exchange rate depreciation of Rupee in relation to foreign currencies, committed to/utilized by India, during the period 1980-81 to 2003-04, both from the multilateral and bilateral sources, and the results are delineated in Table 7.19. A scan of the table shows that out of the 24 sources from which India received foreign aid in the form of loans, Canadian loans proved most concessional having the maximum 91.57 percent grant element, followed by Danish loans with grant element of 89.72 percent, both ways, i.e., without and with incorporating exchange rate depreciation in Rupee, during the above-said period. However, if exchange rate depreciation of Rupee is accounted for, Belgian loans stand third with overall average grant element of 59.62 percent, followed by Russian loans with grant element of 44 percent; IFAD loans with grant component of 41.27 percent; Japanese loans with 40.43 percent; and IDA loans with 37.13 percent. The least grant element (4.77 percent) has been found in the single British loan. The US loans proved costliest with (–)30.25 percent grant element. Even the loans committed by the multilateral agencies like IBRD (–3.27 percent); ADB (–0.81 percent); OPEC Fund (–0.28 percent); and IMF Trust Fund (–13.75 percent) also proved costlier to India if exchange rate depreciation of rupee is included.

Belgian loans also stand third with overall average grant element of 86.87 percent, followed by IDA loans with grant component of 84.35 percent; IFAD loans with grant element of 84.26 percent; German loans with 79.38 percent; Austrian loans with 78.12 percent; Japanese loans with 72.91; and Spanish loan with 70.24 percent, when depreciation of Rupee is left out. In this category, the least grant element (4.77 percent) has also been

Table 7.19
Overall Grant Element in Loans (1980-81 to 2003-04)

Institution/ Country	*No. of Loans*	*Without Depreciation of Rupee*		*With Depreciation of Rupee*		*Loan Amount*
		Percent	*Rs. Crore*	*Percent*	*Rs. Crore*	*Rs. Crore*
(1)	*(2)*	*(3)*	*(4)*	*(5)*	*(6)*	*(7)*
(a) Multilateral Sources						
1. IBRD	163	39.42	21510.73	-3.27	-1784.25	54571.82
2. IDA	201	84.35	47326.09	37.13	20831.12	56107.24
3. ADB	64	32.64	11291.24	-0.81	-280.24	34597.44
4. IFAD	16	84.26	879.12	41.27	430.61	1043.30
5. OPEC Fund	11	61.64	120.68	-0.28	-0.54	195.79
6. IMF Trust Fund	1	48.79	262.75	-13.75	-74.05	538.53
(b) Bilateral Sources						
7. Japan	149	72.91	29936.17	40.43	16598.92	41059.28
8. Germany	127	79.38	6322.72	17.12	1363.35	7964.69
9. USA	25	52.76	213.19	-30.25	-122.21	404.04
10. UK	1	4.77	2.05	4.77	2.05	42.92
11. France	72	55.57	1339.97	-0.44	-10.70	2411.50

12. Italy	13	68.22	234.22	-6.23	-21.38	343.34
13. Canada	9	91.57	187.24	91.57	187.24	204.48
14. Russia	5	61.39	8673.97	44.00	6216.38	14128.56
15. Australia	2	62.93	24.90	10.67	4.22	39.57
16. Austria	6	78.12	45.52	-13.52	-7.88	58.27
17. Belgium	6	86.87	52.98	59.62	36.36	60.99
18. Denmark	6	89.72	105.07	89.72	105.07	117.11
19. Kuwait	6	45.88	96.72	-22.19	-46.78	210.80
20. Netherlands	16	69.91	523.11	-16.72	-125.09	748.29
21. Saudi-Arabia	3	54.10	50.31	-8.88	-8.26	92.99
22. Sweden	3	50.67	288.51	8.80	50.09	569.34
23. Switzerland	2	63.68	60.53	-3.28	-3.12	95.06
24. Spain	1	70.24	53.73	-6.53	-4.99	76.50

Source (Basic Data) : Govt. of India, *External Assistance*, (2003-04 and other issues).

found in the single British loan because the loan was interest free. Grant element inherent in the loans from almost all the sources, which provided loans to India during the above-mentioned period have been found positive, when exchange rate variations in Rupee are ignored.

On the whole, it may be concluded that India should borrow only from those sources which provide assistance on soft terms and conditions, like Canada, Denmark, Belgium, Russia, Japan, IFAD and IDA etc., which yielded the maximum grant element, despite depreciation of Rupee *vis-a-vis* foreign currencies, during the above-mentioned period. Loans on hard terms should be avoided to lighten the debt burden of the country.

8

Effectiveness of Foreign Aid in India

Admittedly, evaluating aid effectiveness is a challenging task, which is possible if the impact of foreign aid on development indicators can be quantified. Quantitative indicators may give some insight into effectiveness but these do not provide a complete picture. Also many effects of aid are difficult to separate from the effects of other factors that influence economic growth—such as : macroeconomic and sectoral policies, availability of the necessary institutions and infrastructure, organizational and management capacity of the government, and last (though not the least in terms of importance) the quality and quantity of natural resources. The impact of aid is, therefore, better evaluated in the broader context of macroeconomic and sector policies (Lele, 1992 : pp. 3-4). In literature, effectiveness of aid has long been a matter of controversy and debate among the policy-makers. Even the results of empirical studies differ markedly. Some studies indicate no relation, either positive or negative, between aid and growth (Mosley, 1987; Boone, 1994, 1996; Dawson and Tiffen, 1999) because it is difficult to isolate the impact of one of the multitude of factors having bearing on growth and quality of life. Some others indicate positive correlation between aid and growth (Gupta and Islam, 1983; Riddell, 1987; Burnside and Dollar, 2000; Holmgren *et al.*, 2001). However, the effectiveness of aid largely depends on, whether it is invested or consumed ? To the extent it is invested, it will be effective in promoting growth.

In the present chapter, an attempt has been made to analyze the effectiveness of foreign aid in the Indian economy through its impact on the development of the diverse sectors, especially on which it has been utilized and also on the whole economy, since 1970.

There has been a widespread impression that India received large sums of foreign aid. This, of course, is true in absolute terms but is not true if the large size of country and its huge population are taken into consideration. Gross utilized aid as ratio of its GDP at 1993-94 prices remained quite low and declined after reaching the peak level of 2.16 percent in 1975-76 to the lowest level of 0.72 percent in 2002-03. The rate of growth of gross utilized aid as ratio of GDP has been worked out as (–)2.131 percent per annum during the period 1970-71 to 2003-04 (Table 8.1), which is significant at one percent level. However, since most of the aid has been utilized for asset generation in the country in the form of setting up industries in diverse areas; power generation projects; creating transport, communication and agricultural infrastructure etc., Index of Gross Utilized Foreign Aid Stock (IGAS) has been prepared as a composite reflector of the quantum of foreign aid utilized in the economy, and has been taken as an independent/explanatory variable. To estimate and analyze its impact on the overall level of economic development of the Indian economy, especially on the sectors on which foreign aid has been utilized, depending upon the availability of statistical information, following indicators have been selected and used :

1. Per Capita GDP (PGDP),
2. Annual Growth Rate of GDP (AGDP),
3. Gross Domestic Capital Formation as Ratio of GDP (GDCF/GDP),
4. Total Expenditure of the Central Government as Ratio of GDP (TECG/GDP),
5. Gross Fiscal Deficit as Ratio of GDP (GFD/GDP),
6. Import of Capital Goods as Ratio of GDP (ICG/GDP),

TABLE 8.1
Gross Utilized Aid as Percentage of GDP_{FC} at 1993-94 Prices

Year	*Gross Utilized Aid (Rs. Crore)*		*GDP_{FC} (Rs. Crore)*	*Aid/GDP Ratio (Percent)*
	At current prices	*At 1993-94 prices*	*At 1993-94 prices*	
(1)	*(2)*	*(3)*	*(4)*	*(5)*
1970-71	791.4	5534.27	296278	1.87
1971-72	834.1	5523.84	299269	1.85
1972-73	666.2	3989.22	298316	1.34
1973-74	1035.7	5152.74	311894	1.65
1974-75	1314.3	5236.26	315514	1.66
1975-76	1840.5	7421.37	343924	2.16
1976-77	1598.9	6319.76	348223	1.82
1977-78	1290.0	4831.46	374235	1.29
1978-79	1215.6	4552.81	394828	1.15
1979-80	1353.1	4336.86	374291	1.16
1980-81	2161.8	5858.54	401128	1.46
1981-82	1864.9	4627.54	425073	1.09
1982-83	2252.0	5323.88	438079	1.22
1983-84	2265.8	4979.78	471742	1.06
1984-85	2359.4	4864.74	492077	0.99
1985-86	2936.0	5802.37	513990	1.13
1986-87	3605.0	6738.32	536257	1.26
1987-88	5051.9	8725.22	556778	1.57
1988-89	5304.4	8527.97	615098	1.39
1989-90	5802.5	8673.39	656331	1.32
1990-91	6704.3	9096.74	692871	1.31
1991-92	11615.0	13843.86	701863	1.97
1992-93	10981.8	11897.94	737792	1.61
1993-94	11781.0	11781.00	781345	1.51
1994-95	10880.5	9671.56	838031	1.15
1995-96	11022.2	9064.31	899563	1.01
1996-97	11978.5	9417.06	970082	0.97

(Contd.)

TABLE 8.1 (*Contd.*)

(1)	*(2)*	*(3)*	*(4)*	*(5)*
1997-98	11744.7	8843.90	1016595	0.87
1998-99	13238.9	9409.31	1082748	0.87
1999-00	14404.6	9913.70	1148368	0.86
2000-01	14254.3	9154.98	1198592	0.76
2001-02	17559.3	10886.11	(P)1267833	0.86
2002-03	15835.9	9488.26	(QE)1318321	0.72
2003-04	18697.4	10629.56	(RE)1426701	0.75
Annual Compound Growth Rate (Percent)				
1970-71 to 1979-80	—	—	3.448** (9.288)	-4.304^{NS} (-2.140)
1980-81 to 1989-90	—	—	5.379** (25.430)	1.654^{NS} (0.999)
1990-91 to 1999-00	—	--	6.187** (29.385)	-8.159** (-5.143)
1990-91 to 2003-04	—	—	5.967** (50.431)	-6.541** (-7.18)
1970-71 to 2003-04	—	—	5.094** (53.099)	-2.131** (-5.919)

N.B. : (i) **Significant at 0.01 level.
^{NS} Indicate non-significant.
(ii) Utilized aid at current prices has been converted into 1993-94 prices by using Spliced Wholesale Price Index (1993-94 = 100) as deflator.
(iii) Aid-GDP ratio and annual compound growth rates have been computed.

Sources (Basic Data): (i) RBI, *Handbook of Statistics on The Indian Economy*, 2003-04, p. 8.
(ii) Govt. of India, *Economic Survey*, 2004-05, p. S-95 and 5.

7. Export of Goods and Services as Ratio of GDP (XGS/GDP),
8. Foreign Exchange Reserves as Ratio of GDP (FORX/GDP),
9. Index of Gross Irrigated Area (IGIA),
10. Index of Foodgrains Production (IFG),
11. Index of Steel (Finished) Production (ISP),
12. Index of Petroleum Refinery Products (IPOL),

13. Index of Electricity Generation (IELE),
14. Index of Fertilizer Production (IFP),
15. Index of Overall Industrial Production (IIP),
16. Index of Transport and Communication (ITC),
17. Index of Employment in Organized (Both Public and Private) Sector (IEMP),
18. Wholesale Price Index for All the Commodities (WPI),
19. Life Expectancy (Health),
20. Literacy Ratio (Education),
21. Percentage of Urban Population,
22. Access to Safe Drinking Water in Households, and
23. Prevention of Environmental Damage.

The present study has been carried out for the period 1970-71 to 2003-04. The analysis has been made for the overall time period along with two sub-periods to delineate the impact of economic reforms, i.e., (1) the pre-reforms period (1970-71 to 1990-91), and (2) the post-reforms period (1991-92 to 2003-04). To examine the nature, degree and extent of the impact of foreign aid on the selected development indicators, techniques of Tabular Analysis, Compound Growth Rate, Correlation, Multiple Linear as well as Log-Linear Regression have been used. An attempt has also been made to capture the lagged impact of utilized foreign aid by incorporating Lagged Index of Gross Aid Stock (IGAS) up to five periods in the Multiple Linear Regression Model.

SECTION I

RELATIONSHIP BETWEEN IGAS AND DEVELOPMENT INDICATORS

In order to study the relationship between the Index of Gross Aid Stock (IGAS) and selected development indicators, Tabular Analysis has been carried out by comparing their annual compound growth rates with the growth rate of IGAS during the three different decades of 1970s, 1980s, and 1990s as well as the overall time period of 1970-71 to 2003-04. These indicators have been divided into two categories: (1) Economic Indicators, and (2) Social Indicators.

1. Economic Indicators

Under this broad category only those variables, which are of economic in nature, related to the structure of body economic and on which foreign aid has been utilized, have been included. These are :

1.1 Gross Aid Stock and Its Index

GAS has been examined in Table 8.2 which shows that it has increased with fluctuations from 82.49 in 1970-71 to 135.07 in 2003-04, at the rate of 1.975 percent per annum during the overall period of 1970-71 to 2003-04. The growth of IGAS has

TABLE 8.2
Index of Gross Aid Stock (1993-94 = 100)

Year	*Gross Aid Stock (Rs. Crore)*		*Index of Gross Aid Stock (IGAS) (1993-94 = 100)*
	At Current Prices	*At 1993-94 Prices*	
(1)	(2)	(3)	(4)
Up to 1970	9059.76	—	—
1970-71	9762.16	68266.85	82.49
1971-72	10289.11	68139.80	82.33
1972-73	10745.23	64342.69	77.75
1973-74	11566.03	57542.44	69.53
1974-75	12649.01	50394.46	60.89
1975-76	14144.23	57033.18	68.91
1976-77	15392.44	60839.68	73.51
1977-78	16352.69	61246.03	74.00
1978-79	17241.24	64573.93	78.03
1979-80	18249.51	58492.02	70.68
1980-81	20046.32	54326.07	65.64
1981-82	21510.30	53375.43	64.49
1982-83	23332.09	55158.60	66.65
1983-84	25131.25	55233.52	66.74
1984-85	26988.02	55645.40	67.24
1985-86	29384.26	58071.66	70.17
1986-87	32401.58	60563.70	73.18
1987-88	36805.45	63567.27	76.81
1988-89	41373.74	66517.27	80.37
1989-90	46348.76	69280.66	83.71

(Contd.)

TABLE 8.2 (Contd.)

(1)	(2)	(3)	(4)
1990-91	52126.08	70727.38	85.46
1991-92	62698.56	74730.11	90.30
1992-93	72426.39	78468.46	94.82
1993-94	82758.86	82758.86	100.00
1994-95	91984.19	81763.72	98.80
1995-96	101166.70	83196.30	100.53
1996-97	111121.87	87359.96	105.56
1997-98	120644.13	90846.48	109.77
1998-99	131470.15	93440.05	112.91
1999-00	143245.35	98585.93	119.12
2000-01	154634.74	99315.82	120.01
2001-02	169101.35	104836.55	126.68
2002-03	181555.22	108780.84	131.44
2003-04	196621.52	111780.28	135.07
Annual Compound Growth Rate of IGAS (Percent)			
1970-71 to 1979-80	—	—	-1.038^{NS} (-1.027)
1980-81 to 1989-90	—	—	2.925** (8.716)
1990-91 to 1999-00	—	—	3.367** (15.461)
1990-91 to 2003-04	—	—	3.417** (30.168)
1970-71 to 2003-04	—	—	1.975** (8.909)

N.B. : (i) ** Significant at 0.01 level.
NS Indicate non-significant.
(ii) Compound growth rates have been computed.

Source (Basic Data) : Govt. of India, *Economic Survey*, 2004-05 and other issues.

been recorded highest (3.417 percent per annum) during the period 1990-91 to 2003-04.

1.2 Growth of GDP and Per Capita GDP

Table 8.3 delineates the growth rates of GDP as well as per capita GDP, which experienced significant growth rates of 5.094 percent and 2.921 percent, respectively, during the overall above-mentioned period. Both have also grown significantly even

TABLE 8.3
Annual Growth Rate of GDP and Per Capita GDP_{FC} at 1993-94 Prices

Year	GDP_{FC} at 1993-94 Prices		Population (Crore)	Per Capita GDP (Rs.)
	Rs. Crore	Annual Growth Rate (percent)		
(1)	(2)	(3)	(4)	(5)
1970-71	296278	5.0	54.1	5476.49
1971-72	299269	1.0	55.4	5401.97
1972-73	298316	-0.3	56.7	5261.31
1973-74	311894	4.6	58.0	5377.48
1974-75	315514	1.2	59.3	5320.64
1975-76	343924	9.0	60.7	5665.96
1976-77	348223	1.2	62.0	5616.50
1977-78	374235	7.5	63.4	5902.76
1978-79	394828	5.5	64.8	6093.03
1979-80	374291	-5.2	66.4	5636.91
1980-81	401128	7.2	67.9	5907.63
1981-82	425073	6.0	69.2	6142.67
1982-83	438079	3.1	70.8	6187.56
1983-84	471742	7.7	72.3	6524.79
1984-85	492077	4.3	73.9	6658.69
1985-86	513990	4.5	75.5	6807.82
1986-87	536257	4.3	77.1	6955.34
1987-88	556778	3.8	78.8	7065.71
1988-89	615098	10.5	80.5	7640.97
1989-90	656331	6.7	82.2	7984.56
1990-91	692871	5.6	83.9	8258.30
1991-92	701863	1.3	85.6	8199.33
1992-93	737792	5.1	87.2	8460.92
1993-94	781345	5.9	89.2	8759.47
1994-95	838031	7.3	91.0	9209.13
1995-96	899563	7.3	92.8	9693.57
1996-97	970082	7.8	94.6	10254.57
1997-98	1016595	4.8	96.4	10545.59
1998-99	1082748	6.5	98.3	11014.73

(Contd.)

TABLE 8.3 (*Contd.*)

(1)	(2)	(3)	(4)	(5)
1999-00	1148368	6.1	100.1	11472.21
2000-01	1198592	4.4	101.9	11762.43
2001-02	(P)1267833	5.8	103.7	12225.97
2002-03	(QE)1318321	4.0	105.5	12495.93
2003-04	(RE)1426701	8.2	107.3	13296.37
Annual Compound Growth Rate (Percent)				
1970-71 to 1979-80	3.448** (9.288)	—	—	1.140* (3.049)
1980-81 to 1989-90	5.379** (25.430)	—	—	3.150* (14.909)
1990-91 to 1999-00	6.187** (29.385)	—	—	4.113** (19.434)
1990-91 to 2003-04	5.967** (50.431)	—	—	3.970** (34.954)
1970-71 to 2003-04	5.094** (53.099)	—	—	2.921** (27.545)

N.B. : (i) ** Significant at 0.01 level.
* Significant at 0.05 level.
(ii) Compound growth rates have been computed.

Source (Basic Data) : RBI, *Handbook of Statistics on The Indian Economy*, 2003-04, pp. 5, 8 and 470.

during the three decades of 1970s, 1980s and 1990s, taken separately. Evidently, lower growth rate of per capita GDP *vis-a-vis* GDP has been due to the rapid growth of population. However, a comparison between the IGAS (Table 8.2) and GDP as well as per capita GDP (Table 8.3) highlights the positive relationship between them during all the sub-periods, except the decade of 1970s, which indicates that utilized foreign aid seems to have encouraged the growth of GDP as well as per capita GDP.

1.3 Growth of Gross Domestic Capital Formation, Total Expenditure of Central Government and Gross Fiscal Deficit

Table 8.4 shows significant growth of the Gross Domestic Capital Formation (GDCF); Total Expenditure of the Central Govt. (TECG); and its Gross Fiscal Deficit (GFD) during the overall

TABLE 8.4
Gross Domestic Capital Formation, Total Expenditure of the Central Govt. and Gross Fiscal Deficit at 1993-94 Prices (Rs. Crore)

Year	Gross Domestic Capital Formation	Aid/GDCF Ratio (percent)	Total Expenditure of Central Govt.	Gross Fiscal Deficit
(1)	(2)	(3)	(4)	(5)
1970-71	64638	8.56	39328.67	9846.15
1971-72	66704	8.28	45642.38	11437.09
1972-73	65287	6.11	47047.90	13047.90
1973-74	77055	6.69	40885.57	8621.89
1974-75	68649	7.63	39585.66	9171.32
1975-76	71655	10.36	49915.32	12213.71
1976-77	80238	7.88	53980.24	15027.67
1977-78	90648	5.33	58074.91	13782.77
1978-79	105080	4.33	70284.64	21385.77
1979-80	92895	4.67	60775.64	20487.18
1980-81	99719	5.87	61701.90	22490.51
1981-82	100425	4.61	62692.31	21503.72
1982-83	100271	5.31	72791.96	25122.93
1983-84	103784	4.80	78096.70	28637.36
1984-85	112567	4.32	89962.89	35909.28
1985-86	123113	4.71	104083.00	43197.63
1986-87	123552	5.45	117600.00	49237.38
1987-88	142152	6.14	117894.64	46708.12
1988-89	160762	5.30	127188.10	49715.43
1989-90	172047	5.04	138875.93	53261.58
1990-91	195650	4.65	142873.81	60559.02
1991-92	171553	8.07	132793.80	43295.59
1992-93	187478	6.35	132847.23	43524.38
1993-94	198412	5.94	141853.00	60257.00
1994-95	243882	3.97	142879.11	51291.56
1995-96	271015	3.35	146607.73	49541.94
1996-97	268435	3.51	158024.37	52463.05
1997-98	289058	3.06	174738.70	66970.63
1998-99	290971	3.23	198535.89	80560.77

(Contd.)

TABLE 8.4 (Contd.)

(1)	(2)	(3)	(4)	(5)
1999-00	351624	2.82	205129.38	72069.51
2000-01	353995	2.59	209114.96	76310.85
2001-02	(P)346907	3.14	224618.72	87386.86
2002-03	(QE)373399	2.54	248149.79	86921.51
2003-04	—	— (RE)	269616.25	75101.19
Annual Compound Growth Rate (Percent)				
1970-71 to 1979-80	5.127** (5.708)	—	5.643** (4.505)	8.331** (3.535)
1980-81 to 1989-90	6.609** (9.580)	—	10.208** (18.277)	11.890** (10.025)
1990-91 to 1999-00	7.642** (8.527)	—	4.835** (5.898)	4.725* (2.542)
1990-91 to 2003-04	6.860** (12.016)[a]	—	5.740** (12.395)	4.906** (4.974)
1970-71 to 2003-04	6.001** (34.906)[a]	—	5.958** (32.788)	7.228** (18.194)

N.B. : (i) 'a' stands for up to 2002-03.
** Significant at 0.01 level.
* Significant at 0.05 level.
(ii) Compound growth rates have been computed.

Source (Basic Data) : RBI, *Handbook of Statistics on The Indian Economy*, 2003-04, pp. 10, 153 and 156.

period (1970-71 to 2003-04) as well as the three decades of 1970s, 1980s and 1990s, taken separately. However, a comparison of these indicators (Table 8.4) with IGAS (Table 8.2) shows that with the growth of Gross Aid Stock, GDCF, TECG and GFD have also increased during the above-mentioned periods, except the decade of 1970s, which means utilized foreign aid also supplemented the GDCF and TECG, though along with growing GFD. But in recent past (since 2001-02), GFD started declining owing, perhaps, to the check on public expenditure and policy of disinvestment of public enterprises etc., of the Govt. of India. However, the share of utilized foreign aid in the GDCF at 1993-94 prices has declined fluctuatingly from the maximum level of 10.36 percent in 1975-76 to the lowest level of 2.54 percent in 2002-03.

1.4 Growth of Electricity and Industrial Production

Foreign aid has been mainly utilized for the development of basic and key industries such as : iron and steel, petroleum refinery products, fertilizers production, power generation, etc., the growth of which has been examined in Table 8.5. The table points out that production in all these above-mentioned industries as well as the overall industrial production increased quite significantly during the overall period (1970-71 to 2003-04) and also during the three decades, taken separately, except for the fertilizer industry in which production has declined, recently, since 2001. However, a comparison of these industrial indicators (Table 8.5) with that of IGAS (Table 8.2) shows that utilized foreign aid appeared to have further strengthened these basic industries.

TABLE 8.5
Indices of Industrial Development (1993-94=100)

Year	Finished Steel Production	Petroleum Refinery products	Electricity Generation	Fertilizer Production	General Industrial Production
(1)	(2)	(3)	(4)	(5)	(6)
1970-71	29.5	36.3	17.0	10.72	28.2
1971-72	31.5	39.4	18.8	12.45	29.8
1972-73	33.0	38.5	19.9	14.02	30.8
1973-74	29.4	40.4	20.0	13.99	31.3
1974-75	32.3	41.2	21.5	15.30	32.0
1975-76	37.8	44.5	24.7	18.77	34.5
1976-77	44.7	45.6	27.6	24.08	37.8
1977-78	45.9	49.7	28.5	27.02	39.1
1978-79	50.3	51.2	31.9	29.76	42.0
1979-80	45.4	54.6	32.6	30.18	41.4
1980-81	44.9	51.0	34.5	30.42	43.1
1981-82	60.8	55.3	38.0	41.40	47.1
1982-83	60.8	56.9	40.2	42.08	48.6
1983-84	53.3	64.8	43.2	45.95	51.9

(Contd.)

TABLE 8.5 (*Contd.*)

(1)	(2)	(3)	(4)	(5)	(6)
1984-85	58.3	65.4	48.4	52.42	56.3
1985-86	65.0	78.9	52.6	58.23	61.2
1986-87	68.4	84.0	58.0	71.50	66.8
1987-88	71.7	87.8	62.4	75.67	71.7
1988-89	76.6	89.8	68.4	90.18	78.0
1989-90	75.0	95.5	75.8	87.48	84.7
1990-91	77.5	95.3	81.7	92.30	91.6
1991-92	93.3	94.5	88.6	107.97	92.2
1992-93	94.2	98.4	93.1	107.27	94.3
1993-94	100.0	100.0	100.0	100.0	100.0
1994-95	117.2	105.9	108.5	110.82	109.1
1995-96	142.9	110.1	117.5	121.52	123.3
1996-97	151.1	117.8	121.9	117.04	130.8
1997-98	160.6	122.1	130.0	138.21	139.5
1998-99	162.8	128.4	138.6	141.89	145.2
1999-00	187.3	161.0	148.6	144.56	154.9
2000-01	199.3	193.8	154.4	147.80	162.6
2001-02	206.4	201.0	159.3	147.80	167.0
2002-03	227.2	210.9	164.3	146.16	176.6
2003-04	242.9	(P)228.1	(P)172.5	(P)143.68	(P)188.8
Annual Compound Growth Rate (Percent)					
1970-71 to 1979-80	6.390** (6.318)	4.476** (14.519)	7.845** (18.389)	13.249** (14.787)	4.772** (14.732)
1980-81 to 1989-90	4.915** (5.293)	7.657** (15.862)	9.096** (55.927)	12.424** (16.059)	7.802** (37.970)
1990-91 to 1999-00	10.145** (15.145)	5.270** (7.530)	6.803** (50.741)	4.829** (7.594)	6.760** (16.475)
1990-91 to 2003-04	9.027** (22.117)	7.718** (11.963)	6.001** (30.197)	3.730** (8.709)	6.208** (26.098)
1970-71 to 2003-04	6.597** (34.097)	5.430** (31.887)	7.707** (77.129)	8.731** (23.777)	6.274** (70.087)

N.B. : (i) **Significant at 0.01 level.
(ii) Compound growth rate have been computed.

Source (Basic Data) : (i) RBI, *Handbook of Statistics on The Indian Economy*, 2003-04, pp. 54, 57 to 59.
(ii) Govt. of India, *Economic Survey*, 1982-83 and other issues.

1.5 Agricultural Development

Foreign aid has also been utilized in the agricultural sector for the expansion of irrigation facilities, water resource management and consequently for the growth of foodgrains production, in particular. The growth of these sectors have been examined in Table 8.6, which indicates that these have grown significantly during the overall as well as during the decadal

TABLE 8.6
Indicators of Agricultural Development, Employment Generation, and Inflation

Year	*Gross Irrigated Area (Million Hectares)*	*Index of food-grains production (1993-94 =100)*	*Total Employment in Organized Sector (Million)*	*Spliced Wholesale Price Index (1993-94 =100)*	*Share of Transport & Communication Sector in GDP at 1993-94 Prices (Rs. Crore)*
(1)	(2)	(3)	(4)	(5)	(6)
1970-71	38.19	58.52	17.83	14.3	13579
1971-72	38.43	57.32	18.65	15.1	14017
1972-73	39.05	52.66	19.12	16.7	15043
1973-74	40.28	56.79	19.48	20.1	15681
1974-75	41.74	53.93	19.92	25.1	17215
1975-76	43.36	65.78	20.42	24.8	18579
1976-77	43.55	59.65	21.13	25.3	19827
1977-78	46.08	68.58	21.84	26.7	20341
1978-79	48.31	71.24	22.81	26.7	21730
1979-80	49.21	58.26	22.36	31.2	22945
1980-81	49.78	69.84	22.88	36.9	24530
1981-82	51.41	71.64	23.81	40.3	25930
1982-83	51.83	69.04	24.14	42.3	26713
1983-84	53.83	81.76	24.58	45.5	27818
1984-85	54.53	78.23	25.01	48.5	29702
1985-86	54.28	82.16	25.05	50.6	31869
1986-87	55.76	77.83	25.63	53.5	33862

(*Contd.*)

TABLE 8.6 (Contd.)

(1)	(2)	(3)	(4)	(5)	(6)
1987-88	56.04	75.57	25.71	57.9	36287
1988-89	61.13	91.94	25.96	62.2	37921
1989-90	61.85	92.61	26.35	66.9	40444
1990-91	62.47	95.67	26.74	73.7	42291
1991-92	65.68	91.61	27.06	83.9	44997
1992-93	66.76	96.07	27.18	92.3	47099
1993-94	68.25	100.00	27.38	100.0	50497
1994-95	(P)70.65	103.80	27.53	112.5	55504
1995-96	(P)71.35	97.27	27.94	121.6	61622
1996-97	(P)73.25	107.12	28.25	127.2	66767
1997-98	(P)73.01	103.66	28.17	132.8	72340
1998-99	(P)77.59	109.99	28.11	140.7	78213
1999-00	(P)78.49	112.98	27.96	145.3	86904
2000-01	—	105.46	27.79	155.7	97603
2001-02	—	(P)114.38	27.20	161.3	106055
2002-03	—	(AE)97.74	—	166.9	118495
2003-04	—	—	—	(P)175.9	—
Annual Compound Growth Rate (Percent)					
1970-71 to 1979-80	3.066** (17.332)	1.926[NS] (1.988)	2.691** (18.054)	8.879** (8.743)	6.299** (31.057)
1980-81 to 1989-90	2.241** (9.418)	2.851** (4.115)	1.415** (12.300)	6.565** (46.865)	5.832** (33.053)
1990-91 to 1999-00	2.386** (16.636)	2.019** (5.787)	0.581** (6.436)	7.770** (14.874)	8.486** (34.057)
1990-91 to 2002-03	—	1.192* (3.005)	0.293* $(2.284)_a$	6.524** $(17.474)_b$	9.104** (41.502)
1970-71 to 2002-03	2.552** (63.114)	2.423** (18.348)	1.426** $(16.797)_a$	8.031** $(59.606)_b$	6.626** (51.824)

N.B. : (i) **Significant at 0.01 level.
* Significant at 0.05 level.
[NS] Indicate non-significant.
(ii) 'a' stands for up to 2001-02.
'b' stands for up to 2003-04.
(iii) Compound growth rates have been computed.

Sources (Basic Data): (i) RBI, *Handbook of Statistics on The Indian Economy*, 2003-04, pp. 28, 34, 50 and 67.
(ii) Govt. of India[e], *National Accounts Statistics*, (2004 and other issues), Central Statistical Organization.

periods of 1970s, 1980s and 1990s taken individually, except for the foodgrains production during the decade of 1970s (when the growth rate was non-significant). A comparison of these indicators with the growth of IGAS (Table 8.2) highlights the fact that foreign aid also seems to have contributed its mite through the expansion of irrigation facilities and water resource management in making India self-reliant in foodgrains production.

1.6 Growth of Transport and Communication Sectors

Foreign aid in India has also been utilized for the development of railways, road network, ports and telecommunication network, etc. The share of these sectors in the GDP has also grown significantly at the rate of 6.626 percent per annum during the overall period of 1970-71 to 2002-03 as well as during the three decades, taken separately, as is evident from Table 8.6. Its comparison with the growth of IGAS (Table 8.2) also highlights the fact that utilized foreign aid seems to have strengthened the transport and communication sector during these above-mentioned time periods as the share of these sectors has grown with the growth of IGAS.

1.7 Employment Generation

Foreign aid utilized for asset generation in industrial, agricultural as well as in the transport and communication activities, etc., might have encouraged the employment generation in the Indian economy. The growth of employment in the organized public and private sectors has also been examined in Table 8.6, which shows that employment avenues have grown quite significantly at the rate of 1.426 percent during the overall period of 1970-71 to 2001-02. It has grown at the highest rate of 2.691 percent during the decade of 1970s. Its comparison with IGAS (Table 8.2) points out that utilized foreign aid appears to have proved useful in the generation of employment avenues during the above-mentioned periods, except 1970s, in the country.

1.8 Inflation

Utilized foreign aid in the various sectors of the economy have pumped in money supply and consequently might have led to hike in the price level in the country as has been assessed in

Table 8.6. The table shows that the Wholesale Price Index for all the commodities have grown significantly at the rate of 8.031 percent per annum during the overall period 1970-71 to 2003-04. Its comparison with the growth of IGAS (Table 8.2) indicates that utilized foreign aid might have been one of the factors responsible for price hike in the country during the period mentioned-above.

1.9 Growth in Foreign Trade

Foreign aid has been utilized for the development of basic and key industries, foodgrains production, transport and communication sector, etc., as well as to import capital goods like machinery including electrical and electronic, machine-tools, manufacture of metals, and transport equipment etc., necessary for these sectors. As a result, the import of capital goods increased quite significantly at the rate of 8.944 percent per annum during the overall period as has been shown in Table 8.7. Consequently, with increased production, both industrial as well as of foodgrains, country has been able to increase, though inadequately, the export of goods and services along with earning record forex reserves at the rate of 8.803 percent and 11.554 percent per annum, respectively, during the overall period of 1970-71 to 2003-04. A comparison of these foreign trade indicators (Table 8.7) *vis-a-vis* IGAS (Table 8.2) shows that utilized foreign aid financed the import of capital goods, and led to the promotion of export of goods and services along with earning forex reserves as these have grown significantly with the

TABLE 8.7
Import of Capital Goods, Export of Goods and Services, and Forex Reserves at 1993-94 Prices

(Rs. Crore)

Year	*Import of Capital Goods*	*Export of Goods and Services*	*Forex Reserves*
(1)	*(2)*	*(3)*	*(4)*
1970-71	2824.97	10736.01	5125.87
1971-72	3196.82	10650.00	5675.50
1972-73	3298.62	11805.15	5317.37

(Contd.)

TABLE 8.7 (Contd.)

(1)	(2)	(3)	(4)
1973-74	3350.65	12554.33	4945.27
1974-75	2881.75	13262.27	4071.71
1975-76	3902.10	16275.24	7604.84
1976-77	4266.44	20326.92	12818.18
1977-78	4301.31	20254.19	18213.48
1978-79	4891.35	21445.92	21801.50
1979-80	4674.58	20571.89	19019.23
1980-81	5176.69	18186.21	15027.10
1981-82	5201.46	19369.48	9987.59
1982-83	6421.58	20811.73	11304.96
1983-84	7301.56	21474.09	13125.27
1984-85	6531.79	24213.77	14934.02
1985-86	8469.21	21530.81	15452.57
1986-87	12126.30	23274.67	15235.51
1987-88	11339.60	27070.22	13274.61
1988-89	11182.64	32526.53	11318.33
1989-90	13160.40	41342.93	9345.29
1990-91	14207.08	44175.89	15489.82
1991-92	12436.53	52493.22	28426.70
1992-93	14219.67	58167.12	33308.76
1993-94	19580.96	69751.39	60420.00
1994-95	21317.72	73488.10	70915.56
1995-96	28416.26	87461.63	61171.05
1996-97	27691.00	93409.65	74632.08
1997-98	27415.04	97967.35	87277.86
1998-99	30093.40	99327.04	98084.58
1999-00	26737.72	109815.13	114186.51
2000-01	26234.30	130745.67	126656.39
2001-02	29218.97	129583.36	163692.49
2002-03	39140.27	152868.35	216578.78
2003-04	(P)44753.97	165765.73	278640.70

TABLE 8.7 (Contd.)

(1)	(2)	(3)	(4)
Annual Compound Growth Rate (Percent)			
1970-71 to 1979-80	6.161** (6.115)	9.585** (9.850)	20.566** (5.111)
1980-81 to 1989-90	11.784** (9.087)	7.843** (6.138)	-1.273NS (-0.607)
1990-91 to 1999-00	10.508** (5.940)	10.394** (13.029)	21.366** (7.353)
1990-91 to 2003-04	8.556** (7.761)	9.910** (23.026)	20.109** (13.389)
1970-71 to 2003-04	8.944** (35.739)	8.803** (26.374)	11.554** (13.040)

N.B. : (i) ** Significant at 0.01 level.
NS Indicates non-significant.
(ii) Compound growth rates have been computed.

Source (Basic Data) : RBI, *Handbook of Statistics on The Indian Economy*, 2003-04, pp. 184, 197-202 and 239.

growth of Gross Aid Stock during the above-mentioned time-periods.

2. Social Indicators

Foreign aid in India has also been utilized in the spread of primary education with special emphasis on children from scheduled castes and tribes, and girls; curing the prevention of certain specific diseases; access to safe drinking water facilities; urban development; and the prevention of environmental damage etc. The growth of these social indicators in relation to the growth of IGAS has been examined as under :

2.1 Progress in Health and Education

Foreign aid has been utilized, though smaller in quantum, with focus on curing certain specific diseases, like : leprosy, blindness, tuberculosis, malaria, HIV/AIDS, SARS, etc., as well as on the increased access to primary education for the disadvantaged, particularly the children from scheduled castes and tribes, and girls. The growth of life expectancy and literacy ratio has been examined in Table 8.8, which shows that these have improved at the rate of 1.1 percent and 2.18 percent per annum, respectively, during the overall period 1971-2001. A comparison of these indicators with IGAS (Table 8.2) points out

TABLE 8.8
Social Indicators

Census Year	*Life Expectancy (years)*	*Literacy Ratio*	*Urban Population (Percentage)*	*Access to Safe Drinking water in Households (Percentage)*
(1)	*(2)*	*(3)*	*(4)*	*(5)*
1971	45.6	34.45	19.9	-
1981	50.4	43.57	23.3	38.19
1991	58.7	52.21	25.7	62.30
2001	63.3	65.85	27.8	77.90
Annual Compound Growth Rate (Percent)				
1971-81	1.01	1.59	1.59	—
1981-91	1.54	1.83	0.99	5.01
1991-01	0.76	2.35	0.79	2.26
1971-2001	1.10	2.18	1.12	3.63*

N.B. : (i) *for the period 1981-2001.
(ii) Compound growth rate have been computed.

Source (Basic Data) : Govt. of India, *Economic Survey*, various issues.

that the growing utilization of foreign aid might have contributed to the improvement in life expectancy as well as literacy ratio.

2.2 Urban Development

Foreign aid has also been utilized on urban development, especially on safe drinking water supply and sanitation projects. The growth of urban population and safe drinking water facilities in India has been assessed in Table 8.8, which shows that these have grown at the rate of 1.12 percent and 3.63 percent per annum during the periods 1971-2001, and 1981-2001, respectively. These might also be attributed to the growth of utilized Gross Aid Stock presented in Table 8.2. However, still "no Indian city today can provide safe water for more than a few hours a day, and most water and sanitation agencies have financial difficulties, and offer inadequate services" (Zanini, 2001: p. 26), while on the average only 75 percent of the rural population has access to public water supplies, which leaves some 175 million people without safe public water (*Ibid.*, p. 29).

2.3 Prevention of Environmental Damage

Since 1990, foreign aid has also been utilized to mitigate the environmental damage caused largely due to price subsidies on water and power utilization in most of the states. The foreign aid for this purpose has mainly been given by the WB, which has lent US $ 1.94 billion to India for 19 projects, since 1990. Another amount of US $ 97 million has been granted under the Global Environmental Facility and Montreal Protocol Trust Fund to protect the global environment (*Ibid.*, p. 30). However, the overall impact to mitigate environmental damage has been modest.

Thus, utilized foreign aid has been a major source for financing the major infrastructure projects including basic and key industries, power and power projects, transport and communication sectors along with projects in social sector, urban development and building up institutional capacity in the Indian economy, since 1970.

Section II

Simple Correlation, Multiple Linear as well as Log-Linear Regression techniques have been applied to estimate the effectiveness of utilized foreign aid through its impact on the various selected development indicators for which time-series data have been available for the period 1970-71 to 2003-04. Lagged Multiple Linear Regression Analysis has also been applied to capture the lagged impact of utilized foreign aid on these selected indicators in this section.

CORRELATION MATRIX

To estimate and analyze the nature, and magnitude of association between the various selected development indicators as well as the IGAS, Karl Pearson's coefficients of correlation have been computed for the period 1970-71 to 1999-2000*, which has been further sub-divided into two sub-periods in order to

* Data for five development indicators viz: GDCF/GDP; IFG; ITC; IEMP; and IGIA have not been available up to the year 2003-04. Hence for the sake of bringing consistency in comparison, coefficient of correlation has been calculated only up to the year 1999-2000 for all the development indicators.

delineate the impact of economic reforms introduced in India : (1) Pre-reforms Period (1970-71 to 1990-91), and (2) Post-reforms Period (1991-92 to 1999-2000).

1. The Overall Period (1970-71 to 1999-2000)

Correlation matrix for the overall study period 1970-71 to 1999-2000 has been presented in Table 8.9, a perusal of which shows that IGAS has been positively and significantly associated with almost all the selected development indicators. During this period, IGAS has grown significantly as its coefficient of correlation has been found positive and significant (0.7767) at one percent level with time variable. IGAS has also grown significantly with all other selected variables. Similarly, most of the other development indicators have been found positively and significantly correlated with each other during this period.

2. The Pre-reforms Period (1970-71 to 1990-91)

During the pre-reforms period, IGAS was also found to be positively associated with almost all the development variables, except with ratio of Forex Reserves to GDP (FORX/GDP). IGAS has also grown during the pre-reforms period as its coefficient of correlation has been found positive (0.1353) with time variable as has been shown in Table 8.10. Most of the other development indicators have been found positively and highly significantly correlated with each other, except the FORX/GDP which has been negatively associated with most of the variables including IGAS, PGDP, AGDP, ICG/GDP, IFG, IPOL, IELE, IFP, IIP, ITC, and WPI.

3. The Post-reforms Period (1991-92 to 1999-2000)

Correlation matrix for the post-reforms period has been amplified in Table 8.11, which indicates that IGAS has been positively and highly significantly associated with most of the development indicators, such as : TIME, PGDP, XGS/GDP, FORX/ GDP, IGIA, IFG, ISP, IPOL, IELE, IFP, ITC, IEMP, and WPI. Positive and significant association (0.9777) with time variable at one percent level indicates that IGAS has grown significantly during this time period. However, IGAS was found to be negatively associated with TECG/GDP which means with growth of Gross Aid Stock, Total Expenditure of the Central

TABLE 8.9
Correlation Matrix: Inter-Correlations between the Various Indicators of Economic Development and Index of Gross Aid Stock (Overall Period: 1970-71 to 1999-2000)

Development Indicator(s)	*TIME*	*IGAS*	*PGDP*	*AGDP*	*GDCF/ GDP*	*TECG/ GDP*	*GFD/ GDP*	*ICG/ GDP*	*XGS/ GDP*	*FORX/ GDP*
(1)	(2)	(3)	(4)	(5)	(6)	(7)	(8)	(9)	(10)	(11)
TIME	1.000	0.7767	0.9525	0.3764	0.7923	0.5753	0.6539.	0.9226	0.8719	0.7217
IGAS	—	1.000	0.9111	0.2433	0.7632	0.2380	0.2527	0.8006	0.8960	0.8212
PGDP	—	—	1.000	0.3845	0.8237	0.4134	0.4817	0.9139	0.9234	0.8038
AGDP	—	—	—	1.000	0.3256	0.1696	0.2105	0.3746	0.2740	0.1898
GDCF/GDP	—	—	—	—	1.000	0.3564	0.3869	0.7784	0.8092	0.7257
TECG/GDP	—	—	—	—	—	1.000	0.9446	0.4985	0.2170	0.0851
GFD/GDP	—	—	—	—	—	—	1.000	0.5786	0.2732	0.1685
ICG/GDP	—	—	—	—	—	—	—	1.000	0.8603	0.7149
XGS/GDP	—	—	—	—	—	—	—	—	1.000	0.8790

(Contd.)

TABLE 8.9 (Contd.)

(1)	(2)	(3)	(4)	(5)	(6)	(7)	(8)	(9)	(10)	(11)
FORX/GDP	—	—	—	—	—	—	—	—	—	1.000
IGIA	—	—	—	—	—	—	—	—	—	—
IFG	—	—	—	—	—	—	—	—	—	—
ISP	—	—	—	—	—	—	—	—	—	—
IPOL	—	—	—	—	—	—	—	—	—	—
IELE	—	—	—	—	—	—	—	—	—	—
IFP	—	—	—	—	—	—	—	—	—	—
IIP	—	—	—	—	—	—	—	—	—	—
ITC	—	—	—	—	—	—	—	—	—	—
IEMP	—	—	—	—	—	—	—	—	—	—
WPI	—	—	—	—	—	—	—	—	—	—

(Contd.)

TABLE 8.9 (Contd.)

Development Indicator(s)	*IGIA*	*IFG*	*ISP*	*IPOL*	*IELE*	*IFP*	*IIP*	*ITC*	*IEMP*	*WPI*
(1)	*(12)*	*(13)*	*(14)*	*(15)*	*(16)*	*(17)*	*(18)*	*(19)*	*(20)*	*(21)*
TIME	0.9939	0.9643	0.9235	0.9670	0.9666	0.9827	0.9602.	0.9483	0.9785	0.9597
IGAS	0.8196	0.8155	0.8997	0.8535	0.9006	0.8517	0.9016	0.8944	0.6524	0.8908
PGDP	0.9705	0.9577	0.9835	0.9762	0.9959	0.9756	0.9979	0.9936	0.8762	0.9915
AGDP	0.3838	0.5153	0.3322	0.3518	0.3473	0.3553	0.3513	0.3408	0.3862	0.3521
GDCF/GDP	0.8071	0.7843	0.8157	0.8161	0.8231	0.8018	0.8289	0.8163	0.7393	0.8104
TECG/GDP	0.5140	0.5369	0.3310	0.5449	0.4325	0.5431	0.4310	0.3926	0.6590	0.3733
GFD/GDP	0.5927	0.6053	0.4046	0.5958	0.5028	0.5964	0.4996	0.4710	0.7333	0.4602
ICG/GDP	0.9172	0.8896	0.8940	0.8981	0.9254	0.9222	0.9240	0.9004	0.8832	0.9255
XGS/GDP	0.9023	0.8636	0.9224	0.8630	0.9312	0.8888	0.9232	0.9156	0.7946	0.9389
FORX/GDP	0.7643	0.7182	0.8470	0.7392	0.8020	0.7219	0.7947	0.8245	0.6338	0.8217
IGIA	1.000	0.9766	0.9444	0.9703	0.9807	0.9855	0.9740	0.9654	0.9582	0.9760

(Contd.)

TABLE 8.9 (Contd.)

(1)	(12)	(13)	(14)	(15)	(16)	(17)	(18)	(19)	(20)	(21)
IFG	—	1.000	0.9091	0.9537	0.9569	0.9640	0.9512	0.9358	0.9364	0.9466
ISP	—	—	1.000	0.9545	0.9789	0.9450	0.9836	0.9922	0.8402	0.9827
IPOL	—	—	—	1.000	0.9794	0.9788	0.9802	0.9768	0.9077	0.9644
IELE	—	—	—	—	1.000	0.9852	0.9980	0.9916	0.8960	0.9961
IFP	—	—	—	—	—	1.000	0.9818	0.9960	0.9350	0.9734
IIP	—	—	—	—	—	—	1.000	0.9944	0.8867	0.9932
ITC	—	—	—	—	—	—	—	1.000	0.8687	0.9906
IEMP	—	—	—	—	—	—	—	—	1.000	0.8869
WPI	—	—	—	—	—	—	—	—	—	1.000

N.B. : r ≥ ± 0.4602 at 28 df. is significant at 0.01 level.
r ≥ ± 0.3609 at 28 df. is significant at 0.05 level.

Source (Basic Data): Tables 8.2 to 8.7.

TABLE 8.10
Correlation Matrix: Inter-Correlations between the Various Indicators of Economic Development and Index of Gross Aid Stock (Pre-reforms Period: 1970-71 to 1990-91)

Development Indicator(s)	*TIME*	*IGAS*	*PGDP*	*AGDP*	*GDCF/ GDP*	*TECG/ GDP*	*GFD/ GDP*	*ICG/ GDP*	*XGS/ GDP*	*FORX/ GDP*
(1)	*(2)*	*(3)*	*(4)*	*(5)*	*(6)*	*(7)*	*(8)*	*(9)*	*(10)*	*(11)*
TIME	1.000	0.1353	0.9387	0.3530	0.6145	0.8752	0.9308.	0.8985	0.5891	0.0174
IGAS	—	1.000	0.4112	0.0726	0.4563	0.4293	0.2750	0.3462	0.2900	–0.1252
PGDP	—	—	1.000	0.4467	0.6665	0.8772	0.8906	0.8929	0.6034	–0.1338
AGDP	—	—	—	1.000	0.1867	0.2160	0.2132	0.2708	0.1395	–0.1587
GDCF/GDP	—	—	—	—	1.000	0.5746	0.5411	0.5397	0.6773	0.2520
TECG/GDP	—	—	—	—	—	1.000	0.9618	0.9353	0.4711	0.0489
GFD/GDP	—	—	—	—	—	—	1.000	0.9318	0.4207	0.0154
ICG/GDP	—	—	—	—	—	—	—	1.000	0.4500	–0.0931
XGS/GDP	—	—	—	—	—	—	—	—	1.000	0.3580

(*Contd.*)

Table 8.10 (Contd.)

(1)	(2)	(3)	(4)	(5)	(6)	(7)	(8)	(9)	(10)	(11)
FORX/GDP	—	—	—	—	—	—	—	—	—	1.000
IGIA	—	—	—	—	—	—	—	—	—	—
IFG	—	—	—	—	—	—	—	—	—	—
ISP	—	—	—	—	—	—	—	—	—	—
IPOL	—	—	—	—	—	—	—	—	—	—
IELE	—	—	—	—	—	—	—	—	—	—
IFP	—	—	—	—	—	—	—	—	—	—
IIP	—	—	—	—	—	—	—	—	—	—
ITC	—	—	—	—	—	—	—	—	—	—
IEMP	—	—	—	—	—	—	—	—	—	—
WPI	—	—	—	—	—	—	—	—	—	—

(Contd.)

TABLE 8.10 (Contd.)

Development Indicator(s)	*IGIA*	*IFG*	*ISP*	*IPOL*	*IELE*	*IFP*	*IIP*	*ITC*	*IEMP*	*WPI*
(1)	*(12)*	*(13)*	*(14)*	*(15)*	*(16)*	*(17)*	*(18)*	*(19)*	*(20)*	*(21)*
TIME	0.9921	0.9197	0.9736	0.9614	0.9668	0.9645	0.9561.	0.9889	0.9904	0.9853
IGAS	0.1661	0.3028	0.2340	0.3350	0.3457	0.3410	0.3759	0.2501	0.0662	0.1999
PGDP	0.9469	0.9634	0.9375	0.9699	0.9880	0.9797	0.9899	0.9719	0.9017	0.9662
AGDP	0.3858	0.5973	0.3585	0.3350	0.3534	0.3717	0.3574	0.3576	0.3521	0.3702
GDCF/GDP	0.6412	0.6059	0.6179	0.6288	0.6639	0.6409	0.6757	0.6451	0.5944	0.6103
TECG/GDP	0.8521	0.8137	0.8933	0.9296	0.8984	0.9098	0.8960	0.8917	0.8564	0.8545
GFD/GDP	0.9082	0.8453	0.9214	0.9424	0.9243	0.9289	0.9149	0.9333	0.9149	0.9143
ICG/GDP	0.8691	0.8160	0.8967	0.9480	0.9228	0.9310	0.9216	0.9202	0.8670	0.9006
XGS/GDP	0.6218	0.5648	0.5867	0.5427	0.6034	0.5639	0.6050	0.5972	0.5862	0.5689
FORX/GDP	0.0322	−0.0497	0.0073	−0.1059	−0.1192	−0.1294	−0.1353	−0.0684	0.1070	−0.1227
IGIA	1.000	0.9394	0.9674	0.9499	0.9642	0.9610	0.9540	0.9830	0.9828	0.9793

(Contd.)

TABLE 8.10 (Contd.)

(1)	(12)	(13)	(14)	(15)	(16)	(17)	(18)	(19)	(20)	(21)
IFG	—	1.000	0.9071	0.9127	0.9321	0.9247	0.9291	0.9296	0.9029	0.9290
ISP	—	—	1.000	0.9518	0.9570	0.9666	0.9500	0.9724	0.9667	0.9586
IPOL	—	—	—	1.000	0.9875	0.9903	0.9862	0.9843	0.9245	0.9720
IELE	—	—	—		1.000	0.9929	0.9990	0.9930	0.9299	0.9870
IFP	—	—	—	—	—	1.000	0.9922	0.9886	0.9293	0.9795
IIP	—	—	—	—	—	—	1.000	0.9877	0.9157	0.9809
ITC	—	—	—	—	—	—	—	1.000	0.9620	0.9949
IEMP	—	—	—	—	—	—	—	—	1.000	0.9568
WPI	—	—	—	—	—	—	—	—	—	1.000

N.B. : r ≥ ± 0.5487 at 19 df. is significant at 0.01 level.
r ≥ ± 0.4329 at 19 df. is significant at 0.05 level.

Source (Basic Data) : Tables 8.2 to 8.7.

TABLE 8.11
Correlation Matrix: Inter-Correlations between the Various Indicators of Economic Development and Index of Gross Aid Stock (Post-reforms Period: 1991-92 to 1999-2000)

Development Indicator(s)	*TIME*	*IGAS*	*PGDP*	*AGDP*	*GDCF/ GDP*	*TECG/ GDP*	*GFD/ GDP*	*ICG/ GDP*	*XGS/ GDP*	*FORX/ GDP*
(1)	*(2)*	*(3)*	*(4)*	*(5)*	*(6)*	*(7)*	*(8)*	*(9)*	*(10)*	*(11)*
TIME	1.000	0.9777	0.9969	0.5046	0.7008	-0.2959	0.1221	0.5656	0.8126	0.8727
IGAS	—	1.000	0.9730	0.4370	0.6192	-0.1598	0.2397	0.4437	0.7508	0.8788
PGDP	—	—	1.000	0.4659	0.6818	-0.2773	0.0898	0.5344	0.7887	0.8424
AGDP	—	—	—	1.000	0.6164	-0.7353	-0.1390	0.7748	0.7252	0.6106
GDCF/GDP	—	—	—	—	1.000	-0.6587	-0.3458	0.6093	0.7712	0.6762
TECG/GDP	—	—	—	—	—	1.000	0.6003	-0.7561	-0.6955	-0.2875
GFD/GDP	—	—	—	—	—	—	1.000	-0.0451	-0.0317	0.3381
ICG/GDP	—	—	—	—	—	—	—	1.000	0.8750	0.5825
XGS/GDP	—	—	—	—	—	—	—	—	1.000	0.7925

(Contd.)

TABLE 8.11 (Contd.)

(1)	(2)	(3)	(4)	(5)	(6)	(7)	(8)	(9)	(10)	(11)
FORX/GDP	–	–	–	–	–	–	–	–	–	1.000
IGIA	–	–	–	–	–	–	–	–	–	–
IFG	–	–	–	–	–	–	–	–	–	–
ISP	–	–	–	–	–	–	–	–	–	–
IPOL	–	–	–	–	–	–	–	–	–	–
IELE	–	–	–	–	–	–	–	–	–	–
IFP	–	–	–	–	–	–	–	–	–	–
IIP	–	–	–	–	–	–	–	–	–	–
ITC	–	–	–	–	–	–	–	–	–	–
IEMP	–	–	–	–	–	–	–	–	–	–
WPI	–	–	–	–	–	–	–	–	–	–

(Contd.)

Table 8.11 (Contd.)

Development Indicator(s)	*IGIA*	*IFG*	*ISP*	*IPOL*	*IELE*	*IFP*	*IIP*	*ITC*	*IEMP*	*WPI*
(1)	*(12)*	*(13)*	*(14)*	*(15)*	*(16)*	*(17)*	*(18)*	*(19)*	*(20)*	*(21)*
TIME	0.9823	0.9085	0.9798	0.9151	0.9971	0.9148	0.9923	0.9908	0.8816	0.9930
IGAS	0.9616	0.9250	0.9397	0.9439	0.9751	0.8852	0.9596	0.9785	0.7947	0.9471
PGDP	0.9827	0.9014	0.9867	0.9241	0.9965	0.9258	0.9968	0.9954	0.8802	0.9873
AGDP	0.5157	0.5867	0.4444	0.3193	0.4705	0.1849	0.4393	0.4093	0.6108	0.5717
GDCF/GDP	0.6689	0.5764	0.7481	0.6739	0.7144	0.5945	0.6979	0.6783	0.6506	0.7439
TECG/GDP	-0.2237	-0.2083	-0.3546	-0.1020	-0.2678	-0.0801	-0.2984	-0.2125	-0.6032	-0.3881
GFD/GDP	0.1406	0.2039	-0.0306	0.0573	0.1086	0.1035	0.0593	0.1076	-0.0788	0.0672
ICG/GDP	0.5208	0.4226	0.5562	0.2611	0.5382	0.3568	0.5511	0.4715	0.7962	0.6456
XGS/GDP	0.7433	0.6807	0.8141	0.6269	0.7921	0.5986	0.8001	0.7506	0.9090	0.8524
FORX/GDP	0.8640	0.9089	0.7968	0.7716	0.8590	0.6756	0.9089	0.8317	0.7335	0.8735
IGIA	1.000	0.9335	0.9536	0.9194	0.9848	0.8933	0.9699	0.9802	0.8282	0.9739

(Contd.)

TABLE 8.11 (Contd.)

(1)	(12)	(13)	(14)	(15)	(16)	(17)	(18)	(19)	(20)	(21)
IFG	—	1.000	0.8411	0.8646	0.8959	0.7299	0.8664	0.8924	0.7426	0.8929
ISP	—	—	1.000	0.9190	0.9850	0.9239	0.9942	0.9834	0.8909	0.9769
IPOL	—	—	—	1.000	0.9331	0.8696	0.9145	0.9513	0.6642	0.8764
IELE	—	—	—		1.000	0.9291	0.9939	0.9961	0.8590	0.9877
IFP	—	—	—	—	—	1.000	0.9375	0.9402	0.7469	0.8929
IIP	—	—	—	—	—	—	1.000	0.9924	0.8915	0.9854
ITC	—	—	—	—	—	—	—	1.000	0.8350	0.9728
IEMP	—	—	—	—	—	—	—	—	1.000	0.9154
WPI	—	—	—	—	—	—	—	—	—	1.000

N.B. : Significant at 0.01 level for $r \geq \pm 0.7976$ at 7 df.
Significant at 0.05 level for $r \geq \pm 0.6664$ at 7 df.

Source (Basic Data) : Tables 8.2 to 8.7.

Government has declined. Positive and significant inter-correlations have been observed between most of the other economic variables, except for TECG/GDP and GFD/GDP.

Thus, on the whole, analysis of correlations for the three selected time periods highlighted positive and mostly significant correlation between IGAS and all other development indicators, except FORX/GDP during the pre-reforms period, and TECG/GDP during the post-reforms period. The Gross Aid Stock variable was positively and highly significantly correlated with almost all the development indicators during the overall study period.

MULTIPLE REGRESSION ANALYSIS

To estimate the impact of utilized gross foreign aid as measured by the IGAS on the selected indicators of development, Linear as well as Log-Linear Multiple Regression Analysis, with selected development indicators as dependent variables and IGAS along with time variable* as independent/explanatory variables have been applied for the period 1970-71 to 2003-04, which has been further divided into two sub-periods, in order to delineate the impact of economic reforms: (1) Pre-reforms Period (1970-71 to 1990-91), and (2) Post-reforms Period (1991-92 to 2003-04).

1. The Overall Period (1970-71 to 2003-04)

The results of Linear Multiple Regression Analysis (LMRA) for the whole period 1970-71 to 2003-04 have been presented in Table 8.12. A glance at the table shows that R^2 of the fitted regression equations have been found significant for almost all the dependent variables, except for AGDP (Annual Growth Rate of GDP). The regression coefficients for most of the dependent variables, such as : PGDP (Per Capita GDP); XGS/GDP (Export of Goods and Services as ratio of GDP); FORX/GDP (Forex reserves as ratio of GDP); IGIA (Index of Gross Irrigated Area); ISP (Index of Steel Production); IPOL (Index of Petroleum Refinery

* Time variable has been included as explanatory variable along with IGAS variable to eliminate the trend component from the available time-series data in order to obtain trend corrected coefficients (Gujarati, 1985: pp. 124-25).

Products); IELE (Index of Electricity Generation); IFP (Index of Fertilizer Production); IIP (Index of Overall Industrial Production); and ITC (Index of Transport and Communication) have been found to be positive and highly significant, which indicated that utilized gross foreign aid proved quite useful for these industries/activities, during the above-mentioned period. Foreign aid also proved highly helpful to check the Gross Fiscal Deficit (GFD/GDP) as indicated by its negative but highly significant regression coefficient. It also had positive, though non-significant, effect on some other dependent variables, such as: GDCF/GDP (Gross Domestic Capital Formation as ratio of GDP); ICG/GDP (Import of Capital Goods as ratio of GDP); and IFG (Index of Foodgrains Production) as indicated by their positive and non-significant regression coefficients. However, for other dependent variables, such as : TECG/GDP (Total Expenditure of the Central Govt. as ratio of GDP) and IEMP (Index of Employment in Organized Sector) regression coefficients were found to be negative and significant, while for AGDP (Annual Growth Rate of GDP) it was found to be negative and non-significant, which implies that foreign aid did not prove useful or proved harmful for these variables, during the overall period. Similarly, utilized aid was found unable to curb the price-rise, instead it fuelled the same, as has been indicated by the positive and significant regression coefficient of WPI (Wholesale Price Index for all the commodities). The highly significant regression coefficients of time variable, which has been taken along with IGAS, in the different equations indicate that the effect of foreign aid, if any, has been carried away by the trend coefficients.

The results of Log-Linear Multiple Regression Analysis (LLMRA) for the overall period have been given in Table 8.13, a perusal of which shows that R^2 of almost all the fitted regression equations were found to be significant. However, the results of LLMRA were different to some extent than those of the LMRA. Under LLMRA utilized gross foreign aid positively and highly significantly affected PGDP; XGS/GDP; FORX/GDP; ISP; IPOL; IIP; and ITC as their regression coefficients were positive and significant at either one or five percent level. The regression coefficients of GFD/GDP and WPI (unlike LMRA) were found negative and highly significant, which means that utilized

TABLE 8.12

Impact of Foreign Aid : Results of Linear Multiple Regression Analysis (Overall Period: 1970-71 to 2003-04)

Equation No.	Dependent Variable	Regression Coefficients: Constant (T-value)	Index of Gross Aid Stock (T-value)	Time (T-value)	R^2	$\bar{R}^2$	F-value	N
(1)	(2)	(3)	(4)	(5)	(6)	(7)	(8)	(9)
1.	(PGDP) Per Capita GDP	574.1142* (2.127)	58.1238** (12.989)	128.3022** (13.386)	0.987**	0.986	1158.143	34
2.	(AGDP) Annual Growth Rate of GDP	4.9432^NS (1.834)	-0.03398^NS (-0.760)	0.16976^NS (1.774)	0.143^NS	0.087	2.577	34
3.	(GDCF/GDP) Gross Domestic Capital Formation as Ratio of GDP	19.1493** (12.585)	0.0398^NS (1.599)	0.1593** (3.107)	0.694**	0.673	34.003	33
4.	(TECG/GDP) Total Expenditure of Central Govt.	19.3528** (11.367)	-0.07819** (-2.770)	0.27431** (4.537)	0.445**	0.409	12.413	34
5.	(GFD/GDP) Gross Fiscal Deficit as Ratio of GDP	8.5773** (8.015)	-0.0778** (-4.387)	0.2406** (6.332)	0.585**	0.558	21.821	34

(Contd.)

TABLE 8.12 (Contd.)

(1)	(2)	(3)	(4)	(5)	(6)	(7)	(8)	(9)
6.	(ICG/GDP) Import of Capital Goods as Ratio of GDP	0.5148^{NS} (1.987)	0.00392^{NS} (0.913)	0.05674** (6.166)	0.849**	0.839	87.169	34
7.	(XGS/GDP) Export of Goods & Services as Ratio of GDP	-1.4102* (-2.096)	0.0705** (6.320)	0.1070** (4.480)	0.926**	0.921	194.678	34
8.	(FORX/GDP) Forex Reserves as Ratio of GDP	-10.5246** (-5.653)	0.1762** (5.707)	0.02755^{NS} (0.417)	0.810**	0.798	66.212	34
9.	Index of Gross Irrigated Area (IGIA)	42.4081** (24.016)	0.1360** (4.913)	1.8544** (36.833)	0.994**	0.993	2094.528	30
10.	Index of Foodgrains Production (IFG)	47.7618** (8.733)	0.0402^{NS} (0.450)	1.8509** (10.044)	0.923**	0.918	180.025	33
11.	(ISP) Index of Steel (Finished) Production	-106.0506** (-8.244)	1.7405** (8.160)	2.6723** (5.850)	0.955**	0.952	327.494	34
12.	(IPOL) Index of Petroleum Refinery Products	-65.7729** (-4.556)	1.2997** (5.430)	2.5152** (4.906)	0.920**	0.915	177.879	34
13.	(IELE) Index of Electricity Generation	-65.7795** (-17.893)	0.9851** (16.161)	3.0933** (23.693)	0.994**	0.994	2652.045	34

14.	(IFP) Index of Fertilizer Production	-30.5008** (-4.568)	0.3714** (3.355)	4.1806** (17.631)	0.980**	0.979	760.796	34
15.	(IIP) Index of Industrial Production	-60.8236** (-11.839)	1.0780** (12.654)	2.8302** (15.512)	0.988**	0.988	1321.914	34
16.	(ITC) Index of Transport and Communication	-94.2945** (-6.955)	1.5477** (6.981)	2.7093** (5.931)	0.944**	0.940	253.735	33
17.	(IEMP) Index of Employment in Organized Sector	83.9796** (42.778)	-0.2505** (-7.916)	1.6223** (26.003)	0.977**	0.975	611.033	32
18.	(WPI) Wholesale Price Index for All the Commodities	-69.7047** (-11.310)	1.0109** (9.893)	3.1498** (14.391)	0.984**	0.983	984.487	34

N.B. : * Significant at 0.05 level.
** Significant at 0.01 level.
NS Indicates non-significant.

Sources (Basic Data) : Tables 8.2 to 8.7.

TABLE 8.13
Impact of Foreign Aid : Results of Log-Linear Multiple Regression Analysis (Overall Period: 1970-71 to 2003-04)

Equation No.	Dependent Variable	Regression Coefficients: Constant (T-value)	Index of Gross Aid Stock (T-value)	Time (T-value)	R^2	$\bar{R}^2$	F-value	N
(1)	(2)	(3)	(4)	(5)	(6)	(7)	(8)	(9)
1.	PGDP	2.9017** (42.588)	0.4260** (11.169)	0.00888** (23.145)	0.992**	0.991	1908.727	34
2.	AGDP	4.2935NS (1.156)	-2.3778NS (-1.144)	0.0467* (2.233)	0.182*	0.129	3.451	34
3.	GDCF/GDP	1.0738** (6.960)	0.1458NS (1.691)	0.00271** (3.186)	0.699**	0.679	34.902	33
4.	TECG/GDP	1.7746** (6.517)	-0.3382* (-2.219)	0.00643** (4.193)	0.433**	0.396	11.829	34
5.	GFD/GDP	2.5826** (4.883)	-1.1106** (-3.751)	0.0182** (6.099)	0.587**	0.560	21.993	34
6.	ICG/GDP	-0.0632NS (-0.189)	0.0152NS (0.081)	0.0155** (8.249)	0.886**	0.879	120.387	34
7.	XGS/GDP	-0.7356* (-2.337)	0.7091** (4.025)	0.00904** (5.097)	0.896**	0.889	133.682	34

8.	FORX/GDP	-2.9837** (-2.905)	1.7625** (3.066)	0.0109NS (1.889)	0.718**	0.700	39.570	34
9.	IGIA	1.7811** (33.640)	-0.0252NS (-0.858)	0.0111** (41.256)	0.993**	0.993	1973.594	30
10.	IFG	1.7969** (9.648)	-0.0382NS (-0.367)	0.0107** (10.445)	0.916**	0.910	163.688	33
11.	ISP	0.5083* (2.286)	0.4978** (3.998)	0.0235** (18.772)	0.982**	0.981	861.563	34
12.	IPOL	0.9742** (4.369)	0.2956* (2.368)	0.0204** (16.282)	0.974**	0.972	584.368	34
13.	IELE	1.3224** (9.515)	-0.0672NS (-0.864)	0.0328** (41.909)	0.995**	0.994	2951.247	34
14.	IFP	3.0479** (8.048)	-1.0850** (-5.118)	0.0456** (21.359)	0.971**	0.969	518.311	34
15.	IIP	0.8840** (9.842)	0.2792** (5.553)	0.0240** (47.535)	0.997**	0.996	4761.262	34
16.	ITC	0.8385** (5.684)	0.2997** (3.636)	0.0254** (31.295)	0.992**	0.991	1879.194	33
17.	IEMP	2.3551** (33.123)	-0.2841** (-7.169)	0.00836** (21.949)	0.965**	0.963	403.856	32
18.	WPI	1.8223** (12.292)	-0.3672** (-4.424)	0.0367** (43.901)	0.995**	0.994	2817.318	34

N.B. : * Significant at 0.05 level.
** Significant at 0.01 level.
NS Indicates non-significant.

Sources (Basic Data) : Tables 8.2 to 8.7.

foreign aid proved highly useful in checking gross fiscal deficit, and the wholesale price level. Besides these, foreign aid also had positive, though non-significant, effect on the GDCF/GDP and ICG/GDP as their regression coefficients were also found to be positive but non-significant. The regression coefficients of AGDP; IGIA; IFG; and IELE, unlike in case of LMRA, were found to be negative, though non-significant, which implies that utilized gross foreign aid did not contribute to their growth. The highly significant regression coefficients of time variable in case of these indicators show that the impact of foreign aid, if any, seems to have been absorbed by the trend coefficients. Similarly, foreign aid contributed negatively in the presence of time variable in case of IFP; IEMP; and TECG/GDP as indicated by the negative and significant regression coefficients of these variables.

2. The Pre-reforms Period (1970-71 to 1990-91)

During the pre-reforms period, the results, under both the LMRA and LLMRA, were also found to be different to some extent, although R^2 for almost all the fitted regression equations were significant under both these analyses. The LMRA, results of which are amplified in Table 8.14, shows that utilized gross foreign aid proved highly useful in most of the activities/ indicators, such as : PGDP; GDCF/GDP, TECG/GDP; ICG/GDP; IFG; ISP; IPOL; IELE; IFP; IIP; and ITC as their regression coefficients have been found to be positive and significant. Similarly, it also proved quite useful, though non-significantly, in some other activities, such as : AGDP; XGS/GDP; and IGIA, for which regression coefficients have been positive but non-significant. However, the regression coefficient for IEMP has been negative and significant, and for FORX/GDP negative but non-significant, which infers that utilized foreign aid has not contributed much to their growth in the presence of time variable. Similarly, it also did not prove useful for checking gross fiscal deficit, and the price level as the regression coefficients of GFD/ GDP and WPI were found to be positive but non-significant in the presence of time variable. The highly significant regression coefficients of time variable in case of these variables indicate that the impact of foreign aid, if any, seems to have been taken away by the highly significant trend coefficients, during the above-mentioned period.

Table 8.14
Impact of Foreign Aid : Results of Linear Multiple Regression Analysis (Pre-reforms Period: 1970-71 to 1990-91)

Equation No.	Dependent Variable	Regression Coefficients: Constant (T-value)	Index of Gross Aid Stock (T-value)	Time (T-value)	R^2	$\bar{R}^2$	F-value	N
(1)	(2)	(3)	(4)	(5)	(6)	(7)	(8)	(9)
1.	PGDP	2161.5996** (5.132)	36.7537** (6.365)	129.6320** (19.784)	0.963**	0.959	237.346	21
2.	AGDP	1.3422NS (0.166)	0.0126NS (0.114)	0.1975NS (1.571)	0.125NS	0.028	1.288	21
3.	GDCF/GDP	14.3532** (4.370)	0.1038* (2.305)	0.1744** (3.414)	0.519**	0.466	9.728	21
4.	TECG/GDP	3.0416NS (1.146)	0.1315** (3.614)	0.3924** (9.501)	0.864**	0.849	57.369	21
5.	GFD/GDP	-0.9941NS (-0.575)	0.0454NS (1.916)	0.3088** (11.485)	0.889**	0.877	72.087	21

(Contd.)

Table 8.14 (Contd.)

(1)	(2)	(3)	(4)	(5)	(6)	(7)	(8)	(9)
6.	ICG/GDP	-0.1506^NS^ (-0.406)	0.0130* (2.558)	0.0560** (9.699)	0.859**	0.843	54.671	21
7.	XGS/GDP	2.2381^NS^ (1.461)	0.0243^NS^ (1.155)	0.0720** (3.019)	0.392*	0.324	5.804	21
8.	FORX/GDP	4.3159* (1.460)	-0.0223^NS^ (-0.551)	0.0068^NS^ (1.148)	0.017^NS^	-0.092	0.154	21
9.	IGIA	48.8879** (14.377)	0.0524^NS^ (1.124)	1.8104** (34.226)	0.985**	0.984	602.591	21
10.	IFG	25.7333* (2.303)	0.3351* (2.188)	1.8744** (10.783)	0.878**	0.865	64.917	21
11.	ISP	6.3275^NS^ (0.769)	0.2426* (2.150)	2.5368** (19.812)	0.958**	0.954	208.151	21
12.	IPOL	-16.750 ^NS^ (-1.860)	0.5968** (4.836)	3.0285** (21.624)	0.967**	0.963	264.483	21
13.	IELE	-36.9560** (-5.650)	0.6094** (6.798)	2.9617** (29.111)	0.982**	0.980	482.445	21

14.	IFP	-64.2380** (-6.070)	0.8324** (5.738)	4.1223** (25.043)	0.975**	0.973	356.013	21
15.	IIP	-31.0834** (-4.274)	0.6799** (6.821)	2.8333** (25.047)	0.976**	0.973	366.779	21
16.	ITC	-1.6075^NS (-0.406)	0.2969** (5.471)	2.7666** (44.931)	0.992**	0.991	1077.369	21
17.	IEMP	72.6796** (21.120)	-0.0998* (-2.416)	1.6374** (34.933)	0.985**	0.984	612.879	21
18.	WPI	-5.0891^NS (-0.739)	0.1715^NS (1.817)	2.8018** (26.155)	0.975**	0.973	356.660	21

N.B. : * Significant at 0.05 level.
** Significant at 0.01 level.
NS Indicates non-significant.

Sources (Basic Data) : Tables 8.2 to 8.7.

On the other hand, LLMRA, results of which are shown in Table 8.15, identified regression coefficients positive and significant for variables, like : PGDP; TECG/GDP; IPOL; IELE; IIP; GDCF/GDP; and ICG/GDP which implies that utilized gross foreign aid proved highly useful in their respective growth. The regression coefficient for WPI (unlike in case of LMRA) has been found negative and significant at one percent level implying thereby that utilized foreign aid proved highly useful in checking the increase in wholesale prices. It was also found to be useful, though non-significantly, for some other activities, such as : XGS/GDP; IFG; ISP; and IFP unlike in case of LMRA. However, the regression coefficient of IEMP under LLMRA also (like in case of LMRA) has been found negative and significant in the presence of time variable. Similarly, for FORX/GDP regression coefficient has been found negative but non-significant under both the analyses. Both of these showed the regression coefficients for gross fiscal deficit (GFD/GDP) as positive and non-significant. This means foreign aid did not prove helpful in generating employment, raising forex reserves and checking the gross fiscal deficit. Unlike in case of LMRA, under LLMRA the regression coefficients for AGDP; IGIA; and ITC are negative and non-significant. This implies that foreign aid had not contributed to the growth of these variables. However, the presence of highly significant regression coefficients of time variable in case of these variables indicate that the effect of foreign aid, if any, might have been absorbed by the trend coefficients.

3. The Post-reforms Period (1991-92 to 2003-04)

During the post-reforms period, results of fitted regression equations were again found to be different to some extent under both the LMRA and LLMRA. The results of LMRA, amplified in Table 8.16, show that R^2 for most of the fitted regression equations were found to be significant, except for the indicators AGDP; GFD/GDP; ICG/GDP; and IFG. A perusal of the table indicate that utilized foreign aid proved useful only in a few activities on which it has been incurred, including TECG/GDP; FORX/GDP; IPOL; and ITC as their regression coefficients were found positive and significant. It also proved helpful in checking the wholesale prices, as the regression coefficient of WPI have been negative and highly significant. Utilized foreign aid also contributed, though non-significantly, to the growth of irrigation

TABLE 8.15
Impact of Foreign Aid : Results of Log-Linear Multiple Regression Analysis (Pre-reform Period: 1970-71 to 1990-91)

Equation No.	Dependent Variable	Regression Coefficients: Constant (T-value)	Index of Gross Aid Stock (T-value)	Time (T-value)	R^2	$\bar{R}^2$	F-value	N
(1)	(2)	(3)	(4)	(5)	(6)	(7)	(8)	(9)
1.	PGDP	3.0358** (26.930)	0.3551** (5.843)	0.0088** (21.517)	0.968**	0.964	270.087	21
2.	AGDP	2.6077^{NS} (0.315)	-1.4884^{NS} (-0.334)	0.0505^{NS} (1.684)	0.137^{NS}	0.041	1.424	21
3.	GDCF/GDP	0.7817** (3.052)	0.3007* (2.178)	0.0031** (3.394)	0.508**	0.453	9.279	21
4.	TECG/GDP	0.0463^{NS} (0.160)	0.5737** (3.675)	0.00928** (9.465)	0.864**	0.849	57.187	21

(Contd.)

TABLE 8.15 (Contd.)

(1)	(2)	(3)	(4)	(5)	(6)	(7)	(8)	(9)
5.	GFD/GDP	-0.5366^NS^ (-0.842)	0.5354^NS^ (1.559)	0.0243** (10.544)	0.870**	0.855	60.053	21
6.	ICG/GDP	-1.1047* (-2.739)	0.5670* (2.608)	0.0168** (11.510)	0.893**	0.881	74.959	21
7.	XGS/GDP	0.1330^NS^ (0.225)	0.2518^NS^ (0.790)	0.0067** (3.151)	0.388*	0.320	5.708	21
8.	FORX/GDP	1.5539^NS^ (0.833)	-0.6359^NS^ (-0.632)	0.00315^NS^ (0.466)	0.029^NS^	-0.078	0.274	21
9.	IGIA	1.8030** (19.258)	-0.0367^NS^ (-0.728)	0.0110** (32.538)	0.983**	0.982	535.972	21
10.	IFG	1.2314** (4.070)	0.2610^NS^ (1.600)	0.0115** (10.470)	0.868**	0.854	59.374	21
11.	ISP	1.2452** (3.359)	0.1089^NS^ (0.545)	0.0224** (16.659)	0.941**	0.934	142.643	21
12.	IPOL	0.7596** (3.703)	0.4069** (3.680)	0.0219** (29.438)	0.981**	0.979	462.669	21

13.	IELE	0.5974**	0.3170**	0.0335**	0.999**	0.999	7456.077	21
		(7.734)	(7.614)	(119.780)				
14.	IFP	0.7551*	0.1283^{NS}	0.0486**	0.989**	0.988	810.279	21
		(2.239)	(0.706)	(39.798)				
15.	IIP	0.4442**	0.5123**	0.0247**	0.996**	0.996	2323.489	21
		(4.287)	(9.170)	(65.728)				
16.	ITC	1.450**	-0.0241^{NS}	0.0248**	0.998**	0.997	3892.912	21
		(18.503)	(-0.570)	(87.526)				
17.	IEMP	2.0689**	-0.1327**	0.00874**	0.978**	0.976	400.914	21
		(24.264)	(-2.886)	(28.303)				
18.	WPI	2.3201**	-0.6287**	0.0351**	0.996**	0.996	2332.29	21
		(16.362)	(-8.225)	(68.292)				

N.B. : * Significant at 0.05 level.
** Significant at 0.01 level.
^{NS} Indicates non-significant.

Sources (Basic Data) : Tables 8.2 to 8.7.

TABLE 8.16
Impact of Foreign Aid : Results of Linear Multiple Regression Analysis (Post-reforms Period: 1991-92 to 2003-04)

Equation No.	Dependent Variable	Constant (T-value)	Regression Coefficients: Index of Gross Aid Stock (T-value)	Regression Coefficients: Time (T-value)	R^2	$\bar{R}^2$	F-value	N
(1)	(2)	(3)	(4)	(5)	(6)	(7)	(8)	(9)
1.	PGDP	7694.102** (5.427)	-0.8396^{NS} (-0.051)	423.9578** (6.917)	0.995**	0.995	1113.585	13
2.	AGDP	25.2654^{NS} (1.134)	-0.2388^{NS} (-0.917)	1.0016^{NS} (1.039)	0.142^{NS}	-0.029	0.831	13
3.	GDCF/GDP	66.6643** (3.745)	-0.4758* (-2.300)	2.0078* (2.680)	0.569*	0.474	5.948	12
4.	TECG/GDP	-9.2168^{NS} (-1.235)	0.3117** (3.576)	-1.0945** (-3.392)	0.580*	0.496	6.898	13
5.	GFD/GDP	-1.5667^{NS} (-0.171)	0.0927^{NS} (0.867)	-0.3450^{NS} (-0.871)	0.071^{NS}	-0.115	0.380	13
6.	ICG/GDP	7.1706^{NS} (1.527)	-0.0584^{NS} (-1.065)	0.2678^{NS} (1.319)	0.308^{NS}	0.170	2.227	13
7.	XGS/GDP	9.3070^{NS} (1.498)	-0.0207^{NS} (-0.285)	0.3737^{NS} (1.392)	0.853**	0.824	29.122	13

8.	FORX/GDP	-42.5990* (-2.324)	0.5275* (2.464)	-0.9037^{NS} (-1.140)	0.895**	0.874	42.805	13
9.	IGIA	91.5059** (4.035)	0.0207^{NS} (0.080)	2.2732* (2.621)	0.965**	0.953	82.485	9
10.	IFG	139.5792^{NS} (1.878)	-0.5146^{NS} (-0.596)	3.0668^{NS} (0.980)	0.416^{NS}	0.286	3.208	12
11.	ISP	104.9443^{NS} (1.323)	-0.4017^{NS} (-0.434)	14.3010** (4.170)	0.985**	0.982	330.531	13
12.	IPOL	-302.2983^{NS} (-1.899)	4.2545* (2.289)	-3.8014^{NS} (-0.552)	0.935**	0.922	71.832	13
13.	IELE	110.5790** (5.408)	-0.3569^{NS} (-1.495)	8.5228** (9.640)	0.997**	0.996	1574.078	13
14.	IFP	234.8296* (2.811)	-1.5912^{NS} (-1.631)	10.1235* (2.803)	0.874**	0.849	34.734	13
15.	IIP	122.0592** (3.803)	-0.4957^{NS} (-1.322)	10.0419** (7.237)	0.994**	0.993	830.941	13
16.	ITC	-162.8040^{NS} (-1.635)	2.6111* (2.255)	3.6923^{NS} (0.881)	0.977**	0.972	192.597	12
17.	IEMP	141.5027** (8.327)	-0.4810* (-2.452)	1.8587* (2.722)	0.537*	0.421	4.642	11
18.	WPI	167.4930** (11.616)	-1.0269** (-6.098)	11.2377** (18.026)	0.998**	0.998	3415.170	13

N.B. : * Significant at 0.05 level.
** Significant at 0.01 level.
^{NS} Indicates non-significant.

Sources (Basic Data) : Tables 8.2 to 8.7.

facilities as the regression coefficient of IGIA was positive and non-significant. For all other indicators including PGDP; AGDP; GDCF/GDP; ICG/GDP; XGS/GDP; IFG; ISP; IELE; IFP; IIP; and IEMP regression coefficients have been found negative and non-significant in the presence of time variable, which means utilized foreign aid has not proved useful or proved harmful for these activities, during the post-reforms period. Similarly, it also did not prove helpful in checking gross fiscal deficit (GFD/GDP) in the country. However, the presence of significant regression coefficients of time variable in case of most of these above-mentioned variables infers that the impact of foreign aid, if any, seems to have been carried away by the trend coefficients.

Whereas, under LLMRA, results of which are shown in Table 8.17, R^2 of all the fitted regression equations have been found significant, except for AGDP; TECG/GDP; GFD/GDP; ICG/GDP; IFG; and IEMP. A glance at the table shows that utilized foreign aid contributed significantly to the total expenditure of the Central Government as the regression coefficient of TECG/GDP has been found positive and significant. It also proved useful in checking the wholesale price level in view of the negative but significant regression coefficient of WPI. The regression coefficients of FORX/GDP; IFG; and IPOL under LLMRA have been found positive but non-significant, unlike in case of LMRA, which implies that utilized foreign aid proved useful for these areas of economic activity. For all other areas/activities including PGDP; AGDP; GDCF/GDP; ICG/GDP; XGS/GDP; IGIA; ISP; IELE; IFP; IIP; ITC; and IEMP under LLMRA, like in case of LMRA, utilized foreign aid did not prove useful during the post-reforms period as their respective regression coefficients have been found negative but mostly non-significant. However, the presence of significant regression coefficients of time variable in case of most of these equations again indicate that the impact of foreign aid, if any, seems to have been absorbed by the trend coefficients. Consequently, utilized foreign aid did not contribute significantly to the development of these above-mentioned areas of activity in the presence of time variable.

LAGGED MULTIPLE REGRESSION ANALYSIS

In order to examine the impact of utilized foreign aid during the current year and in the preceding years on the level of

TABLE 8.17
Impact of Foreign Aid : Results of Log-Linear Multiple Regression Analysis (Post-reforms Period: 1991-92 to 2003-04)

Equation No.	Dependent Variable	Regression Coefficients: Constant (T-value)	Index of Gross Aid Stock (T-value)	Time (T-value)	R^2	$\bar{R}^2$	F-value	N
(1)	(2)	(3)	(4)	(5)	(6)	(7)	(8)	(9)
1.	PGDP	4.7087** (11.616)	-0.4180 NS (-2.003)	0.0234** (7.812)	0.996**	0.995	1161.058	13
2.	AGDP	5.2360 NS (0.298)	-2.3889 NS (-0.265)	0.0525 NS (0.404)	0.126 NS	-0.049	0.720	13
3.	GDCF/GDP	5.1912* (2.627)	-1.9458 NS (-1.913)	0.0326 NS (2.238)	0.526*	0.420	4.987	12
4.	TECG/GDP	-2.4722 NS (-1.585)	1.9115* (2.381)	-0.0261* (-2.262)	0.389 NS	0.267	3.182	13
5.	GFD/GDP	-5.6840 NS (-1.403)	3.3383 NS (1.600)	-0.0480 NS (-1.601)	0.204 NS	0.045	1.285	13

(Contd.)

TABLE 8.17 (Contd.)

(1)	(2)	(3)	(4)	(5)	(6)	(7)	(8)	(9)
6.	ICG/GDP	5.6764 ^{NS} (0.963)	-2.7516 ^{NS} (-0.907)	0.0492 ^{NS} (1.128)	0.304 ^{NS}	0.165	2.185	13
7.	XGS/GDP	1.9616 ^{NS} (0.990)	-0.5542 ^{NS} (-0.543)	0.0215 ^{NS} (1.464)	0.854**	0.825	29.374	13
8.	FORX/GDP	-6.1247 ^{NS} (-1.103)	3.4728 ^{NS} (1.215)	-0.00295 ^{NS} (-0.072)	0.899**	0.879	44.692	13
9.	IGIA	2.1042** (4.249)	-0.0678 ^{NS} (-0.267)	0.0106* (2.990)	0.970**	0.960	96.151	9
10.	IFG	1.9487 ^{NS} (0.916)	0.0159 ^{NS} (0.015)	0.00496 ^{NS} (0.316)	0.396 ^{NS}	0.261	2.946	12
11.	ISP	7.0812** (5.119)	-2.6520** (-3.725)	0.0743** (7.250)	0.989**	0.986	438.198	13
12.	IPOL	-1.2364 ^{NS} (-0.413)	1.6114 ^{NS} (1.046)	0.0117 ^{NS} (0.528)	0.944**	0.933	84.462	13
13.	IELE	3.7509** (4.299)	-0.9358 ^{NS} (-2.083)	0.0381** (5.892)	0.990**	0.988	501.951	13

14.	IFP	5.3770* (2.559)	-1.7375 NS (-1.606)	0.0397* (2.550)	0.866**	0.840	32.457	13
15.	IIP	4.7888** (5.428)	-1.4674** (-3.231)	0.0478** (7.315)	0.991**	0.990	581.798	13
16	ITC	1.9912* (2.341)	-0.0514 NS (-0.117)	0.0396** (6.324)	0.996**	0.995	1037.445	12
17.	IEMP	2.7622** (5.190)	-0.3923 NS (-1.433)	0.00634 NS (1.650)	0.356 NS	0.195	2.209	11
18.	WPI	5.0974** (4.048)	-1.6302* (-2.515)	0.0489** (5.247)	0.981**	0.977	261.642	13

N.B. : * Significant at 0.05 level.
** Significant at 0.01 level.
NS Indicates non-significant.

Sources (Basic Data) : Tables 8.2 to 8.7.

development through the selected development indicators, Lagged Multiple Linear Regression Analysis has been carried out with a time lag up to five years, the results of which are amplified in Appendix 8.1. A scanning of the Appendix indicates that R^2 has been improved for most of the regression equations as compared to the without lag LMRA, and found highly significant at one percent level for almost all the dependent variables, except AGDP and GFD/GDP, for which it was non-significant. Most of the regression coefficients worked out for the utilized foreign aid for their selected respective development indicators during the current year have been found positive, either significant or non-significant. During the preceding t-1, t-2, t-3, t-4 and t-5 years, for most of the development indicators, the regression coefficients presented fluctuating and non-significant results. The utilized foreign aid in the current and past five years, under Lagged Multiple Linear Regression Analysis, proved useful only for the variables, like IGIA; ISP; and ITC. Similarly, foreign aid also proved useful for petroleum refinery products (IPOL), overall industrial production (IIP), and employment generation (IEMP) with lagged effect.

On the whole, it can be concluded that utilized foreign aid proved useful and effective for the development of most of the areas/activities of Indian economy on which it has been utilized, under both the LMRA as well as LLMRA, particularly during the overall period (1970-71 to 2003-04), and during the pre-reforms period (1970-71 to 1990-91). However, the effectiveness of utilized foreign aid weakened during the post-reforms period (1990-91 to 2003-04), owing to the fact that country got either a little or negative net foreign aid, during this period, as the country has been repaying the amortization and interest payments from its own precious forex reserves in the recent past to relieve off the burden of debt payments. The Lagged Multiple Regression Analysis indicated that utilized foreign aid was not significantly useful for most of the selected indicators during all the time periods.

APPENDIX 8.1
Impact of Foreign Aid : Results of Lagged Multiple Linear Regression Analysis (1970-71 to 2003-04)

Equation No.	Dependent Variable	Constant (T-value)	$IGAS_t$ (T-value)	$IGAS_{t-1}$ (T-value)	$IGAS_{t-2}$ (T-value)	$IGAS_{t-3}$ (T-value)
(1)	(2)	(3)	(4)	(5)	(6)	(7)
1.	Per-Capita GDP (PGDP)	-1208.6119^{NS} (-2.043)	91.6253^{*} (2.772)	-15.1381^{NS} (-0.347)	34.9658^{NS} (0.821)	-3.6745^{NS} (-0.085)
2.	Annual Growth Rate of GDP (AGDP)	1.1454^{NS} (0.393)	0.2604^{NS} (1.598)	-0.6266^{**} (-2.913)	0.6217^{**} (2.963)	-0.2914^{NS} (-1.366)
3.	Gross Domestic Capital Formation as Ratio of GDP (GDCF/GDP)	18.8069^{**} (11.010)	-0.0415^{NS} (-0.462)	0.1528^{NS} (1.292)	0.0732^{NS} (0.628)	0.0457^{NS} (0.378)
4.	Total Expenditure of Central Govt. as Ratio of GDP (TECG/GDP)	23.3219^{**} (13.952)	0.3099^{**} (3.318)	-0.1097^{NS} (-0.890)	-0.03899^{NS} (-0.324)	-0.0891^{NS} (-0.729)
5.	Gross Fiscal Deficit as Ratio of GDP (GFD/GDP)	10.1472^{**} (6.996)	0.1458^{NS} (1.800)	-0.0389^{NS} (-0.364)	-0.0173^{NS} (-0.166)	-0.0266^{NS} (-0.250)
6.	Import of Capital Goods as Ratio of GDP (ICG/GDP)	0.3278^{NS} (0.734)	0.0378^{NS} (1.514)	-0.00677^{NS} (-0.206)	0.00255^{NS} (0.079)	-0.0110^{NS} (-0.337)
7.	Export of Goods and Services as Ratio of GDP (XGS/GDP)	-3.1311^{**} (-4.465)	0.0429^{NS} (1.096)	0.0788^{NS} (1.524)	-0.0465^{NS} (-0.921)	0.0324^{NS} (0.632)

(Contd.)

APPENDIX 8.1 (*Contd.*)

(1)	(2)	(3)	(4)	(5)	(6)	(7)
8.	Forex Reserves as Ratio of GDP (FORX/GDP)	-15.6015** (-8.089)	-0.1763^{NS} (-1.636)	0.2801^{NS} (1.969)	0.0431^{NS} (0.311)	-0.0190^{NS} (-0.135)
9.	Index of Gross Irrigated Area (IGIA)	21.2373* (2.209)	0.6898^{NS} (1.639)	0.0487^{NS} (0.084)	0.2901^{NS} (0.508)	0.0318^{NS} (0.055)
10.	Index of Foodgrains Production (IFG)	37.5785** (3.510)	1.3712* (2.438)	-0.9866^{NS} (-1.331)	1.0169^{NS} (1.392)	-0.5564^{NS} (-0.734)
11.	Index of Steel Production (ISP)	-170.3773** (-11.065)	1.0235^{NS} (1.190)	0.5840^{NS} (0.514)	0.2664^{NS} (0.240)	0.8108^{NS} (0.720)
12.	Index of Petroleum Refinery Products (IPOL)	-102.3177** (-4.721)	1.5148^{NS} (1.251)	0.4376^{NS} (0.274)	0.1850^{NS} (0.119)	0.0131^{NS} (0.008)
13.	Index of Electricity Generation (IELE)	-97.7895** (-7.734)	2.0030* (2.835)	-0.1515^{NS} (-0.163)	0.4178^{NS} (0.459)	0.0398^{NS} (0.043)
14.	Index of Fertilizer Production (IFP)	-45.2866* (-2.350)	3.1469** (2.923)	-0.7750^{NS} (-0.545)	0.1509^{NS} (0.109)	-0.1573^{NS} (-0.112)
15.	Index of Industrial Production (IIP)	-94.9843** (-7.603)	1.8348* (2.629)	-0.0448^{NS} (-0.049)	0.3717^{NS} (0.414)	0.0360^{NS} (0.039)
16.	Index of Transport and Communication (ITC)	-156.8246** (-8.598)	1.0834^{NS} (1.131)	0.6853^{NS} (0.543)	0.1439^{NS} (0.116)	0.7904^{NS} (0.612)
17.	Index of Employment in Organized Sector (IEMP)	75.9187** (10.686)	0.5603^{NS} (1.623)	-0.0227^{NS} (-0.049)	0.0022^{NS} (0.005)	0.0272^{NS} (0.056)
18.	Wholesale Price Index for All Commodities (WPI)	-114.6662** (-8.425)	1.4475^{NS} (1.904)	0.1187^{NS} (0.118)	0.5387^{NS} (0.550)	0.1194^{NS} (0.120)

(*Contd.*)

APPENDIX 8.1 (Contd.)

Equation No.	Dependent Variable	$IGAS_{t-4}$ (T-value)	$IGAS_{t-5}$ (T-value)	R^2	$\bar{R}^2$	F-value	N
(1)	(2)	(8)	(9)	(10)	(11)	(12)	(13)
1.	Per-Capita GDP (PGDP)	13.5099NS (0.315)	-14.1123NS (-0.492)	0.964**	0.954	98.835	29
2.	Annual Growth Rate of GDP (AGDP)	-0.1365NS (-0.645)	0.2241NS (1.586)	0.424NS	0.267	2.702	29
3.	Gross Domestic Capital Formation as Ratio of GDP (GDCF/GDP)	-0.1355NS (-1.134)	-0.0175NS (-0.225)	0.781**	0.718	12.454	28
4.	Total Expenditure of Central Govt. as Ratio of GDP (TECG/GDP)	0.0199NS (0.165)	-0.1804* (-2.227)	0.603**	0.495	5.571	29
5.	Gross Fiscal Deficit as Ratio of GDP (GFD/GDP)	0.0122NS (0.116)	-0.1331NS (-1.893)	0.425NS	0.268	2.709	29
6.	Import of Capital Goods as Ratio of GDP (ICG/GDP)	0.0288NS (0.891)	-0.0347NS (-1.603)	0.726**	0.651	9.720	29
7.	Export of Goods and Services as Ratio of GDP (XGS/GDP)	0.0233NS (0.459)	-0.0144NS (-0.423)	0.954**	0.941	76.169	29
8.	Forex Reserves as Ratio of GDP (FORX/GDP)	-0.0605NS (-0.433)	0.1965* (2.103)	0.894**	0.865	30.957	29

(Contd.)

APPENDIX 8.1 (Contd.)

(1)	(2)	(8)	(9)	(10)	(11)	(12)	(13)
9.	Index of Gross Irrigated Area (IGIA)	0.1573^{NS} (0.287)	0.6898^{NS} (1.639)	0.887**	0.849	23.445	25
10.	Index of Food grains Production (IFG)	0.00644^{NS} (0.009)	-0.3321^{NS} (-0.681)	0.798**	0.740	13.827	28
11.	Index of Steel Production (ISP)	0.1597^{NS} (0.143)	0.3414^{NS} (0.458)	0.964**	0.955	99.322	29
12.	Index of Petroleum Refinery Products (IPOL)	0.6021^{NS} (0.383)	-0.4602^{NS} (-0.438)	0.900**	0.873	33.060	29
13.	Index of Electricity Generation (IELE)	0.6234^{NS} (0.680)	-0.9279^{NS} (-1.515)	0.960**	0.949	88.347	29
14.	Index of Fertilizer Production (IFP)	0.8775^{NS} (0.628)	-1.9273^{NS} (-2.064)	0.895**	0.866	31.129	29
15.	Index of Industrial Production (IIP)	0.6198^{NS} (0.684)	-0.7353^{NS} (-1.215)	0.961**	0.950	90.382	29
16.	Index of Transport and Communication (ITC)	0.0364^{NS} (0.029)	0.2168^{NS} (0.261)	0.946**	0.930	61.073	28
17.	Index of Employment in Organized Sector (IEMP)	0.0913^{NS} (0.195)	0.5603^{NS} (1.623)	0.715**	0.630	8.377	27
18.	Wholesale Price Index for All Commodities (WPI)	0.7347^{NS} (0.745)	-0.7242^{NS} (-1.098)	0.956**	0.945	80.699	29

N.B. : ** Significant at 0.01 level.
* Significant at 0.05 level.
^{NS} Indicates non-significant.

Sources (Basic Data) : Tables 8.2 to 8.7.

9

Government Policy Regarding Foreign Aid

It is essential to analyze the Government policy regarding foreign aid/capital, for, it decides whether to encourage or discourage borrowing of funds from abroad. The present chapter reviews the Government of India (GOI)'s policy towards foreign aid, which has been outlined in two sections. Section-I analyzes the constitutional provisions and the mechanism regarding borrowing of funds from abroad, while Section-II evaluates the Government policy and attitude towards foreign aid, since independence, and the recent changes therein.

SECTION I

CONSTITUTIONAL PROVISIONS

The political independence of India on August 15, 1947 paved way for economic transformation and social change in the economy. GOI adopted the Constitution on November 26, 1949 which became fully operative on January 26, 1950. The Article 1(1) of the Constitution states that "India, that is Bharat, shall be a Union of States" (Basu, 2004: p. 51). In other words, a political federation comprising the Union and the State governments within the context of a democratic socialistic society has been one of main salient features of the Indian Constitution. Hence, for the successful working of the federal set-up, the Union and the States should have adequate financial powers at their disposal to discharge their respective responsibilities under the Constitution. The Seventh Schedule of the Constitution specifies the legislative and financial powers of both the Union and the States.

The Article 292 of the Constitution states that "the Union shall have unlimited power of borrowing, upon the security of the revenues of India, either within India or outside. The Union Executive shall exercise the power subject only to such limits as may be fixed by Parliament from time to time. However, the borrowing power of a State is subject to a number of Constitutional limitations: (i) It cannot borrow from outside India. Under the Government of India Act, 1935, the States had the power to borrow outside India with the consent of the Centre. But this power is totally denied to the States by the Constitution; the Union shall have the sole right to enter into the international money market in the matter of borrowing. (ii) The State Executive shall have the power to borrow, within the territory of India upon the security of the revenues of the State, subject to the following conditions: (a) limitations as may be imposed by the State Legislature; (b) if the Union has guaranteed an outstanding loan of the State, no fresh loan can be raised by the State without consent of the Union Government; (c) the Government of India may itself offer a loan to a State, under a law made by Parliament. So long as such a loan or any part thereof remains outstanding, no fresh loan can be raised by the State without the consent of the Government of India. The Government of India may impose terms in giving its consent as above (Article 293)" (*Ibid.*, p. 332). Thus, the States are not allowed to borrow from outside India. Only the Centre can do so.

However, in case a State may be interested in taking up a project with forex component, the Centre, subject to its own approval of the project and assisted by the State concerned, may negotiate with a donor agency such as : IBRD or IDA, to secure the necessary foreign aid, which may be procured either as an outright grant or as a loan. But irrespective of the terms of foreign aid to the Centre, the State receives only a part of it from the Centre and that too in the form of a loan. The duration of loan from the Centre to the States is shorter than the maturity of original foreign loans, while extending it to the States, this assistance is referred to as 'Additional Central Assistance' (ACA) and it is given on the same terms and conditions as normal Central assistance for State plans (Govt. of India, 2001c : p. iii). It "carried interest at the rate of 12.5 percent which was reduced to 10.5 percent, and 9.5 percent per annum for all disaster reconstruction and rehabilitation programmes assisted by the WB and ADB in 2003-04, and further to 9.0 percent with effect from April 1, 2004 "(*Business Standard*, Budget Speech, 2004 : p. II). Similarly, there might be a situation where a State finds itself unable to spare funds for a particular project and the Centre also expresses its inability to help the State. In such a situation, the donor, if convinced of the desirability and feasibility of the project, would agree to help by a grant or a loan specifically committed to the said project. As a result, here, the Centre agrees to extend to the State a loan equivalent to a part of the foreign aid (including outright grants, if any) and the State is required to arrange the rest of the rupee finance. In the process, thus, the Centre acquires some forex, while the State get indebted to the Centre (Bhatia, 1981: p. 31). In sum, under the present Centre-State financial relations, foreign aid has become a tool in the hands of Centre with which it burdens the States under ever-increasing indebtedness to itself.

THE MECHANISM

All activities relating to external assistance in India are dealt with by the *External Finance Wing* (EFW) of the *Department of Economic Affairs* (DEA) within the Ministry of Finance (MOF), GOI. It is the principal nodal agency through which India negotiates with donors; administers the documentation of aid inflows; receives, allocates and monitors the implementation of Externally Aided Projects (EAPs) within the country; and arranges for servicing and repayment of foreign loans. The EFW is headed by a special secretary. Within EFW, various Divisions/Units deal with different multilateral/bilateral external donors, such as: *ADB Division*, which handles all the matters relating to Asian Development Bank and the projects financed by it; *Aid,*

Accounts and Audit (AA&A) Division, which is responsible for the disbursement of loans and grants from multilateral/bilateral donor agencies, their debt servicing, accounting of external assistance, export promotion audit, and supply of management information to credit divisions; *America-Canada Division*, deals with official development assistance from USA and Canada, and policy matters relating to exchange control in India; *EEC Division*, which is primarily responsible for processing official development assistance from the European Economic Community and other European countries, except the 'Commonwealth of Independent States' (CIS); *Foreign Trade Division* renders advice to the Ministry of Commerce, especially from forex angle, on policies pertaining to Indian foreign trade including matters connected with WTO and various multilateral trade blocks, like SAARC, SAFTA, ASEAN, etc. Matters related with CIS countries, Colombo Plan, Indian Aid, and African Development Bank are also handled in this Division; *Fund-Bank Division* deals with all the matters relating to IMF, IBRD, IDA, IFC, Global Environment Facility (GEF), and Multilateral Investment Guarantee Agency (MIGA); *Japan Division* deals with foreign assistance from Japan, Australia, New Zealand and Korea; *Project Management Unit* handles the monitoring of the progress of the implementation of 'Externally Aided Projects' (EAPs) along with the release of 'Additional Central Assistance' (ACA) to the States; and *United Nations Unit* handles the financial assistance proposals under UNDP, etc. In other words, out of the total 22 Divisions under the DEA, MOF, GOI, at least nine Divisions are responsible for handling matters relating with external assistance from various multilateral/bilateral donor agencies (http://finmin.nic.in:2004). These Divisions deal with tying up of external assistance, and covering activities, like project identification, source of external funding, negotiations and conclusions of agreements, etc. However, AA&A Division, which deals with all the matters connected with financial components in the aid agreements, is the designated authority to withdraw funds from loan/grant account. It is responsible for scrutinizing claims received from project implementing agencies as to their eligibility as per relevant credit agreement and submitting the same to the donors for obtaining disbursement. For release of ACA to the concerned States, State-wise disbursement particulars are sent on weekly basis to the Project Management Unit of the

DEA, which recommends release of ACA to the *Plan Finance Division* of the Department of Expenditure, under the MOF. The AA&A Division is also responsible for framing the budget estimates relating to foreign loans/grants for receipts and repayments under both relevant Capital, and Revenue heads. Timely discharge of debt service payments to all the donors and maintaining of loan account under each loan agreement is also handled by this Division. It also maintains comprehensive external debt database relating to sovereign debt from all the multilateral and bilateral donors including debt contracted by parastatals guaranteed by the GOI (http://finmin.nic.in/caaa:2004).

As stated earlier, the EFW of the DEA under the MOF is the apex agency, which prepares the estimates of required aid-funds in India at the beginning of each fiscal year; enters into negotiations with the foreign donor agencies regarding the quantum, terms and conditions of aid funds on which they are willing to grant these funds to India; and if all goes well, aid agreements are finalized. The GOI, through diplomatic channels, UN forums, visits of Union Ministers, Secretaries, special delegations and specific agencies, tries to create congenial atmosphere for inter-governmental aid on a significant scale. Who signs an agreement depends upon, at what level the agreement is negotiated and finalized. For instance: agreement concerning the Petroleum refinery is signed by the Indian Minister of petroleum and Kuwaiti Minister of Commerce, or the agreement between the ICAR and IFAD is signed by these two institutions. These agreements are negotiated, and finalized at different levels of Divisions/Ministries but the terms and conditions of the loans are always approved by the MOF of the GOI.

These aid agreements can be specific or general, in nature, regarding the terms and conditions. "Often, though not always, the agreement to give and receive aid itself stipulates the terms and conditions attached to it. It specifies the projects to be financed out of aid, the rate of interest chargeable on the loan, the manner and period of its repayment, and other pertinent details, i.e., specific aid agreements are complete in all respects. Sometimes, the agreement is couched in more general terms, leaving the details to be worked out and incorporated into later agreements" (Rao and Narain, 1963: p.19). For example: an agreement between GOI and Govt. of Japan for 'Yamuna Action Plan Project', dated December 21, 1992, specified the terms of credit, while the 'Indo-US Technical Cooperation Agreement' signed between the GOI and the Government of USA did not deal with specific offers of aid, and provided for determining the policies and for the general supervision of projects receiving assistance under the US Technical Cooperation Mission.

The entire amount of loan is not disbursed to the borrower at the time the loan agreement is signed but is disbursed for specific purposes, such as to finance imports by the donors through three kinds of procedures: (1) The Reimbursement Procedure, (2) The Commitment Procedure, and (3) The Transfer Procedure.

1. The Reimbursement Procedure

The Reimbursement Procedure, which is more common, has been *mutatis mutandis* applied for the disbursement of loan proceeds made to the Supplier(s) of the Eligible Source Country(ies). Under this the Borrower (GOI) initially finances the import of goods and services through the normal channels. Thereafter the Borrower collect the relevant documents like : the bills of lading, invoices, a certificate of the origin of goods, etc., evidencing each payment, and its usage on goods and services in conformity with the conditions of the loan agreements. Then the Suppliers reimburse the same to the Borrower (GOI). This method has been in vogue in respect of most of the government to government credits that India has received.

2. The Commitment Procedure

The Commitment Procedure for ODA loans has been *mutatis mutandis* applied for the disbursement of loan proceeds for the purchase of goods and services from the Supplier(s) of the Eligible Source Country(ies) as per the agreement. Under this, the Supplier/donor(s) issues a letter of commitment to a forex bank in the donor country chosen by the Borrower (in this case GOI) agreeing to reimburse the bank for any payment made by it at the direction of the Borrower for those items of equipment, materials or supplies mentioned in the 'letter of commitment'. In this case, the forex bank collects the necessary documents from the Suppliers and obtains the reimbursement from the donor agency.

This method has been in vogue in respect of credits made available by the multilateral agencies, like the WB, IFAD, etc.

3. The Transfer Procedure

The Transfer Procedure has been applied to the disbursement of the loan proceeds for the payment to be made to the Supplier(s) with respect to the portion of contract stated in Indian currency. Under this procedure, when the Borrower (GOI) receive claims for the payments from the Supplier(s) through the Executing Agency, the Borrower requests the authorized forex bank to make disbursement for a sum not exceeding the amount actually claimed by the Supplier(s) by sending the bank a 'Request for Disbursement'. Each request should be accompanied by the Summary Sheet of Payments; claims for payments evidencing the amount to be paid to the Supplier(s); received invoice for the amount to be paid; and bills of lading or similar documents evidencing shipment/delivery of the goods and/or services listed on the invoice, etc. After receiving the disbursed amount, the authorized forex bank shall immediately transfer the exact amount mentioned in the 'Transfer Instructions' to the respective Supplier's Bank in the Borrower's country. The credited amount shall in turn be credited into the corresponding account of the Supplier by the Supplier's Bank. The Borrower shall submit to the bank a copy of the 'Transfer Instructions' immediately after the issuance of the original.

In brief, the aid process in India is much more orderly than in other countries. Control of aid receipts has been centralized in one department of the government, investment planning takes account of anticipated aid receipts, and considerable experience has been built up in the field of international price comparisons (Cassen and Associates, 1994: p. 258).

Section II

GOVERNMENT POLICY

The Constitution of India has enunciated certain 'Directive Principles of State Policy' in Articles 36 to 51 that the State shall strive to promote the welfare of the people by securing and protecting as effectively as it may, a social order in which justice;

social, economic and political; shall prevail in all the institutions of national life, and shall direct its policy towards securing, among other things, equality of opportunity, measure of social security for all the citizens and raising the overall standard of living of the people. For attaining these ends, these Directives enjoin that ownership and control of material resources of the country should be distributed in such a way that the operation of economic system should not result in the concentration of wealth and means of production in a manner which is detrimental to the common good. In other words, "these Directives emphasize that the goal of the Indian polity is not *laissez faire* but a Welfare State, where the State has a positive duty to ensure to all its citizens, social and economic justice, and dignity of the individual. These would serve as an 'instrument of instructions' upon all the future governments, irrespective of their party creeds" (Basu, 2004: p. 149). "These general principles were given a more precise direction in December, 1954 when Parliament adopted the 'socialistic pattern of society', as the objective of social and economic policy . . . had its roots deep in India's struggle for freedom" (Govt. of India, 1961: p. 4). The socialistic approach has further been emphasized by the 42nd and 44th Amendment Acts of the Constitution. Though, these Directives do not prescribe any rigid economic and social framework, yet provide the guidelines for the State policy. So, the economic policy of the State/GOI must be governed by these guidelines along with certain Fundamental Rights of the citizens (Articles 14 to 32).

The Constitution of India recognizing the respect for these Directive Principles, "Fundamental Rights and the existence of a multi-party system, ruled out forced savings. There was also the possibility of creating money for financing investments, but the risks of disruption in the monetary system and inflationary pressures, inherent in a context in which the production would not satisfy the demand thus generated, restricted its use" (Gilles, 2003: p. 33). Similarly, economic openness was viewed with suspicion at that time. Hence, in furtherance of these Directives as well as the declared objectives of the Government to promote a rapid rise in the standard of living of the people by efficient exploitation of the resources of the country, increasing production and offering opportunities to all for employment in the service of community, GOI set-up a non-statutory permanent body, the Planning Commission, in March, 1950 as an agency to formulate five year economic plans, and to advise the Government on their effective execution.

The Five Year Plans (FYPs), apart from their philosophy, and institutional, organizational and legislative recommendations, are essentially a series of projects for economic and social development in various fields, classified vertically under the different ministries of the GOI and their associated and subordinate agencies, and horizontally under the various State Governments and their Ministries. State Governments, Central Ministries and other agencies associated with the Central Government submit their projects, and all these are brought together, processed, scrutinized, amended and then consolidated into the National Plan. Many of the projects that come up for consideration have their requirements of foreign aid, either for purchase of equipment or materials or technical skills, and their forex requirements have to be consolidated into a forex budget. Private enterprises also indicate their requirements for foreign aid and this also comes into the forex budget in so far as their projects get included in the Plan. Altogether, therefore, the Plan provides a measure of the total forex required and the balance that remains to be met by foreign aid after taking into account expected receipts from export earnings. And it is this gap that, broadly speaking, determines the country's need for foreign aid (Rao and Narain, 1963: p. 16). In other words, FYPs are the prisms which reflect the GOI's policy regarding foreign aid requirements along with Annual Budgets.

The GOI's policy regarding foreign aid has been reviewed in three phases: (1) The Phase of Structuralism (1951-69); (2) The Transitional Phase (1969-92); and (3) The Phase of Global Orientation (1992-onwards).

1. The Phase of Structuralism (1951-69)

Though, the 'Industrial Policy Resolution' issued in April 1948, soon after India's independence, spoke of liberal but regulated (in national interest) attitude towards foreign aid and capital, yet an event of considerable significance to the future economic policy of the country was the publication of *First Five Year Plan, A Draft Outline* in July, 1951 by the Planning

Commission, for the national economic development covering the period 1951-56. The final version of the Plan, adopted by the Parliament in early December, 1952 relied mainly on the internal resources for financing development, its formulation on a realistic basis has generally improved the projects of foreign aid, both official and private, which was essential for the complete execution of the Plan. The Draft Outline stated, "there is no gainsaying that if India is to progress at a rate which will ensure a fair measure of improvement in standards of living to the vast masses of its population, without imposing on them a degree of suffering and regimentation which would endanger the further development of democratic institutions, it will have to receive assistance for some years from countries more advanced than itself. At the same time, it is of utmost importance that no effort should be spared for making the maximum utilization of the resources available within the country" (Govt. of India, 1951: p. 4). Thus, it is evident that when the planning process started, there existed much favorable opinion for foreign aid at the government level, and the country has been using the same since then to supplement its domestic rupee finances like many other countries of this universe. "Even the United States of America, for instance, which is the most developed country of the world today, also relied a great deal in the initial stages of its development on foreign capital" (Govt. of India, 1952: p. 26).

As a consequence of the policy statements of the First 'FYP', India was enabled to present a revised six-year development programme under the 'Colombo Plan' to the meeting of its 'Commonwealth Consultative Committee' held at Karachi (Pakistan) in March, 1952 so as to secure its approval. In furtherance of the Plan, India received substantial external assistance from the USA and some members of the 'Colombo Plan' (RBI[b], 1952: p. 30). Over the period of the First Plan (1951-56), a total of Rs. 298 crore of external assistance was made available to India for her development programmes in the public sector, of which about Rs. 201.7 crore, i.e., 10.3 percent of the total public sector outlay of Rs. 1960 crore was actually utilized. Even then, the BOP deficit on current account during this Plan period amounted to Rs. 1100 crore. After allowing for a withdrawal from forex reserves of Rs. 200 crore, there remained a gap of Rs. 900 crore at the end of First Plan in 1956 (Govt. of India, 1956c:

pp. 102-03). Thus, despite India's realistic attitude towards foreign aid and capital, its availability remained limited during the initial years of her development.

To fill the resource gap of Rs. 900 crore, the Second FYP (1956-61) decided to: (a) float public issues in foreign money markets; (b) arrange for banker's credits and export credits for supply of goods from foreign countries; (c) borrow from IBRD and the newly formed International Finance Corporation; (d) borrow loans and grants from other international institutions such as : United Nations Technical Assistance Administration or the proposed Special United Nations Fund for Economic Development; (e) borrow loans and grants from friendly governments; and (f) through private foreign investment (*Ibid.*, p. 103). The Government considered it necessary to take advantage of all these sources of finance for meeting the forex requirements of the Plan. Besides these, India also received technical assistance from the United Nations and its specialized agencies under the Expanded Technical Assistance Programme, from the USA under Point Four Programme, and from Commonwealth countries under the 'Colombo Plan'. This assistance included the services of experts, training facilities for Indian nationals, and supply of demonstration equipment including the UNESCO programme for the Western Higher Technical Institute and the Indian Statistical Institute. The Second Plan envisaged to raise Rs. 800 crore in the form of external assistance and Rs. 100 crore in the form of investment programmes in the private sector. With regard to the requirements of public sector, the Second Plan stated that an unutilized balance of Rs. 94 crore was available from past authorizations. In addition to this, arrangements were already made for a net credit of Rs. 43 crore from the then USSR (now Russia) Government for financing the Bhilai Steel Plant, and Rs. 33 crore were promised by the British Government and British bankers for financing the Durgapur Steel Plant, thereby assuring resources amounting Rs. 170 crore, and leaving a balance of Rs. 630 crore for which arrangements were to be made in the beginning of the Second Plan (*Ibid.*, p. 104).

However, as a consequence of the encouraged response and cooperation of friendly foreign governments and international financial institutions, GOI emphasized rapid industrialization, particularly of the basic and heavy industries such as : the establishment of three huge steel plants (Rourkela in 1954 with German assistance; Bhilai in 1955 with the then USSR assistance; and Durgapur in 1956 with British assistance), heavy engineering, chemical fertilizers, cement units, etc., along with the reorganization of rural economy through agrarian reforms, community development and cooperation, etc. Infact, it was only with the entry of the (former) Soviet Union and other Communist countries into the field that Western countries also began displaying some enthusiasm for offering aid to the underdeveloped countries at the governmental level (Rao and Narain, 1963: p. 72). However, both the United States and the Soviet Union gave aid less in view of a wide identity of political and economic ideological affinities than in order to prevent India, acknowledged as a leading non-aligned country, from falling into the sphere of influence of enemy camp, either as the result of economic contingency or because of a military threat (Gilles, 2003: p. 398). Owing to all this, the amount of actual utilization of external assistance went up to Rs. 1430.4 crore against the original estimate of Rs. 800 crore, i.e., 30.6 percent of the actual public sector outlay of Rs. 4672 crore during the Second Plan (Govt. of India, 2004a: p. 50). The USA with nearly Rs. 1515 crore of authorized aid accounted for 59 percent of the total assistance granted, during the Second Plan, followed by the (then) USSR with authorization of Rs. 319 crore. The USA under its PL-480 programme agreed to supply 27 million tons of wheat in addition to substantial quantum of rice, tobacco, cotton, corn and dried milk etc., worth Rs. 1113 crore during this Plan (RBI[b], 1961: pp. 108-09).

Following the pattern and trend set during the Second Plan, GOI continued its liberal policy towards receiving foreign assistance, emphasizing thereby on the development and strengthening of basic capital goods, and machine-building industries along with the development of mining, power, and transport during the Third FYP. The Third Plan was formulated on the basis that "it would be advantageous from the point of view of the recipient country (India) as well as the donor countries to plan for substantial amounts of external assistance for a relatively short period albeit to proceed in terms of varying and uncertain amounts of assistance over an indefinite period.

Development effort in India over the Third and Fourth Plans has to concentrate on the expansion of capital goods and machine building industries—together with corresponding development of mining, power and transport—on a scale that would enable the country to build up in this period, sufficient capacity to produce domestically the bulk of capital goods and machinery, that it would require in subsequent periods for supporting high levels of investment. This was a priority that followed as much from the objective of maximizing the rate of growth of the economy as from the need to attain a viable external accounts position within a foreseeable future" (Govt. of India, 1961: p. 107). That is "in order to minimize external interference, priority was given to a development policy oriented towards the domestic market and designed to promote an import substitution strategy, notably in the case of capital goods. It was in this perspective that the concept of 'self-reliance' was put forward, itself rooted in the Swadeshi movement which had been an integral part of the nationalist movement—aiming at not to be dependent upon external assistance for the import of life-line supplies and to the extent possible it should have the capacity to withstand the vicissitudes of international markets" (Gilles, 2003: p. 36). Evidently, it was in this context the forex and hence external assistance requirements in the Third Plan were substantial.

The total outlay of the Third FYP (1961-66) was finalized at Rs. 10,200 crore, out of which Rs. 6200 crore were allocated for public sector, and the remaining Rs. 4000 crore for the private sector. The Plan aimed at raising the level of investment from about 11 percent of the national income by the end-Second Plan to about 14 percent by the end-Third Plan. But, the actual savings rate at that time in the economy was around 8 percent of the national income. Hence, the balance represented inflow of resources from abroad (Govt. of India, 1960: p. 43). The total external assistance required for the Plan was estimated at Rs. 3200 crore. Of this Rs. 450-500 crore were required for repayments of external obligations; Rs. 300 crore for the private sector; and Rs. 200 crore represented buffer stocks (four million tons of wheat and one million tons of rice), which would not yield rupee resources. Thus, from the external assistance of Rs. 3200 crore after deducting Rs. 1000 crore for these three heads, the net balance of Rs. 2200 crore remained available for the public sector as budgetary resources (*Ibid.*, pp. 48-49). But the increasing import of machinery and equipment due to the long gestation period of capital goods, and machine-building industries; diversion of public sector outlay towards defence production and industries due to the Chinese aggression in 1962; the cut-off in aid in response to Indo-Pak conflict of autumn 1965, both by the US and the UK; and the inability to increase export earnings, aggravated the forex problems and financial difficulties for the GOI. In addition to all this, bad weather conditions adversely affected the agricultural production in relation to rapidly growing population/aggregate demand, which compelled the Government to import large intake of foodgrains under the US PL-480 programme. Consequently, the actual utilization of net external assistance increased to Rs. 2423 crore against the earlier estimate of Rs. 2200 crore, i.e., 28.25 percent of the actual public sector outlay of Rs. 8577 crore (Govt. of India, 1970: p. 73). That is, aid utilized during the Third Plan was practically 1.5 times more than the entire aid utilized during the first two Plans.

The years of 1966-67 and 1967-68 were extremely difficult for India, when the country faced acute shortages of foodgrains due to widespread drought; forex problems due to the US pressure for a virtual silence on Vietnam issue and certain changes in agricultural policy; the US and British role against India during Indo-Pak war in 1965; and undue pressure of the US and the IMF to devalue Indian Rupee in 1966. India, the largest recipient of the US agricultural commodities under the PL-480 programme at that time, had to wait anxiously month after month for the next instalment of foodgrains due to arm-twisting tactics. Till 1967, India used to make payment for such purchases entirely in Indian Rupees, but since 1967 all agreements provided for payments partly in Indian Rupees, and partly against long-term credits called 'convertible local currency credits' (Banerjee, 1977: p. 217), and that too on harder terms. As a result, the budgetary receipts corresponding to external assistance, during the three years of 'plan holiday' (Annual Plans), increased to Rs. 2426 crore, i.e., 35.9 percent of the public sector outlay amounting to Rs. 6756 crore (Govt. of India, 1970: p. 75). This was Rs. 341 crore lower than the original estimates adjusted for the devaluation of Rupee. This shortfall was entirely under non-PL-480 assistance, and was accounted for mainly by the suspension of aid following Indo-Pak war in 1965. The PL-480 assistance was of about the same order.

In sum, during the period up to the late 'sixties', external capital financing was dependent almost entirely on the foreign aid, reflecting Government's policy aversion to the Private Foreign Investment and External Commercial Borrowings, mainly due to the concessionality associated with it. The sense of vulnerability prevailing in India at the time, partly due to the country's increasing dependence on aid, exacerbated sensitivities about outside interference. India sought to receive foreign aid keeping in view the economic considerations and guarding against political implications. Indian policy-makers tried to keep the burden of foreign loans (amortization and interest payments) within the country's repaying capacity as much as possible by securing them on favorable terms like low interest rates with longer maturity and grace periods. During this period, India had drawn wide benefits from the aid granted by the two superpowers (the USA and Soviet Union) of the time by following the policy of non-alignment. Such external resources were essential to hasten the economic growth of the country, particularly at a time when highest priority was being given to the basic and strategic industries which were necessary for export earnings, and import savings. These were also necessary to create conditions in which dependence on external assistance should disappear as early as possible. For all this "India has been able to receive aid without foregoing her independence or injuring her self-respect, and there has been no serious tension or any real ill-will between her and donor countries caused by the giving and receiving of aid" (Rao and Narain, 1963: p. 38). This ability to obtain aid from both the superpowers, from the mid-1950s, constituted a remarkable trump card in the face of a growing dependence on foreign aid. Apart from a few accommodations, India did not allow itself to be dictated to on its fundamentals and continued to pursue its policy goals without unduly jeopardizing its national development (Gilles, 2003: p. 401). Although in certain cases, it has been alleged that India had followed the dictates of the multilateral agencies and other donors in policy adoption.

2. The Transitional Phase (1969-92)

After learning lessons from the past experience of about two decades of economic planning, particularly from the increasing dependence on external assistance in the form of political pressures, grave uncertainties and instabilities, the Fourth FYP (1969-74), which should have ordinarily been commenced in 1966 but delayed due to severe stresses which developed during the Third Plan, envisaged a distinct departure from the earlier plans. It has been especially designed to promote progress towards 'self-reliance' and removal of poverty in order to serve the objective of growth with stability. In fact, the objective of 'self-reliance' to be realized within a definite time schedule was formulated explicitly for the first time in the Third Plan: "the balance of payment difficulties, the country is facing are, it must be stressed, not short-term or temporary; they will continue for several years to come. The external assistance is essential for this period but the aim must be to make the economy more and more self-reliant so that it is able to support within a period of ten or twelve years, an adequate scale of investment from its own production and savings. Normal inflow of capital may continue but self-reliance on special forms of external assistance has to be reduced progressively and eliminated. The Third Plan represents a very crucial stage in this process" (Govt. of India, 1961: p. 115).

The Third Plan objective of self-reliance contained three essential ideas: (a) self-reliance meant elimination of special forms of external assistance; (b) self-reliance could not be achieved forthwith and had to be phased over time; and (c) the justification for external assistance during the intervening period was that it helped to build up the growth potential of the economy to the level where it could support an adequate level of investment from its own production and savings (Govt. of India, 1974, Part I : p. 3).

The Fourth FYP sought to concretize the time phasing for realizing the goal of self-reliance. Consequently, the share of external assistance (net of loan repayments but without allowing for the interest payments) for the public sector plan was reduced from 28 percent in Third Plan and 35.9 percent in the three Annual Plans to nearly 17 percent of the original estimated total resources in the Fourth Plan. As percentage of total net investment, foreign aid, net of debt servicing (repayment as well as interest), was estimated to be only 8.2 percent during the Fourth Plan. The share of domestic budgetary resources such as : domestic savings, both public and private, the surpluses of public enterprises, etc., was raised to about 78 percent in comparison to 59 percent in the Third Plan and 54 percent in the three Annual Plans (Govt. of India, 1970: p. 76). The Approach document also indicated the policy objective of reducing foreign aid, net of debt servicing (inclusive of interest payments), to half the current level of aid by the end of the Fourth Plan and to eliminate it altogether as speedily as possible, thereafter (*Ibid.*, p. 88). In other words, the objective of self-reliance, which the Third Plan proposed to achieve by mid-seventies, was postponed in the Fourth Plan to 1980.

All this was decided, despite the forex requirements of Rs. 10,150 crore estimated for the Fourth Plan due to massive maintenance imports of raw materials and components, import of foodgrains, and the project import of capital goods, etc. The Plan estimated to meet these requirements by way of export earnings of Rs. 8300 crore and from the external assistance, net of debt servicing, amounting to Rs. 1850 crore (*Ibid.*, pp. 88-89), which was later on revised to Rs. 2614 crore (Govt. of India, 1974, Part I : p. 54). But the widespread drought in 1972-73 once again obliged the country to go in for large import of foodgrains, particularly at a time when global prices had risen to an unprecedented level. The import prices of other essential items like: petroleum and petroleum products, chemical fertilizers, iron and steel, non-ferrous metals, and newsprint had also risen. The unilateral stoppage of aid by the United States in June, 1973 further aggravated the forex problem. To safeguard the economy, GOI drew a contingency plan and the Govt. was able to set a proper rate of exchange for Indian Rupee, independent of British Pound Sterling (£). The Indian Rupee moved from the 'monogamy' of Pound Sterling to a 'flexible polygamy' of the basket of major international currencies. Consequently, the country became able to take its own decisions and need not depend on any other currency because "India would be divising its own basket, it would do justice to the pattern of its trade and would keep the fluctuations to the minimum. De-linking reflected the intrinsic strength of Indian Rupee" (Banerjee, 1977: p. 49). However, the bumper *kharif* crop and the two million tonne Soviet wheat loan saved the situation to some extent. Vigorous export promotion measures succeeded in boosting export earnings. As a consequence, the actual utilization of net external assistance during the Fourth Plan placed at Rs. 1739 crore, i.e., 33.5 percent lower than the originally envisaged and 11.02 percent of the actual total public sector outlay of Rs. 15,778.8 crore (Govt. of India, 2004a: p. 50). Thus, the GOI was able to reduce the dependence on external assistance for the first time, after independence and favored the acceptance of that external assistance which was either without strings or with minimal strings, i.e., the actual progress during the Fourth Plan period has been in line with the anticipation.

The projections of the Fifth FYP (1974-79) emphasized the importance of proper planning of the BOP if the objectives of accelerated growth and greater self-reliance were to be achieved. For this purpose, the Plan assumed among other measures, the availability of the bulk of envisaged foreign aid on soft terms; adoption of effective measures to neutralize the recent adverse trend in the terms of trade, thereby bringing about a sufficient improvement in the BOP, so as to meet, by 1978-79 the maximum amount of forex requirements other than debt service charges from its own sources; increase in the output of foodgrains, oil-seeds, raw cotton, raw jute, tea, coffee, tobacco, etc., commensurate with the country's requirements for domestic consumption and exports; efficient management of the food economy to avoid large scale food imports; and large increases in the output of ferrous and non-ferrous metals, machinery and equipment, essential chemicals, and newsprint, etc. The Fifth FYP projected that the forex gap to be met by the net external assistance amounting Rs. 1451 crore as against the original provision of Rs. 1850 crore in the Fourth Plan. Moreover, in the Fifth Plan GOI also made a provision of Rs. 300 crore for providing foreign aid mainly to the neighbouring countries, like: Bhutan, Nepal and Bangladesh, etc. Hence, if this amount was set-off against the net foreign aid taken credit of for the Fifth Plan, the total of latter as budgetary resources for the public sector reduced to Rs. 1151 crore. Even without this set-off, the net aid worked out to 3.1 percent of the total investment, and 4.6 percent of the public sector investment envisaged in the Fifth Plan as against the corresponding figures of 8.2 percent and 13.6 percent in the Fourth Plan (Govt. of India, 1974, Vol. I : p. 74).

However, the Fifth Plan was knocked sideways, mainly by the 1973 oil price explosion and the Planning Commission's refusal to recognize the implications (more taxes or a smaller Plan) which led to a considerable loss of public confidence in the Commission. Donors, too, weakened the Commission by public utterances that increasingly appeared to equate planning with misplaced economic interventionism. When, as often happened, Plans had to be pared to the core in order to meet the forex crises that core was determined largely by pressures from Chief Ministers (of the States), secondly, by the Ministers (at the Centre) and least by the Planning Commission priorities. During the 1970s, the growth of a 'parallel economy' fuelled by money from tax evasion and other illegal activities further reduced the role of planners (Lipton and Toye, 1990: p. 87). As a consequence, the actual utilization of net external assistance (exclusive of debt service payments) gone up to Rs. 3489 crore, i.e., 8.85 percent of the actual public sector plan outlay of Rs. 39,426 crore for the Fifth Plan period of five years (1974-79) as originally envisaged (Govt. of India, 2004a: p. 50), though the Plan was actually terminated during 1977-78, a year earlier, by the Janta Party Government. The 'Janta Government' introduced its own Sixth FYP (1978-83) which was later on abandoned by the Congress (I) Government in 1980. Hence, the plan for the year 1979-80 has been treated as 'Annual Plan' here, during which the net external assistance utilization amounted only to Rs. 552 crore (Govt. of India[b], 1984: p. 71), i.e., 4.53 percent of the actual public sector plan outlay of Rs. 12,176.50 crore (Govt. of India, 2004a: p. 50), which was quite low as compared to the original Plan external assistance estimate of Rs. 5954 crore (Govt. of India, 1978: p. 62) and the previous plans, perhaps, due to political instability in the country during 1978-80.

The Congress (I) Government reformulated a new Sixth FYP (1980-85) and a new Industrial Policy after coming back to power in January, 1980. The Plan and Policy was launched under difficult conditions of acute inflationary pressures which prevailed since March, 1979; a set back in the functioning of critical sectors such as : power, coal, railways, steel, etc.; and the steep rise in the prices of petroleum products resulting in an increasing deterioration in the nation's terms of trade, and balance of payments. "The global economy was also in a much more disturbed state since the mid-seventies than at any time in the past three decades and there was an atmosphere of confrontation rather than cooperation in international economic relations" (Govt. of India, 1981 : p. 10). In such a situation, the objective of self-reliance needed to be pursued with continuous vigor. To achieve the said objective and the annual growth rate of 5.2 percent, the Sixth FYP provided for a total outlay in the public sector amounting to Rs. 97,500 crore at 1979-80 prices, which in real terms was 80 percent higher than the outlay in Fifth FYP (*Ibid*., pp. xix and xx). The net inflow of external resources to this public sector plan was fixed at Rs. 9929 crore, i.e., about 10.2 percent of the public sector outlay, of which Rs. 5889 crore in the form of net aid and Rs. 4040 crore in the form of other flows from abroad (*Ibid*., p. 66) including commercial borrowings, withdrawl of forex reserves etc. However, due to sharp increase in the non-plan expenditure, partly resulting from inflationary pressures developed during the Sixth Plan period, and partly due to increase in defence expenditure, subsidies, interest liabilities, cost of maintenance of normal services, additional DA instalments, etc., the actual public sector plan outlay rose to Rs. 1,10,467 crore at current prices (Govt. of India, 2004a: p. 50). But the actual net external assistance (exclusive of debt service payments) contributed only 5.52 percent of the actual public sector plan outlay, worked out at Rs. 6095 crore (RBI, 2004: p. 236). This declining trend was mainly due to "the substantial cuts in the real value of IDA aid—plus major redirection (actual and planned) of IDA aid away from India, largely in response to the US judgements and pressures—. Even a big rise in IBRD (non-concessional) flows to India can hardly make up for significant falls in IDA flows" (Lipton and Toye, 1990: p. 113); and rising costs of debt servicing as 44 percent of total utilized aid was paid back in the form of amortization and interest payments (RBI, 2004: p. 236).

Though the Seventh FYP (1985-90) was finalized in an atmosphere of robust confidence (due to the highest overall realized growth rate of 5.4 percent in previous 25 years), yet the development financing structure, which emerged during the Sixth Plan, showed serious limitations in the matter of generation of resources to cope with the increasing demand for development expenditure in the country. In the face of resource crunch, mobilization of financial resources, particularly in a non-inflationary manner, presented a real challenge to be faced during the Seventh Plan period by the GOI, besides providing enough incentives for savings and growth in production, removal of poverty, and attainment of self-reliance. Dr. Manmohan Singh, then the Deputy Chairman of the Planning Commission, stated, "removal of poverty, the building of modern society making maximum possible use of science and technology, and attainment of self-reliance are the basic objectives of planning in India" (Govt. of India, 1985, Vol. I : p. ix). In this challenging scenario, GOI estimated the net inflow of external resources amounting to Rs. 18,000 crore (i.e., 10 percent) to finance the proposed public sector plan outlay of Rs. 1,80,000 crore at 1984-85 prices for the Seventh Plan (*Ibid.*, pp. 52 and 56). However, the budget deficit of the GOI far exceeded the projections of the Plan, due to the Government's felt need to make large investment commitments, not included in the Plan, in public speeches not previously discussed with the Planning Commission (Lipton and Toye, 1990: p. 87). Expenditure on pay and allowances, interest payments, and other non-plan revenue expenditure items, notably subsidies, also increased, which led to pressures on the BOPs necessitating external borrowings on a much larger scale. But the GOI was able to utilize net external assistance (exclusive of interest payments) amounting to Rs. 16,124 crore, constituting 9.0 percent of the actual Seventh Plan public sector outlay of Rs. 1,78,377 crore at 1984-85 prices (Govt. of India, 1992, Vol. I : p. 109). The amount of net external assistance (exclusive of amortization and interest payments) worked out to Rs. 10,048 crore (RBI, 2004: p. 236), i.e., 4.6 percent of the Seventh Plan actual public sector outlay of Rs. 2,18,729.60 crore at current prices (Govt. of India, 2004a: p. 50). This was again mainly due to cut in the real value of IDA aid, with China claiming its share from IDA funds for the first time, since 1985 (Commerce Research Bureau, 1985: p. 8) and the rising costs of debt servicing. There was increased dependence on non-concessional foreign inflows and substantial draw down on the country's forex reserves.

The Annual Plan (1990-91) was formulated, initially as a part of the Eighth FYP envisaged for the period 1990-95, but due to political instability, economic policies devoid of direction, and shocks engineered by the Gulf crisis postponed the launching of this Plan. Consequently, there was again a virtual 'plan holiday', during the period 1990-92 with the Annual Plans of 1990-91 and

1991-92. However, as a consequence of 'plan holiday', considerable uncertainty about the future policy stand of the Government resulted in lower utilization of net external assistance and public sector plan outlays. During the year 1990-91, net inflow from abroad in the form of loans and grants was actually estimated at Rs. 2421 crore (against the total of Rs. 7359 crore including commercial borrowings by the public enterprises) compared to the Annual Plan/Budget Estimates of Rs. 4327 crore (against the total of Rs. 5793 crore). Thus, net external assistance (exclusive of debt service payments) contributed 3.94 percent of the actual public sector plan outlay of Rs. 61,508 crore during 1990-91 (Govt. of India, 2004a: p. 70). It has, *inter alia*, been decided in pursuance of the recommendations of the National Development Council, which met in October, 1990 that the entire external aid (compared to 70 percent earlier), meant for externally aided projects implemented by the States, would be passed on to them. Similarly, during 1991-92 net inflow of loans and grants from abroad has actually been came out Rs. 4959 crore (against the total of Rs. 7892 crore including commercial borrowings by the public enterprises and drawing down from forex reserves) compared to the Annual Plan of Rs. 6379 crore, financing thereby 7.64 percent of actual public sector Annual Plan outlay of Rs. 64,953 crore (Govt. of India, 2004a: p. 71).

Evidently, GOI was compelled to borrow foreign aid to fulfil the Plan outlays, though on a declining scale, during the transitional period (1969-92) as compared to the phase of structuralism (1951-69). However, Government remained unable to achieve the long cherished goal of self-reliance, even during this period, although it followed the policy of 'give and take' with regard to foreign aid, i.e., GOI, on the one hand, authorized assistance comprising loans and outright grants to the friendly countries, like Vietnam, Bhutan, Nepal, Bangladesh, Sri Lanka, etc., amounting to Rs. 2437 crore up to end-March 1992 (RBI[b], 1992, Vol. I : p. 409), and on the other hand, borrowed/utilized cumulative external assistance amounting Rs. 71,926 crore during the same period (*Ibid*., p. 399). Up to end-March 1992, India borrowed roughly 53 percent from the multilateral sources, of which the WB (IBRD and IDA) accounted for about 86 percent of the total multilateral assistance, while the USA (with 9.1 percent), Japan (with 9.0 percent), Germany (with 6.5 percent),

UK (with 6 percent) and the (then) USSR (with 3.7 percent) were the main bilateral donors (*Ibid.*, p. 404). India's official stand remained that it preferred to gave up aid, whatever be the consequences, albeit to make concessions that would compromise its national interests. During this period, India continued to follow the policy of non-alignment till the end of cold war in the late eighties and gained more in terms of aid from both the superpowers than it would have had by aligning itself with either of the power.

3. The Phase of Global Orientation (1992-Onwards)

On July 24, 1991 a series of reforms in the form of new economic policy, featuring 'Liberalization, Privatization and Globalization' (LPG), was introduced in the back drop of widespread changes which had altered the global socio-economic order. These could not leave India untouched. In such a trying and turbulent times, GOI launched Eighth FYP (1992-97) to respond and adjust to these changes quickly and creatively, and to face the number of challenges, such as : growing fiscal deficit, poor performance of public enterprises, almost 30 percent of population living below poverty line who were denied of the basic minimum needs even after the four decades of planning, etc. This necessitated the formulation of the Eighth Plan with a difference. It has been a plan for managing the transition from inward-looking centrally planned economy to a market led more globally-oriented economy without tearing its basic socio-cultural fabric. Consequently, the role of Planning Commission and the Government also underwent change from a highly centralized planning system to the one gradually moving towards indicative planning. The Planning Commission was expected to play an integrative role and help in the development of a holistic approach to the policy formulation in the critical areas of development. It was to play a mediatory and facilitating role for managing the change smoothly, and creating a culture of high productivity and efficiency in the Government machinery. In addition to the resource allocation, the Commission was expected to concern itself with resource mobilization for development as well as with efficient utilization of the funds (Govt. of India, 1992, Vol. I : p. ii).

For mobilization of funds, especially from abroad, GOI decided to woo the foreign capital in the form of 'Private Foreign

Investment' (PFI), in general, and FDI, in particular, even up to 100 percent in certain specific high priority areas along with lot of facilities and incentives, instead of depending more on foreign aid. Correspondingly, GOI decided to finance the Eighth FYP in a non-inflationary manner by avoiding debt trap, both internally and externally. For this purpose the Eighth Plan, thus, aimed at performance improvement, quality consciousness, competitiveness, efficiency of operations and completion of projects in time. The Plan proposed an annual growth rate of 5.6 percent for the period 1992-97 with national investment proposed at Rs. 7,98,000 crore, and the public sector plan outlay of Rs. 4,34,100 crore, of which Rs. 28,700 crore in the form of net capital inflow from abroad, all estimated at 1991-92 prices (Govt. of India, 1992, Vol. I : pp. 106 and 115). In other words, net capital inflow from abroad was expected to finance only 6.6 percent of the public sector plan outlay, indicating a reduced contribution as compared to the earlier FYPs, and the balance was expected to be financed from domestic budgetary sources by improving the performance of central public enterprises; containing the growth of staff and expenditure on them; and reduction on non-developmental expenditure such as : subsidies, etc. Some hard decisions were also required to make the socio-economic services yield their due. It was believed that unless such decisions were taken, the viability of financing the Plan would be jeopardized.

However, the actual public sector plan outlay worked out at Rs. 4,85,457.24 crore, at current prices (Govt. of India, 2004a: p. 50), while the net inflow of external assistance (exclusive of amortization and interest payments) actually estimated at Rs. 3331 crore during the Eighth FYP (RBI, 2004: p. 236), which was only 0.69 percent of the actual public sector plan outlay to be financed from net external assistance. In nominal terms, the debt service payments increased from Rs. 8749 crore in the initial year to Rs. 11,940 crore in the terminal year of the Eighth Plan, while the gross inflows of external assistance tended to have risen only merely from Rs. 10,982 crore to Rs. 11,979 crore during the same period (*Ibid.*, p. 236). Thus, increased principal repayments of the past disbursements falling due; fiscal stringency since 1991; and extensive procedural difficulties faced by the implementing agencies contributed mainly to the significant decline in the utilization of net external assistance.

Similarly, conversion of the 'Aid India Consortium' into 'India Development Forum' (IDF), and the invitation to private investors to participate in the meeting of IDF during June 30—July 1, 1994 reflected the growing importance of PFI in the global capital inflows and India's enhanced capacity to attract such flows. Owing to such developments, "the share of net external assistance in aggregate net foreign capital inflows went down from 61 percent in 1980-81 to 26 percent in 1990-91. After a brief spurt in its share in 1991-92 to 64 percent, mainly due to large availability of exceptional finance in that year to finance the BOP crisis, the share again declined thereafter and was below 20 percent in 1993-94" (Govt. of India[b], 1995: p. 88). Hence, the consequent decline in the net availability of external assistance left almost little for development purposes for the domestic budgetary resources during the Eighth Plan.

The Ninth FYP (1997-2002), unique in a number of ways, commenced from April 1, 1997, in the 50th year of India's independence, taking the country into the new Millennium, though formal necessary approval and adoption was made nearly two years after its implementation due to political instability. The NDA Government deliberately chose to continue with the development strategy articulated by the previous United Front Governments and endorsed by the 'National Development Council', first, to avoid the 'plan holiday' which proved detrimental, in the past, to the development process. Second, the development strategy of the Ninth Plan aimed at strengthening efforts to build self-reliance along with to augment domestic resource generation through enhanced inflows of external savings in order to accelerate the growth rate. "The requirements of external capital inflows were given not only by the current account deficit but also by the desired increase in forex reserves which provided the precautionary cushion against the sudden disruptions" (Govt. of India, 1999, Vol. I : pp. 63-64). The calculations of sustainable 'current account deficit' implicitly assumed that all the future external inflows would be in the form of commercial debt, and ignored the possibility of concessional debt (foreign aid) on the one hand and foreign investments, on the other (*Ibid.*, p. 64). The trend of concessional debt suggested that it would steadily decline as a proportion of total external inflows into the country. This view even has also been supported by the overall trend in the international availability of concessional funds. Third, the deficit financing has to be kept at zero level in this plan when balance from current revenue turned negative.

Taking into consideration these above-mentioned points, the Ninth Plan (1997-2002) envisaged GDP growth rate of 6.5 percent per annum, with public sector plan outlay placed at Rs. 8,59,200 crore at 1996-97 prices, representing a step up of 48 percent, and 33 percent in real terms over the anticipated Plan expenditure and the approved Plan outlay, respectively, of the Eighth Plan. Of this, almost seven percent, amounting to Rs. 60,018 crore, were to be in the form of net inflows from abroad, consisting of external loans amounting to Rs. 49,956 crore and external grants amounting to Rs. 10,062 crore (*Ibid.*, pp. 166-67). However, the actual realizations for the public sector plan outlay were estimated at Rs. 7,05,818 crore at 1996-97 prices, i.e., nearly 82 percent of the project target. In other words, the Plan outlay has been reduced in size by 18 percent. Similarly, the realizations from net income from abroad has been recorded paltry Rs. 17,452 crore, i.e., just 2.47 percent of the actual public sector plan outlay as against the expectations of Rs. 60,018 crore, represented a serious slippage in the net inflow from abroad. Consequently, GOI was forced to resort to market borrowings. As against the projection of Rs. 4,60,179 crore from market borrowings, the actual realization was of the order of Rs. 6,71,216 crore, i.e., nearly 95 percent of the total resource mobilization. If market borrowings and net inflow from abroad are taken together, then nearly 98 percent of the Plan resources were generated from them. The entire resource mobilization projection has gone haywire. It is a matter of deep concern that the entire Plan was financed by the market borrowings and external resources which burdened the government in the form of interest payments, eating into the State revenues (Govt. of India, 2002, Vol. I : p. 84). The actual public sector plan outlay, when estimated at current prices, worked out at Rs. 8,13,997.90 crore (Govt. of India, 2004a: p. 50), while the contribution of net external assistance (exclusive of total debt service payments) was estimated to be Rs (–)3433 crore (RBI, 2004: p. 236), which meant all the utilized external assistance amounting to Rs. 71,202 crore along with draw down of Rs. 3433 crore from country's forex reserves was used just to service the debt repayments. In other words, nothing net from external assistance was available for the country's development, albeit 4.82 percent of the utilized aid was drawn from country's precious forex reserves to repay the amortization and interest payments, which was a matter of serious concern.

This was mainly due to certain reasons like punitive sanctions in the form of fully suspending foreign aid (except humanitarian aid) to India by the major donor countries including primarily the USA, and then followed by Japan, Germany, Sweden and Denmark, etc., due to the Pokhran nuclear test explosions conducted by her on May 11 and 13, 1998; 24 years after such test was conducted in 1974. Japan even refused to host the meeting of the WB coordinated IDF scheduled in Tokyo in June, 1998. No IDF meeting was held in 1998 and 1999 as a sequel to the sanctions; while in 2000, the meeting of IDF was held in Paris on June 22-24 but no specific pledges were made by any country. However, Germany already decided to resume its development assistance to India, while Japan, the largest bilateral donor, lifted these sanctions on October 26, 2001 (Govt. of India[c], 2003: pp. 25 and 45). The RBI estimated total loss of inflow of forex due to the suspension of foreign aid to India at US $ 2.8 billion as a combined total of such aid from all the donor countries (Wadhwa, 1998: p. 1604). At the same time, higher repayments resulting in pre-payments of about US $290 million against eight fixed interest IBRD currency pool loans (interest rate ranging between 9.25 to 11.6 percent per annum) during May 2000 (Govt of India[b], 2001: p. 124) left nothing net for the domestic budgetary resources. India appeared to be in the situation of 'debt trap', when the country borrowed funds from abroad to meet the debt-service obligations. Consequently, the policy-makers started questioning the overall benefits of external assistance. Dr. Y.V. Reddy, then the Deputy Governor, RBI, while delivering the 27th Frank Moraes Memorial Lecture in Chennai on July 14, 2000 called for "conscious efforts to free the economy from the dependence on non-commercial sources of funding, such as bilateral or multilateral aid, in normal times" (*The Hindu*, 2000: p. 4).

The Draft Tenth FY (2002-07) adopted on October 5, 2002 envisaged the total public sector plan requirements of Rs. 15,92,300 crore, which were later on reassessed at

Rs. 15,25,639 crore at 2001-02 prices, of which paltry sum of Rs. 27,200 crore, i.e., just 1.7 percent of the total was expected in the form of net inflow from abroad including net external assistance, net commercial borrowings, net FDI, etc. The projections for the Tenth Plan estimates, worked out on the basis of past trends and likely developments in the future, show that net external assistance is expected to rise from US $ 1, 117 million in 2001-02 (P) to US $ 1,572 million in the year 2006-07 (Govt. of India, 2002, Vol. 1 : p. 112). Evidently, despite the situation of almost 'debt trap', country is unable to get rid off of the external assistance, and make itself fully self-reliant, even after the end of the Tenth Plan. Though, it is a matter of some respite that GOI has decided to pre-pay the high cost currency pool loans of the WB and of the ADB in the year 2003-04. The then Finance Minister Mr. Jaswant Singh, while presenting the Budget for 2003-04, told the Parliament, "taking the advantage of our comfortable forex reserves and lower domestic interest rates, the Government has effected pre-mature repayment of 'high cost' currency pool loans of the World Bank, and of the Asian Development Bank totalling around US $ 3 billion. We intend to continue with this policy of prudently managing the external liabilities and of proactively liquidating relatively higher cost component of our external debt" (*The Economic Times,* Budget Speech, 2003 : p. 1). Following these Union Budget Policy Guidelines enunciated in February, 2003 the Government decided to continue receiving bilateral development assistance only from five major donors : Japan, USA, Germany, UK and the Russian Federation, i.e., GOI decided not to receive bilateral assistance from all other countries. Government also decided to pre-pay its outstanding bilateral debt, except to Japan, USA, Germany and France. Those bilateral development partners, from whom it has been decided not to receive development assistance at Government level, have been advised to consider providing their development assistance to non-government organizations (NGOs), universities and research institutes, etc., in India, subject to certain guidelines issued by the DEA, MOF, GOI. It has further been suggested that they may also consider routing their development assistance through multilateral development agencies (Govt. of India[a], 2004: p. 43). In other words, the country will continue to depend on external assistance provided by the multilateral institutions along with assistance given by these five major bilateral donors.

However, the country would prefer more net income from abroad in the form of private capital inflows, such as : FDI and Portfolio investment, NRI deposits, etc., in the near future mainly because of the rising costs of debt service payments of foreign loans, and burgeoning forex reserves. It was clarified that this was only the first part of a three step policy. The next stage would extend these new arrangements to all the bilateral, and finally to multilateral agencies like the WB, ADB and European Commission, etc. It has been further clarified that India now did not require concessional finance. India has prematurely repaid sovereign loans, both multilateral and bilateral, amounting to US $ 2.9 billion in 2002-03, and US $ 3.8 billion during 2003-04. As on end-March 2004, bilateral loans received from Sweden, Netherlands, Austria, Australia, Canada, Spain, Denmark, Kuwait and Saudi Arabia stood completely liquidated (Govt. of India[d], 2004: p. 1). The country is in the process of changing its status from a net recipient of foreign aid to a net disburser to other friendly countries like Nepal, Vietnam, Bhutan etc. To these countries, India has provided assistance, in cumulative terms, amounting to Rs. 3310 crore, comprising a loan component of Rs. 1544 crore and a grant element of Rs. 1766 crore up to the end-March, 1998 (RBI[b], 1998, Vol. I : p. X-3).

On September 20, 2004, GOI reviewed the existing policy of bilateral development cooperation to affirm the liberalization and reform orientation in India's economic policy. It was decided that hence forth bilateral development assistance would be accepted from all the G-8 countries: Japan, USA, UK, Germany, France, Canada, Italy and Russian Federation alongwith the European Commission. The aid from countries of the European Union outside the G-8, providing a minimum bilateral aid package of US $ 25 million per annum to India, was also to be welcomed. The other countries not covered by this policy might consider providing bilateral aid directly to autonomous institutions, universities, NGOs, etc., as before (Govt. of India, 2004b: PIB-15).

On the whole, it may be concluded that GOI preferred foreign aid as a source of finance to ease the financing constraints in the initial stages of development, particularly up to the end-March 1969. Afterwards, realizing its political and economic adverse effects, Government tried to reduce the dependence on foreign aid to achieve the objective of self-reliance, introduced in the Third FYP. But the ground realities always compelled the Government to continue its dependence on this source of finance. Even after the recent policy changes on bilateral assistance, enunciated in February, 2003 and September, 2004 the country is unable to fully end its dependence on foreign aid, not even by the end of the Tenth Plan, mainly, due to the lower cost and longer maturity of aid in relation to the commercial loans. Donors also have gradually de-emphasized the role of foreign aid in the international economic relations resulting in a significant decline in the aid flows as percentage of GDP of the donors. In India, the accretion to higher level of forex reserves, brought about primarily by the non-debt creating capital flows during the preceding decade, has ensured the sustainability of external debt, which led India to be classified as a 'less indebted country' by the WB, since 1999, and enhanced the credibility of the Indian economy in the global fora. This indicates that the importance of foreign aid has been waning gradually, over the years, in the Indian economy. The country is trying to change its status from a net recipient of foreign aid to a net disburser of the same.

10

Problems of Foreign Aid in India

The present chapter is an endeavor to identify and analyze certain major practical problems, specifically those which are associated with the day-to-day mechanics of foreign aid, and the extent to which these are exacerbated by the nature of aid process limiting the effectiveness of aid in India. Most of these problems are inter-related. Some reinforce each other, while some others are inversely related. The most mundane problems encountered in foreign aid utilization in India are discussed below:

1. UNDUE DELAYS IN THE IMPLEMENTATION OF PROJECTS

It is a rare occurrence that externally aided projects (EAPs) in India, in almost all the sectors, in general, and power sector and highways, in particular, have been completed within specified time schedule. The implementation of such projects have been characterized by varying degrees of undue delays attributable to a variety of reasons, such as:

1.1 Under-Provisioning

An EAP require funds upfront for incurring expenditure

before its share of cost is to be reimbursed from the donor(s), known as foreign aid, is received. Hence, adequate provisioning of funds has to be made by the concerned authorities in Govt. of India. Unfortunately, adequate provision for these projects has not mostly been made in the budgetary estimates of the Govt. Planning Commission also treated 'additional central assistance' (ACA) to the States always as residual expenditure. Even in the case of Central Ministries, Government insisted on accommodating the provision for EAPs of the Central Ministries in the overall plan ceiling only, but these Ministries have been unwilling to cut back their other programmes to accommodate EAPs. Similarly, in a situation of fiscal constraint, the first charge on the plan funds has to be the allocations for EAPs, as the receipts of external assistance on the resource side are contingent upon project expenditure. But normally it did not happen. Although pre-financing of EAPs has been introduced in 1993 to make start up of these projects easier and improve their implementation, yet the ground realities remained almost the same. For instance: 'Sarva Shikhsha Abhiyan', the mother scheme for primary education, launched in 1999-2000 by the HRD Ministry with financial assistance from the European Commission, was afflicted by a major resource gap in the very first year due to insufficient allocation by the Finance Ministry (Sethi, 2003: p. 4422). Consequently, drop in the receipts on account of external assistance delayed the implementation of such EAPs. Interlinked with this was the issue of new commitments and the funds required to absorb these. However, insistence of the Planning Commission on accommodating new external assistance commitments within the existing outlays has resulted in Central Ministries being unwilling to take on the new commitments.

1.2 Lack of Commitment and Coordination

Lack of seriousness, commitment and coordination, on the part of those entrusted to implement the EAPs, in India, has also been responsible for undue delays in their implementation. It must be admitted that the implementing agencies viz:—the Department of Economic Affairs, the Planning Commission and the Budget Division of the Govt. of India have not taken the task of provisioning for central projects, and ACA to the States seriously enough. There has been little or even no coordination between these agencies to come to a mutually agreeable figure. In the past, divergence was of little consequence as it was possible to make additional provisioning at the stage of revised estimates. However, the process of fiscal consolidation has made this task far more difficult (Govt. of India, 1994, Part I : p. 3).

1.3 Inadequate Counterpart Rupee Funding

Fiscal adjustments and the associated budgetary stringencies have also acted as a further constraint on the execution of the EAPs. The disbursements on Japanese side were adversely affected due to the inability of concerned States to provide counterpart rupee funds during the early 1990s. "Assam Gas (NEEPCO/Power Grid), Raichur TPP (Karnataka), Teesta HEP (West Bengal) and Anpara (UP) registered a shortfall of US $ 45, US $ 54, US $ 5 and US $ 42 million, respectively, on account of State budgetary constraints" (*Ibid.*, p. 3). The paucity of rupee resources, both in case of Central Ministries and State Governments reflecting inadequate preparedness, budgetary constraints, and non-convergence of the project-interests and plan priorities (RBI, 1993: p. 1161; Rangarajan, 2004, Vol. 2 : p. 282) have also been responsible for undue delays in the implementation of EAPs. Similarly, non-adherence to financial and other formal undertakings such as : property tax reforms, water tax revision, electricity tariff revision, etc., due to inadequate counterpart funding also delayed the implementation of EAPs in India, because donors never pay for such duties and taxes.

1.4 Protracted Procurement and Contracting Delays

Probably, the most serious cause for delays in the implementation of EAPs in India involved difficulties associated with the procurement of goods and services along with contract awarding. This has also been universally cited as a factor in delaying projects (Sobhan, 1982: p. 96). The stages for procurement of goods and services under the foreign loan agreements, broadly, consisted of donor's concurrence to bid documents, publication of invitation to bids, pre-bid conference, donor's concurrence to the evaluation of awards and recommendations, letter of awards, and signing of awards, etc. In case of procurement of civil works, in addition, there existed steps like pre-qualification of civil contractors. However, all these stages do not feature in case of a large number of bilateral donors as they do in case of the WB and ADB funded projects. Thus, due to the complexity of process involved in the entire procurement cycle, there occurred significant delays in the award of contracts and hence in the implementation of EAPs also.

A 'reasonable' period of time for bid evaluation of contract award is somewhat dependent on the size and complexity of the proposed contract. In some cases a period of 90 days will suffice, in most cases a period of 120 days is considered 'reasonable' or at most 180 days. On the basis of a study conducted by the WB, estimated sector-wise average time taken for bid-evaluation and award in India has been shown in Table 10.1.

TABLE 10.1

Sector-wise Average Time for Awarding Contracts in India

Sector	*No. of days*
Agriculture	179
Power	262
Water Supply	356
Transport	409

Source : Govt. of India, *External Assistance: A Performance Review* 1993-94, Part I, Ministry of Finance, Deptt. of Economic Affairs; Aid, Accounts and Audit Division, p. 11.

The experience showed that the evaluation of bids at the initial level generally proceeded satisfactorily in time but the delay was mostly at the review and decision-making levels. However, a sample review made for the Kerala Power Project, for 14 international competitive bids, the period elapsed from the date of invitation to the date of order ranged between 10 to 28 months, while the time taken from the date of the invitation to the date of contract varied between 6 to 24 months (Govt. of India, 1994, Part I : p. 3). Similarly, a 'Task Force on the Standard Bidding Documents' (M.C. Gupta Committee : Govt. of India, 1993 and 1994) mentioned that the delays in the award of contracts for the WB projects in India ranged between 6 to 14 months (Sarkar, 1999: pp. 11-12). Following the recommendations of the 'Task Force', in this regard, Government has Indianized some standard bidding documents for use in the WB and ADB aided projects. A similar step is yet to be taken in case of the other donors.

Similarly, inordinate delays in India also occurred in the internal evaluation of bidding documents. Frequent interventions at every stage of internal evaluation process and absence of confidentiality in the decision-making process made the contract award process more complicated, and slow. Such delays were often further compounded in many cases by the fact that procurement staff were not familiar with the complex procurement procedures of the different donors. However, recently (2004) the Administrative Staff College, Hyderabad and National Institute of Financial Management, Faridabad have started imparting training regarding procurement procedures under the WB assistance. This should be continued on sustainable basis (*Ibid.*, pp. 12-13)

1.5 Start up and Other Procedural Delays

Many EAPs in India faced delays in the start up activities due to the shortage of requisite funds, basic infrastructure including staff, lack of procurement planning, problems in land acquisition, forest and environmental clearances, water rights, etc. Generally, the administrative sanction, which allows the project authority to incur the project expenditure, has been granted only after the loan was approved by the donor agency. Consequently, there arose time gap between the project approval and the commencement of work. Similarly, personnel staff for manning the key positions in the project were sanctioned, mostly, after the project was approved and the loan was sanctioned. Identification of the project implementing staff and setting up the implementing unit were, thus, delayed. In most of the cases, detailed project design, its specifications, project bid documents, etc., were prepared after the approval of the project, resulting thereby delays in starting the EAPs. However, it should be noted in this regard that only in case of the WB and ADB funded projects, the issue of advance procurement actions have been addressed, which should also be followed in case of the other donors.

1.6 Ignorance about Contract Management

During the execution of certain EAPs, sometimes, the project authorities were not fully aware of the international conditions of contract, and other provisions relating to the punitive actions against defaulting suppliers and contractors. This made the punitive process slower than expected. It may be noted that in case of international competitive bidding contracts for the WB and ADB projects, the *Federation International Des Ingenieurs Conseils (FIDIC)* conditions of credit were followed as the general conditions of credit. Thus, application of domestic practices instead of the FIDIC conditions in civil contracts often resulted in long civil disputes. Similarly, for attracting domestic contractors, the project authorities packaged the size of contract into smaller units. Consequently, global contractors have been reluctant to participate in the bids. Due to a large number of contracts, the executing agency often found it difficult to manage. Further, there was high turnover of staff in the project implementation cell, resulting in the loss of expertise, which developed over a period of time (Sarkar, 1999: p. 13).

1.7 Project Specific Issues

Any kind of delay in the resolution of project specific issues, such as : land acquisition, land alienation, various clearances, resettlement and rehabilitation problems, shifting of utilities, staff and training equipment, etc., also put a brake in the implementation of EAPs, and in the utilization of foreign aid in India. Such delays have hold up two Japanese OECF financed irrigation projects in Orissa, apart from the Japanese assisted Ghatghar hydel power project (Shirali and Chatterjee, 1993: p. 7). The WB stipulations that transcend economic and financial criteria to include environmental factors further slackened the implementation of EAPs. Sometimes, major changes were sought to be made, even after the finalization of these projects, which also delayed the utilization of foreign aid as well as the implementation of EAPs. Sometimes, the nature of these projects, particularly in the power sector, themselves was such that it took on an average about five years to be implemented (RBI, 1993: p. 1161; Rangarajan, 2004, Vol. 2 : p. 282).

Thus, undue, unnecessary and inordinate delays in the implementation of EAPs resulted in the under-utilization of authorized foreign aid, wasting thereby the precious resources of the country, both foreign as well as the counterpart domestic. In addition, when time and costs overrun, project cost escalated also due to the depreciation of rupee value necessitating supplementary loans, which donors usually found it difficult to process. For instance: 112 projects of the Govt. of India with original estimated investment of Rs. 51,493 crore were delayed up to end-March 2004. The overrun cost of these projects was expected to be Rs. 92,344.3 crore, i.e., an escalation of Rs. 40851.3 crore (RBI, 2004: p. 66). As a consequence of inordinate delays, authorized aid amounting to Rs. 81,122.93 crore (Table 5.6) remained un-disbursed upto the above-mentioned period, out of which Rs. 33,438.12 crore (41.22 percent) were sanctioned by the WB (both IBRD and IDA) alone (Govt. of India[c], 2004: pp. 299-300). There have been instances where committed amounts of aid had been cancelled as a result of such delays, and commitment charges were paid on unutilized aid (RBI, 1993: p. 1162; Rangarajan, 2004, Vol. 2 : p. 283). All this restricted the effectiveness of utilized foreign aid in India.

2. UNWANTED SIDE EFFECTS

The externally aided projects (EAPs) have some side effects which have been unforeseen, undesirable and unwanted, and proved detrimental to the effective utilization of aid-funds in India. These are analyzed below :

2.1 Hasty Preparation of Project Proposals

Mostly, EAPs were undertaken in haste without any research basis and evaluation of their feasibility reports for borrowing funds from the donor agencies. Preparation and evaluation of feasibility reports require sufficient time. For instance : an average period of ten years from conception to completion on the WB projects is taken and environmental impact studies may involve still more time (McNeill, 1981: p. 70). However, Indian experience, particularly in respect of bilateral assistance, showed that some projects were taken up merely because foreign exchange was available only through bilateral credit (RBI, 1993: p. 1162; Rangarajan, 2004, Vol. 2 : p. 282). EAPs were undertaken in haste without sufficient study of their possible consequences, which created various unwanted side effects such as : the disputes regarding the project site, clearances from various departments, cost escalations, etc., resulting sometimes in project losses questioning their very existence. But for the successful completion of EAPs, use of aid-resources must be well planned before these are received.

2.2 Capital Bias of Projects

It has been a common practice, particularly for the multilateral donor agencies, to meet only the forex component of the capital costs of an EAP, and not the local costs in domestic currency, mainly due to the reason that at least recipient country must demonstrate its interest and commitment to the project by meeting its local costs. To make use of forex component, "there were pressures towards choices of excessively capital-intensive and/or excessively import-intensive techniques, despite a general awareness that an 'appropriate' technology is what is required" (Lipton and Toye, 1990: p. 128). This resulted in sectoral disparities in India because the Government borrowed more for projects which had larger capital component, such as : iron and steel, petroleum refineries, transport and communication, etc., as compared to agriculture which remained at disadvantage. A similar bias operated in favor of certain other types of projects and of course the choice of technique has been distorted considerably. For example : of the three equivalent fertilizer plant projects (Nangal, Sindri and Haldia), the first two, financed by the multilateral agencies, had a 25 percent higher forex content than the latter, which was funded bilaterally and was undertaken by a domestic main contractor, the Fertilizer Corporation of India (*Ibid.*, p. 129). Similarly, massive prestigious projects, like power generation, steel plants, road highways network, etc., had great appeal to the political leaders, both in India as well as in donor countries, which also resulted in sectoral disparities, delay in the implementation of EAPs, and restricted the effectiveness of utilized foreign aid.

2.3 Problem of Involuntary Resettlements

EAPs in India also faced certain serious unwanted problems mainly caused by the poor involuntary resettlement and rehabilitation practices, and implementation shortcomings for land and other assets, especially in sectors like: major irrigation, power generation and road/highway projects, which has seriously damaged the reputation of the country. "Numerous projects were cancelled, suspended or restructured including withdrawal of the WB support for the Sardar Sarovar Dam and a power project on the Narmada river" (Zanini, 2001: pp. 33 and 62; Sharma, 2005: p. 29). The Indian settlement laws and practices were quite different as compared to the WB approach. The major discrepancy is that, while the Indian approach is limited only to the compensation for loss of land and other assets, the Bank standards require that attention should also be given to the potential loss of livelihood for poor and vulnerable people. Thus, Bank-supported projects require a broader set of supportive measures for affected people, which was quite contradictory, albeit in conformity with, Indian laws and practices. However, GOI and some State Governments have now adopted sectoral resettlement policies in accordance with the WB safeguards for the coal sector and highways. Nevertheless, so far, the high level policy dialogue has been insufficient at national and state levels. Drafts of a new national resettlement policy and proposed amendments to the Land Acquisition Act in line with 'the Bank' guidelines have been awaiting cabinet approval for the past five years. The perception of unreasonableness among some senior officials regarding 'the Bank's application of its guidelines in Central Ministries and the NTPC remains an area of concern' (Zanini, 2001: p. 34).

2.4 Lack of Maintenance of EAPs

Lack of proper maintenance of most of the EAPs in India also created delays in the authorization as well as utilization of foreign aid. Most commonly, Government's capital expenditure was quite excessive in relation to its recurrent expenditure, which in many cases has damaging and wasteful effects, especially on the maintenance of assets. Government spent more money on such projects which have glamor and fanfare, while recurring expenditure on maintenance is not so visible, and hence remained mostly neglected. For instance: the well grounded 'Universal Immunization Programme' assisted by the UNICEF still has many problems like the lack of maintenance budget for repair and upkeep of cold chain equipment, misuse of programme vehicles, staff vacancies as revealed by the recent report of the Comptroller and Auditor General of India. Aid agencies can give drum sterilizers for sterilizing needles/ syringes, even a stove, but the Government must provide funds for kerosene and consumables. In some States medical officers and health workers do not have even funds for kerosene. All this resulted in the wastage of aid-funds on EAPs, which do not have maintenance facilities. There are other examples too. Consequently, "EAPs have a tendency to become 'grandiose' if they are not merged or dissolved with the ongoing programmes of the state" (An Aid Worker, 1993: p.1398). Thus, the lack of donor finance for local maintenance expenditure can distort the investment programming, with too many resources directed towards new capital investment, and too few towards the maintenance in good operating order of the previous slices of investment (Lipton and Toye, 1990: p. 138).

2.5 Inequitable Benefits

Another aspect creating adverse/unwanted effects of EAPs in India is that gainers of such projects are actually not those in need. This may be due to a number of reasons such as : the project is too capital-intensive or built for prestige purposes; selection of beneficiaries may be determined by the political patronage; and/or inequitable distribution of gains is built into the method of project appraisal. For instance, aid funds given by IDA in 1985 used to build 'Sardar Sarovar Narmada River Development Project' have adversely affected the residents of the surrounding areas by submerging their villages. Similarly, 'Indira Sagar Dam' (in Madhya Pradesh) is likely to cause the largest impoundment in Asia by submerging a large proportion of the flora, fauna and human settlements in 2.25 lakh acres of land including 700-year old Harsud town (*Tribune*, 2004: p. 14; Sharma, 2005: pp. 27-28). Gainers of such projects reside far away, and the losers living near the project site resort to agitations against the construction of these projects. Similar is the case of aid-funds used for the construction of express or national highways. It is true, in theory, that beneficiaries can be charged in the form of tolls/taxes so that redistribution of gains is effected, but in practice this is rarely done. Thus, inequitable benefits emanating from EAPs delayed the implementation of numerous such projects, leading to cost escalations and restricting effectiveness of utilized foreign aid in the country.

2.6 Political Pressures and Interferences

One of the most serious side effect of foreign aid, in general, and bilateral aid, in particular, has been the undue political pressures and interferences of the donor countries, especially the USA and allies, on India's economic policies, not to talk of foreign policy. The US-led Western influence has been visible in the recent shift of emphasis from capital goods industries to consumer goods industries, more reliance on private sector for industrial development, encouragement to private foreign investment, particularly FDI since 1991, etc. Similarly, failure to finance the agreed construction of Bokaro Steel Plant in 1960s by the US administration of the day (Lipton and Toye, 1990: p. 122); devaluation of rupee in 1966; unilateral stoppage of aid to India during Indo-Pak war in 1965 and again in December 1971; refusal to supply nuclear fuel to Tarapur Atomic Power Plant in 1978; devaluation of rupee in July, 1991 under the WB-US pressure; and the punitive economic sanctions against India in May, 1998 for conducting Pokhran-II nuclear tests by the US and allies are some such glaring examples of the unwanted side effects of foreign aid, which have delayed the timely implementation of EAPs, and adversely affected the development strategies.

Thus, undesirable and deleterious side effects of the EAPs in the form of above-mentioned problems had unnecessarily delayed the implementation of projects, leading to cost escalations, payment of commitment charges on unutilized aid in pipeline and sometimes even led to the cancellation of projects, resulting in wastage of funds, both local as well as foreign, limiting thereby the effectiveness of foreign aid in India.

3. PROBLEM OF ABSORPTIVE CAPACITY

The problem of absorptive capacity has been another major problem in the use of foreign aid resources in India. The recipient country must be in a position to provide appropriate policy environment and useful projects that could successfully absorb foreign aid funds. Though measuring absorptive capacity is like trying to catch a will-o'-the wisp, yet it has different dimensions:

3.1 Institutional Problems

Institutional limitations, like the lack of an able, efficient, honest, transparent and strong administrative machinery; red-tapism and an administration, which may not have the will for initiative, and taking responsibility at lower levels; frequent references to the administrative ministries, especially the Finance Ministry; lack of an effective carrot and stick system for encouraging productive work; arbitrary job assignments with little regard for specific skill capabilities; and assignments with little meaningful work content, etc., inhibited the speedy implementation of EAPs, and effective utilization of foreign aid resources in India. These have led to increases in the costs of EAPs and non-adherence to time schedules (Rao and Narain, 1963: pp. 78-81).

3.2 Inadequate Basic Infrastructure

The effective use of foreign aid requires strong and well-built basic infrastructure, social overhead capital, and external economies in the form of efficient transport amenties, quality highway/road network, effective banking and insurance facilities, etc. These are considered imperative because these constitute a 'permissive factor' facilitating the forces of initiative and enterprise, creating thereby an environment conducive to economic growth. But, India found it difficult to absorb foreign aid funds to the desired extent, in the absence of such appropriate arrangements.

3.3 Nature and Extent of the Market

Another problem pertaining to the capital absorptive capacity in India is, whether foreign aided investment is domestic-market oriented or export-market motivated. Obviously, if foreign-aided investment, i.e., EAPs are made to meet the domestic requirements then the limited size of market will restrict the use of foreign aid funds, as has mostly happened in India. On the flipside, if EAPs are required to strengthen the export-motivated sector—as has been in the case of iron ore mines in Venezuela and copper mines in Zambia—then vast export market provides ample avenues for the use of foreign aid funds.

3.4 Tied Aid

Bulk of the foreign aid funds, especially from the bilateral sources, to India has mostly been tied in nature, either to the project or to the source and sometimes to the both. This has also been responsible for the under-utilization of authorized external assistance, high cost imports, reduced real value of aid inflows and consequently, restricted effectiveness. Under tied aid, the loan proceeds are required to be spent on the goods and services purchased exclusively from the donor country. The reasons for tying vary from country to country. In 1998 almost a quarter of ODA was tied. Driven by domestic political interests, this practice goes against the very free-market principles that most donors are trying to encourage in the developing countries and results in the inefficient use of aid. It has been estimated that tying aid reduces its value by 15-30 percent (The World Bank, 2000: p. 200). Thus, under this disguised trading in the name of foreign aid, donors have taken back bulk of the aid provided in the form of loans or outright grants to India, through a continuous process of drainage of precious forex reserves, which also reduced the ultimate absorptive capacity of aid funds in the economy.

3.5 Shortage of Skilled Manpower and Entrepreneurial Abilities

Basically, the effective use of foreign aid resources requires the availability of technically trained skilled manpower along with able entrepreneurial skills. Unfortunately, such abilities were virtually conspicuous by their absence during the pre-reforms period, particularly in the initial years of planning, in India. The trouble further expanded, partly due to the inadequate training facilities to the staff employed, and partly due to the pressure imposed on the administration by the rapidity with which the country was transformed into a predominantly welfare-oriented development state (Rao and Narain, 1963: p. 80). Consequently, resources spent on the development including those furnished by foreign aid were not utilized effectively to the extent possible.

Thus, the limited absorptive capacity in India due to the above-mentioned reasons also resulted in the under-utilization of authorized foreign aid, delayed the implementation of EAPs, escalated the project costs, and even reduced the possible continued support from the donor agencies.

4. EXTERNAL PROBLEMS

EAPs in India also faced certain problems on external front relating to the inflow of foreign aid, such as:

4.1 Reduction in the Global Aid Flows

During 1970s, the UN resolved that one percent of the GNP of the donor advanced industrialized countries should be transferred as net resources, including 0.7 percent of the GNP as ODA, to the developing countries. But, ODA flows actually remained only about half of the above-said target, which in itself has been quite inadequate for the developing countries. Recently, there has been a further gradual decline in the net transfers to all the developing countries, particularly on account of multilateral assistance from US $ 28.2 billion in 1995 to 21.3 billion in 2002 (RBI 2003[c]: p. 175) due to the reasons, like the entry of new and larger claimants, especially China, structural changes in the global capital flows, etc. These aid flows to India have already been quite low, when compared to her population and GNP: per capita aid being US $ two in 2001 (The World Bank, 2004: p. 260); aggregate authorized aid being 0.4 percent of GNP in 2001 (*Ibid.*, p. 260); and 0.75 percent of GDP in 2003-04 (Table 8.1). Due to the repayment obligations, net utilized aid was being Rs (–)17,872 crore in 2002-03 (Table 5.4).

4.2 Balance of Payment Problems

Among the BOP aspects that have created problems for the EAPs in India, particularly during the pre-reforms period, two most pertinent were: (a) need to import complementary factor inputs in order to ensure the effective utilization of aid resources, and (b) inadequate increase in exports. The former problem would not have largely arisen, had foreign aid received was 'untied' which could have been used to import the required complementary inputs, not available in the country or were in short supply. However, the situation has been to some extent helped by two factors: first, the country has been able to obtain the resources, which India required most, through aid channels, and second, aid has been committed to projects which had a large forex component, like steel projects, for which aid had been in the form of package deals, supplying the import basket, etc. (Rao and

Narain, 1963: p. 81). The latter problem, i.e., inadequate growth of exports has been due to various reasons such as : low exportable surplus resulting from ever increasing domestic consumption, petering out of the effect of 'Green Revolution', failure of industrial production to rise up to the desired levels, shortage of basic infrastructure, lack of proper incentives, etc. Consequently, the share of India in global exports, which was 0.6 percent in 1970, attenuated to the lowest level of 0.4 percent in 1980 (Govt. of India[b], 2001: pp. S-93 and S-94), and then rose to 0.7 percent in 2001 (Govt. of India[b], 2004: p. S-93), but remained below one percent level.

Even the balance of trade remained unfavorable and the trade deficit has been burgeoning, since 1950. Liberalization and Globalization has further widened it. The trade deficit has been record highest Rs (–)62,870 crore in 2003-04 (*Ibid.*, p. S-78). As a result, the capacity to repay through exports has been further inhibited, due to the needs for even larger volume of imports during the post-reforms period. The prospects for larger increase in exports appear none too bright. Thus, it is obvious that with rising imports, the country has no other alternative but to accept the received 'wisdom' of liberalism : 'export or perish'. The irony is that the same developed countries promoting overall liberalization of imports in India have been the first ones to adopt, hidden or overt, protectionist policies hampering Indian exports. In short, the Hegelian 'cunning of reason' becomes always the 'cunning of capital'. The advice in crude terms would run as follows: "liberalize imports so that I can sell my goods and services to you, and if, by chance or necessity, you run a deficit, do not worry, I am ready to lend it to you at market prices" (Franco, 2000: p. 162). Thus, the unstated fact is that the advanced donor countries have gained from the liberalized imports as well as from the accrued interest on debt by exploiting the country, and adversely affecting her EAPs and the overall development process.

4.3 Burden of External Debt Servicing

Another major problem India faces, today on external front, is the burden of external debt service payments on the public and publicly guaranteed external debt in the form of repayments of amortization along with accrued interest, contributing to the worsening conditions of country's BOPs, even though the renewed policy focus has helped in containing the accumulation of external debt. In the initial years of planning, India got loans on concessionary terms for the implementation of long-term development projects. However, as a consequence, debt-service payments started putting pressure on the net transfer of fresh assistance, rendering the net value for development purposes insignificant, and recently, even negative (Table 5.4). Such state of affairs has been mainly due to the reasons: (a) excessive use of short-term debt in the form of supplier's debt/credit for 180 days up to one year and buyer's credit of all maturities, and (b) unsatisfactory management of overall financial affairs, especially up to early 1990s. Following the recommendations of the 'Report of High Level Committee on BOPs' (Chairman: C. Rangarajan, 1993) short-term credits have been strictly restricted for import purposes, in addition total outstanding under short-term credits are subject to a ceiling.

However, as a result of the cautious and prudent approach towards the management of external debt pursued by the Govt. of India, since 1991, country's rank has improved from third debtor after Brazil and Mexico in 1991 to eighth in 2002 after Brazil, China, Russian Federation, Mexico, Argentina, Indonesia and Turkey, among the top fifteen debtor countries of the world (Govt. of India[d], 2004: pp. 6-7; The World Bank[b], 2004, Vol. II : pp. xxxiv-xxxvi). The total external debt-GDP ratio declined from the peak level of 38.7 percent in 1991-92 to 20.2 percent in 2002-03 and the debt-service ratio from the maximum level of 35.3 percent in 1990-91 to 15.8 percent in 2002-03 (Govt. of India[d], 2004: p. 2, Exhibit 2), although the absolute magnitude of total outstanding external debt has increased from US $ 83.8 billion in 1990-91 to US $ 104.87 billion at the end of March 2003 (*Ibid*., p. 15). Thus, due to the burden of external debt, net availability of aid for development purposes has declined. The long-term solution of this problem depends, among other things, upon the effectiveness of overall economic policies including policies to promote exports and efficient utilization of foreign aid resources.

4.4 Uncertainty and Volatility

Another problem which EAPs, in almost every recipient country including India, facing is the uncertainty and volatility of the magnitude, and the purpose for which aid is likely to become available over a period of time. In India, for instance, the inflow of gross authorized aid always remained volatile and uncertain (Table 5.1). It was Rs. 3847 crore in 1980-81, declined continuously to Rs. 2088 crore in 1983-84; rose to Rs. 13,070 crore in 1988-89, but again declined to Rs. 8123 crore in 1990-91, and after experiencing fluctuations rose to Rs. 17,105 crore in 2003-04 (Govt. of India[b], 2005: p. S-98). This happened not only because the aid disbursements were subject to the vagaries of the numerous donor countries' budgetary processes, in which aid competed with their domestic priorities, but also because it has been allocated to the recipient countries according to the donor's political and strategic priorities, albeit for reducing poverty, and variations in the recipients' currency (Rupee for India) value in relation to the foreign currencies. The latter adversely affect the amount of foreign currency resources available against rupee expenditure. "Moreover aid disbursements are usually subject to the IMF's 'seal of approval'—donors disburse aid only when an IMF supported program is on the track. IMF conditionality is an important factor in aid receipts but not the only one" (Bulir and Lane, 2002: pp. 29-30). These interruptions in aid inflows associated with conditionality aggravate the problems of uncertainty and volatility, which stands in the way of effective implementation of fiscal plans, and even in the execution of EAPs, which presume not only an adequate estimate of forex requirements but also an estimate of their availability.

Thus, EAPs in India faced shortage of resources due to the above-mentioned extraneous constraints, resulting in the under-utilization of authorized external assistance and weak effectiveness. Consequently, the net aid inflows to India fell sharply from the maximum level of US$ 2001 million in 1991-92 to the lowest level of US $ (–)3813 million in 2002-03 (RBI, 2004: p. 236).

5. MISCELLANEOUS PROBLEMS

Besides the above-mentioned problems, which EAPs are facing in India, there are also some other major problems, which are discussed on the next page.

5.1 Donor Coordination

India received foreign aid from more than 40 donor bilateral countries/multilateral agencies, since 1949, for financing various EAPs. Just to maintain coordination between them for supporting a coherent development strategy, even at a sector level, is a challenging task. "When different donor priorities and project related conditions (including donor-specific reporting and procurement requirements) are multiplied many times over, they can create an unworkable environment for a recipient government" (The World Bank, 2000: p. 193). During the 1980s, about 30 donor agencies/countries financed more than 420 EAPs, simultaneously in India, while about 300 EAPs received foreign assistance from the same number of agencies during the 1990s, in the form of loans only (Govt. of India[c], 2004: pp. 87-221). All these agencies/countries are dealt with by the 'External Finance Wing', a single nodal agency of the Department of Economic Affairs in the Ministry of Finance, Govt. of India, through the various Divisions, which in itself causes procedural delays, both in receiving and disbursing aid funds to the EAPs running under the various Central Ministries and State Governments.

5.2 Problem of Ownership

Ownership of EAPs is a key determinant of aid effectiveness in the recipient countries including India, since both the donors and recipients often disagree regarding disbursements of aid funds after the completion of projects. Donors often look for their own ways to ensure that their money is spent as they intend. They want to run their own projects, demand detailed reports from the recipient countries on the projects, and even attach policy-oriented conditions usually to the use of funds. Generally, donors dominate the project life cycle and pay inadequate attention to the preferences of the recipient government or project beneficiaries. However, as a matter of fact, for the success of EAPs, policy reforms must foster ownership by the people for whom the project is ostensibly being implemented (The World Bank, 2000: p. 193). In India, usually this did not happen. Most of the EAPs have been run either by the Central or State Governments without local public participation, which resulted in the wastage of aid-resources without proper maintenance and management.

5.3 Fungibility and Conditionality

'Assessing Aid', a path breaking report undertaken by a group of enthusiastic scholars at the World Bank (The WB, 1998), argued that utilized foreign aid always remained fungible, i.e., intentionally (ab)used elsewhere by the recipient government for the purposes for which it was not sanctioned, whatever conditions might be put to it. This means that in funding specific projects or sectors, donors may actually be helping the sectors which they do not intend to finance such as : military. "The dynamics between the donors and the recipients explain why conditionality fails. Recipients do not see the conditions as binding and most donors are reluctant to stop giving aid when conditions are not met. As a result, compliance with conditions tends to be low, while the release rate of loan trenches remains high. Thus, aid has often continued to flow despite the continuation of bad policies" (*Ibid.*, p. 193), which has profound implications for development cooperation. The time, government officials in the recipient countries including India, spent negotiating and monitoring such conditions, can better be utilized for analyzing development problems, and designing development strategies. All this also hampers the timely execution of EAPs, utilization of authorized aid and its effectiveness.

5.4 Unrealistic Government Policy

Following the budgetary guidelines of February, 2003, Govt. of India announced its three stage policy regarding obtaining foreign aid, without sensing ground realities and without consulting the needy State Governments. Though these policy guidelines have been somewhat revised in September, 2004 yet the situation almost remained the same. Following these revised guidelines, in the first stage, Central, State and parastatal institutions will no longer receive the bilateral assistance from all other countries, except the G-8 members: Japan, Germany, USA, UK, France, Canada, Italy and Russia along with the European Commission (Govt. of India, 2004b:PIB-15). These policy guidelines indicate as if India with burgeoning forex reserves, no longer requires concessional finance. The country is keen to revise its status from an aid-recipient to aid-donor, but the ground realities are quite different. The number of development projects are facing the problem of resources crunch. It is also possible that many 'smaller donors', especially the Scandinavians, from whom India has unilaterally stopped accepting aid, who in per capita terms, were the largest donors to the multilaterals, like the UN, the WB, the IMF, etc., and are occupying crucial positions on the boards of the WB and the IMF, are unlikely to support Indian claims for resources from these bodies (Sethi, 2003: p. 4422). At the same time, it is also illogical on the part of Govt. of India to search for less expensive and concessional flow of funds, particularly in an atmosphere of liberalization, with strenuous efforts being made to enhance the inflow of foreign capital. Consequently, the development projects, especially the EAPs, will face more problems in their implementation, thereby adversely affecting the country's overall development process.

On the whole, the problems relating to foreign aid, detailed above, are though not exhaustive yet include all the major problems, which limited the effectiveness of utilized foreign aid in India by creating undue delays in the implementation of EAPs, generating adverse side effects owing to the limited absorptive capacity of the economy, and due to certain external and miscellaneous problems. Most of these problems are interrelated. As a result, country is still unable to leave the crutches of foreign aid, even after more than five decades of economic planning. Although, Govt. of India has unilaterally decided in September, 2004 not to accept bilateral assistance on government to government level from all the countries, except G-8 and the European Commission, yet it allowed the NGOs, universities, research institutions, etc., to receive aid from all these sources. For the realization of long cherished goal of 'self-reliance', the country should adopt corrective measures to improve the effectiveness of the utilization of foreign aid, whatsoever is available, in India in the near future. This requires improvement in the overall policy environment.

11

Policy Measures for Improving Foreign Aid Effectiveness

Foreign aid has been a post WW-II phenomenon. It has proved highly effective, totally ineffective and everything in between at different times in different countries. The present study has been undertaken with the prime objective of examining its effectiveness in India, particularly during the period 1970-71 to 2003-04, alongwith the review of Government policy regarding foreign aid. For this purpose, grant element inherent in the utilized/committed loans has been estimated to work out the real worth of foreign aid, and its impact has been examined in the various sectors of the body economic, especially for which it was sanctioned and utilized.

The specific objectives of the study were:

1. to examine the various theoretical and empirical issues involved in the utilization of foreign aid;
2. to analyze the source-wise and purpose-wise nature, extent and utilization of foreign aid in India, and the changes there-in;
3. to analyze the loan-wise terms and conditions of foreign aid, especially the loans utilized by India, both from the

multilateral and bilateral sources, in order to estimate grant element inherent there-in;
4. to examine the effectiveness of utilized foreign aid through its impact on the various sectors of the Indian economy;
5. to review the policy of Government of India regarding foreign aid; and
6. to identify the problems, especially in the authorization as well as in the utilization, of foreign aid in India and to suggest policy measures.

PLAN OF THE STUDY

The study consisted of 11 chapters. Chapter 1 introduced the topic. Chapter 2 explained the various concepts of foreign aid along with database and methodology applied in the study. Important theoretical issues involving major aspects of foreign aid to the developing countries have been discussed in Chapter 3. A brief review of the important empirical investigations relating to foreign aid, particularly concerning India, has been made in Chapter 4. In Chapter 5, source-wise and purpose-wise utilization of foreign aid in the Indian economic system has been examined. Chapter 6 dealt with the estimation of grant element inherent in the multilateral loans to India, while in Chapter 7 estimation of grant element in the bilateral loans to India has been discussed. In chapter 8, an attempt has been made to examine the effectiveness of utilized foreign aid through its impact on the different sectors of the Indian economy. Chapter 9 outlined the policy of the Government of India regarding foreign aid. Chapter 10 focussed upon the various problems involved in the utilization of foreign aid faced by the country. Chapter 11 summarized the discussion and main findings of the study, and also suggested certain policy measures for improving the effectiveness of foreign aid in India.

DATA BASE AND METHODOLOGY

The study, being country specific in nature, had to rely primarily on the secondary data, which were mainly obtained from the various reports published by the MOF, GOI; RBI; CMIE;

the WB; OECD; and UNDP. The data regarding source-wise and purpose-wise nature, extent, and distribution of foreign aid, both authorized as well as utilized, were collected from the *Economic Survey* (various issues : 1970-71 to 2004-05), published annually by the Economic Division, MOF, GOI; *Report on Currency and Finance, Vol. I and II* (various issues : 1950-51 to 1997-98), *Report on Currency and Finance* (various issues : 1998-99 to 2002-03), *Annual Report* (various issues : 1970-71 to 2003-04), and *Handbook of Statistics on The Indian Economy (2003-04)*, all annually published by the RBI; and the *External Assistance (2003-04)*, annual publication of the Aid, Accounts and Audit Division of the DEA, MOF, GOI. For cross-checking the data, reports of the 'Development Assistance Committee' of the OECD and the WB were also consulted. The data regarding external debt burden were cross-checked from *India's External Debt : A Status Report*, (various issues: 2000 to 2004), an annual publication of the DEA, MOF, GOI.

For estimating loan-wise grant element inherent in the loans utilized (committed to, in case of loans in pipeline) by India, information regarding the source-wise and loan-wise terms and conditions, and the historical exchange rate of Rupee for various foreign currencies during the period 1980-81 to 2003-04 were obtained from the *External Assistance* (various issues: 1970-71 to 2003-04). For this purpose the *Global Development Finance*, formerly *World Debt Tables, Vol. I and II*, (various issues: 1990-2005) published yearly by the WB were also consulted. The data regarding the domestic market sensitive discount rates used in the estimation of grant element were collected from the *Handbook of Statistics on The Indian Economy (2003-04)*.

For examining the effectiveness of utilized gross foreign aid in India, through its impact on the various sectors of the Indian economy, the data were obtained from the *Handbook of Statistics on The Indian Economy (2003-04)*; *Economic Survey*, (various issues: 1970-71 to 2004-05); *National Accounts Statistics* (various issues: 1990 to 2004), annual publication of the Central Statistical Organization, Ministry of Statistics and Programme Implementation, GOI; and *Foreign Trade & Balance of Payments*, (various issues: 2000 to 2004), one of the monthly publications of the CMIE.

For evaluating the policy of the GOI regarding foreign aid, in addition to the above, information were obtained from the

Annual Report (various issues: 1997-98 to 2003-04) published by the MOF, GOI; *Indian Public Finance Statistics, (2003-04)*, annually published by the Economic Division, DEA, MOF, GOI; and the various Drafts, Overviews and Mid-term Reviews of the Five Year Plans published from time to time by the Planning Commission, GOI.

For analyzing the data, especially for estimation of effectiveness of foreign aid, ratios and index numbers were used. Wherever these were not available, these were calculated from the quantity figures available at constant prices (1993-94=100). In some cases, where constant price figures were not available, these were converted from current price figures, by utilizing the 'spliced WPI' (1993-94=100) as deflator for the period 1970 -71 to 2003-04. In case of Index of Foodgrains (IFG) base year (triennium ending 1981-82=100) was shifted to the year 1993-94 in order to make it comparable with other variables.

Statistical techniques like: Tabular Analysis; Linear Trend; Annual Compound Growth Rates; estimation of 'grant element' using domestic market sensitive discount rates; Correlation Analysis; Multiple Linear as well as Log-Linear Regression Analysis; and Lagged Multiple Linear Regression Analysis were applied to analyze the data.

MAIN FINDINGS

The linear trend values of the aggregate authorized foreign aid during the pre-eighty period (1966-67 to 1979-80); the post-eighty period (1980-81 to 2003-04); and for the overall study period (1966-67 to 2003-04) were estimated to be 104.7688; 809.5364; and 588.8303, respectively, which were all positive as well as highly significant at one percent level. Similarly, the trend values for loans as well as outright grants, for the above-mentioned corresponding periods, were also worked out as positive and highly significant, especially during the overall period, as has been discussed in Chapter 5. Loans under the US Public Law-480/665 showed a downward trend from Rs. 392.7 crore in 1966-67 to Rs. 22.8 crore in 1977-78. Thereafter no such loan was authorized to India.

The linear trend value of the overall utilized foreign aid (41.41208) was found to be positive and significant at five percent level for the pre-eighty period, while the trend values for the post-eighty period (732.05980), and for the whole period (470.42900) were positive and significant at one percent level. The study also showed that the share of loans in the overall utilized aid always remained dominant as compared to outright grants with share ranging between the maximum level of 98.2 percent (taken together of loans and PL-480 loans) in 1972-73 and the minimum level of 77.50 percent in 1979-80. During the post-eighty period, the share of outright grants in the overall utilized assistance reduced to 5.1 percent in 2000-01, but thereafter slightly rising to 11.95 percent in 2003-04. The linear trend values for the utilized loans as well as outright grants, individually, for the pre-eighty period, post-eighty period, and for the overall period were all found to be positive and significant at one percent level. However, gross utilized overall aid as ratio of country's GDP at 1993-94 prices remained quite low and declined with fluctuations from the peak level of 3.98 percent in 1966-67 to the bottom level of 0.72 percent in 2002-03.

If the cost of debt-servicing is taken into consideration, the net utilized assistance showed a negative trend, while the gross utilized aid showed a positive trend which was significant at one percent level during the overall period. The net assistance declined to its lowest level of Rs. (–)17,872 crore in 2002-03, which meant that instead of providing budgetary support to the domestic resources, aid became a liability because country was repaying its servicing costs from its own precious forex reserves. Even during the pre-eighty period, the linear trend value for net external assistance was worked out as negative though non-significant, while the same for gross utilized aid was positive and significant at five percent level. Thus, net external assistance remained low and showed a negative trend as compared to positive trend shown by gross utilized foreign aid.

India received foreign aid mainly (62.2 percent of the utilized aid up to end-March 2004) from the multilateral institutions, like the WB (both IBRD and IDA), ADB, OPEC Fund, IMF Trust Fund, EEC, UNDP, ISO and IFAD. On the other hand, bilaterally, Japan was the largest contributor with a share of 17.4 percent of the total utilized assistance followed by Germany, UK, USA and Russia with relative shares of 4.7, 4.2, 3.2, and 1.8 percent of the total utilized assistance, respectively, during the above-mentioned period. About 90 percent of the total utilized aid was contributed by only the eight sources: IDA, IBRD, ADB, Japan, Germany, UK, USA, and Russia. The relative share of all other sources was marginal.

The linear trend values of the utilized multilateral assistance during the pre-eighty period; the post-eighty period; and the overall period were found to be positive and significant at one percent level, but the trend values of the bilateral assistance during the pre-eighty period worked out to be negative and non-significant, while the same during the post-eighty period as well as during the overall period were found to be positive and significant at one percent level. Thus, multilateral utilized assistance proved more dominant and significant *vis-a-vis* bilateral assistance in India.

The evaluation of purpose-wise utilization of aid was carried out for the two time periods (in view of the comparability problem) for which it was utilized: (1) April 1, 1951 to March 31, 1985, and (2) April 1, 1985 to March 31, 2004. During 1951-1985, on the average maximum 42.3 percent (Rs. 9519.54 crore) of the total utilized foreign aid was used for the development of industries, followed by 20.3 percent (Rs. 4563.06 crore) on agricultural development; 11.3 percent (Rs. 2543.79 crore) on the development of power and power projects; 9.3 percent (Rs. 2089.81 crore) on the development of transport and communication; and 4.3 percent (Rs. 970.67 crore) on the steel and steel projects. During the period 1985-2004, the average maximum of 28.65 percent (Rs. 46,039.28 crore) of the total utilized foreign aid was spent on the development of total energy sector [out of which power sector used the maximum of 24.6 percent (Rs. 39,526.97 crore) of aggregate utilized foreign aid], followed by social sector with 15.49 percent (Rs. 24,888.39 crore); total infrastructure sector with 10.97 percent (Rs. 17,614.30 crore); and structural adjustment with 10.44 percent (Rs. 16,771.67 crore) share. The lowest proportion of 1.43 percent (Rs. 2303.32 crore) was spent for the development of fertilizers sector. Thus, the significance of energy, particularly the power sector; water resources management; and social and urban development sector in the use of foreign aid has increased, while the importance of agricultural, industrial, fertilizers and infrastructural sectors has declined during the post-1985 period, although it was utilized in almost all the strategic sectors of the Indian economy.

During the period 1980-81 to 2003-04 India borrowed aid funds from different multilateral agencies and bilateral donor countries. Grant element inherent in loans borrowed from the multilateral agencies such as : the WB (both IBRD and IDA), Asian Development Bank, International Fund for Agricultural Development, OPEC Fund, and IMF Trust Fund, etc., during the above mentioned period was estimated in Chapter 6. IBRD, a parent body of 'the WB Group', has so far (up to end-March 2004) financed 195 development projects in India in the form of outright grants as well as loans at near market rates of interest. It authorized outright grants amounting to Swiss Francs 16.454 million (fully utilized); Japanese Yen 2184.336 million; SDRs 3.8 million; and US $ 130.80 million up to end-March 2004, out of which Yen 1622.839 million (74.3 percent); SDRs 0.79 million (20.8 percent); and US $ 78.176 million (59.8 percent) were utilized during the same period. During the period 1980-81 to 2003-04, IBRD committed 163 semi-concessional loans to India, which on the average had overall grant element 39.42 percent, if depreciation of Rupee in relation to US $ is ignored. However, these loans proved non-concessional with overall average grant element (–) 3.27 percent, if exchange rate depreciation of Rupee was incorporated, during the above-mentioned period. On the other hand, IDA, the 'soft loan window' of the WB, granted 201 interest free loans (with 0.75 percent service charges only) to India during the above mentioned period. These loans were found quite concessional with overall average grant element of 37.13 percent by incorporating depreciation of Rupee in relation to SDRs and US $, and highly concessional with overall average grant element of 84.35 percent, when exchange rate depreciation of Rupee was ignored. IDA also authorized outright grants amounting to Swiss Francs 6 million; Japanese Yen 144.477 million; Dutch Guilder 0.8 million; US $ 53.428 million; and SDRs 18.5 million to India up to end-March 2004, out of which Swiss Francs 3.76 million (62.6 percent); Yen 133.167 million (92.2 percent); Guilder 100 percent; US $ 32.510 million (60.8 percent); and SDRs 2.771 million (15 percent) were utilized during the same period. Asian Development Bank, another multilateral institution, was providing development assistance to

India, since 1986, in the form of outright grants as well as loans. India utilized US $ 25 million (50 percent) out of the total authorized US $ 50 million as outright grants up to the end-March, 2004. ADB committed 64 loans to India during the period 1986-2004, which proved non-concessional on the average as their overall average grant element worked out to be (–) 0.81 percent, if exchange rate variations in Rupee in relation to US $ were included. These were found concessional with overall average grant element of 32.64 percent, during the same period, when depreciation of Rupee was ignored. IFAD, a specialized agency of the UN, provided interest free 16 loans (with 0.75 percent as service charge only) to India during the period 1980-2004, which proved quite concessional, both without depreciation of Rupee against SDRs with overall average grant element of 84.26 percent as well as with incorporating exchange rate variations in the overall average grant element of 41.27 percent. It also provided outright grants amounting to US $ 7.29 million up to end-March 2004, out of which US $ 1.506 million (20.7 percent) were utilized during the same period. Another multilateral organization, which provided assistance to India in the form of loans during the period 1980-2004, was the OPEC Fund, which committed 11 loans to the country during the fore-said period. These loans proved non-concessional to India with overall average grant element (–) 0.28 percent, when depreciation of Rupee *vis-a-vis* US $ was accounted for, and worked out to be highly concessional with overall average grant element of 61.64 percent, if depreciation of Rupee was neglected. The IMF Trust Fund provided only a single loan to India in 1980 during the above-mentioned period, which proved non-concessional (grant element –13.75 percent) if depreciation of Rupee in relation to SDRs was incorporated, and proved quite concessional (grant element 48.79 percent) when these exchange rate variations were excluded.

A brief evaluation of the role of those multilateral agencies were also made, which provided assistance in the form of outright grants only, to India during the period 1980-81 to 2003-04 such as : UNDP inclusive of UNICEF, WFP, and WHO; Global Fund Organization; and the European Commission, etc. UNDP, a largest source of development cooperation under the UN system, was providing outright grants to India, since 1966. India fully utilized Rs. 43.83 crore, and US $ 42.653 million (56.8 percent) out of the authorized US $ 75.084 million up to end-March, 2004 for the sustainable human development, poverty alleviation, gender equality and environmental protection. UNICEF, a special organization of the UN to help the children, authorized outright grants amounting to US $ 0.364 million, out of which India utilized US $ 0.329 million (90.4 percent) up to the same period, while the WFP helped Govt. of India through the donation of food aid in the socio-economic development projects in the form of outright grants amounting to Rs. 0.141 crore, of which India utilized Rs. 0.113 crore (80.14 percent) up to the above-mentioned period. WHO provided technical assistance to India in the implementation of National Health Programmes. For this purpose India utilized the WHO grants amounting to Rs. 0.015 crore (25 percent) out of the sanctioned Rs. 0.06 crore up to end-March, 2004. Similarly, the 'Global Fund' sanctioned US $ 53.67 million in the form of outright grants for the prevention of HIV/AIDS, TB and Malaria, out of which unfortunately, India utilized nothing up to end-March, 2004. The European Commission, another multilateral source of providing assistance entirely in the form of outright grants since 1976, authorized the same amounting to € 1380.145 million up to the end-March 2004, out of which € 918.315 million (66.54 percent) were utilized during the same period, for the sectors, like watershed management, irrigation, forestry, health and education.

The contribution of the US-based two private philanthropic organizations viz. : the Ford Foundation and the Rockefeller foundation, in providing economic assistance in the form of outright grants to India, was also examined in Chapter 6. Although the share of aid provided by these two charitable institutions in the overall development assistance to India is almost negligible, yet these contributed towards the building up of a number of scientific and technical institutes, and medical colleges; control of diseases; and development of rural health, etc. The Ford Foundation was providing grants to India since December, 1951. Its activities ceased in 1983. On the other hand, the Rockefeller Foundation was operating in India since 1920, but its activities were terminated by the Govt. of India in 1976. However, both have again been allowed to operate in India since

1998-99, after a gap of almost two decades. Subsequently, Ford Foundation authorized outright grants amounting to US $ 0.267 million, which were fully utilized up to end-March 2004, while the Rockefeller Foundation granted since then US $ 2.60 million up to end-March 2000. Thus, these multilateral as well as private charitable institutions, on the whole, contributed significantly in the form of loans as well as outright grants, during the period 1980-2004.

Chapter 7 dealt with the estimation of grant element inherent in the loans obtained from the friendly bilateral sources (committed to, in case of loans in pipeline) utilized in India during the period 1980-81 to 2003-04. First, grant element in bilateral loans was estimated regarding those countries from which India is continuing to borrow, even after the revised bilateral development cooperation policy of September 2004, both without as well as with exchange rate depreciation of Rupee *vis-a-vis* concerned foreign currencies. These included all the G-8 countries: Japan, Germany, USA, UK, France, Italy, Canada and Russia. Japan, the largest bilateral donor to India, provided 149 soft loans, which were found quite concessional during the above-mentioned period, with an overall average grant element of 40.43 percent when depreciation of Rupee in relation to Yen was incorporated, and 72.91 percent if depreciation of Rupee was ignored. Japan also authorized outright grants amounting to Yen 81.745 billion through the JICA, out of which India utilized Yen 81.063 billion (99.2 percent) up to end-March 2004. Germany, another bilateral donor, provided financial assistance in the form of soft loans, commercial credit and outright grants. The German 127 loans committed to/utilized by India, during the above-mentioned period, also proved concessional with overall average grant element of 17.12 percent, if depreciation of Rupee against Deutsche Mark (up to end-March 1993) and Euro (afterwards up to end-March 2004) was included. These loans were highly concessional with overall average grant element of 79.38 percent, otherwise when exchange rate variations in Rupee were ignored. Germany also provided outright grants inclusive of technical assistance amounting to Deutsche Mark 445.052 million (totally utilized by India), € 327.427 million and US $ 0.750 million, out of which € 199.033 million (60.8 percent) and US $ 0.234 million (31.2 percent) were utilized by India up to end-March 2004.

However, the US assistance to India in the form of loans was available only up to end-March, 1986. During 1980-2004, India utilized 25 US committed loans, which proved quite costly and non-concessional with an overall average grant element of (–)30.25 percent, when exchange rate depreciation of Rupee *vis-a-vis* US $ was accounted for, but proved quite concessional with overall average grant element of 52.76 percent otherwise, if depreciation of Rupee was ignored. India also utilized US $ 896.161 million (79.4 percent) in the form of outright grants inclusive of technical assistance, available from the USAID since mid-1980s, out of the total authorized US $ 1128.195 million. The UK was extending development assistance to India since 1958, mainly in the form of loans up to 1975, and thereafter in the form of outright grants only. India utilized British £ 2326.332 million (82.4 percent) out of the total authorized British £ 2822.794 million in the form of outright grants inclusive of technical assistance. During the period 1980-2004, UK provided only a single loan to tide over the BOP crisis in 1991-92, which proved concessional with grant element of 4.77 percent, both without as well as with exchange rate variations in Rupee (as the loan was interest free). However, the French assistance to India was mostly in the form of loans, and that too as mix of soft and commercial loans. India utilized 72 French loans during the period 1980-2004, which proved marginally non-concessional with overall average grant element of (–)0.44 percent, if depreciation of Rupee was accounted for, and proved quite concessional with overall average grant element of 55.57 percent, otherwise, when depreciation of Rupee was ignored. India also utilized the French outright grants amounting to French Francs 251.495 million (100 percent) and Euros amounting to 0.311 million (38.2 percent) out of the authorized amount € 0.815 million up to end-March 2004. Italy, on the other hand, provided only 13 loans during the above-mentioned period to India, which also proved non-concessional with overall average grant element (–)6.23 percent, when exchange rate variations were incorporated and found highly concessional with overall average grant element of 68.22 percent, otherwise if these exchange rate variations in Rupee were neglected. However, Canada provided nine interest free loans to India during this fore-said period, which proved highly concessional with grant element of 91.57 percent, both without as well as with incorporating exchange rate depreciation of Rupee *vis-a-vis* CAN $. Canada also authorized outright grants amounting CAN $ 1348.649 million, out of which India utilized CAN $ 1324.078 million (98.2 percent) up to the end-March, 2004. Following the disintegration of USSR, bilateral arrangements for development assistance were entered into with Russia in 1993, which provided five loans including three non-rescheduled and one rescheduled loan to India, during the period 1992-93 to 2003-04. These loans proved quite concessional to India both without and with depreciation of Rupee. The overall average grant element was worked out to 44 percent with incorporating exchange rate variations in Rupee, and 61.39 percent if depreciation of Rupee was ignored. Russia also provided outright grants to India amounting to Rs. 9.63 crore, which were fully utilized by her up to end-March 2004.

The grant element implicit in the loans committed to/ utilized by India from those bilateral sources from which it would not borrow on government to government level in accordance with the new policy on bilateral development cooperation September, 2004 was also examined. These included Australia, Austria, Belgium, Denmark, Kuwait, Netherlands, Saudi Arabia, Sweden, Switzerland, Spain, and Norway, etc. During the period 1980-81 to 2003-04, Australia authorized only two loans to India, which proved quite concessional, both without incorporating exchange rate variations in Rupee *vis-a-vis* US $ (grant element on the average 62.93 percent) and after including depreciation of Rupee (grant element on the average 10.67 percent). Besides these loans, India has also fully utilized the Australian outright grants amounting to Australian $ 166.16 million up to end-March 2004. On the other hand, Austrian six loans were found non-concessional with overall average grant element (–)13.52 percent when exchange rate variations in Rupee in relation to Austrian Shillings were accounted for, and estimated as concessional with average grant element 78.12 percent when such variations were ignored. India also fully utilized the outright Austrian grants amounting to Shillings 55.96 million up to the end of March, 2004. However, the six Belgian loans during the period 1980-2004 proved highly concessional with overall average grant element 59.62 percent and 86.87 percent, both with and without incorporating exchange rate depreciation of Rupee in relation to

Belgian Francs, respectively. India also wholly utilized Belgian Francs 46.95 million authorized to her in the form of outright grants up to the period fore-mentioned. Similarly, the six interest free Danish loans were also found to be highly concessional with overall average grant element 89.72 percent, both with and without including depreciation of Rupee *vis-a-vis* Danish Kroner, during the above-mentioned period. India likewise utilized Danish Kroners 2228.895 million (79.7 percent) out of the authorized Danish Kroners 2796.355 million in the form of outright grants up to end-March, 2004. But, the Kuwaiti six loans proved non-concessional with overall average grant element (–)22.19 percent if exchange rate variations in Rupee against Kuwaiti Dinar were incorporated, and proved concessional with average grant element of 45.88 percent when these variations were ignored. India also fully utilized the Kuwaiti outright grants amounting to the Rs. 12.03 crore up to the end-March, 2004. Similarly, the Dutch 16 loans committed to/utilized by India proved non-concessional with overall average grant element (–)16.72 percent when exchange rate depreciation of Rupee against Dutch Guilder and Euro were incorporated during the period 1980-2004, while these proved highly concessional with average grant element of 69.91 percent when depreciation of Rupee was ignored during the same period. € 182.168 million (62.8 percent) out of € 290.047 million; Rs. 0.446 crore (0.8 per cent) out of Rs. 55.081 crore; and Dutch Guilder 1584.129 million (100 percent) authorized as outright grants by the Netherlands, up to end-March 2004 have also been utilized by India. Similarly, the three Saudi-Arabian loans also proved non-concessional with average grant element (–)8.88 percent after incorporating exchange rate changes in relation to Saudi-Riyals during the above-mentioned period, and worked out concessional with grant element of 54.10 percent by ignoring depreciation of Rupee during the same period. However, the three Swedish loans proved concessional, both without as well as after accounting for exchange rate variations in Rupee *vis-a-vis* Swiss Francs and US $, during the above-mentioned period, with grant element of 50.67 and 8.8 percent, respectively. India also utilized Swedish Kroner 5184.623 million (99 percent) out of the Swedish Knoner 5235.696 million authorized as outright grants up to the period ending March, 2004. But, the two Swiss loans proved non-concessional, with average grant element (–)3.28 percent after incorporating exchange rate depreciation of Rupee in relation to Swiss Francs, during the period 1980-81 to 2003-04. The same proved highly concessional with average grant element of 63.68 percent if depreciation of Rupee was ignored. India likewise utilized the Swiss outright grants amounting to Swiss Francs 408.049 million (93.9 percent) out of the authorized amount of Swiss Francs 434.521 million and cent percent utilized Rs. 26.267 crore (given in local currency) up to the period ending March, 2004. Similarly, a single Spanish loan utilized by India, during the above-mentioned period, proved non-concessional with grant element (–)6.53 percent after incorporating depreciation of Rupee in relation to US $, and found otherwise highly concessional with grant element of 70.24 percent if exchange rate variations were neglected. However, grant element in single Norwegian loan extended to India, outside Annual Budget of the Govt. of India, could not be estimated as its terms and conditions were not available. India utilized Norwegian outright grants amounting to Kroner 1354.116 million (99 percent), out of the sanctioned Kroner 1366.478 million during the period ending-March, 2004.

An endeavor has also been made to compare and contrast the average grant element inherent in the loans, both multilateral as well as bilateral, committed to/utilized by India during the period 1980-81 to 2003-04, both without as well as with incorporating exchange rate depreciation of Rupee in relation to foreign currencies. The results showed that average grant element implicit in all the loans sanctioned by all the sources proved concessional/highly concessional when exchange rate depreciation of Rupee was ignored. The maximum average grant element was found in Canadian nine loans (91.57 percent), followed by Danish six loans (89.72 percent); Belgian six loans (86.87 percent); IDA 201 loans (84.35 percent); and IFAD sixteen loans (84.26 percent) if depreciation of Rupee was ignored. The lowest grant element was estimated in single British loan (4.77 percent). However, average grant element was found negative in most of the loans when depreciation of Rupee *vis-a-vis* foreign currencies was accounted for during the above mentioned period. The grant element with incorporating exchange rate variations was found maximum in nine interest free Canadian loans (91.57

percent), followed by Danish six interest free loans (89.72 percent); Belgian six loans (59.62 percent); Russian five loans (44 percent); IFAD 16 loans (41.27 percent); Japanese 149 loans (40.43 percent); and IDA 201 loans (37.13 percent). The least grant element was found in 25 US loans (–30.25 percent) during the above mentioned period.

In Chapter 8, an endeavor was made to analyze the effectiveness of foreign aid utilized in the Indian economy through its impact on the development of diverse sectors, especially on which it was utilized and also on the whole economy, since 1970. For this purpose, 'Index of Gross Utilized Aid Stock' (IGAS) was prepared as a composite reflector of the quantum of foreign aid utilized in the economy and was taken as an independent/explanatory variable along with time variable. To estimate, its impact on the different sectors of the economy, 23 social and economic variables were selected, and out of these, 18 variables for which time-series data were available, for the period 1970-71 to 2003-04, have been used as dependent variables. The analysis was made for the overall time period 1970-71 to 2003-04 along with two sub-periods to delineate the impact of economic reforms, i.e., (1) the pre-reforms period (1970-71 to 1990-91), and (2) the post-reforms period (1991-92 to 2003-04).

The study showed that the Index of Aid-Stock (IGAS) was positively and significantly correlated with almost all the selected variables during the whole period 1970-71 to 1999-2000. During this period, IGAS had also grown significantly as indicated by its positive coefficient of correlation (0.7767) with the time variable. However, during the pre-reforms period (1970-71 to 1990-91), IGAS was also found positively associated with almost all the selected development indicators, except Forex Reserves as ratio of GDP (FORX/GDP). IGAS had also grown over the time during this period (coefficient of correlation being 0.1353 with time variable). Similarly, during the post-reforms period (1991-92 to 1999-2000), IGAS was positively and significantly correlated with most of the development indicators, except the Total Expenditure of the Central Govt. as ratio of GDP (TECG/GDP) with which it was negatively associated. IGAS had also grown significantly during this period as its coefficient of correlation was found positive and significant (0.9777) with time variable at one percent level.

The study also estimated the impact of utilized foreign aid in the form of IGAS along with time variable on the selected development indicators with the help of Linear as well as Log-Linear Multiple Regression Techniques. The results of Linear Multiple Regression Analysis showed that utilized foreign aid proved quite useful for most of the activities/areas, during the overall period (1970-71 to 2003-04), on which it was utilized because their regression coefficients were found positive and highly significant, such as : PGDP; XGS/GDP; FORX/GDP; IGIA; ISP; IPOL; IELE; IFP; IIP; and ITC, etc. Utilized foreign aid also proved significantly useful to check the Gross Fiscal Deficit (GFD/GDP) as proved on the basis of its negative and significant regression coefficient. It also had positive, though non-significant, effect on some other dependent variables, like GDCF/GDP; ICG/GDP; and IFG. However, for other dependent variables, such as : TECG/GDP and IEMP, regression coefficients were found to be negative and significant, while for AGDP, it was found negative but non-significant, which implied that utilized foreign aid did not prove useful for these variables, during the above-mentioned overall period. Similarly, it failed to curb the price-rise in the economy as was indicated by the positive and significant regression coefficient of WPI. Highly significant regression coefficients of time variable in case of these variables indicated that the effect of foreign aid, if any, might have been carried away by the trend coefficients.

However, the results of Log-Linear Multiple Regression Analysis were found to be different to some extent *vis-a-vis* the results of Linear Multiple Regression Analysis for the overall period. Under Log-Linear Analysis, utilized foreign aid positively and highly significantly affected PGDP; XGS/GDP; FORX/GDP; ISP; IPOL; IIP; and ITC as their regression coefficients were positive, and significant either at one or five percent level. The utilized foreign aid also proved useful in checking gross fiscal deficit (GFD/GDP) and the wholesale price level (WPI) due to negative, and highly significant regression coefficients. Besides these, foreign aid also had positive, though non-significant, effect on the GDCF/GDP and ICG/GDP. But the regression coefficients of AGDP; IGIA; IFG; and IELE, unlike Linear Multiple Analysis, were found to be negative, though non-significant, which inferred that utilized foreign aid did not contribute to their growth. The highly significant regression coefficients of time variable in case of these indicators showed that the effect of foreign aid, if any, might have been taken away by the trend coefficients. Similarly, foreign aid contributed negatively in the presence of time variable in case of IFP; IEMP; and TECG/GDP.

During the pre-reforms period (1970-71 to 1990-91), the study, under both the Linear Multiple as well as Log-Linear Regression Analysis, showed that utilized foreign aid proved highly useful in most of the areas/activities, such as : PGDP; GDCF/GDP; TECG/GDP; ICG/GDP; IFG; ISP; IPOL; IELE; IFP; IIP; and ITC. Similarly, aid also proved quite useful, though non-significantly, in some other areas, such as : AGDP; XGS/GDP; and IGIA, as shown by the results of both the analyses. During the post-reforms period (1991-92 to 2003-04), both the Linear as well as Log-Linear Analysis found utilized foreign aid useful only in few areas/activities, either significantly or non-significantly. The Linear Analysis proved its usefulness only in activities/areas, such as : TECG/GDP; FORX/GDP; IPOL; ITC; WPI; and IGIA. On the other hand, Log-Linear Analysis found it useful for variables, like TECG/GDP; WPI; FORX/GDP; IFG; and IPOL. For all other remaining indicators, such as : PGDP; AGDP; GDCF/GDP; ICG/GDP; XGS/GDP; ISP; IELE; IFP; IIP; and IEMP, utilized foreign aid did not prove useful, during the above mentioned period. However, the significant regression coefficients of time variable in case of most of these variables indicated that the impact of foreign aid, if any, might have been absorbed by the trend coefficients.

An attempt was also made to capture the lagged impact of utilized foreign aid, during the overall period (1970-71 to 2003-04), by incorporating Lagged Index of Aid-Stock up to five periods, in Multiple Linear Regression Analysis. The results indicated that R^2 was found highly significant at one percent level for almost all the dependent variables, except AGDP and GFD/GDP for which it was non-significant. At the same time, regression coefficients for most of the selected development indicators for the preceding years t-1, t-2, t-3, t-4 and t-5, presented fluctuating non-significant results.

Chapter 9 examined the constitutional provisions, mechanism, and Govt. of India's policy regarding obtaining and utilizing foreign aid in the country. The constitutional provisions in Article 292 clearly stated that only the Govt. of India could borrow from abroad subject to the conditions fixed by the Parliament from time to time. This borrowing power was totally denied to the State Governments. All the activities relating to the foreign aid are dealt by the 'External Finance Wing' (EFW) of the Department of Economic Affairs under the Ministry of Finance, Govt. of India. It has been the principal nodal machinery, through which India negotiated with the donors; administered the documentation of aid inflows; received, allocated and monitored the implementation of externally aided projects within the country; and arranged for the servicing and repayment of foreign loans. Within EFW at least nine Divisions/Units, such as : ADB Division; Aid, Accounts and Audit Division; America-Canada Division; EEC Division; Fund-Bank Division; Japan Division; Project Management Unit, etc., dealt with the various multilateral and bilateral sources. The authorized loan amount has been disbursed to India for specific purposes, such as to finance imports by the donors through three kinds of procedures: (1) the Reimbursement Procedure, (2) the Commitment Procedure, and (3) the Transfer Procedure.

The Government policy regarding foreign aid was reviewed in three phases: (1) The Phase of Structuralism (1951-69), during which external capital financing was almost entirely dependent on foreign aid, reflecting Government's policy aversion to the private foreign investment and external commercial borrowings, mainly due to the concessionality associated with it. During this period, India has drawn wide benefits from aid, especially granted by the two superpowers of the time (the USA and the then Soviet Union) by following the policy of non-alignment. Such external resources were even essential at that time to hasten the economic growth of the country, particularly at a time when high priority was being given to the basic and strategic industries which were necessary for export earnings, and import savings. During this phase, India received foreign aid without foregoing her self-respect and independence. Apart from few accommodations, India did not allow itself to be dictated to on its fundamentals, although in certain cases, it was alleged that India had to follow the dictates of multilateral agencies and other donors in policy adoption. (2) The Transitional Phase (1969-92), during which Government continued to borrow aid funds to meet the plan outlays, though on a declining scale as compared to the earlier phase, to achieve the goal of self-reliance, which remained unfulfilled. Government also continued to follow the policy of non-alignment, till the end of cold war in late eighties, despite the pressure tactics of the United States (unilateral stoppage of aid in June, 1973) and gained more in terms of aid from both the superpowers than it would have had by aligning itself with either of the power. During this phase, Government also espoused the policy of 'give and take' with regard to foreign aid, i.e., on the one hand it borrowed aid from the donors, and on the other, it granted the same to the friendly neighbouring countries, like Nepal, Bhutan, Bangladesh, Sri Lanka, etc. (3) The Phase of Global Orientation (1992-onwards), during which, in the backdrop of widespread changes in the global socio-economic order, Govt. of India decided to woo foreign capital in the form of PFI, in general, and FDI, in particular, as against foreign aid. Though the Government continued to borrow funds to achieve self-reliance, yet it decided in February, 2003 to discontinue borrowing aid-funds from all the bilateral countries, except five major donor countries, which were later on expanded to G-8 countries in September, 2004, mainly due to the lower domestic interest rates and comfortable forex reserves. Government even effected the pre-mature repayment of high-cost currency pool loans of some sources such as : the WB and ADB, etc. Government has also been trying to reduce its dependence on foreign aid funds, although the possibility is dim in the near future, at least up to end-March 2007, the terminal year of the Tenth FYP.

Chapter 10 of the study focussed upon certain major practical problems associated with the authorization as well as utilization of foreign aid in India, such as : undue delays in the implementation of externally aided projects (EAPs) due to under provisioning, lack of commitment and coordination, inadequate counterpart rupee funding, protracted procurement and contracting delays, start up and other procedural delays, ignorance about contract management and project specific issues; unwanted side effects in the form of hasty preparation of project proposals, capital bias of projects, problem of involuntary resettlements, lack of maintenance of EAPs, inequitable benefits, political pressures and interferences; problem of absorptive capacity due to institutional limitations, shortage of basic infrastructure, domestic-market oriented nature of projects, tying of aid, lack of skilled manpower and entrepreneurial abilities; external problems due to the reduction in global aid flows, BOP problems, burden of external debt-servicing, uncertainty and volatility in aid flows; and some miscellaneous problems, like the problem of donor coordination, ownership of EAPs, fungibility and conditionality, unrealistic Government policy, etc.

POLICY MEASURES

To improve the effectiveness of utilized foreign aid in India, some policy measures are recommended below:

First, to reduce the high cost of debt-servicing either 'loan-swapping' should be arranged, i.e., high-cost loans should be pre-paid by borrowing new low-cost soft loans or such high cost loans should be pre-paid from country's own comfortable forex reserves.

Second, country should reduce its dependence on foreign aid and should borrow from only those sources which provide either liberal outright grants or loans on soft terms or a mixture of both.

Third, foreign aid should be utilized only in those critical areas/sectors, which private foreign investment finds unattractive and is not forthcoming.

Fourth, 'sector specific' albeit 'project specific' approach, in which donors provide funds for the sector and the recipient Government designs an overall sector specific strategy, should be encouraged. This will help in improving the effectiveness of foreign aid because complementary activities can be planned in a better way through, both, own and borrowed funds.

Fifth, the practice of publishing loan-wise terms and conditions in the brochure *External Assistance,* which has been discontinued since 1995, should be restored in order to make it a more useful conspectus of data base regarding foreign aid utilization in India.

Sixth, in order to avoid undue and inordinate delays in the utilization of foreign aid, adequate counterpart rupee funds to the externally aided projects (EAPs) should be allocated in time; contracting procedure should be streamlined and decentralized so that reference to the Government should be minimal; all the EAPs should be timely planned in accordance with their respective feasibility project reports; and monitoring mechanism should be reviewed from time to time in order to ensure adequate preparedness, and timely actions.

Last, either adequate funds should be earmarked for the maintenance of EAPs or local public participation (through NGOs) and private sector participation be encouraged for the purpose.

Bibliography

Abusni, Ahmad Ibrahim (1982), "*Foreign Aid and Development*", *Development Policy and Administrative Review,* 8 (1 & 2), Jan.-June, pp. 1-18.

Aggarwal, M.R. (ed.) (2002), *International Institutions And Economic Development of Underdeveloped Countries,* New Delhi: Deep & Deep Publications (P) Ltd.

Akbar, Mohammad (1995), "Does Aid Distort Development? A Case Study of Pakistan", *The Asian Economic Review,* 37(2), August, pp. 358-69.

An Aid Worker (1993), "Aid and Development Policy", *Economic and Political Weekly,* 13(26), June 26, p.1398.

Apthorpe, Raymond (ed.) (1998), *Towards Emergency Humanitarian Aid Evaluation,* Canberra: Asia Pacific Press.

Arnold, Guy (1985), *Aid and The Third World: The North South Divide,* London: Robert Royace Ltd.

Arnold, H.J.P. (1962), *Aid for Developing Countries: A Comparative Study,* London: The Bodley Head.

Arun, T.K. (1991), "Aid Utilisation, What Should be Done?", *The Economic Times,* New Delhi, Oct. 19, p. 6.

Asian Development Bank (2000 to 2004), *Annual Report,* Various Issues, Manila.

Avramovic, Dragoslaw *et al.* (1964), "*Economic Growth and External Debt,* Baltimore: John Hopkins Press.

Azam, Jean-Paul; Shantayanan Devarajan; and Stephen A.O'Connell (1999), *Aid Dependence Reconsidered,* Policy Research Working Paper-2144, July, Washington D.C: The World Bank Research Group, Public Economics, pp. 1-14.

Bacha, Edmar L. (1990), "A Three-Gap Model of Foreign Transfers and the GDP Growth Rate in Developing Countries", *Journal of Development Studies,* Vol. 32, pp. 279-96.

Banerjee, Brojendra Nath (1977), *Foreign Aid to India,* Delhi: Agam Prakashan.

Basu, Durga Das (2004), *Introduction to The Constitution of India,* Nagpur and New Delhi: Wadhwa & Co., 19th Edition, Reprint.

Bauer, Peter (1979), *Dissent on Development,* Cambridge, Massachusetts: Harvard University Press, 2nd Printing, Chapter 2, pp. 96-135.

Bauer, Peter (1981), *Equality, the Third World and Economic Delusion,* London: Weidenfeld and Nicolson.

——— (1993), *Development Aid: End it or Mend It,* International Centre for Economic Growth, Occasional Paper No. 43, San Francisco: ICS Press, pp. 1-22.

Bauer, Peter and Basil Yamey (1982), "Foreign Aid: What is at Stake", *Public Interest,* Summer, pp. 53-57.

Bauer, Peter Tamas (1984), *Reality and Rhetoric: Studies in the Economics of Development,* London: Weidenfeld and Nicolson.

Behari, Bipin (1968), *The Facets of Foreign Aid,* Bombay: Vora & Co.

Bhagwati, J.N. (1971), *The Economics of Underdeveloped Countries,* London: Weidenfeld and Nicolson.

Bhagwati, Jagdish and Richard S. Eckaus (eds.) (1970), *Foreign Aid,* Harmondsworth: Penguin Books.

Bhatia, H.L. (1981), *Does Foreign Aid Help?,* New Delhi: Allied Publishers.

Bhatia, Sneh Lata (1993), "Quantum of Unused Overseas Aid Mounts to Rs. 65,940 crore", *The Economic Times,* New Delhi, August 9, p. 6.

Black, Lloyd D. (1968), *The Strategy of Foreign Aid,* Princeton: D. Von Nostrand Co. Inc.

Boone, Peter (1994), *The Impact of Foreign Aid on Savings and Growth,* Mimeo, London School of Economics.

Boone, Peter (1996), "Politics and the Effectiveness of Foreign Aid", *European Economic Review,* Vol. 49, pp. 767-76.

Brahmbhatt, Milan; T.G. Srinivasan; and Kim Murrell (1996), *India in The Global Economy,* PRWP-1681, International Economics Department, Analysis and Prospects Division, Washington D.C: The World Bank.

Brakman, Steven and Charles Van Marrewijk (1998), *The Economics of International Transfers,* New York and Melbourne: Cambridge University Press.

Brautigam, Deborah A. and Stephen Knack (2004), "Foreign Aid, Institutions and Governance in Sub-Saharan Africa", *Economic Development and Culture Change,* 52(2), January, pp. 255-85.

Bulir, Ales and Timothy Lane (2002), "Managing The Fiscal Impact of Aid", *Finance and Development,* 39(4), December, Washington D.C: IMF, pp. 28-30.

Burnside, Craig and David Dollar (2000), "Aid, Policies and Growth", *American Economic Review,* 90(4), September, pp. 847-68.

Casella, Alessandra and Barry Eichengreen (1996), "Can Foreign Aid Accelerate Stabilisation?", *The Economic Journal,* Vol. 106, May, pp. 605-19.

Cassen, Robert & Associates (1994), *Does Aid Work? Report to an Intergovernmental Task Force,* Oxford: Clarendon Press.

Chalker, Lynda (1995), "British Aid Focus on Social Sector", *The Economic Times,* New Delhi, December 9, p. 7.

Chandavarkar, Anand (1990), *Macro-Economic Aspects : Foreign Flows and Domestic Savings Performance in Developing Countries: 'A State of the Art' Report,* Technical Paper No. 11, Paris: OECD Development Centre, February, pp. 28-33.

Chang, Charles C.; Eduardo Fernandez-Arias; and Luis Serven (1999), *Measuring Aid Flows : A New Approach,* Policy Research Working Paper–2050, February, Washington, D.C: The World Bank Development Research Group, pp. 1-28.

Chenery, Hollis B. and Michael Bruno (1962), "Development Alternatives in an Open Economy: The Case of Israel", *Economic Journal,* 72(285), March, pp. 79-103.

Chenery, Hollis B. and Alan M. Strout (1966), "Foreign Assistance and Economic Development", *American Economic Review,* 56(4), September, pp. 679-733.

Clark, D.P. (1991), "Trade Versus Aid: Distributions of Third World Development Assistance", *Economic Development and Cultural Change,* 39(4), July, pp. 829-37.

CMIE (2000 to 2004), *Foreign Trade & Balance of Payments,* Various Issues, Economic Intelligence Service, Mumbai: Centre for Monitoring Indian Economy.

Commerce Research Bureau (1985), "Declining Role of Foreign Aid in 7th Plan", *Financial Express*, New Delhi, July 3, p 8.

Dawson, P.J. and Richard Tiffen (1999), "Is There a Long Run Relationship Between ODA and GDP ?: The Case of India", *Applied Economic Letters*, 6(5), May, pp. 275-77.

Deininger, Klaus; Lyn Squire; and Swati Basu (1998), "Does Economic Analysis Improve the Quality of Foreign Assistance?", *The World Bank Economic Review*, 12(3), September, pp. 358-418.

Devarajan, Shantayanan; David R. Dollar; and Torgny Holmgren (eds.) (2001), *Aid and Reform in Africa: Lessons From Ten Case Studies*, Washington, D.C: The World Bank.

Dewald, Michael and Rolf Weder (1996), "Comparative Advantage and Bilateral Foreign Aid Policy", *World Development*, 24(3), March, pp. 549-56.

EPW Research Foundation (2002), *National Accounts Statistics of India (1950-51 to 2000-01): New Linked Series with 1993-94 as Base Year*, Mumbai, July, pp. 190-95.

Fei, J.C.H. and Douglas S. Paauw (1965), "Foreign Assistance and Self Help: A Reappraisal of Development Finance", *The Review of Economics and Statistics*, Vol. 47, pp. 251-67.

Franco, Fernando (2000), "India's External Debt : The Cost of Liberalisation", *Social Action*, 50(2), April-June, New Delhi, pp. 129-77.

Friedman, Milton (1958), "Foreign Economic Aid: Means and Objectives", *Yale Review*, Vol. 47, pp. 24-38, reprinted in Bhagwati, Jagdish and R.S. Eckaus (eds.) (1970), *Foreign Aid*, Harmondsworth: Penguin, pp. 63-78.

Friedman, Wolfgang G.; George Kalmanoff; and Robert F. Meagher (1966), *International Financial Aid*, New York and London: Columbia University Press.

Gang, Ira N. and Haider Ali Khan (1990), "Some Determinants of Foreign Aid to India (1960-85)", *World Development*, 18(3), March, pp. 431-42.

Gangadharan, S. (1991), "Unutilised Foreign Aid Rs. 48,107 Crore", *The Economic Times*, New Delhi, February 26, p. 5.

Gilles, Boquerat (2003), *No Strings Attached ?: India's Policies and Foreign Aid, 1947-66*, New Delhi: CSH-Manohar.

Goldar, B.N. (1986), *Productivity Growth in Indian Industry*, New Delhi: Allied Publishers.

Gounder, Rukmani (1996), "The Political Economy of Australia's Foreign Assistance: Asia-Pacific Region", *Indian Journal of Quantitative Economics*, 11(2), July, Amritsar, pp. 1-24.

Govt. of India (1951), *The First Five Year Plan : A Draft Outline*, July, New Delhi: Planning Commission.

——— (1952), *The First Five Year Plan*, New Delhi: Planning Commission.

——— (1956a), *The Second Five Year Plan: A Draft Outline*, February, New Delhi: Planning Commission.

——— (1956b), *Five Year Plan Progress Report for 1954-55*, May, New Delhi: Planning Commission.

——— (1956c), *Second Five Year Plan*, New Delhi: Planning Commission.

——— (1960), *Third Five Year Plan : A Draft Outline*, June, New Delhi: Planning Commission.

——— (1961), *Third Five Year Plan*, New Delhi: Planning Commission.

——— (1970), *Fourth Five Year Plan, 1969-74*, New Delhi: Planning Commission.

——— (1974), *Fifth Five Year Plan, Part I*, New Delhi: Planning Commission.

——— (1978), *Draft Five Year Plan, 1978-83*, New Delhi: Planning Commission.

——— (1981), *Sixth Five Year Plan, 1980-85*, New Delhi: Planning Commission.

——— (1983), *Sixth Five Year Plan, (1980-85), Mid Term Appraisal*, August, New Delhi: Planning Commission.

——— (1985), *Seventh Five Year Plan, 1985-90, Vol. I*, October, New Delhi: Planning Commission.

——— (1992), *Eighth Five Year Plan, 1992-97, Vol. I*, July, New Delhi: Planning Commission.

——— (1994), *External Assistance, 1993-94, A Performance Review, Part I*, New Delhi: Ministry of Finance, Department of Economic Affairs.

——— (1999), *Ninth Five Year Plan, 1997-2002, Vol. I, Development Goals, Strategy and Policies*, July, New Delhi: Planning Commission.

——— (2000), *Mid Term Appraisal of Ninth Five Year Plan*, October, New Delhi: Planning Commission.

Govt. of India (2001a), *National Accounts Statistics Back Series: 1950-51 to 1992-93*, April, New Delhi: Central Statistical Organisation, Ministry of Statistics and Programme Implementation.

——— (2001b), *Indian Planning Experience: A Statistical Profile*, New Delhi: Planning Commission.

——— (2001c), *External Assistance Manual*, New Delhi : Ministry of Finance, Department of Economic Affairs, Project Management Unit.

——— (2002), *Tenth Five Year Plan, 2002-07, Vol. I, Dimensions and Strategies*, New Delhi: Planning Commission.

——— (2004a), *Indian Public Finance Statistics, 2003-04*; August, New Delhi: Ministry of Finance, Department of Economic Affairs, Economic Division.

——— (2004b), *Policy On Bilateral Development Cooperation*, New Delhi: Press Information Bureau, PIB-15, September 20.

Govt. of India[a] (1997-98 to 2003-04), *Annual Report*, Various Issues, New Delhi: Ministry of Finance.

Govt. of India[b] (1970-71 to 2004-05), *Economic Survey*, Various Issues, New Delhi: Ministry of Finance, Economic Division.

Govt. of India[c] (1960-61 to 2003-04), *External Assistance*, Various Issues, New Delhi: Ministry of Finance, Department of Economic Affairs; Aid, Accounts and Audit Division.

Govt. of India[d] (2000 to 2004), *India's External Debt : A Status Report*, Different Issues, New Delhi: Ministry of Finance, Department of Economic Affairs.

Govt. of India[e] (1990 to 2004), *National Accounts Statistics*, Various Issues, New Delhi: Central Statistical Organisation, Ministry of Statistics and Programme Implementation.

Goyal, Ashima (1993), "The Role of Foreign Aid and The Foreign Exchange Constraints in Growth : Some Extensions", *Journal of Foreign Exchange and International Finance*, 7(1), April-June, Pune, pp. 30-43.

Griffin, K.B. and J.L. Enos (1970), "Foreign Assistance: Objectives and Consequences", *Economic Development and Cultural Change*, 18(3), April, Chicago, pp. 313-27.

Guillaumont, Patrick and Lisa Chauvet (2001), "Aid and Performance: A Reassessment", *Journal of Development Studies*, 37(6), London, pp. 66-92.

Gujarati, Damodar (1985), *Basic Econometrics,* Singapore : McGraw-Hill.

Gulati, Umesh C. (1976), "Foreign Aid, Savings and Growth : Some Further Evidence", *Indian Economic Journal,* 24(2), October-December, pp. 152-60.

Gurumurthi, Sitaraman (1989), "Externally Funded Projects and State Plans", *Economic and Political Weekly,* 24(3), January 21, pp. 127-28.

Hawkins, E.K. (1970), *The Principles of Development Aid,* Harmondsworth: Penguin Books.

Hayter, Teresa (1974), *Aid as Imperialism,* Harmondsworth: Penguin Books.

Hayter, Teresa (1982), *The Creation of World* Poverty, New Delhi: Select Book Service Syndicate.

Healy, J.M. (1971), *The Economics of Aid,* London : Routledge and Kegan Paul.

Helleiner, G.K. (1984), "Aid and Liquidity : The Neglect of the Poorest in The Emerging International Monetary System", *Monthly Commentary on The Indian Economic Conditions,* 26(5), December, New Delhi, pp. 67-74.

Herbst, Jeffrey and Charles C. Soludo (2001), "Nigeria" in Devarajan, Shantayanan *et al.* (eds.), *Aid and Reforms in Africa: Lessons From Ten Case Studies,* Washington, D.C: The World Bank, pp. 645-78.

Higgins, Benjamin (1959), *Economic Development,* London: Constable and Co.

Hill, Marianne T. (1988), "Modelling the Macroeconomic Impact of Aid", *The Bangladesh Development Studies,* 16(1), March, pp. 1-24.

Holmgren Torgny; Louis Kasekende; Michael Atingi-Ego; and Daniel Ddamulira (2001), "Uganda" in Devarajan Shantayanan *et al.* (eds.), *Aid and Reforms in Africa: Lessons From Ten Case Studies,* Washington D.C: The World Bank, pp. 101-65.

Iqbal, Badar Alam (1991), "Japan's ODA, Aid Should Not Follow Trade", Calcutta : *Business Standard,* December 20, p. 5.

——— (1994), "India's Foreign Aid Scenario", *Monthly Commentary on the Indian Economic Conditions,* 35(6), January, New Delhi, pp. 85-86.

Iqbal, Zafar (1995), "Constraints to Economic Growth of Pakistan: A Three Gap Approach", *Pakistan Development Review,* 36(2), Summer, pp. 115-29.

Iqbal, Zubair and Ravi Kambur (ed.) (1997), *External Finance for Low Income Countries,* Washington, D.C: IMF Institute.

Islam, Anisul M. (1999), "Foreign Assistance and Development in Bangladesh", in Gupta, Kanahya L. (ed.), *Foreign Aid: New Perspectives,* Boston : Kluwer Academic Publishers, pp. 211-31.

Jalan, Bimal (1992), "Balance of Payments 1956 to 1991" in Jalan, Bimal (ed.), *The Indian Economy : Problems and Prospects,* New Delhi: Viking Penguin, pp. 163-94.

Jha, Shikha and Vinaya Swaroop (1999), "Foreign Aid to India, What Does It Finance ?", *Economic and Political Weekly,* 34(19), May 8, pp. 1142-46.

Joshi, Nawin Chandra (1988), "Foreign Aid, Impact Depends on Domestic Policy", *Business Standard,* Calcutta, July 30, p. 5.

Kakkar, Renu, M.R. (1991), "Foreign Funds, India's Apathy Amazing", *Financial Express,* New Delhi, April 5, pp. 1 and 12.

Katz, S.S. (1968), *External Assistance and Indian Economic Growth,* Bombay: Asia Publishing House.

Kausaliya, R.; Michael Debabrata Patra; and Sitikantha Pattanaik (1995), "External Assistance, The Phenomenon of Unutilised Balance", *Reserve Bank of India Occasional Papers,* 16(3), September, Bombay, pp. 197-222.

Khadka, Narayan (1995), "Foreign Aid and the Economy : The Case of Nepal", *Asian Economies,* 24(3), September, Seoul, pp. 59-81.

Khan, Haider Ali and Eiichi Hoshino (1992), "Impact of Foreign Aid on the Fiscal Behaviour of LDC Governments", *World Development,* 20(10), October, Oxford, pp. 1481-87.

Killick, Tony (1991), *The Developmental Effectiveness of Aid to Africa,* Policy, Research and External Affairs Working Papers, April, International Economics Department, Washington, D.C: The World Bank.

Krauss, Melvyn (1997), *How Nations Grow Rich: The Case for Free Trade,* New York and Oxford: Oxford University Press, Chapter 5, pp. 61-84.

Krishna Prasad, K. (1997), "Some Thoughts on Development Assistance", *Economic and Political Weekly*, 32(41), October 11, pp. 2594-98.

Krueger, Anne O. (1991), "Aid in The Development Process", in Singer, H.W. *et al* (eds.), *Aid and External Financing in the 1990s*, New Delhi: Indus Publishing Co., New World Order Series: Nine.

Kulwant Singh and P.S. Raikhy (2004), "Trends in Foreign Aid to India : Source-wise and Purpose-wise Analysis," *PSE Economic Analyst*, 24 (1 & 2), Amritsar, pp. 23-53.

Lele, Uma (ed.) (1992), *Aid to African Agriculture: Lessons From Two Decades of Donor Experience*, Baltimore and London : The John Hopkins University Press.

Lensink, Robert and Howard White (2001), "Are There Negative Returns to Aid ?", *Journal of Development Studies*, 37(6), pp. 42-65.

Lindert, Peter H. (1995), *Kindleberger's International Economics*, Illinois: Richard D. Irwin Inc.

Lipton, Michael and John Toye (1990), *Does Aid Work in India?: A Country Study of the Impact of Official Development Assistance*, London and New York: Routledge.

Maizels, Alfred and Machiko K. Nissanke (1984), "Motivations for Aid to Developing Countries", *World Development*, 12(3), September, Oxford, pp. 879-900.

Mavrotas, George (1998), *Foreign Aid and Fiscal Response: A New Model*, Working Paper No. 9802, School of Economic Studies, University of Manchester.

Mavrotas, George (2002), "Aid and Growth in India: Some Evidence from Disaggregated Aid Data", *South Asia Economic Journal*, 3(1), Jan.-June, New Delhi, pp. 19-49.

McGillivray, Mark and Akhtar Ahmad (1994), "Aid, Savings and Investment Re-explored : The Cases of Bangladesh, India, Nepal, Pakistan and Sri Lanka", *The Asian Economic Review*, 36(3), December, Hyderabad, pp. 736-46.

McGillivray, Mark and Oliver Morrissey (1998), "Aid and Trade Relationships in East Asia", *World Economy*, 21(7), September, pp. 981-95.

McKinnon, Ronald I. (1964), "Foreign Exchange Constraints in Economic Development and Efficient Aid Allocation", *Economic Journal*, 74(294), June, pp. 388-409.

McNeill, Desmond (1981), *The Contradictions of Foreign Aid*, London : Croom Helm Ltd.

Meier, G.M. (ed.) (1995), *Leading Issues in Economic Development*, New Delhi : Oxford University Press.

Menon, Usha (1988), "Technology and Development Aid, The Case of Ganga Action Plan", *Economic and Political Weekly*, 23(33), August 13, pp. 1693-01.

Mikesell, Raymond F. (1968), *The Economics of Foreign Aid*, Chicago: Aldine Publishing Co.

Mikesell, Raymond F., *et al* (1983), *The Economics of Foreign Aid and Self-Sustaining Development*, Colorado : West View Press.

Mishra, Sudhakanta (1965), *Foreign Aid to India (1951-64)*, Allahabad: Tirabhukti Publications.

Mishra, T.K. (1994), "Aid that Cripples", *Financial Express*, New Delhi, October 28, p. 7.

Mitra, P.K. (1990a), "Foreign Aid : Donor's Perspective", *Indian Journal of Economics*, 70(279), April, Allahabad, pp. 401-13.

Mitra, P.K. (1990b), "Foreign Aid : Recipient's Perspective", *Indian Journal of Economics*, 71(281), October, Allahabad, pp. 255-67.

Mittal, A.C. (1988), *Foreign Aid and India's Economic Development*, New Delhi : Commonwealth Publishers.

Mosley, Paul (1987), *Overseas Aid: Its Defence and Reform*, Sussex Brighton: Wheat Sheaf Books.

Mydral, G. (1957), *Economic Theory and Underdeveloped Regions*, London: Duckworth.

Naqvi, Syed Nawab Haider (1971), *The Incubus of Foreign Aid*, Essays in Development Economics No. 2, Karachi: Pakistan Institute of Development Economics, pp. 1-20.

Narain, Veena (1988), *US Financial Aid and India's Economic Growth*, New Delhi : Commonwealth Publishers.

Nurkse, Ragnar (1986), *Problems of Capital Formation in Underdeveloped Countries*, Delhi : Oxford University Press.

O'Connell, Stephen A. and Charles C. Saludo (2001), "Aid Intensity In Africa", *World Development*, 29(9), Oxford, pp. 1527-52.

OECD (1990 to 2002), *Development Cooperation (or Development Assistance)*, Efforts and Policies of the Members of the Development Assistance Committee, Various Issues, Paris : DAC Report.

Ohlin, Goran (1966), *Foreign Aid Policies Reconsidered*, Paris: OECD Development Centre.

Opeskin, Brian R. (1996), "The Moral Foundations of Foreign Aid", *World Development,* 24(1), pp. 21-44.

Owens, Edgar and Robert Shaw (1972), *Development Reconsidered,* New Delhi : Oxford and IBH.

Papanek, Gustav F. (1972), "The Effects of Aid and Other Resource Transfers on Savings and Growth in Less Developed Countries", *The Economic Journal,* 82 (327), pp. 934-50.

Patil, R.H. (1987), "Trends and Issues in Resources Flows to Developing Countries", *Journal of Foreign Exchange and International Finance,* 1(4), October, Pune, pp. 391-96.

Pederson, Karl R. (1996), "Aid, Investment and Incentives", *Scandinavian Journal of Economics,* 98(3), Oxford, pp. 423-38.

Perera, Nelson (1991), "An Analysis of External Assistance to Sri Lanka : 1960-1984", *Indian Economic Journal,* 38(3), Jan.-March, Bombay, pp. 60-70.

Pincus, J.A. (1963), "The Cost of Foreign Aid", *The Review of Economics and Statistics,* 45(4), pp. 360-67, reprinted in Bhagwati and Eckaus (eds.) (1970), *Foreign Aid,* Harmondsworth: Penguin Books.

Poduyal, Sriram (1982), *Foreign Aid in Nepal,* Kathmandu: Centre for Economic Development and Administration, Tribhuvan University, December, pp. 1-67.

Ranaweera, Thilak (2003), *Foreign Aid, Conditionality and Ghost of the Financing Gap: A Forgotten Aspect of the Aid Debate,* PRWP-3019, Washington, D.C: The World Bank Development Data Group, April, pp. 1-28.

Rangachari, K. (1991), "Re-appraisal Aid: New Priorities Needed", *The Statesman,* New Delhi, June 10, p. 6.

Rangarajan C. (2004), "Report of High Level Committee on Balance of Payments", in Kannan, R. (ed.), *Select Essays On Indian Economy,* Vol. 2, New Delhi: Academic Foundation, pp. 241-331.

Rao, J. Mohan (1994), "Judging Givers : Equity and Scale in Aid Allocation", *World Development,* 22(10), October, Oxford, pp. 1579-84.

——— (1997), "Ranking Foreign Donors: An Index Combining the Scale and Equity of Aid Giving", *World Development,* 25(6), Oxford, pp. 947-61.

Rao, V.K.R.V. and Dharm Narain (1963), *Foreign Aid and India's Economic Development,* Bombay: Asia Publishing House.

Reddy, Y.V. (2000), *27th Frank Moraes Memorial Lecture,* July 14 (reported in *The Hindu,* Chennai, July 15, 2000, p. 4).

Reserve Bank of India (1993), "Report of High Level Committee on Balance of Payments", (Chairman: Dr. C. Rangarajan), *RBI Bulletin,* August, Bombay, pp. 1139-80.

——— (2004), *Handbook of Statistics on The Indian Economy 2003-04,* Mumbai.

Reserve Bank of India[a] (1970-71 to 2003-04), *Annual Report,* Various Issues, Mumbai.

Reserve Bank of India[b] (1950-51 to 1997-98), *Report on Currency and Finance, Vol. I and II,* Various Issues, Bombay.

Reserve Bank of India[c] (1998-99 to 2003-04), *Report on Currency and Finance,* Different Issues, Mumbai.

Riddell, Roger C. (1987), *Foreign Aid Reconsidered,* Baltimore: John Hopkins University Press.

Rosenstein-Rodan, P.N. (1961), "International Aid for Underdeveloped Countries", *Review of Economics and Statistics,* 43(2), pp. 107-38, reprinted in Bhagwati and Eckaus (eds.) (1970), *Foreign Aid,* Harmondsworth: Penguin.

Roy, Durgadas (1991), "Foreign Aid, Present Form is a Lever to Control", *Business Standard,* Calcutta, July 16, pp. 5-8.

Roy, K.C; Y.R. Vadlamudi; and N.D. Karunaratne (1997), "The Impact of Domestic and Foreign Debt on Indian Development Process", *Indian Journal of Quantitative Economics,* 12(2), pp. 85-103.

Ruttan, Vernon W. (1989), "Why Foreign Economic Assistance ?", *Economic Development and Cultural Change,* 37(2), January, pp. 411-24.

Sanghvi, Jitendra (1985), "Status Quo in Foreign Aid", *Commerce,* 150(3866), June, Bombay, pp. 1232-34.

Sarkar, S.K. (1999), "India's Foreign Aid Management: Next Steps", *Management in Government,* 31(1) April-June, New Delhi, pp. 1-17.

Seiber, Marilyn J. (1982), *International Borrowing by Developing Countries,* New York : Pergamon Press.

Sengupta, Arjun (1993), "Aid and Development Policy in the 1990s", *Economic and Political Weekly,* 28(11), March 13, pp. 453-64.

Sengupta, Arjun (2002), "Official Development Assistance: The Human Rights Approach", *Economic and Political Weekly,* 37(15), April 13, pp. 1424-36.

Sethi, Harsh (2003), "Doing Without Aid ?", *Economic and Political Weekly,* 38(42), October 18, pp. 4421-23.

Sharan, Vyuptakesh (1989), "IDA flows to the Least Developed Countries : The South-Asian Experience", *Journal of Foreign Exchange and International Finance,* 3(2), April-June, pp. 154-60.

——— (1993), "External Aid and Indebtedness Among Least Developed Countries, A South-Asian Experience", *Foreign Trade Review,* 28(34), July-December, New Delhi, pp. 172-88.

Sharma, Betwa (2005), "Oustees of Indira Sagar Dam: Saga of Harsud", *Economic and Political Weekly,* 40(1), January 1, pp. 27-29.

Sharma, R.K. (1977), *Foreign Aid to India, An Economic Study,* New Delhi: Marwah Publications.

Sharma, Sheela (1994), "Development Aid : Private Resource Flows Hold the Key", *PTI Economic Service,* 18(17), May 1, New Delhi, pp. 62-68.

Sharma, Subhash (1997), "Changing Pattern of External Resource Flows", *Social Scientist,* 25(7 & 8), November-December, New Delhi, pp. 49-63.

Shirali, Rajiv and Patralekha Chatterjee (1993), "Donor's Worry, India's Luxury", *The Economic Times,* New Delhi, August 22, p. 7.

Singer, H.W.; Neelamber Hatti; and Rameshwar Tandon (eds.) (1991), *Aid and External Financing in The 1990s,* New Delhi: Indus Publishing Co., New World Order Series: Nine.

Singer, Hans and Javed Ansari (1978), *Rich and Poor Countries,* London: George Allen and Unwin.

Singh, Rama Shankar (1988), "Impact of External Assistance on Indian Economy", *Mainstream,* 26(46), August 27, New Delhi, pp. 11-13 and 30.

Snider, Delbert A. (1987), *Introduction to International Economics,* Delhi: Surjeet Publications, 7th Edition, First Indian Reprint, pp. 427-47.

Sobhan, Rehman (1982), *The Crisis of External Dependence : The Political Economy of Foreign Aid To Bangladesh*, Dhaka: The University Press.

Sobhan, Rehman and Tajul Islam (1988), "Foreign Aid and Domestic Resource Mobilisation in Bangladesh", *The Bangladesh Development Studies*, 16(2), June, Dhaka, pp.. 21-44.

Somanathan, T.V. (1994), "World Bank Aid to India : Money, Advice Ratio Inverse", *Business Line*, New Delhi, October 31, p. 8.

Srivastava, D.K.; C. Bhujanga Rao; and T.S. Rangamannar (1998), *External Assistance to States : Terms and Conditions of Transfer*, (Interim Report), February, New Delhi: National Institute of Public Finance and Policy.

Streeten, Paul (1983), "Why Development Aid", *Banca Nazionale Del Lavoro Quarterly Review*, 147, December, Rome, pp. 379-85.

Streeten, Paul and Roger Hill (1971), "Aid to India" in Chaudhuri, Pramit (ed.), *Aspects of Indian Economic Development*, London : George Allen and Unwin, pp. 160-79.

Sudarshan, R. (1995), "International Development Aid", *The Hindu*, New Delhi, February 16, p. 8.

Sundari, S. (1996), "Utilisation of Foreign Loans: A Matter of Concern", *Southern Economist*, 35 (12), October 15, Bangalore, pp. 10-12.

Taylor, L. (1994), "Gap Models", *Journal of Development Economics*, Vol. 45, pp. 17-34.

Tendler, Judith (1975), *Inside Foreign Aid*, Baltimore: John Hopkins University Press.

The World Bank (1995a), *Economic Developments in India: Achievements and Challenges*, October, A World Bank Country Study, Washington, D.C.

—— (1995b), *India, Recent Economic Developments and Prospects*, March, A World Bank Country Study, Washington, D.C.

—— (1995c), *Strengthening the Effectiveness of Aid: Lessons for Donors*, Development in Practice Series, May, Washington, D.C: The World Bank.

The World Bank (1997), *India, Achievements and Challenges in Reducing Poverty,* July, A World Bank Country Study, Washington, D.C.

——— (1998), *Assessing Aid: What Works, What Doesn't, and Why ?* A World Bank Policy Research Report, December, New York: Oxford University Press.

——— (2000), *World Development Report 2000/2001: Attacking Poverty,* September, New York: Oxford University Press.

——— (2002a), *A Case for Aid: Building A Consensus For Development Assistance,* June, Washington, D.C.

——— (2002b), *India : Country Assistance Strategy Progress Report,* December, Washington, D.C.

——— (2002c), *World Development Report 2002: Building Institutions For Markets,* New York: Oxford University Press.

——— (2003), *World Development Report 2003: Sustainable Development in a Dynamic World,* New York: Oxford University Press.

——— (2004), *World Development Report 2004: Making Services Work for Poor People,* New York: Oxford University Press.

The World Bank[a] (2000 to 2004), *Annual Review of Development Effectiveness,* Different Issues, Washington, D.C: Operations Evaluation Department.

The World Bank[b] (1990 to 2005), *Global Development Finance* (Formerly, *World Debt Tables*) *Vol. I and II,* Various Issues, Washington, D.C.

The World Bank[c] (1990 to 2004), *World Development Indicators,* Various Issues, Washington D.C.

Thirlwall, A.P. (1995), *Growth and Development with Special Reference to Developing Economies,* Hampshire: ELBS with Macmillan.

Thomas, T. (1990), "India, Self-reliance is an Outmoded Concept", *The Economic Times,* New Delhi, September 27, 28, 29, Three Parts, p. 8.

Thorp, Willard J. (1971), *The Reality of Foreign Aid,* New York: Praeger Publishers.

Tiwari, Madan Mohan (1982), *External Resources and Economic Development in India with Special Reference to US Aid,* Delhi : B.R. Publishing Corporation, 1st Edition.

Todaro, Michael P. and Stephen C. Smith (2004), *Economic Development,* Delhi: Pearson Education (Singapore), 8th Edition, 2nd Indian Reprint, Chapter 15, pp. 634-69.

Trumbull, William N. and Howard J. Wall (1994), "Estimating Aid Allocation Criteria with Panel Data", *Economic Journal,* July, pp. 876-82.

UNDP (2004), *Human Development Report, 2004, Cultural Liberty in Today's Diverse World,* New Delhi: Oxford University Press.

US House of Representatives Committee on International Relations (1976), *Foreign Economic Assistance Program, Part I,* Historical Series, Washington, D.C.

Vaidyanathan, P. (1993), "Undisbursed Aid", *The Financial Express,* New Delhi, May 13, p. 7.

——— (1993), "Aid Receipts and Debt-Service Payments", *The Financial Express,* New Delhi, July 8, p. 7.

Wadhva, Charan D. (1998), "Costs of Economic Sanctions: Aftermath of Pokhran II", *Economic and Political Weekly,* 33(26), June 27, pp. 1604-07.

Wall, David (1973), *The Charity of Nations, The Political Economy of Foreign Aid,* London: Macmillan.

Wane, Waly (2004), *The Quality of Foreign Aid, Country Selectivity or Donors Incentives ?,* Development Research Group, Washington, D.C: The World Bank.

White, Howard (1992), "The Macroeconomic Impact of Development Aid : A Critical Survey", *The Journal of Development Studies,* 28(2), January, London, pp. 163-240.

White, Howard and J. Luttick (1994), *The Countrywide Effects of Aid,* Policy Research Working Paper-1337, Washington, D.C: The World Bank, pp. 1-130.

White, John (1974), *The Politics of Foreign Aid,* London: The Bodley Head.

Yukio, Shibuya and Yamashita Shoichi (1968), *Foreign Aid and Economic Growth of Developing Asian Countries,* Tokyo: Institute of Asian Economic Affairs Occasional Paper Series No. 2, pp. 3-11 and 19-25.

Zaidi, Naseem A. (1996), "External Capital Inflows and Structural Adjustment Programme in India", *Indian Journal of Economics,* 77(304), July, pp. 49-62.

Zanini, Gianni (2001), *India: The Challenges of Development, A Country Assistance Evaluation*, OED, Washington, D.C: The World Bank.

Zuvekas, Clarence (1979), *Economic Development : An Introduction*, London : Macmillan.

——— (1968), *International Encyclopaedia of The Social Sciences*, Vol. 5, The Macmillan Company and The Free Press, USA, pp. 513-29.

——— (1997), *The New Encyclopaedia Britannica*, Vol. 1, 4, 5 and 10 (15th ed.), Chicago.

——— (2003), "Budget 2003-04 : The Speech", *The Economic Times*, New Delhi, March 1, p. I.

——— (2004), "Budget 2004 Speech", *Business Standard*, New Delhi, July 9, p. II.

——— (2004), "NBA: Villages Around Harsud Ignored", *The Tribune*, Chandigarh, September 8, p. 14.

WEBSITES

www.epw.org.in
http://finmin.nic.in
http://finmin.nic.in/caaa
www.planningcommission.nic.in
www.rbi.org.in
www.worldbank.org.in
www.nic.in/stat
www.oecd.org
www.developmentgoals.org

Index